Corazón de Dixie

THE DAVID J. WEBER SERIES IN THE
NEW BORDERLANDS HISTORY

Andrew R. Graybill and Benjamin H. Johnson, *editors*

Editorial Board
Sarah Carter
Kelly Lytle Hernandez
Paul Mapp
Cynthia Radding
Samuel Truett

The study of borderlands—places where different peoples meet and no one polity reigns supreme—is undergoing a renaissance. The David J. Weber Series in the New Borderlands History publishes works from both established and emerging scholars that examine borderlands from the precontact era to the present. The series explores contested boundaries and the intercultural dynamics surrounding them and includes projects covering a wide range of time and space within North America and beyond, including both Atlantic and Pacific worlds.

Published with support provided by the William P. Clements Center for Southwest Studies at Southern Methodist University in Dallas, Texas.

JULIE M. WEISE

Corazón de Dixie

Mexicanos in the U.S. South since 1910

The University of North Carolina Press CHAPEL HILL

Published with support provided by the Oregon Humanities Center and the University of Oregon College of Arts and Sciences.

© Julie M. Weise
All rights reserved
Manufactured in the United States of America
Designed and set in Arno Pro by Rebecca Evans

The paper in this book meets the guidelines for permanence and durability of the Committee on Production Guidelines for Book Longevity of the Council on Library Resources. The University of North Carolina Press has been a member of the Green Press Initiative since 2003.

Cover illustrations: Courtesy (clockwise from top left) Humberto Marín; Marcos Zervigón; Library of Congress; *La Noticia*; and Richard Enriquez; background: depositphotos.com/© day908; photograph frames: depositphotos.com/© strelov; center taped panel: depositphotos.com/© creisinger

Library of Congress Cataloging-in-Publication Data
Weise, Julie M., author.
Corazón de Dixie : Mexicanos in the U.S. South since 1910 / Julie M. Weise.
pages cm — (The David J. Weber series in the new borderlands history)
Includes bibliographical references and index.
ISBN 978-1-4696-2496-9 (pbk : alk. paper)
ISBN 978-1-4696-2497-6 (ebook)
1. Mexicans—Southern States—History—20th century. 2. Mexican Americans—Southern States—History—20th century. 3. Mexicans—Southern States—History—21st century. 4. Mexican Americans—Southern States—History—21st century. 5. Mexicans—Southern States—Social conditions. 6. Mexican Americans—Southern States—Social conditions. 7. Southern States—Race relations—History—20th century. I. Title. II. Series: David J. Weber series in the new borderlands history.
F220.M5W45 2015
305.8968′72073075—dc23
2015018768

This book was digitally printed.

For MATTHEW
*and for my
mentors, teachers,
and students*

Contents

INTRODUCTION 1

CHAPTER ONE
Mexicans as Europeans: Mexican Nationalism and
Assimilation in New Orleans, 1910–1939 14

CHAPTER TWO
Different from That Which Is Intended for the Colored Race:
Mexicans and Mexico in Jim Crow Mississippi, 1918–1939 51

CHAPTER THREE
Citizens of Somewhere: Braceros, Tejanos, Dixiecrats, and
Mexican Bureaucrats in the Arkansas Delta, 1939–1964 82

CHAPTER FOUR
Mexicano Stories and Rural White Narratives: Creating
Pro-immigrant Conservatism in Rural Georgia, 1965–2004 120

CHAPTER FIVE
Skyscrapers and Chicken Plants: Mexicans, Latinos, and Exurban
Immigration Politics in Greater Charlotte, 1990–2012 179

CONCLUSION 217

Acknowledgments 225

Appendix: Historical Sampling Methodology 233

Notes 235

Bibliography 293

Index 323

For a selection of original historical sources from this book, see
http://corazondedixie.org (http://dx.doi.org/10.7264/N3SJ1HWV).

Maps, Figures, and Tables

MAPS

1 New Orleans and Mexico's Gulf Coast, showing popular steamship routes, 1920s–1930s 18
2 Mexicanos' residences in New Orleans, 1930 29
3 Mexicanos in Mississippi Delta counties, 1930 54
4 Arkansas Delta counties and towns 84
5 Mexicanos' presence in Georgia 123
6 "Hispanic" population in Charlotte, Mecklenburg County, and surrounding area, 2000 182
7 The geography of race and class in Indian Trail, North Carolina, 2012 183
8 Suburban and exurban districts of primary sponsors of anti-immigrant state legislation in the West and South 216

FIGURES

1 "Goldcrest Beer 51—Café-bar" 2
2 Hortensia Horcasitas, New Orleans, Louisiana, ca. 1925 15
3 Robert Canedo, New Orleans, Louisiana, ca. 1945 15
4 "Day laborers picking cotton on Marcella Plantation, Mileston, Mississippi Delta, Mississippi, 1939" 52
5 "Mexican seasonal labor, contracted for by planters, emptying bags of cotton on Knowlton Plantation, Perthshire, Mississippi Delta, Mississippi" 52
6 "Mexican and Negro cotton pickers inside plantation store, Knowlton Plantation, Perthshire, Mississippi Delta, Mississippi" 53
7 Landrove family photograph, Mississippi Delta, ca. 1930 75
8 "Wike's Drive Inn (Restaurant)" 83
9 "Come In Café (restaurant and bar)" 106

10   African American cotton day laborers in Memphis, July 14, 1954   112

11   Bracero reception center in Arkansas, probably Phillips County, exact date unknown   114

12   Bracero reception center in Arkansas, probably Phillips County, exact date unknown   115

13   A page from an Avalos family album: picking cabbage in Georgia in the 1970s   121

14   A page from a Marín family album, 1970s   143

15   Gómez family album, Florida, 1970s   144

16   Gómez family album, Georgia, 1980s   145

17   Gómez family photograph of agricultural labor in Georgia, ca. 1983   146

18   Westfield School students and migrant children at an Easter egg hunt, 1990   155

19   Janis Roberson hugs H2A workers arriving at her farm, ca. 1990   158

20   Wendell Roberson and migrant workers at a quinceañera on the Robersons' farm   159

21   H2A workers' photos in the albums of employer Janis Roberson, 1995   160

22   H2A workers' photos in the albums of employer Janis Roberson, 1991   161

23   English class at St. Juliana Catholic Church, Fort Valley, Georgia, ca. 1988   163

24   Ruth and Sonny Bridges and Mexican workers at Ruth's birthday party in the early 2000s   163

25   Mary Ann Thurman in her home with migrant workers at Christmas, 1988   164

26   Sonny Bridges teaching a Mexican agricultural worker how to make ice cream   164

27   Mexican migrant family, Fort Valley, Georgia, ca. 1988   165

28   Funeral program of former employer Roscoe Meeks, 2006   167

29   Angelina Marín and supervisors, Toombs Manufacturing, 1989   168

30   Christmas card sent from employer Hank Dodson to crew leader Slim Avalos and his wife, Andrea   169

31 Kindergarten class picture from Berryhill Elementary School, Charlotte, 1994 180
32 Third-grade class picture from Poplin Elementary School, Indian Trail, Union County, North Carolina, 2010 181
33 Family outing to a shopping mall in North Carolina, ca. 2009 214
34 Mercedes R.'s daughter Jacqueline 215
35 Mercedes R. at the North Carolina Zoo, ca. 2009 215
36 Immigrants' rights vigil in Marshall Park, Charlotte, May 1, 2006 218
37 Photo postcard of the author's grandmother, Beverly Millman (later Weise), with friend, 1945 226

TABLES

1 Occupations of Mexicano men age sixteen and over in New Orleans, 1920 and 1930 25
2 Occupations of Mexicana women age sixteen and over in New Orleans, 1920 and 1930 27
3 Marriage partners of Mexicano men in New Orleans, 1920 and 1930 31
4 Marriage partners of Mexicana women in New Orleans, 1920 and 1930 32

Corazón de Dixie

Introduction

A dark-skinned man, his face under the shadow of a brimmed hat, leans back against a corrugated metal wall (fig. 1). A beer advertisement marks the place as a bar. In the distance, two still darker figures walk along an unpaved street in a commercial district. It is November 1949 at the close of the cotton picking season in Marked Tree, Arkansas. The setting is the black side of town; the man in the foreground is Mexican. A Mexican Foreign Service officer, Rubén Gaxiola, took this photo in the fall of 1949. He had it printed and added a caption: "Goldcrest Beer 51—Café-bar. Corrugated metal construction. At the side of this establishment there is a sign that says, 'Garzias Mexicanas Servesa.' In this place, blacks and also Mexicans are served."[1] Then the bureaucrat placed the photo in an envelope with nine other images documenting Mexicans' racial position in Marked Tree and mailed it off to Mexico City, where another bureaucrat would review them and consider banning Mexican workers from Marked Tree's cotton fields.

Why was this Mexican man picking cotton in Arkansas in 1949 when so many poor white and black people still lived there? What did he hope to achieve in Arkansas, and what were his experiences while there? Why did he willingly associate himself with a group, African Americans, that had been systematically subjected to violence and deprived of social, economic, and political power? What was a Mexican bureaucrat doing in Marked Tree, and why did he and other elite officials care about the racial position of this poor Mexican laborer in the first place?

These are new questions in the histories of the United States and Mexico. When Latino migration to the U.S. South became visible seemingly out of nowhere in the 1990s, the newness of this "Nuevo" South went unquestioned.[2] Journalists asked, "Will fajitas replace Moon Pie?" as though Mexican food had no history in the region;[3] anti-immigrant activists decried the coming of "Georgifornia," as though Georgia itself had not relied on Mexican and Mexican American laborers for more than forty years.[4] Extrapolating from individual case studies, some social scientists wondered whether anti-black prejudices born in Latin America would doom attempts at political coalition building while others pointed to possibilities for cooperation.[5] Southern

FIGURE 1 "Goldcrest Beer 51—Café-bar. Corrugated metal construction. At the side of this establishment there is a sign that says, 'Garzias Mexicanas Servesa.' In this place, blacks and also Mexicans are served." Attachments to letter from Consul Rubén Gaxiola, Memphis, to Ministry of Foreign Relations, Mexico City, November 19, 1949, TM-26-32, Archivo Histórico de la Secretaría de Relaciones Exteriores, Mexico City.

teachers discussed Jim Crow as a matter of only black and white, and Latino elementary school students responded, "Which water fountain would I be able to drink from?"[6] Observers, activists, scholars, and educators could reasonably argue that the Latino influx would remake southern race relations entirely or would reinforce old regional patterns in the form of "Juan Crow."[7] It seemed there was little precedent available to discern patterns or possibilities from an examination of the past.

Yet as the photograph from the bar in Marked Tree, Arkansas, shows, immigrants from Mexico and Americans of Mexican descent have been migrating to the U.S. South in significant numbers for decades—in fact, as far back as the early twentieth century.[8] This book recovers and recounts their histories. It reveals the myriad different ways that earlier migrants defined and pursued progress while living between a transnational Latin America and a South imagined as black-and-white. And it shows us how white and black southerners recruited or reacted to Latin American newcomers in light of changing ideas about their own lives in the region and world. In so doing, the pages that follow reveal Mexicanos' strategies and responses to shifting U.S., southern, and Mexican circumstances, giving sharper perspective to observers and activists in the Latino present by revealing narratives, possibilities, and disjunctions from the past.

At the same time, these stories about particular people in a particular place deepen understandings of race, class, citizenship, and national belonging throughout greater Mexico and the United States. Beginning their lives in Mexico or South Texas, migrants came to the U.S. South with diverse aspirations depending on where and when they had come of age. In the South, they encountered a distinct kind of borderland, a place where for much of the twentieth century, white elites successfully resisted the liberal promises of U.S. federal power so they could exert near-total control over African American laborers having no claim on the state.[9] Local southern subcultures defined by race and class developed layered ideologies and practices toward black and white, but their stance toward brown and foreign remained more ambiguous in advance of Mexicanos' actual arrival.[10] In the interactions that ensued, all parties revealed essential dimensions of their beliefs, investments, and ambitions. This book therefore argues that to more completely understand even supposedly provincial spaces in U.S. and Mexican history, scholars must look beyond national borders, for the deeds of seemingly marginal actors can illuminate more clearly the main characters and plotlines that have long preoccupied historians. U.S. and Mexican citizens, African American second-class citizens, bureaucrats, capitalists, and activists made the Mexican

American history of the U.S. South in ways seldom predictable. Their stories over the course of a turbulent century offer new ways of understanding the changing regimes of race, class, and citizenship that shaped the lives of ordinary citizens and aliens in both countries.

American Migrations in Myth and History

To derive meaning from this longer history of the South's Latinization, one must be able to see the region's invisible Mexican American history at all. The photograph of a Mexican immigrant in 1940s Arkansas might seem surprising in light of these migrants' near-total absence from extant written histories. Yet key features of southern, western, and Mexican history suggest that Mexican migration to the U.S. South, while perhaps not inevitable, was also not entirely unpredictable. On the one hand, popular understandings of the postbellum South suggest that there, racially oppressed black laborers performed agricultural work because they had no other choice. Having not received their promised "40 acres and a mule" after emancipation from slavery, African Americans became stuck in sharecropping arrangements that rarely afforded them enough profit to acquire their own land, tools, and seeds. From the demise of Reconstruction through World War II, discrimination and subpar segregated educational systems excluded them from most urban jobs, and in any case, farmers in cahoots with local authorities routinely used violence to keep blacks at work in the fields.[11] They were able do so because by the early twentieth century, the reigning ideology of white supremacy insisted in a quasi-biological fashion that black people had inherited irredeemable inferiority in their very blood.[12] In this context, there would seem to be no need for white southern planters to recruit Mexican laborers from Texas and points south. Indeed, some have argued that the South's longtime dependence on agriculture rather than innovation fostered its isolation from global forces throughout most of the nineteenth and twentieth centuries.[13]

But history is driven by more than simple economics. In this case, it was driven also by culture and ideas—particularly ideas about race and labor. Since Emancipation, southern planters scorned their African American workers for alleged noncooperation, seeking to replace them with immigrants from China, Italy, and beyond.[14] A few southern planters briefly recruited Mexicans in 1904, but in that and other cases the early immigrant experiments were short-lived.[15] Large-scale black out-migration in the 1910s–60s gave farmers immediate justification for their long-standing efforts to attract immigrants to the fields. An agricultural economy and paternalistic labor systems had not isolated the South from the world surrounding; rather, they had spawned a specific set of global interests on the part of powerful white southerners.[16]

Unlike the South's, the Southwest's borderlands are well known to popular and academic observers. After all, the United States wrested the region from Mexico in the U.S.-Mexican War of 1846–48. A trickle of Mexican immigrants arrived to the new U.S. Southwest in subsequent decades, but the inflow of white newcomers was far stronger.[17] But in the 1910s, rapid economic change and then revolution shook the Mexican countryside, displacing millions and wreaking havoc on livelihoods just as a wartime economy prompted U.S. farmers and other employers to actively recruit labor in Mexico.[18] From 1913 to a peak in 1924, annual Mexican immigration to the United States increased tenfold.[19] As federal legislators moved to restrict European and Asian immigration, labor-hungry business interests ensured that Mexican immigration would continue unhindered. Notwithstanding the anti-immigrant sentiment and deportations of the Depression era, Mexican immigrants became a staple of agricultural labor throughout the Southwest by the 1940s, and their position as such became even more entrenched during the bracero "guest worker" program of 1942–64.

As Mexicans crossed and recrossed the border and journeyed to locations across the United States, they brought with them distinct outlooks and experiences with race, class, and citizenship. That is, they saw themselves and others in particular terms of biological or quasi-biological inheritance, economic and cultural status, and relationship to nation-states. The Mexican Revolution of 1910–17 ousted a development-focused dictatorship seen as "mother to foreigners and stepmother to Mexicans" and heralded a new era of working-class Mexican nationalism. Some emigrants drew on this politics to become active in U.S. labor movements while others called on Mexican consulates for help. In addition to class, the new government formulated new ideologies of race, eschewing the old regime's focus on whitening through culture and instead celebrating Mexicans' "mixed" genetic background— mixed, officially, between white and Indian but not Chinese or African. Still, popular conceptions of race in Mexico focused on cultural traits far more than biological inheritance, making racial identities seem more malleable than their U.S. counterparts.[20]

As these postrevolutionary Mexicans crossed the border into the United States, they found that the U.S. Southwest was no haven of acceptance and mobility. In the early twentieth century, a typical Mexican immigrant family would arrive first to South Texas, where they confronted a Jim Crow system that had evolved specifically to oppress Mexicans alongside blacks.[21] Labor recruiters might bring them to California or Arizona, where their children would attend inferior segregated schools.[22] Mexicanos in the Southwest were also subject to harassment and violence, and they became the victims of lynching nearly as frequently as African Americans in the South.[23]

And so, just as white southerners have sought alternative sources of workers since the nineteenth century, so have Mexican immigrants sought alternative places to work since the 1910s. Scholars have begun to document their journeys to the Northwest and Midwest during that decade and afterward.[24] As this book will show, the two quests—of Mexicanos, for new routes to social and economic mobility, and of white southerners, for a new class of laborers they hoped would be more pliant—joined each other time and again throughout the twentieth century.

New Histories of the "Viejo" New South

What Mexicanos found in the South and what southerners found in Mexicans fulfilled some of those mutual expectations but upended others. The following pages trace their encounters in five times and places: 1910s–30s New Orleans, the Mississippi Delta during the same period, the Arkansas Delta during the 1940s–60s, rural southern Georgia from the 1960s to the early 2000s, and Charlotte's exurbs since 1990. Texas and Florida appear here as stops on migrants' journeys but not subjects of primary research in their own right. Texas's embrace of slavery, the Confederacy, King Cotton, and Jim Crow surely make it a southern as well as a southwestern state; Florida's multiethnic heritage also does not remove it from the region.[25] Still, this study does not dwell in Texas and Florida because it focuses on times and places where southerners and Mexicans encountered each other for the first time in local memory.

The narrative interrogates these encounters with two overarching questions in mind. First, what specific aspirations led Mexicans and Mexican Americans to work and struggle for rights in the U.S. South, and how did they leverage the power within their grasp—locally, nationally, and internationally, within families, communities, or distant bureaucracies—to pursue their goals? And second, how did white and African American southerners in different economic positions respond to the newcomers, in turn revealing their own strategies for advancement?

The answers to these questions changed over time and place, and this book tries to show how. It draws inspiration from those works of migration history, cultural studies, and anthropology that have helped illuminate how places of origin, transit, and destination shaped migrants' worldviews, identities, and politics—and did so differentially, depending on qualities such as gender, age, social class, and physical appearance.[26] Traditional historical sources such as newspapers, church records, census reports, and government documents are used here in new ways to interpret the experiences and perspectives of long-deceased migrants—even, in many cases, those who were marginal, poor, and illiterate. In particular, the archives of migrants' countries of origin, in this case Mexico, prove critical to the narration of life histories lived across international borders. I also use nontraditional forms of evidence, including oral history interviews and migrants' photo albums, to comprehend the imaginative lives that migrants led outside the surveillance of local, national, or international institutions.[27] Accordingly, *Corazón de Dixie* traces a century of developments in Mexicano migrants' expectations and beliefs about race, class, citizenship, and progress; migrants' relationships to two national states; and the changing politics of segregation, white supremacy, and political liberalism and conservatism in the U.S. South. African Americans' perspectives on Mexicano newcomers are clearest after World War II, the moment when living witnesses' memories can fill gaps in the written sources. Priests and religious institutions sometimes appear as critical actors, though a full consideration of the theological and practical attitudes of Christian denominations toward Mexicano newcomers is beyond the scope of this book.[28]

These sources show that Mexicans' reasons for migration to the South and the results of their struggles once there were determined in incredibly fragile, contingent, and—for most of the twentieth century—local ways. There was no timeless "Mexican perspective" on the South's cotton-picking jobs, or African Americans, or political structures. Rather, there were a myriad of perspectives shaped in particular Mexican migration routes, individual southern communities, and specific moments in the histories of the Mexican and U.S. states. While works on U.S. immigration and ethnicity have well placed their subjects in the changing contours of U.S. history and explored transnational dynamics in locally and temporally bounded case studies, *Corazón de Dixie* is among the first to think seriously about how changes in Mexican national culture and state power shaped Mexican immigrants in generationally and regionally distinct ways across the twentieth century. It shows how migrants' ideas about race, gender, rights, material well-being, and the role of the state in their lives shifted over the course of the twentieth century and into the twenty-first, placing the present in relief against an unfolding past. The focus on the South's Mexican immigrants and Mexican Americans rather than

Latinos as a whole enables this nuanced analysis. Yet because the research provisionally accepts the national boundary of "Mexican" as its subject of analysis, it offers explorations but not definitive conclusions about the ways that migrants from distinct places in Mexico experienced the U.S. South differently. New scholarship, I hope, will build on this book's foundation to probe those distinctions more deeply, complementing and challenging the findings I have offered here.[29]

Not only was there no consistent and unchanging "Mexican reaction" to the U.S. South; there also was no unchanging southern "white perspective" or "black perspective" on the newcomers' arrival. Rather, location, occupation, political ideology, and particularly economic status structured differing black and white reactions over time. This insight builds on several emergent strands in southern history. Scholars have begun to dismantle the truism that "the South's" monolithic white residents have been singularly responsible for the nation's racial woes.[30] Others have probed southern African Americans' perspectives on Mexicans and Mexican Americans, focusing on Texas prior to 1990 and various southern locations thereafter.[31] This latter research has shown, yet again, that the study of "in-between" groups such as Chinese or Native Americans can reveal the complex interests at stake in the South's racial systems.[32]

Engaged with these research strands, *Corazón de Dixie* shows that there was no easy, predictable continuity of whites' racial exclusion or inclusion of Mexicans, nor of African Americans' competition or solidarity with them. Rather, local actors engaged selectively with the regional and national politics of race, class, and citizenship to create a variety of outcomes throughout the twentieth century. In every case, white and African American southerners in different economic positions offered Mexicans complex combinations of acceptance and rejection, oppression and opportunity. Their attitudes and actions changed, in turn, as Mexicanos pursued their goals in ways that complemented, accepted, or resisted the local status quo. Only later, at the turn of the twenty-first century, did the national politics of immigration overpower local interests to definitively push Mexican and other Latino immigrants outside the boundaries of whiteness and Americanness—a turn some immigrants openly resisted, with limited effect on the legal and social politics of exclusion.

Attempts to critically examine the composition of racial groups inevitably run up against the restrictions of language, particularly over a hundred-year period. Southern observers often used the term "Mexican" to denote not only Mexican nationals but also U.S. citizens of Mexican descent; this language accurately represented the latter's inability to access the benefits of their U.S. citizenship. Yet legal nationality mattered in varied and sometimes critical ways throughout the century. So this book uses the term "Mexicans" to refer to Mexican nationals, "Mexican Americans" to refer to U.S. citizens of Mexican descent, "Tejanos" to refer to Mexican Americans born in Texas, and "Mexicanos" to refer to Mexicans and Mexican Americans simultaneously. When referring to census data, that agency's category, "Hispanic," is used. The term "U.S. American" denotes U.S. citizens of any racial identity, acknowledging that the Americas extend far beyond the borders of the United States. Along with "white," "black," and "African American," these terms convey significant though not comprehensive aspects of historical actors' identities and legal positions even as those markers remained in flux.

Into the Heart of Dixie

This story begins in the 1910s with a transformative surge in two of the twentieth-century Americas' most important human migrations: Mexicans to the United States and African Americans out of the U.S. South. While the story of Mexican migration to Texas during this time is well known, New Orleans was also a migration destination for thousands of Gulf Coast Mexicans who arrived by ship. These immigrants are the subjects of Chapter 1. They arrived into a city that was in many respects Caribbean more than southern—a place where race was not as simple as black and white.[33] Yet they also came at the height of the Jim Crow system regionally and nationally, a time when that system was beginning to have its way with the city of New Orleans. There, Mexican immigrants chose to identify themselves as "Mexican" while deliberately shaping the meaning of that category. Together with the Mexican consul, they succeeded in presenting Mexico as a Europeanized land whose citizens could integrate unproblematically into white New Orleans. And integrate into white New Orleans they did. New Orleans is the only place historians have yet documented where Mexicans' path to white assimilation unfolded with relative ease in the interwar period.

The subjects of Chapter 2 traversed a longer path to both the South and the white status they decided to pursue there. They emerged from the more prototypical milieu of interwar Mexican migration: north-central Mexicans who fled their country's bloody revolution or were recruited to Texas in the years that followed it. In Texas, they encountered violence of a different sort: racial violence designed, in large part, to keep an increasingly important labor force "in its place" both physically and economically.[34] By the 1920s, rapid employment growth throughout the United States offered these immigrants and their families an escape to faraway points, from the citrus groves of California to the auto factories of Michigan and indeed the cotton plantations of Mississippi.[35] Tens of thousands of Mexicans and Mexican Americans initially traveled to Mississippi in seasonal work crews; they were met with widespread violence and abuse that convinced many never to return. But a significant minority of Mexicanos found ways to defend their families while finding opportunity in "the most Southern place on Earth."[36] They pursued social mobility as sharecroppers and sought integration into the white side of the color line. When their children were expelled from the white school because of their race, these immigrants fought back; they won by drawing on the transborder power of the newly established postrevolutionary Mexican state. Although the Depression decimated any economic progress they made in their early years in Mississippi, the racial gains remained in place, and by the 1950s a "Mexican" in the Mississippi Delta was someone with brown skin and a Spanish surname who was nonetheless considered "white."

During and after World War II, the U.S. and Mexican economies once again expanded, as did federal bureaucracies, and liberal ideas increased once-marginalized peoples' expectations of citizenship. During those years, white southern farmers finally won a decades-long battle to enlist the U.S. government in recruiting labor from Mexico. From the perspective of both states, this modernist vision allowed for control over who crossed the international boundary line.[37] Chapter 3's subjects, the Tejanos and more than 300,000 bracero contract workers who worked in Arkansas between 1939 and 1964, frustrated white farmers' seemingly strategic use of the U.S. federal government by successfully enlisting the Mexican federal government to help them win greater rights. Thousands of Mexicans struck and protested on farms and appealed to the Mexican consulate for political support. An activist consul helped them recover wages, improve working conditions, and secure the right to enter white establishments. Yet braceros still existed on the margins of Arkansas Delta society, and although they were stereotyped with positive adjectives, they earned low wages and certainly were not considered equal to the area's white people. All would eventually leave the area.

Many of the Mexicans and Mexican Americans who left Arkansas returned to Texas or moved on to Florida, where large-scale agriculture rapidly expanded in the immediate postwar years. They remained in Texas or Florida during winters and journeyed north through the Atlantic South during summers, eventually settling in its rural areas. Although the Mississippi and Arkansas Deltas had hosted relatively large and highly visible Mexicano populations in the past, the 1970s in Georgia and beyond was the first time these migrations spread throughout the U.S. South as a whole. Over the coming three decades, millions of Mexicanos would come through the region as migrant workers or put down roots there.[38] Those Mexicanos, the subjects of Chapter 4, came to hold privileged positions in the white southern imagination between 1965 and 2004, years of globalization, shrinking federal states, and conservative or neoliberal ideologies in both places. Focusing on rural Georgia's agricultural communities, the chapter shows that conservative white people now articulated racial ideas in seemingly cultural more than biological terms.[39] Mexican and Mexican American migrants' cultural traits, it was supposed, included hard work, morality, and assimilability—the opposite of blacks' racial descriptors in this period. Yet the benefits Mexicans gained from being on the receiving end of these stereotypes were limited. Hailing from a crisis-era Mexico, they had more partial expectations of citizenship and less ability to leverage the power of the Mexican state than their predecessors had. The foreign-born among them were largely undocumented, as the 1965 Immigration Act imposed numerical restrictions on Latin American immigration for the first time. Georgia's Mexicans and Mexican Americans appealed to conservative white patrons at work and church rather than to the Mexican or U.S. federal governments. They neither sought nor received full political and labor rights in southern Georgia. The prize was social acceptance in white communities and some freedom from racial harassment; the cost was a meaningful ability to challenge authorities or labor conditions.

During this same period, both Mexican and southern elites cultivated global ambitions: Mexicans to pursue economic development through free trade, and southerners to situate the region's major cities as key nodes in the global economy.[40] Urban areas grew in both countries as free trade agreements displaced Mexican farmers while rapid service-driven growth in the South accelerated the spatial and political creep of metropolitan communities into formerly rural territory.[41] Members of all social classes in both countries were drawn into an increasingly ubiquitous consumer consciousness. Both pushed and pulled by the globalization of cultures and economies, Mexican migrants flocked to construction and low-wage service jobs in metropolitan centers like Atlanta, Nashville, and Charlotte, and immigrants from throughout Latin America quickly followed them.[42] Those who moved to greater Charlotte between 1990 and 2012 are the subjects of Chapter 5. As women joined male migrants there, they moved to suburbs and exurbs to raise families, taking advantage of these places' better-funded schools, cheaper housing, and proximity to peripheral work sites in construction, poultry, and light manufacturing. They embraced a consumerist version of the middle-class ideal that had emerged unevenly in Mexican culture as in so many others by the 1990s.[43] They hoped that long hours of low-wage work would allow their comparatively smaller families to make economic progress through education, eventually acquiring disposable income, family vacations, and an ability to become middle-class consumers, if not necessarily citizens with political rights. Even as many achieved their modest economic goals, they suffered increased persecution at the end of the twenty-first century's first decade.

When Latinos first arrived to Charlotte, they were met by a welcoming climate in the name of business friendliness. Soon, however, they came to transgress racial boundaries not by protesting or striking but rather by simply living. As women joined men and families rooted themselves in the exurbs, they unwittingly entered bastions of unchecked conservative white populism. There, white home owners in pursuit of durable middle-class status resented Mexican and other Latino immigrants not because of job competition but rather because immigrants had joined them as consumers of public services such as schools, roads, and parks. This historically new role for the South's Mexican immigrants violated white middle-class sensibilities about taxes and racial entitlement.[44] In response, these white citizens mounted the region's first large-scale anti-immigrant movement targeted at working-class Latinos. But unlike the previous four case studies, this struggle was not waged within the confines of one community, city, or agricultural subregion. Rather, Greater Charlotte's anti-immigrant activists worked in conjunction with an Internet-based community of like-minded leaders, most themselves suburbanites and exurbanites, throughout the United States. Meanwhile, media coverage of immigrants' rights activism elsewhere in the country inspired small groups of exurban Mexican and Mexican American youths to protest, mostly in high schools. But few exurban immigrants had sufficient transportation to participate in the burgeoning immigrants' rights movement of Charlotte's downtown and inner suburbs. From the perspective of Mexican American history, the South had joined the nation as its migrant experiences and immigration politics followed the familiar contours that had emerged in western metropolitan areas and spread throughout the country over the previous two decades.

In 2011, Alabama's governor signed HB56 into law; the anti-immigrant bill was hailed as the toughest in the country. In legislative debate, primary cosponsor state representative Micky Hammon boasted, "This [bill] attacks every aspect of an illegal immigrant's life. They will not stay in Alabama."[45] To many observers, Hammon's exclusionary rhetoric fit perfectly into generalized ideas about race politics in the U.S. South. It easily reinforced the popular narrative emphasizing the region's "exceptionally" poor track record in matters of race.[46]

But this interpretation is faulty. *Corazón de Dixie* shows that from the perspective of Mexican American history, there is no regional continuity of racial exclusion in the U.S. South. There is no continuity of expectation on the part of Mexicans, nor of reaction on the part of white and African American southerners. Rather, Mexicanos engaged in intensely local struggles to determine their place in racial and social hierarchies. They created flows of ideas and power, in which Mexican immigrants and the Mexican government at times played decisive roles in determining outcomes and in which southern communities nearly always emerged as more receptive to Mexicans than western ones. The emergence in the early 2000s of an apparently unified anti-immigrant conservative South was not that at all. After all, Hammon hailed from the state's largest metropolitan area, not a rural backwater, and he openly acknowledged that he modeled his bill on similar legislation in Arizona.[47] Furthermore, his bill was met with resistance from Alabama's conservative rural areas and Christian religious leaders. Rather than regional exceptionalism, the anti-immigrant tide devastated the South's immigrant communities due to the region's integration into national trends of spatial segregation in exurban areas, as well as the neoliberal trajectory that inspired Mexican immigrants to seek consumer goods over civic rights and neutralized their government's once-politicized emigration bureaucracy. The assault helped politicize these immigrants' children, though, and many forsook their parents' cautious attitudes to lead the South's newest movement for civil and human rights.

When narratives of region and nation structure not only our answers but also our questions, they limit our ability to comprehend the complex dynamics of history. To challenge our assumptions, then, let us follow little-remembered Mexican Americans and Mexican immigrants into the heart of Dixie—a place not exceptional or isolated but rather a *corazón* pulsing through veins both local and global.

CHAPTER ONE

Mexicans as Europeans
Mexican Nationalism and Assimilation in New Orleans, 1910–1939

Photographs of Hortensia Horcasitas (fig. 2) and Robert Canedo (fig. 3) seem typical of Mexican immigrant portraits from the U.S. Southwest in the first half of the twentieth century.[1] The Horcasitas photograph recalls countless others of the "Mexican generation," Mexican immigrants of the 1910s and 1920s. This generation fled revolution and economic hardship in Mexico; once in the United States, they adapted Mexican culture and nationalism to their new environment, using it to buffer themselves from a society that increasingly saw them as racially and culturally suspect.[2] Canedo, too, came to the United States from Mexico as a young child during the 1920s. His portrait evokes the "Mexican American generation," for whom service in World War II was an integral component of a new political strategy and in some cases an identity shift, emphasizing U.S. citizenship. That generation embraced Americanism in the hope that white America would, in turn, embrace Mexican Americans.[3]

These photos, however, were not taken in Los Angeles or San Antonio but rather in New Orleans, where they told a different story. For Horcasitas and her family, embracing Mexican national culture was not a means of protection against white society but rather a way to join it. In the Crescent City, as New Orleans was known, middle-class Mexican immigrants of the 1920s successfully engaged Mexico and shaped the image of "Mexicans" in ways that secured their place among European-style white immigrants. They acquired a different racialization from their counterparts elsewhere in the United States, who had come to be seen as a group distinct from and inferior to white people. In the Southwest, the limited success of the Mexican American generation's politics caused their children to adopt a more radical stance in the 1960s. In New Orleans, by contrast, the "Mexican generation" already lived as white people during the 1920s.

To see a selection of original historical sources from this chapter, go to http://corazondedixie .org/chapter-1 (http://dx.doi.org/10.7264/N3FB517W).

(left) FIGURE 2 Hortensia Horcasitas, New Orleans, Louisiana, ca. 1925. Courtesy of Carlos Zervigón and family.

(right) FIGURE 3 Robert Canedo, New Orleans, Louisiana, ca. 1945. Courtesy of Hazel Canedo and family.

Canedo first acquired his U.S. citizenship during World War II but had enjoyed most of its benefits for decades—benefits not enjoyed by those New Orleans citizens who were African American. Though his skin was dark and his mother was a poor widow raising a family on the proceeds of her sister's boardinghouse, in 1930 young Robert attended kindergarten with white children; meanwhile, his Mexican immigrant counterparts in the Southwest faced school segregation, deportation, and racial violence.[4] By the time he enlisted in the army, Canedo had already fallen in love with his future wife, a U.S.-born white woman named Hazel, to whom the photograph's inscription was addressed.[5] The couple's children went on to live as white people in New Orleans, their Mexican heritage a curiosity rather than a determining factor of their life course.[6] While the Southwest's Mexican Americans hoped military portraits like this one would mark a turning point in their experiences

Mexican Nationalism and Assimilation in New Orleans

of race, Canedo's photograph simply projected the assured patriotism of any white soldier at war.

Between 1910 and World War II, nearly all of the roughly 2,000 Mexican immigrants who lived for a time in New Orleans—even those like Canedo, who hailed from working-class backgrounds and had darker skin—assimilated into white society.[7] During those same years, pro-segregation white southern Democrats took hold of the city and imposed a binary racial system onto what had once been a multilayered social and racial landscape. The Supreme Court case named after New Orleans's most famous Creole color line transgressor, Homer Plessy, ruled in 1896 that ancestry and biological race would determine who sat in which train car—who was black and who white. Since Plessy had just one black great-grandparent, the decision marked the "one-drop" rule's continuance into the twentieth century. Faced with an increasingly rigid Jim Crow system, a variety of in-between groups, such as Italians and the mixed-race French-Spanish group known as Creoles, pursued distinct strategies toward social mobility and status.[8]

Yet racialization—the process of demarcating biological and quasi-biological categories of people, imbuing those categories with meaning, and assigning them to human beings—has never been the province of judges alone.[9] Though biological, blood-based ideas of race were at their height in the United States in the interwar period, Horcasitas, Canedo, and thousands of other Mexican immigrants used culture to wedge their way into white New Orleans.[10] They had learned this strategy in Mexico, where cultural ideas of race nearly always asserted themselves into biological ones. Though Horcasitas went on to marry a Cuban man and her descendants self-identified as Latin American throughout the twentieth century, this cultural identity was subsumed into a broad white racial category from the 1920s onward.[11] The experiences of her family and countless others show that the South's binary, blood-based racial system could not remain fully insulated from the more cultural forms of racial thought prevalent elsewhere in the world.[12] Mexican immigrants secured their white status in large part by ignoring the elements of Mexican nationalism that valorized their nation's self-proclaimed identity of "mixed" biological inheritance. Thus, their stories also illuminate the powerful influence of U.S. white supremacy on other nations' projects of self-definition, in this case Mexico's.

Identifying sources to understand the lives of those who deliberately declined to identify as "Mexican" poses a challenge to historians. Nonetheless, Mexican sources, combined with a close analysis of original manuscript census pages and the family photographs and documents held by immigrants' descendants, together begin to tell a story. They show how a group of middle-class Mexican immigrants like Horcasitas created a Europeanized version of *Mexicanidad*, perceptions of Mexicanness, that in turn allowed the Canedos and other poor Mexicans to quietly assimilate into white New Orleans geographically, culturally, economically, socially, and religiously. Like their counterparts in the Southwest, these working- and middle-class immigrants were considered "Mexican." But "Mexican" in New Orleans quickly acquired a very different meaning than it had elsewhere.[13]

A sociologist wrote in 1949 that Latin American immigrants "are naturally associated with and identify themselves with the white rather than the colored element," but there was nothing natural about Mexicans' strategies for navigating New Orleans.[14] Other immigrant and "in-between" groups made a variety of choices when confronted with the political dominance, and even the violence, of white supremacy during this period. That Mexican immigrants pursued assimilation into whiteness rather than antiracist politics, and achieved that assimilation by crafting a specific image of Mexican culture while remaining silent about biology, thus reveals as much about the history of Mexico as that of the U.S. color line.

Gulf Coast Routes

Though the first significant wave of Mexican migration to Jim Crow New Orleans began during the early twentieth century, the cultural, economic, and political history of the Gulf of Mexico gave this encounter deeper roots (see map 1). Like Latin America, Louisiana was first colonized by Spain and attracted a large population of Spanish emigrants from the eighteenth century forward.[15] Even under French and later U.S. American rule in the eighteenth and nineteenth centuries, Spanish-language culture thrived in New Orleans. In the nineteenth century, steamship connections through the Gulf of Mexico reinforced cultural and economic ties between Louisiana and Latin America, and New Orleans became a major center of Hispanophone journalism linking Spanish-speaking communities throughout the hemisphere.[16] Culture, too, crossed the Gulf, as many of the Mexican musicians who first arrived for the 1884 World's Fair remained in New Orleans and influenced its music scene.[17] The city periodically became embroiled in Latin American political struggles, as exiles including Mexican liberals Valentín Gómez Farías and Benito Juárez lived there for periods of time. Meanwhile, U.S. soldiers departed from New Orleans for their military incursions into Latin America, including the U.S.-Mexican War, as did small groups of U.S. American men

MAP 1 New Orleans and Mexico's Gulf Coast, showing popular passenger steamship routes, 1920s–1930s. Information from U.S. Department of Commerce, *Commercial Traveler's Guide to Latin America*, 1926 and 1931. Map by the author.

who set out for self-designed invasions of Latin America in expeditions that came to be known as filibusters.[18]

The Mexican Revolution of 1910–17 created political and economic instability that affected the United States through immigration and the spillover of revolutionary politics. The majority of the era's U.S.-bound migrants hailed from north-central Mexico, a hotbed of revolutionary activity and within close reach of the Mexico-U.S. border. These poor, rural emigrants journeyed mostly to Texas during the 1910s–20s, and from there, many continued on to all parts of the United States, from Arizona to Alaska, Michigan to California. Meanwhile, some Mexican revolutionaries like the Flores Magón brothers took refuge in U.S. cities like Los Angeles and San Antonio.[19]

Linked to Mexico through the Gulf's watery borderlands, New Orleans saw these same effects from the Mexican Revolution. Though larger numbers of Cubans and Hondurans later moved to New Orleans, in the 1910s–20s refugees from the Mexican Revolution constituted the city's most numerically important group of Latin American immigrants, numbering at least 1,400 in

1920.[20] Revolutionary conflict also straddled the Gulf of Mexico, as Yucatán's future socialist governor, Felipe Carrillo Puerto, retreated to New Orleans for a time.[21] On the other side of the political spectrum, conservative leaders including Aureliano Urrutia and Francisco Carvajal plotted counterrevolution from New Orleans in 1914, arousing suspicion from U.S. authorities.[22] The forces of reactionary Adolfo de la Huerta, while based in Veracruz, later used the Crescent City for refuge and supplies in 1923, spawning a migration of Mexican "soldiers of fortune, political plotters, and ammunition salesmen" to New Orleans.[23]

Though migrant political leaders sought refuge in New Orleans for the same reasons as their counterparts in Los Angeles or El Paso, Mexican migrants to New Orleans had generally experienced the turbulent 1910s differently. Would-be emigrants from north-central Mexico walked or rode railroads to the Texas border, while those who lived near Mexico's Gulf Coast ports boarded ships bound for U.S. Gulf Coast ports. Mexican consulate records suggest that Veracruz was by far the most common state of origin among New Orleans's Mexican immigrants, with others hailing from coastal states Yucatán, Campeche, and Tabasco.[24]

New Orleans–bound Gulf Coast migrants and their counterparts who journeyed from northern Mexico to the southwestern United States had overlapping yet different outlooks and reasons for migration, which in turn shaped the choices they made in the United States. In the late nineteenth and early twentieth centuries, Mexico's dictator Porfirio Díaz brought rapid capitalist development and social transformation to the country's heartland as well as its Gulf Coast. Still, the coast's tropical climates and proximity to shipping routes made the development of agriculture for export particularly dramatic there. Plantations in Veracruz grew coffee, tobacco, and sugar, while those in Yucatán produced the fibrous cactus known as henequen, which ultimately was used to fabricate rope. Economic expansion led to labor shortages, and some foreign-owned plantations notoriously used violence to keep workers on the job.[25] Simple unemployment, then, would not have motivated emigration from the Gulf Coast.

The revolution's trajectory in the Gulf fomented some but not all of the political and economic disruptions that motivated north-central Mexicans to emigrate.[26] Yucatán's poor and isolated plantation laborers did not seize the revolutionary moment to rebel themselves, nor did displaced rural dwellers in Veracruz.[27] Still, the towns and cities of Veracruz were centers of labor radicalism in the early years of the twentieth century. From coffee bean sorters to textile factory laborers, the state's urban workers—many recent transplants from rural areas—initiated strikes and riots in 1906–7.[28] When revolutionary leader Venustiano Carranza installed a sympathetic governor there in 1914, it was apparently with instructions to make major concessions to the working-class agenda.[29] The following year, a revolutionary governor arrived in Yucatán as well.[30] Though neither these leaders nor subsequent socialist governors succeeded in upending the Gulf Coast's stratified economic order, their arrival initiated more than a decade of negotiation with peasant groups over land reform. In the case of Veracruz, continued labor unrest during and after the revolutionary years secured greater rights and protections for urban workers.[31] Thus, while north-central Mexicans undoubtedly experienced more and earlier violence and economic disruption during the revolution, the Gulf Coast's laboring classes also underwent rapid economic change in the early twentieth century—change with which many eventually voiced their dissatisfaction.

That Veracruz produced fewer out-migrants as compared with north-central Mexico thus attests to the critical role of railroad transportation and labor recruitment—beyond simply economic supply and demand—in jump-starting more than a century of Mexican emigration. During World War I, U.S. labor recruiters focused their efforts at the Texas border. Governors, mayors, and local authorities in northern Mexico were instructed to spread the word about job opportunities, though many refused to do so, believing they needed the labor at home. Mexican workers who did hear about recruitment efforts during and after World War I walked days to reach the border or paid the train fare of around $13 to arrive there; then, *enganchadores*, recruiters, paid to transport them to work sites throughout the United States.[32] State government officials in Veracruz also received requests for laborers, such as one in 1918 seeking men to work in the United States and outlining a specific procedure for contracting them.[33] Yet like their counterparts in northern Mexico, local officials in rapidly developing Veracruz were not eager to part with their workforce. "There is not anyone here that wants to abandon their land to go to a foreign country," wrote the mayor of Veracruz highlands village Xoxocotla in response to the 1918 request for laborers, "but if the situation does arise, care will be taken to follow your instructions."[34] Meanwhile, New Orleans–based Mexican import/export agent J. de la Torre saw that employers in the U.S. South, too, were hungry for Mexican labor and tried to start contracting them via ship from Veracruz to New Orleans. His requests that the Mexican government exempt him from the usual contract requirements and subsidize laborers' train fare to the Mexican port city fell on unsympathetic ears, and the plan went nowhere.[35] In the end, then, the serious labor recruitment efforts that helped jump-start emigration in north-central Mexico in the interwar years did not reach the Gulf Coast.

Without the impetus and subsidy of organized labor recruitment, Veracruzanos and other Gulf Coast residents who did board New Orleans–bound ships bore the entire cost of migration and readjustment themselves and thus were more likely to be middle and upper class. Still, they hailed from villages, towns, and cities and from a range of economic positions. The Enseñat family, for example, ran a successful business in Yucatán's capital, Mérida. There, they manufactured and serviced machines that crushed and processed Yucatán's most important crop, henequen.[36] Family lore recalls a bullet hitting a windmill in the Enseñats' backyard in 1916, signifying the revolution's threat to the family's economic status and safety. Originally from Cuba, father Francisco Enseñat moved his family via ship to New Orleans that year, where he purchased a car for the family and enrolled his children in Catholic schools. Leaving his wife and children in New Orleans, he continued to commute between the Crescent City and the family home and business in Mérida.[37] Like the Enseñats, many of these upper- and middle-class migrants feared rather than supported the revolution, making New Orleans a stronghold of conservative sentiment during the 1910s.[38]

Immigrants to New Orleans from the Gulf Coast's rural areas had more to gain than lose from the revolution, yet many still left because of the upheavals it caused. Immigrant Peter Nieto was raised in a rural area near Jalapa, Veracruz, where he managed birth and death records for his town. The feeling of lawlessness in the aftermath of the revolution prompted him to take a banana boat to New Orleans in 1924. Within a year he had found work as a watchmaker and married Laura, a woman of Cajun descent from Cutoff, Louisiana.[39] Another immigrant, a farmer's son, recalled growing up in rural Veracruz. When his father died, the immigrant's mother, like many other rural women in her time, moved the family to the port of Veracruz.[40] But when the city's labor market failed to yield economic stability, she and her children boarded a boat bound for New Orleans.[41] These rural emigrants, then, emerged from a milieu of political and economic flux.

Though Mexican consulate records suggest that the vast majority of New Orleans's Mexican immigrants hailed from the Gulf Coast, census records show that a few families found their way to New Orleans through the more traditional route of passage, from northern Mexico to Texas. For example, the Mexican Hernández, Flores, and Trentes families each had one child in Texas before moving on to New Orleans.[42] Mary and Jesús Reséndez were Tejanos who brought their family to New Orleans, where Jesús found work driving a truck.[43] Francisco Cervantes hailed from Parras, in the border state of Coahuila. A trained machinist, Cervantes crossed the border to San Antonio in 1911 but could not find work in his profession. Indeed, Cervantes's arrival in Texas coincided with an upswing in anti-Mexican violence and Jim Crow practices that affected middle- and working-class Mexicans alike.[44] As Mexican agricultural laborers tried to escape Texas for California and the Midwest, Cervantes heard of an opportunity in New Orleans. Now on the white side of the color line, he did find work as a machinist there. He married Raquel Ramos, a Parras-born woman of upper-middle-class background who had been sent to New Orleans to attend Catholic school.[45] The family settled into a rental home near Clay Square, where their neighbors were almost all Louisiana-born white families whose heads of household practiced skilled trades.[46]

Yet those who came through Texas were the exception, as most Mexicans of all social classes arrived in New Orleans on ship decks, in a context of international trade rather than violent racial threat. Some paid at least $50—a steep sum for poor Mexicans—to ride as proper passengers on a United Fruit Company or Mexican American Fruit Corporation steamship.[47] Men with less means who traveled without families could earn their passage by working menial jobs aboard ships, while others were skilled crew members who might disappear into the city as their vessels sailed on to the next port.

In addition to sailors from around the world, Mexican arrivals shared decks with agricultural goods and import/export businessmen; these businessmen aggressively promoted the idea that trade with Mexico and Latin America was key to their city's future. Though few ships sailed under Mexico's flag, in 1928 and 1929 more Honduran ships docked at New Orleans than did ships from any foreign country, and most of these, as well as several European and U.S. American lines, connected New Orleans to ports along Mexico's Gulf Coast.[48] New Orleans businessmen rejoiced as the United States normalized relations with Mexico's postrevolutionary regime, expecting to see a million dollars of monthly trade between Mexico and New Orleans;[49] "Mexico's Trade Belongs to City" proclaimed a headline in the *Times-Picayune*.[50] In the following years, New Orleans accurately declared itself the "gateway to the Americas," to the chagrin of globally ambitious coastal cities like Miami and Galveston who vied for the same title.[51] Recognizing the need to keep maritime traffic flowing through New Orleans rather than its competitor ports, Louisiana's governor hired a Mexican man to represent the state at trade-related events in Latin America in the late 1920s.[52] With so much public discussion of Latin America's importance to New Orleans's future, it is perhaps no surprise that the city's correspondent from San Antonio's *La Prensa* noted that even New Orleans's major newspaper, the *Times-Picayune*, "has always shown evenhandedness towards Mexico" at a time when papers elsewhere usually did not.[53] Although an economic courtship with Mexico was no guarantee of "evenhandedness" for actual Mexican people, the prominence of trade-related dialogue about the country created an international frame into which such immigrants could insert themselves from the moment of their shipboard arrival.

Attempts to encourage trade with Latin America meant Mexicans' arrival experiences in New Orleans bore little resemblance to those of their counterparts who left Mexico via its northern borderlands. Historians have observed that the U.S.-Mexico land border, and movement across it, was ill policed and even ill demarcated when the Mexican Revolution began. By the early 1920s, the experience of crossing the border became an increasingly humiliating one for Mexicans and indeed a foundational moment for their racialization as a distinct and undesirable group.[54] In El Paso, for example, public health inspectors forced border-crossing Mexicans to strip naked, then searched their scalps for lice and sprayed them with a mixture of soap, kerosene, and water—all because they believed Mexicans were genetically predisposed to carrying disease.[55]

In contrast, New Orleans elites' emphasis on promoting Latin American trade gave Mexicans a more welcoming arrival there in the 1910s–20s. As their steamships neared the port, migrants could see the city's low-profile skyline across the waterfront. They first docked near the new three-building immigration station in Algiers, across the Mississippi River from New Orleans, for immigration and public health inspectors to come on board. Health inspections took place in crowded conditions on deck and, unlike examinations at the southwestern border, were cursory at best. When public health officials tried to implement more thorough screenings in 1910, New Orleans's immigration commissioner discouraged them, saying, "Commerce and trade relations between the port of New Orleans and Central and South America needs stimulating and encouraging."[56] The city's elites wanted the port to welcome, not deter, newcomers, and they successfully pressured federal agencies to fall in line.[57] As boats carrying Mexican migrants continued into the maze of wharves, warehouses, and train tracks that comprised the city's vast international port, inspectors checked passports and distributed six-month visitor permits to those who declared their intention to stay temporarily. Fewer than one in a hundred were barred entry.[58]

Once the ships reached their docks, Mexican crew members may have unloaded bananas or performed final shipboard duties while migrants who could afford passenger fare disembarked into the city's downtown. To the right down Chartres Street, the Cabildo building reigned over Jackson Square, evoking for Mexicans the Spanish colonial architecture in the *zócalos*, town squares, of their home country's state capitals. Italians, Filipinos, and African Americans mingled among Creoles on the French Quarter streets and narrow alleys of their shared neighborhood. Walking onward or boarding a streetcar through New Orleans's dense neighborhoods, Mexicans encountered Irish, German, and Chinese immigrants scattered among white and black residents, their homes often boasting the distinctive Creole iron balustrades that evoked Caribbean architecture.[59] This was hardly a dusty border station like the ones that admitted or excluded Mexicans at El Paso's Santa Fe or Stanton Street bridges, nor was it Los Angeles's railroad depot, which delivered newcomers to a decaying downtown plaza peopled almost exclusively by recently arrived Mexican, Italian, and Eastern European low-wage laborers.[60]

The revolution's final years and ultimate triumph brought Mexicans to New Orleans at a quickened pace. The majority of those present in 1920 had arrived since 1917, suggesting that many considered themselves refugees from the new regime.[61] Their numbers were small but not insignificant: by 1920, the federal census listed 1,242 Mexican-born whites living in New Orleans, slightly more than were living in Chicago that year.[62] It is likely that an additional 10 percent lived there as well, classified by census workers as Negro or mulatto.[63] As these new arrivals adjusted to New Orleans, they would quickly learn to navigate a geography not just physical but, increasingly over the 1910s–20s, racial as well.

Crossing into White New Orleans

Beginning with their maritime border crossings, Mexicans' trajectories in New Orleans were different from their counterparts elsewhere in the United States. In the early years following the revolution, most of the New Orleans Mexican immigrants entered middle-class professions; this reflected their more educated and financially secure origins as well as the relative fluidity of their racial position in the city. The highest number of Mexican immigrant men who arrived by 1920 performed white-collar jobs: they were import/export managers, doctors, teachers, clerks, artists, and musicians, or they worked as ship captains and in other maritime occupations (see table 1). Many of these professionals considered themselves temporary refugees from the revolution, "without power, waiting to return on a moment's notice to our

TABLE 1 Occupations of Mexicano men age sixteen and over (as percentage of all Mexicano men over age sixteen) in New Orleans, 1920 and 1930

	1920	1930
White collar total	45%	32%
Professional/student	11	10
Clerical/sales	17	17
Artist/musician	3	2
Maritime	14	3
Blue collar total	32	51
Skilled	9	12
Semiskilled	10	12
Unskilled	9	27
Not employed/unknown	28	17

Source: 1920 and 1930 manuscript census analysis. See Appendix for methodology.

country," in the words of one upper-class man.[64] Conversely, a sizable minority—about a third of Mexican men—entered blue-collar jobs of various skill levels: they were carpenters, shoemakers, cooks, busboys, or, like Francisco Cervantes, machinists. In contrast, Spanish-surnamed men in Santa Barbara, California, that same year counted just 10 percent of their ranks in white-collar professions, and Mexican immigrants who naturalized in Los Angeles were about a quarter white collar during the 1920s–30s. In both California cities, the vast majority of Mexican men worked as laborers.[65] White perceptions of Mexicans as uniformly working class helped solidify their racialization as a distinct group in the Southwest. In New Orleans, by contrast, Mexicans did not coalesce in any one employment category and thus did not experience the same brand of racialization in the early years of their arrival.

The Catholic Church, however, did attempt to transplant some southwestern understandings of Mexican identity to New Orleans. When Archbishop John Shaw was transferred to New Orleans from San Antonio, he quickly assumed that New Orleans's Mexican arrivals would be just like those he had served in his previous post. New Orleans's Catholic leadership had resisted racial segregation for decades longer than their counterparts elsewhere in the United States, but in the late 1910s Shaw was instrumental in ejecting African Americans from their traditional mixed parishes and sending them instead to newly formed black parishes, usually in run-down buildings on small side streets.[66] For Mexicans, he invited the Oblates of Mary Immaculate, whose work with Mexicans he had admired in San Antonio, to New Orleans, asking them to found a Spanish-speaking parish.[67] Unlike blacks' parishes, Mexicans' parish would be housed in one of New Orleans's finest buildings: the Old Mortuary Chapel on Rampart Street, a large classical revival–style building with expansive arches.[68] The church was renamed Our Lady of Guadalupe, the patron saint of Mexico, and in the 1920s, priests held both Spanish and English masses and delivered sermons in both languages.[69] Shaw believed Mexicans belonged in their own parish, yet his choice of a stately building on a central thoroughfare likely reflected his perception that newly arrived Mexicans were mostly high-class refugees from their country's dangerously radical revolution.[70]

As happened so often in the history of Mexico, paths blazed by emigrants with financial resources were soon trod by those who were poorer.[71] By the 1920s, revolutionary violence had quieted, and many of New Orleans's middle-class refugees returned home while more working-class Mexicans began arriving, largely but not exclusively from the Gulf Coast. While the number of Mexicans in New Orleans was about the same in 1930 as a decade before, 1930 manuscript census pages show that over half of Mexican immigrant men in New Orleans that year occupied blue-collar positions, as middle-class refugees returned home and more working-class immigrants arrived (see table 1). The fastest growth was in the ranks of unskilled labor: by 1930, more than a quarter of Mexicano men in New Orleans were performing unskilled common labor just like their counterparts in the Southwest, and over half worked in blue-collar jobs of all skill levels. For example, Jesús Elizondo arrived in New Orleans in 1928 and found work at a dredging company. In 1930, he lived in a boardinghouse on Bancroft Drive with eleven other recently arrived single Mexican dredge workers, all ages twenty-four through thirty-seven, as well as Italian and black single boarders.[72] Even those who had arrived prior to 1920 reflected this new, more working-class balance of occupations since middle-class emigrants of the revolution years were more likely to have returned home. Shipyard laborer Vicente González, for example, arrived during the revolution but did not follow the self-proclaimed "refugees" home when it ended.[73] By 1930, then, outsiders could well have perceived that most Mexicans worked blue-collar jobs—a stigma that could have branded the entire group as racially inferior.

Changes in women's migration and labor patterns also signaled the increasingly working-class character of New Orleans's Mexican population over the course of the 1920s, as more single Mexican women came to work in the city. Women comprised 42 percent of New Orleans's adult Mexicanos

TABLE 2 Occupations of Mexicana women age sixteen and over (as percentage of all Mexicana women over age sixteen) in New Orleans, 1920 and 1930

	1920	1930
White collar total	5%	13%
Professional/student	1	10
Clerical/sales	4	3
Blue collar total	13	21
Skilled blue collar	0	1
Semiskilled blue collar	5	10
Unskilled blue collar	2	1
Domestic	6	9
Not employed/unknown	82	65

Source: 1920 and 1930 manuscript census analysis. See Appendix for methodology.

immigrants in 1920 and 49 percent in 1930, a gender balance similar to that among Mexican immigrants in the United States as a whole in those years.[74] Just one in six New Orleans Mexicana immigrants counted in the 1920 census were single working women, but by 1930 that share had doubled.[75] Those who immigrated after 1920 had an even higher percentage of single blue-collar working women than their counterparts who had arrived prior to 1920 and remained to be counted on the 1930 census.[76] These women worked as housekeepers, laundresses, seamstresses, or waitresses (see table 2). Mexican widow Analeta Cruz, for example, did not know how to read and write and so supported her Louisiana-born son and niece by working as a housekeeper in a private home.[77] Never-married Ethel Sastre, age forty-two, lived as a roomer in a boardinghouse of native-born white people.[78] She worked as a seamstress—in Spanish, *sastre*—suggesting that the census enumerator might have misconstrued her profession for her last name. Again, Mexican immigrants' increasing deviation from the white middle-class norm could—and did, in other U.S. locations—shape the racial ideas that white Americans held about them by the early years of the Depression.[79]

Yet even as changing immigration patterns lowered the occupational statuses of the Mexican community as a whole, individual Mexican immigrants did not experience downward mobility as their counterparts in Los Angeles did during this time.[80] On the contrary, some were edging their way up. Laborer Manuel Villa and musician Florencio Ramos both listed the same profession in 1920 and 1930, but others experienced upward mobility.[81] Miguel Henriquez, for example, migrated to the United States as a teenager before the Mexican Revolution and in 1920 was working as a laborer in New Orleans and living with his white Louisiana-born wife. By 1930, he had left blue-collar life to become the proprietor of a store.[82] León and Margarita Rodríguez immigrated during the later years of the revolution, and he quickly found work as a salesman; by 1930, he had become the captain of a steamship.[83] While it is likely that at least some Mexican immigrants experienced employment discrimination, long-standing immigrants as a whole were upwardly mobile.[84] In all, by 1930 New Orleans's Mexican immigrant population was more white collar than its southwestern and midwestern counterparts yet sufficiently blue collar that, under the right circumstances, white New Orleaneans could have started to see them as a distinct, inferior racial group just as white Californians, Texans, and Chicagoans had done by this time.

New Orleans did not follow the trajectories of those other places in the 1910s–30s. Mexican immigrants' memories, residential concentration in white neighborhoods, and ability to choose white marriage partners all demonstrate that rather than becoming identified as a distinct racial group, Mexicans quickly came to occupy a spot within the white racial category in New Orleans. When a sociologist interviewed Mexican immigrants in New Orleans in the late 1940s, several interviewees who had been there since the 1920s reported that they had never faced discrimination in the Crescent City. "There was too much discrimination in Texas is another reason why I wanted to get away from there," said one interviewee. "I thought New Orleans would be better. I have not found any discrimination in New Orleans so far. See, if I was in Texas I would not be able to be a Mason," he added.[85] Mexicans also did not file any discrimination-related protests to the local Mexican consulate despite the fact that Mexican immigrants regularly complained of discrimination to consuls elsewhere in the United States, including in nearby Mississippi.[86] Finally, interviews conducted in the 2000s with widows and descendants of New Orleans's Mexican immigrants revealed that stories of discrimination, if they existed, had not been passed down in family memory.[87] Some noted that the first time they had felt different from other white New Orleaneans was in the late 1960s, when the Chicano Movement elsewhere drew attention to the concept of Mexican ethnicity, or in the twenty-first century, when anti-Latino sentiments followed Latino immigrants to the city after Hurricane Katrina.[88] Of course, memories collected seventy years after the fact or passed down intergenerationally do not necessarily capture migrants' historical experiences with precision.

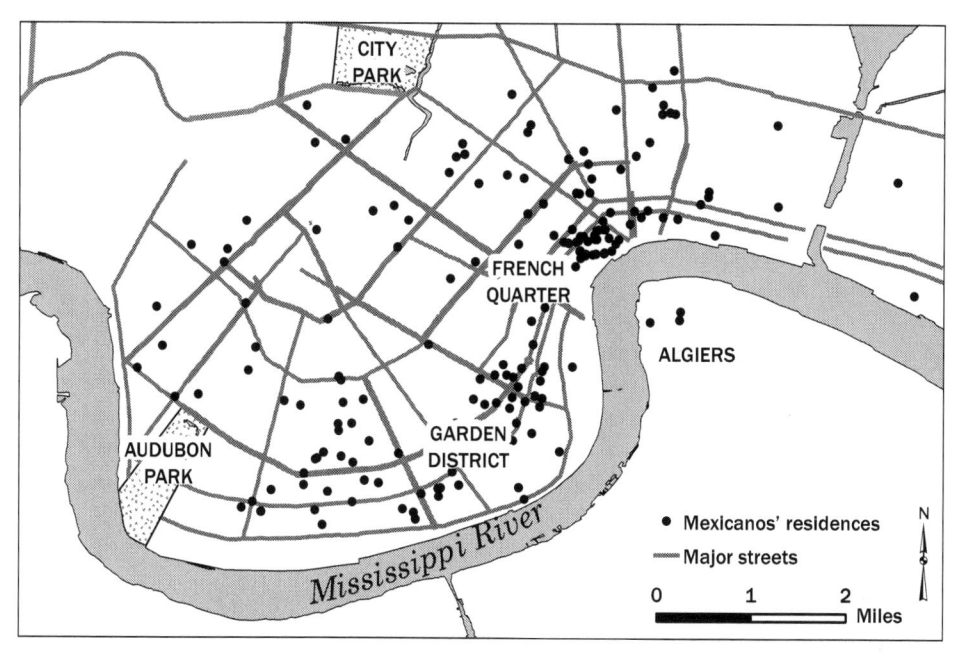

MAP 2 Mexicanos' residences in New Orleans, 1930. Data from U.S. manuscript census pages (see Appendix). Map by the author.

In this case, however, both residential and marriage patterns suggest that these historical memories do reflect the majority of Mexicans' actual experiences in interwar New Orleans. In this period, the Southwest's urban Mexicans tended to live in distinct enclaves that were heavily but not exclusively Mexican, while those in Chicago spread out through the west side of town. In those places, Mexicans shared their neighborhoods with Italians, Poles, Japanese, Jews, and sometimes a few African Americans.[89] Indeed, in every other case of interwar Mexican settlement that historians have studied to date, residential segregation contributed importantly to emerging ideas that Mexicans comprised a distinct and inferior race. In New Orleans, by contrast, a notable concentration of Mexicanos lived in the French Quarter alongside Creole and immigrant neighbors, but larger numbers spread throughout the entire city, including the Garden District and Uptown neighborhoods associated with the Anglophone elite (see map 2). In both 1920 and 1930, a typical Mexican immigrant household contained the only Latin Americans on the block, and no block was majority Mexican or Latin American.[90] New Orleans had no barrio.

Segregation as a whole looked different in this and other cramped southern port cities, such as Charleston, that came of age in antebellum times.

Mexican Nationalism and Assimilation in New Orleans   29

These centers of the Old South were less segregated in the 1920s than Chicago or rapidly growing Los Angeles; their comparative integration was the legacy of a time when servitude demanded proximity, and racial inequality required no forcible reminder in order to persist.[91] Yet New Orleans's residential segregation increased through the 1920s, and the Louisiana legislature legalized it in 1924.[92] Mexicans thus arrived in New Orleans exactly as its new, segregated order was taking shape.

An examination of Mexicanos' neighbors in 1920 and 1930 reflects this changing order and shows that overall, they did not experience the nonwhite spatial categorization that their peers in the Southwest and Chicago did during these years. Characteristic of the city's mixed composition in 1920, 54 percent of Mexican immigrants lived in neighborhoods that included both native-born white and black residents that year, while 45 percent lived among native-born whites but not native-born blacks. By 1930, however, the city was more segregated. Though the Mexicanos present that year were more working class than a decade before, now just 36 percent lived in mixed neighborhoods while 59 percent shared their streets with native-born white but not native-born black neighbors. In both years, fewer than 3 percent of Mexicanos lived in all-black neighborhoods.[93] Observers in the early 1930s also noted that "the Spanish, French, and Latin-Americans have their national clubs, but their homes are to be found in various residential sections."[94] Mexicanos thus experienced increasing inclusion in white New Orleans at exactly the moment that blacks were increasingly excluded.

Mexicanos who had immigrant neighbors also had distinct experiences and opportunities as compared with their counterparts elsewhere. In Los Angeles and Chicago, Mexicans lived among immigrant groups, like Italians and Eastern Europeans, that fell somewhere between black and white. Not so in New Orleans. In 1920 and 1930, more than half of Mexicanos lived in neighborhoods that included at least some Italians or Eastern Europeans, but an equal or larger number shared their blocks with Northern and Western Europeans, those considered whiter in the logic of the time.[95] August Pradillo, for example, had a few Italian and French neighbors on his all-white block in the Bayou St. John neighborhood, while Mexican Ralph Gutiérrez and German Frederick Swartz and their families were the only two foreign households on their all-white block in Uptown.[96] This distribution roughly mirrored the slightly larger number of Northern and Western Europeans in the city as compared with Italians, yet it still suggests that Mexican immigrants did not experience the same spatial segregation as their peers elsewhere.[97] Unlike their counterparts in Los Angeles and Chicago, Mexicanos

TABLE 3 Marriage partners of Mexicano men (as percentage of married Mexicano men) in New Orleans, 1920 and 1930

	1920	1930
Mexican*	59%	52%
U.S.-born white	29	39
U.S.-born Negro/mulatto	7	3
Spanish/Latin American	3	5
European immigrants (not Spanish)	2	0

Source: 1920 and 1930 manuscript census analysis. See Appendix for methodology.
*Mexican refers to both individuals listed as Mexican-race and Mexican nationals listed as white or Negro. See Appendix for more information on these determinations.

in New Orleans were spread throughout the city as a whole, more likely to live among native-born whites and Northern and Western Europeans than to be relegated to the neighborhoods of Italians and Eastern Europeans, let alone blacks. Residential segregation with "undesirable" immigrant groups, a critical marker of Mexicans' nonwhiteness during the interwar period in every other case that historians have probed, was absent for New Orleans's Mexicanos.

Mexicanos, particularly Mexican men, also freely crossed into white New Orleans in their search for marriage partners—a significant fact in the context of the era's scientific racism and antimiscegenation laws and attitudes. Since the nineteenth century, Mexican women in the Southwest had been considered eligible marriage partners while Mexican men were more likely to be seen as a racial threat.[98] These gender-specific racial ideas persisted, and in interwar Los Angeles, 33 percent of Mexican immigrant women married white men while only 16 percent of Mexican immigrant men married white women.[99] Men in New Orleans had the opposite experience. By the time the Mexican population was more settled there in 1930, 41 percent of Mexican and Mexican American men had U.S.-born white wives (see table 3). Even working-class men classified as "Mexican" race on the census, like ice cream peddler Gerino Morantes, married white women and started families with them.[100] The statistic has particular significance in the context of the Jim Crow South, where trumped-up fears of black male sexuality led to countless lynchings, structuring the entire system of segregation.[101]

A comparatively smaller share of New Orleans's Mexican and Mexican American women—17 percent in 1930—were married to U.S.-born white men

TABLE 4 Marriage partners of Mexicana women (as percentage of married Mexicana women) in New Orleans, 1920 and 1930

	1920	1930
Mexican*	60%	63%
U.S.-born white	26	17
Spanish/Latin American	9	12
U.S.-born Negro/mulatto	3	2
European immigrants (not Spanish)	2	6
Filipino	0	1

Source: 1920 and 1930 manuscript census analysis. See Appendix for methodology.
*Mexican refers to both individuals listed as Mexican-race and Mexican nationals listed as white or Negro. See Appendix for more information on these determinations.

(see table 4). That year, 6 percent of Mexicana women were married to European immigrant men from countries including Ireland, France, and Poland, and 12 percent were married to immigrants from Spain or Latin American countries including Peru, Honduras, and Guatemala. Mexican men's higher rates of marriage to non-Mexicans in this period reflect the fact that they were more likely to come to the city alone and find marriage partners there, while adult women were more likely to arrive married. In fact, many marriages between Mexican women and non-Mexican men had begun in Mexico, presumably when those men had lived there as immigrants or businessmen. Leonor Sánchez, for example, came to the United States with her Spanish-born husband, Joaquín, and the couple's four young children, all Mexican born, in 1917. They then had five more children once in New Orleans.[102] Another Mexican woman, Ernestine Bowling, arrived in 1928 along with her Louisiana-born husband Benjamin, a salesman, as well as the couple's three Mexican-born children. Families like the Bowlings solidified Mexicans' image as an "international" element in a port city that fancied itself a gateway to Latin American trade, rather than as a denigrated, working-class, nonwhite immigrant group.

Indeed, while "Mexican" came to be seen elsewhere as not just a national origin but a distinct racial group, the racial identity of "Mexican," bureaucratically enshrined for the first and last time in its own category on the 1930 census, did not cohere in New Orleans. The Census Bureau gathered its data through hired surveyors, known as enumerators, who went house to house during a two-week period in April, recording information about the "usual" residents of a household and asking at-home family members for details about those who happened to be out.[103] In their instructions for racial categorization, enumerators across the country were told, "Practically all Mexican laborers are of a racial mixture difficult to classify, though usually well recognized in the localities where they are found. In order to obtain separate figures for this racial group, it has been decided that all persons born in Mexico, or having parents born in Mexico, who are not definitely white, Negro, Indian, Chinese, or Japanese, should be returned as Mexican ('Mex')."[104] Like most understandings of Mexicans' racial identities at the time, this bureaucratic definition of "Mexican" conflated social and cultural markers with biological ones. It equated "Mexican" with laborer, a racial identity scientifically imprecise yet "well recognized" by enumerators who understood the contours of their own communities. In western cities like Los Angeles, a Mexican was "well recognized" indeed: he was a Spanish-speaking foreigner in a specific part of town who occupied the lowest rung on the economic ladder; the exact tone of his skin or color of his eyes was less material. There, just 5 percent of Mexicans received the "white" racial categorization, and nearly all others were labeled "Mexican" on the 1930 census.[105]

In New Orleans, by contrast, cultural, class, and spatial characteristics were of no help for enumerators trying to "recognize" who was or was not racially Mexican, since Mexicans were not concentrated in any particular industry or neighborhood or in the working class. In New Orleans, more than four in every ten Mexican-born individuals were categorized as white in 1930, 3 percent were categorized as Negro, and just over half were logged as Mexican.[106] How did New Orleans's census enumerators decide who was Mexican and who was white? One clue lies in the selections of those enumerators who were charged with surveying multiple Mexican families. These enumerators were themselves white, and most were women.[107] While some categorized all Mexican-born people as "Mexican," many assigned different categories not only to different households of Mexican-born individuals but even to different members of a household, thus defying the period's basic logic of race as biologically inherited. Their choices reveal that no social, economic, or geographic characteristics determined someone's assignment to the Mexican racial category. Census worker Louise Jung, for example, coded one Mexican man married to white women as Mexican, another man in the same situation as white. She returned a Mexican laborer as Mexican and a Mexican prisoner as white. Another enumerator, Karl Gille, coded a Mexican-born man married to a white woman as white. The couple's children, however, were listed as Mexican, suggesting that they had darker skin than both of their parents. Indeed, with the Mexican racial category not at all "well recognized" in New Orleans, census enumerators likely relied on visual cues in inconsistent ways, attempting to apply biological criteria to a racial category that the census itself admitted eluded biology. The category "Mexican," generated for national use, had little social and cultural meaning for the enumerators who tried to apply its bureaucratic definition in the Crescent City.

Even the sole recorded observation of Mexicans' discrimination in New Orleans demonstrates that white New Orleaneans did not see "Mexican" as a distinct racial group. When a sociologist writing in 1949 claimed that New Orleans's Latin Americans did not experience discrimination, he added a footnote: "In extremely rare cases some Anglos tend to shy away from those Latins who, because of Indian (?) ancestry, are somewhat dark.... The Anglos think they recognize the Latin as a member of the Negro race and tend to treat him categorically according to their conception of the 'stereotyped negro.'"[108] Like census enumerators, the offending white New Orleaneans in the sociologist's example placed Latin American immigrants into the area's traditional racial categories rather than imagining that they occupied their own. Though marriage, residential, and occupational patterns show that Mexicans were not segregated or discriminated against systematically, it is difficult to know how many Mexicans—perhaps on an errand away from their white spouse or neighborhood—were perceived as black and treated accordingly in stores, streetcars, or other public spaces.

While white New Orleaneans recognized "Mexican" as a national identity rather than a race, it is more difficult to determine how African Americans considered them. Black newspapers including the nationally distributed *Chicago Defender* and the local *Louisiana Weekly* had their eye on Mexicans' desegregation efforts in Texas and elsewhere, but neither acknowledged the Mexican presence in New Orleans.[109] The National Association for the Advancement of Colored People (NAACP) official magazine, *The Crisis*, lauded Mexican–black labor solidarity, including nearby in a 1913 rural Louisiana timber workers' strike.[110] But the magazine did not devote regular coverage to Mexicans and thus had little effect on black New Orleaneans' views of the subject. Records of African Americans' personal lives show that many did interact with Mexicans. Both black painter Blair Legendre and Pullman porter Joseph Ducoing married Mexican women, and countless others shared streets with Mexican families in racially mixed neighborhoods.[111] Yet these scant clues leave unanswered the question of whether most African Americans understood, resented, or simply did not know that the city's Mexicans managed to defy strict racial categorization just as Afro-descended people of varying skin tones and identities became bound by it.

By 1930, "Mexican" was mostly, if not entirely, a national identity within the white category rather than a racial identity unto itself in New Orleans. Though lower in the racial hierarchy than the Anglo-Saxon upper class, Mexicans were classed among white ethnics and immigrants rather than as a distinct racial group.[112] They lived among native-born whites and European immigrants; Mexican men married white women almost as often as they married Mexican women. While a small handful joined African American households and communities, the vast majority integrated themselves into white New Orleans. Even once working-class migrants replaced middle-class refugees, the community continued to elude racial categorization as a distinct group.[113]

Up the Road, across the Racial Line

Yet if Mexicans had, over the course of the 1910s–20s, acquired degraded racial connotations in congressional debates, academic discourse, and popular culture in all of their significant migration destinations, would New Orleans continue to be an exception? In the interwar period, systematic racial oppression plagued Mexicanos not only in their major western population centers but even in places where their numbers were few. From Michigan to Kansas in the rural Midwest, preexisting negative ideas about Mexicans prompted varying degrees of racial discrimination from the late 1910s onward.[114] In the urban Midwest, Mexicans lived in mixed neighborhoods but were often excluded from dance halls and relegated to the worst jobs in industrial plants. Though Anglo-Mexican divides were not structured into society as thoroughly in the Midwest as in the Southwest, they nonetheless affected Mexicans' lives, politics, and identities from the earliest moments of their arrival at these new destinations.[115]

Furthermore, concerned Mexicans in New Orleans did not have to look as far as the Midwest for examples of small Mexican communities that experienced harsh treatment based on race; such communities lived just up the road in Louisiana. Within 100 miles of New Orleans lay sugar-producing areas of the state where planters recruited Mexican workers exclusively for low-wage agricultural work otherwise performed by black laborers. In these places, Mexicans were definitively not considered to be white. These rural racial experiences pointed to the potential precariousness of Mexicans' seemingly easily assimilation into white New Orleans and did not escape the notice of the city's Mexican community leaders.

As in the Midwest, rural Louisianans had formed ideas about Mexicans prior to their actual arrival in town. Most white sugar industry managers and planters read about them in their widely circulated trade publication, the *Louisiana Planter and Sugar Manufacturer*. There, frequent accounts of Mexico's sugar industry described Mexican workers as having distinct and innate racial characteristics. One author described Mexicans as "childlike Indians or mixed breeds who have no more notion of a white man's method of working than they have wireless telegraphy. They can pick their food, and so to speak, their houses off the wild jungle trees."[116] These Mexicans, characterized as racially Indian and climatically prone to backwardness, received significantly more negative portrayals than even Southern Europeans in the publication.[117]

Even so, sugar planters had tried to recruit thousands of Mexicans to rural Louisiana as early as 1905.[118] Such schemes faded during the years of Mexico's revolution, only to return shortly afterward. In 1918, Louisiana's sugar industry embarked on a concerted lobbying effort to bring 50,000 Mexicans to rice and sugar parishes in rural Louisiana at federal government expense. The discussion among sugar plantation owners and managers employed racial descriptions that distinguished among Mexicans from different regions. A sugar impresario who had worked in Mexico claimed that workers could be found in southern Mexico who were "a very desirable class of laborers and excellent substitutes for the ordinary Louisiana field laborers." Such workers, he assured his audience, "are not of the banditti type found in Northern Mexico, but quiet and good workers."[119] When the U.S. federal government proved unwilling to help subsidize the cost of southern Mexicans' transport to Louisiana, sugar industry advocates despaired.[120] Since the cost would not be subsidized, lamented the *Louisiana Planter and Sugar Manufacturer*, "it means that the cheapest Mexican labor is labor from Northern Mexico and that the cost of bringing laborers from the peaceful districts of southern Mexico will be too great to bring the very desirable Mexicans from there and compel the Louisiana sugar men to rely upon the reputed shiftless greasers of Chihuahua and her sister states, always the birthplace of riot and revolution."[121] These contrasting depictions of Mexican workers shared an assumption that all of the workers in question bore inherent racial traits unfit for assimilation into white Louisiana. Census enumerators in rural Louisiana held similar racial assumptions: in Sabine Parish, every one of 1,906 Mexican-born people enumerated in 1930 was classified as racially Mexican.[122] In rural Louisiana, unlike New Orleans, the Mexican racial category quickly became "well recognized." And that race was definitely not white. Indeed, Mexicans in at least one rural Louisiana town, Westlake, socialized with African Americans in their leisure time.[123]

Several thousand Mexicans did arrive to work in the state's sugar and lumber industries in the 1910s, though their numbers fell well short of planters' hopes.[124] Mexicans at Bogalusa's Great Southern Lumber Company were "very satisfied" with their working conditions and "unbeatable wages" in 1918 according to Texas's Spanish-language press, but soon thereafter the workers experienced their subjugated racial status in the form of violence.[125] In 1923, more than sixty Mexican workers employed by the company lodged a complaint with the New Orleans Mexican consulate alleging that not only were their wages lower than those promised by the contractors who had recruited them in Texas, but "if they attempt to quit and see other places of employment they are brought back to the quarters by guards and placed in confinement."[126] Planters thus attempted to use on Mexicans the same violent labor controls that had long confined blacks in the lowest rungs of southern agricultural labor. Mexican consulate officials, called to respond in this and other cases of violence and discrimination in rural Louisiana, could not take for granted Mexicans' more advantageous position in New Orleans. In a national and even local context of Mexicans' systematic racialization and exclusion, New Orleans's Mexican leaders would have to keep the question of their compatriots' racial image foremost in their minds.[127]

Giving Meaning to "Mexican"

Such leaders were few, as Mexican New Orleaneans' geographic and occupational dispersion left the community with little potential for organizational life. This distinguished them not only from their Mexican counterparts elsewhere but also from Caribbean immigrants to the Gulf port of Tampa, who rallied around both nationalism and labor politics in their predominant industry, cigar rolling.[128] In New Orleans, no local labor union represented more than a handful of Mexicans, and the community never created Mexican Comisiones Honoríficas or other nationalist mutual aid societies, like their counterparts in the West, Midwest, and even nearby Shreveport, Louisiana, and the Mississippi Delta.[129] Our Lady of Guadalupe, the Catholic church dedicated just for Mexicans, never drew the majority of Mexicans to its pews.[130] Thus, other than Latin American student groups at local universities, the Mexican consulate provided the only formal structure for collective activity among Mexican immigrants, and the only avenue for Mexicans' collective self-representation in the city.[131] White neighbors and power holders assigned no clear racial meaning to the idea of "Mexican," and most immigrants like Robert Canedo, the soldier whose portrait began this chapter (fig. 3), declined to fill the void in any vocal way. The charge of representing Mexico to New Orleans thus fell to a core group of middle-class families who actively maintained a Mexican cultural life—families like that of Hortensia Horcasitas, whose Mexican dance photograph also began this chapter (fig. 2). While consulates sought to influence Mexico's image in locations throughout the United States, the New Orleans Mexican consulate was in the unique position of being the only visible representative of Mexicans in the city and even the region.[132]

In protecting their advantageous position in the Jim Crow South, consular officials and elite Mexican families could have pursued several different strategies. They could have emphasized the difference between themselves—whiter, Europeanized, and middle class—and poor Mexican laborers, protecting their own interests and racialization at the expense of others. Anglos in Texas had made such distinctions among Mexicans for decades, and white Louisianans likely would have accepted them, too. Prior to the advent of the "Mexican" racial category on the 1930 census, for example, a New Orleans enumerator in 1920 listed Mexican merchant Agustín Valles's race as "white," while recording his two Mexican servants, Rosa García and Teresa Vargas, as "Indian."[133] Reinforcing notions of intra-Mexican racial distinctions, such as those held by this census enumerator, might have proven a successful strategy for ensuring the continued privileges of middle-class Mexicans in New Orleans.

Mexican elites could also have followed the lead of New Orleans's other racially questionable groups, whose strategies for negotiating Jim Crow varied widely. Italians, for example, freely formed families with blacks in the late nineteenth century, advocated labor unionism at a time when the movement flirted with interracialism, and paid the price for these transgressions when eleven Italians died at the hands of a white lynch mob in 1891.[134] For its part, the mixed-race French-Spanish cultural group long known as "Creole" split along race lines in the wake of emancipation and Reconstruction. Creoles who considered themselves "white" created discourses of "purity of blood," actively refuting allegations about their mixed racial ancestry and adopting an emphatically white racial identity that persisted into the late twentieth century.[135] Those who identified differently or had darker skin now became known as "Creoles of color." Some tried to "pass" as white but others adopted an antiracist ideology inspired by the liberal and egalitarian ideals of the French Revolution; Supreme Court plaintiff Homer Plessy, who had just one black great-grandparent, emerged from this milieu.[136] For him and many other Creoles of color, Jim Crow was not to be eluded but rather challenged.

White Creoles' strategy to make outright claims about their nonblack racial inheritance had some recent precedent in the history of Mexico, as did the antiracist politics pursued by Creoles of color. In 1923, as the Mexican Revolution's competing factions continued to vie for power, the Mexican embassy in Washington responded to the expulsion of Mexicans and blacks from Johnstown, Pennsylvania, by eugenically distinguishing the two groups. "The percentage of negroes is far lower in Mexico than in the United States, and there is no justification for Mayor Cauffield's act in classifying them with negroes," protested Charge d'Affairs Manuel Tellez.[137] In this case, Mexican elites, like New Orleans's emphatically white Creoles, claimed a form of "purity of blood" and explicitly distanced themselves from black ancestry. Conversely, from the 1890s onward, many prominent Mexican and Latin American intellectuals advocated direct resistance to Jim Crow.[138] Mexico's most well-known theorist of racial nationalism, José Vasconcelos, wrote deliberately against white supremacy and the discrimination he had witnessed as a student in Eagle Pass, a Texas border town.[139] The postrevolutionary elite's anti-imperialist outlook easily fostered a tradition of disdain for white supremacy even as bureaucrats facing off with the United States sometimes adopted its eugenic discourses.

But Mexican immigrants in interwar New Orleans chose neither of these paths, drawing instead on a different strain in Mexican cultural history. Though "Mexican" had not solidified as a distinct racial category in New Orleans, it certainly had in Mexican elite discourse by 1930. The ideology of *mestizaje*, which valorized white–Indian mixture as the foundation of Mexicanness, first emerged in colonial times and became modernized in the late nineteenth century during the reign of Porfirio Díaz, the conservative strongman the revolution overthrew.[140] The progress-oriented positivist intellectuals that surrounded Díaz, known as the *científicos*, advanced the ideology of mestizaje to reconcile Mexico's reality—that of a majority-Indian, caste-divided society—with the ideals of a modern, homogenous nation. They emphasized the potential of all Mexicans to whiten through eugenic means like race mixing and European immigration, as well as cultural means like education, hygiene, clothing, and cosmopolitanism. In this worldview, culture and class could enable mestizos to overcome biology.[141] European physical features were valued inasmuch as they were believed to bring with them the benefits of economic progress and modernity, but for mestizos—particularly urban mestizos—the latter could be achieved without the former.[142] By the late 1920s, the *raza cósmica* or "cosmic race" ideology fashioned itself as a new part of a "revolutionary" cultural program that celebrated race mixing and explicitly rejected U.S.-style white supremacy.[143] Historians have since observed that mestizaje, too, was a eugenic ideal that celebrated white and Indian over black and Chinese blood. Depending on who invoked it, mestizaje could potentially be white supremacy's mirror image rather than its subversion.[144] Nonetheless, by 1930 the consolidating Mexican government's official investment in mestizaje made it unfashionable and even impractical for Mexican elites in New Orleans to make or win a eugenic argument for whiteness. By their own accounts, they were not white.[145]

Notwithstanding the admonitions of Mexican and Latin American intellectuals, both the political dominance of white supremacy in New Orleans and the international imbalance of power between Mexico and the United States mitigated against a potential strategy to challenge Jim Crow itself, as Creole plaintiff Homer Plessy had done. Mexican politicians in this period constantly struggled to balance opposition with accommodation in their relationship with the United States, given their northern neighbor's repeated interventions in Mexican political and economic affairs. As a result, the New Orleans consulate and the Mexican Foreign Service in general often cooperated with white supremacy in matters affecting relations between the two countries. Taken together, a series of confusions and rulings on Mexico's relationship to African Americans shows that Mexican bureaucrats were very willing to distinguish between white and black Americans in their day-to-day business. Whatever their theoretical ruminations on the desirability of race mixing and the injustices of Jim Crow, in practice the postrevolutionary government cooperated with white supremacy as a matter of survival.[146]

In 1922, Mexican president Alvaro Obregón invited black Americans to settle in Mexico, but between the mid-1920s and the late 1930s Mexican policy changed repeatedly on this count.[147] At various times, blacks were singled out, required to furnish bonds to prove that they would not be an economic burden on Mexico as a condition of entry, or denied admission to Mexico entirely. In the late 1920s, Mexican border agents refused African American boxer Harry Willis entry into Mexico to participate in a scheduled fight. When the director of the Tuskegee Institute asked the Mexican embassy in Washington for a policy clarification, the embassy indicated that in fact there was no prohibition on African American immigration to Mexico.[148]

No Mexican government ever articulated a justification for having separate immigration policies for black and white U.S. Americans, but Marcus Garvey speculated that Mexico wanted to avoid its historical association as a haven for U.S. blacks, lest the U.S. government have additional pretexts for intervention.[149] Whether or not Garvey's speculation was accurate, by the 1930s Mexican bureaucrats dealing with the United States had developed at least a basic sensitivity to the politics of white supremacy and had established a precedent of willingness to comply with it.

Yet unlike the consulate's racial arguments in the case of Mexicans' and blacks' expulsion from Johnstown, Pennsylvania, in 1923, in the early 1930s Mexican elites in New Orleans did not argue that their countrymen were genetically white or not black. They also did not put their compatriots at risk by openly decrying the Jim Crow system. Rather, they focused on Mexicans' cultural compatibility with the white United States even as they remained silent about their biological bona fides. Mexican revolutionary nationalism contained a tension between a race-based celebration of mestizaje and the legacy of Porfirian positivism's emphasis on whitening. The cultural program of Mexico's New Orleans consulate demonstrates just one way in which intense contact with the United States long favored the dominance of the Porfirian legacy.[150]

The social and racial identities and ideologies of Armando Amador, vice-consul and later consul at New Orleans from 1928 to 1932, exemplified his government's conundrum. Amador was, for a time, the most prominent representative of *Mexicanidad* in New Orleans. A native of Zacatecas, Amador was well educated and multilingual; he worked as a journalist, novelist, and poet before, during, and after his time in the consular service. At the same time, his identity documents defined his race as "trigueño," literally wheat-colored, or "moreno claro," light-dark.[151] Both mestizo and modern, Amador was the quintessential representative of the new Mexican nationalist ideal, but in Louisiana his racial descriptors might have earned him a spot in the black train car alongside another mixed-race intellectual, Homer Plessy.

In his representations of race in Mexico, Amador never attempted to assert that Mexicans were biologically European, but he also did not espouse the ideologies of mestizaje that by then had become the favored radical rhetoric of Mexico's moderate "Sonoran Dynasty" leaders as they consolidated rule between 1920 and 1934. Hemmed in by an unequal international power dynamic, New Orleans's self-identified upper-class Mexicans understood that they could not successfully challenge white supremacy. Yet, as representatives of a national program celebrating Indian bloodlines, and often adopting mestizo identities themselves, they could not claim to be biologically white. Middle-class Mexican nationalists like young dancer Hortensia Horcasitas's father, Andrés, and the Mexican consuls he befriended walked a careful line, remaining silent about mestizaje and race while drawing on Mexico's positivist tradition of whitening through culture and class. They secured their place in white New Orleans not through claims about legal or biological race but rather through promises of international cooperation, the neutralization of the revolution's political legacy, and the transformation of racial difference into folk culture.

To this end, Amador gave speeches throughout the state of Louisiana to educate its populace about Mexico and was also active in the city's Latin American intellectual circles.[152] As trading partners, objects of touristic fascination, and willing workers on both sides of the border, Mexicans in Amador's portrayal carried with them a folk heritage but ultimately were committed to full cooperation with the United States as a whole and the Jim Crow landscape of New Orleans more specifically. In his representations of race in Mexico, Amador never asserted that Mexicans were biologically European nor that they were biologically mestizo.

Rather than biologically inherited race, Amador discussed culture. Specifically, he emphasized the compatibility of Mexican culture with European culture, describing its indigenous elements as beautiful yet inevitably subordinate to European ones. For example, in 1929 at Tulane's Latin American Center, Amador delivered a lecture in Spanish titled "The Renaissance of Mexican Art." Amador's speech praised the art of the Maya and the Nahua, yet claimed that the dominance of white men over the continent was "unavoidable" from the day Columbus landed in the Americas. "Nonetheless," he said, "the artistic soul of the conquered race was not dead, but rather . . . little by little inserted itself into the new culture, wrapping itself in this new spirit, learning to think and to feel within the new philosophical and ethical norms."[153] The following year, he gave a speech on New Orleans radio, describing Mexico's emergence from "two races possessing high standards of civilization." He then went on to describe Mexico's "floating gardens in which the Indians cultivate flowers unequaled for their color and aroma."[154] In both cases, Amador valued Indians' contribution to Mexican culture while assuring listeners that their backward ways would not hinder the nation's European-style modernization. In this sense, he reflected Mexican intellectual currents of the time that prized Indian cultures as the "raw material" for an emerging national aesthetic tradition that would ultimately be shaped by educated men.[155]

In the same vein, Amador's public accounts of Mexican history deliberately presented a moderate political image of the Mexican Revolution. The revolution's perceived radicalism, a useful image within Mexico for a new regime seeking broad legitimacy, had prompted Anglos to react violently and repress Mexicans further in the Southwest.[156] Revolutionary leader Emiliano Zapata's demand for land redistribution from foreign and domestic wealthy landowners to peasant cooperatives threatened U.S. business interests and concerned white observers not only along the border but also in Louisiana. The *Louisiana Planter and Sugar Manufacturer*, for example, decried the "abuses and crimes" of the "so-called Zapatistas"[157] who had filled "the indifferent Mexican peon" with "hatred of the gringoes and foreigners."[158] In a 1930 speech to a fraternity at Louisiana State University, Consul Amador combatted this image directly, asserting that Mexico had had just one "real" revolution—that of moderates Francisco Madero and Venustiano Carranza, not the more radical Zapata and Pancho Villa. Just as elites within Mexico began to mythologize Zapata and Villa as heroes of a revolution that in reality had defeated them, Amador's account of the revolution to Louisianans minimized them.[159] Once again, though Amador could not affirm Mexicans' biological whiteness, he could neutralize the threat their difference posed in the minds of elite white southerners.

Most strikingly, Amador freely discussed the African influences in Mexican culture, in defiance of official mestizaje's denial of Mexico's African roots. While New Orleans's racially suspect white Creoles had insisted that their bloodlines were pure and free of African influences, Amador made no such insistence, instead casting Mexico's African heritage as an object of folk fascination. In 1930, he sponsored a gala event at the Jung Hotel, one of the city's largest and priciest, in honor of Mexico's Independence Day.[160] He did so together with the Mexico Society of New Orleans, a group of white businessmen that promoted business ties with Mexico. The Mexican and U.S. flags hung from the walls, and the Mexican national anthem was met with a "warm and prolonged applause." Democratic mayor T. Semmes Walmsley, a white conservative segregationist, was on the program and offered his personal greetings and congratulations, which were broadcast through the city on a popular radio station.[161] For Walmsley, apparently, Mexicans and blacks fell into entirely different categories of appropriate social interaction.

And then, right in front of Walmsley and the city's white business elites, young Mexican women performed a "typical" Mexican jarocho song and dance. Jarocho music was typical to Mexico's Gulf Coast state of Veracruz, whose port provided New Orleans's most significant entry into the country.

Even after its adoption as national "folk" by revolutionary dance artists in the 1920s and 1930s, Mexicans and American businessmen familiar with the country would have immediately identified jarocho as an African-influenced dance style in both aesthetics and lyrics.[162] Like the U.S. South, Veracruz had a long history of African slavery. Though he usually described Mexico as being white and Indian, Amador did not fear admitting African influences even in front of a segregationist mayor; rather, he transformed these influences into folk culture. Amador could claim Mexicans' place as politically, culturally, and historically European, without arguing that they qualified biologically. The strategy departed sharply from his own government's insistence, seven years before in Johnstown, Pennsylvania, that "the percentage of negroes is far lower in Mexico than in the United States."

Assimilating Mexicans

While the consulate's nationalistic lectures and performances helped maintain a culturally upper-class and European image of Mexicans in New Orleans, they seemed to resonate little with most of the city's working-class and middle-class Mexicans. Unlike those in Amador's earlier post of Chicago, New Orleans's Mexican immigrants hailed from the Gulf Coast, a region on the fringe of revolution-era struggles and the constellation of key power brokers that took charge in their wake.[163] They mostly bypassed Texas, where their northern Mexican counterparts founded Mexican mutual aid societies and invoked Mexican nationalism as a defense against racism.

Hundreds of Mexicans did reach out to the New Orleans consulate for assistance, but they did so for individual rather than communal matters. They sought legal assistance after arrest or in the deportation process, letters of recommendation for potential employers, and, after the Depression set in, help finding work or repatriating to Mexico.[164] Yet these appeals for Mexican government help did not beget a working-class Mexican nationalism nor did they foster the creation of a distinct Mexican community life. Ordinary Mexicans likely understood the whitening potential of mestizaje but knew little about their new nation's ideology of the cosmic race, and while Mexico's Gulf Coast had a more visible black population than the rest of the country, Afro-Mexicans lived mostly in distinct communities that newly arrived migrants may not have encountered and likely did not identify with.[165] With white New Orleans giving them little additional reason to consider themselves a distinct group, Mexicans likely felt a weak connection to the new government, its revolutionary promises, or even the reimagined Mexican nation it claimed to represent. Indeed, at least some migrants selected New Orleans precisely because they had heard it lacked a distinct Mexican community. One man considered migration to both New York and New Orleans but, upon hearing that New York had a "Mexican colony," chose New Orleans instead.[166] This immigrant likely perceived that where Mexican immigrant communities became visible, a distinct and disparaged racial category followed them.

Indeed, the "Mexican" racial category became a particular target of hostility throughout the United States during the Depression. As white and Mexican elites celebrated Mexico's independence at a fancy New Orleans hotel, thousands of Mexican workers around the country had already begun to lose their jobs and face deportation. Though the U.S. federal government encouraged the deportation of Mexican and other immigrants during this time, city and county-level officials provided critical assistance to immigration agents in an attempt to reduce public relief rolls and the burdens on charitable institutions.[167] In Los Angeles, for example, a concerted deportation campaign targeted the city's main plaza, ultimately deporting 300 people to Mexico, some U.S. citizens, and scaring thousands of others into initiating their own journeys to Mexico.[168] Local officials and social workers also encouraged Mexicans to repatriate "voluntarily" and subsidized the cost of doing so; scholars have found that local officials in the Southwest were more likely to coerce immigrants into leaving while those in the Midwest and Northwest often refused to cooperate with repatriation efforts.[169] Nationally, about 400,000 Mexicanos were deported or repatriated under pressure during the 1930s, including untold numbers of immigrants' U.S. citizen children.[170] Mexicans constituted 44 percent of all deportees from the United States in the early 1930s, the single largest national group, with European and Asian immigrants making up most of the remainder.[171]

The Depression and deportation years did not play out as dramatically for Mexicans in New Orleans, but they did generate a measure of instability and uncertainty. Even a few months before the stock market crash of October 1929, New Orleans's Mexicans found themselves on edge when rumors spread that those who did not take advantage of a new legal provision for naturalization would be deported.[172] "Hard-working people who have lived here for years," wrote a New Orleans–based correspondent for San Antonio's *La Prensa*, were hurriedly preparing trips to border cities where they could legalize their status under the new law.[173] Though ultimately untrue, the rumors unsettled even the city's long-standing Mexican residents.

Threats to Mexicans' privileged status in New Orleans next arrived in the form of poor unemployed compatriots. As the Depression set in, rural

Louisiana planters fired their Mexican workers who in turn streamed into New Orleans, while "an army of laborers," newly unemployed in Chicago, descended on the city to return to Mexico via steamship.[174] Brothers Bernardo and Manuel Velasco Mendoza, natives of the western Mexican state of Colima, had first crossed the Mexico-U.S. border in April 1929 to join their cousin in Chicago.[175] The Depression soon left them unemployed and penniless, and so they walked from Chicago to New Orleans and contacted the consulate, which secured them free passage back to Mexico on an American Petroleum ship.[176] In other cases, U.S. immigration authorities used the port of New Orleans to carry out deportations of Mexicans they had apprehended in nearby states.[177] The sudden appearance of so many indigent Mexicans threatened the upper-class image that Mexican bureaucrats and middle-class families had so carefully cultivated in the city.

Ultimately, though, the Depression years provide further evidence that in New Orleans, Mexicans were treated more like European immigrants than Mexicans elsewhere in the United States. They faced the prospect of deportation like all immigrants in those years, but evidence shows that they were not singled out among immigrant groups. Neither the Mexican consulate, the U.S. Immigration and Naturalization Service (INS), the *Times-Picayune*, nor Texas's Spanish-language press reported on a deportation campaign targeted at New Orleans's Mexicans, even though consuls, federal correspondence, and newspapers documented and reported widely on deportation campaigns elsewhere.[178] For every Mexican immigrant who permanently departed Louisiana for any reason between July 1, 1929, and June 30, 1930, six were admitted to residence there. In comparison, the ratio for British immigrants was 1:3.[179] The dispersed geography, economic diversity, and smaller numbers of Mexicans in New Orleans meant that no spaces or industries in the city were racialized as Mexican. Had a deportation campaign been mounted, it would have had no logical target.

Federal, not local, officials initiated the deportations that did take place in New Orleans, again suggesting that intense local animosity toward Mexicans was lacking there. While local prisons and charitable institutions did cooperate with requests from the Immigration Service to report aliens who had committed a crime or become a public charge, they did not go out of their way to do so and certainly did not instigate the deportation efforts as their counterparts in Los Angeles and other places had done.[180] Federal immigration agents in New Orleans found that only "frequent visits" to those institutions would procure the desired knowledge of which immigrants were in their custody.[181] These officials sought to exert some control over the flow of humans through the city's international port. They responded to shipping companies' reports of no-shows who absconded into the port city rather than reboard their boats, and they "checked up" on visitors who had overstayed their visas to ensure that they departed the country.[182] The Immigration Service maintained a searching squad to find these immigrants and also relied on the help of the New Orleans Police Department to apprehend their suspects.[183] While these efforts did not explicitly target any one national group, official correspondence mentioned Chinese and European immigrants more often than Mexicans, even though "the vast majority of aliens entering here are those coming from Mexico, Cuba, Central America, and the West Indies Islands."[184]

Though immigration enforcement in New Orleans did not target Mexicans, it did produce Mexican deportees. The New Orleans Mexican consulate processed fifty deportations in 1930, though many of those affected had not been living in New Orleans when they were apprehended.[185] Of those who had been living in New Orleans, most had arrived as shipping crew members. Gregorio López of Ameca, Jalisco, arrived on a Panamanian ship with permission to remain on land for sixty days. When he overstayed the visa, immigration agents apprehended and deported him to Veracruz.[186] Agents were less successful in their pursuit of twenty-year-old Antonio Benavides, who hailed from the Mexican state of Puebla. Benavides worked on the ship *Agua Prieta* but deserted it while docked at New Orleans. U.S. Immigration agents attempted to track him down in 1931, but it appears that they did not succeed.[187] He would arrive again in New Orleans port more than sixty times in the 1930s, performing a variety of shipboard duties from barber to general laborer as he sailed around the Gulf of Mexico.[188] When the United Fruit Company ship *Santa Marta* left the docks at New Orleans two days after arriving from Havana in June 1936, a crew member was reported missing: Antonio Benavides had once again disappeared into New Orleans.[189]

Mexicans in other parts of the United States were not only targeted for deportation but were also coerced by social service workers into initiating their own repatriations. But in New Orleans, Mexicans' repatriations were more often voluntary, and social workers there did not actively encourage repatriation as their counterparts had elsewhere, particularly in Los Angeles.[190] The Mexican consulate did record a single case of a social welfare agency requesting repatriation: in 1931, Catholic Charities sought help repatriating Nacario Hernández and his wife because she was under their charge due to mental illness.[191] Yet such cases were rare. Indeed, the lack of funds within Catholic Charities to send the Hernándezes home suggests that Mexican repatriation was not a priority for local agencies in New Orleans. In Los Angeles, the efforts of charity workers to encourage their clients' departure meant that three-quarters of Depression-era repatriation cases involved families with children, the group considered to be the greatest burden on welfare and charity rolls. By contrast, just six of the thirty-four repatriations the New Orleans consulate handled in 1930 involved women and children, and of these only three originated from the city of New Orleans.[192] Because the vast majority of repatriates were men traveling alone, it is unlikely that their return to Mexico was encouraged by local social welfare workers.

Yet the consulate's responses to Mexicans' requests for repatriation assistance suggest the office was aware that a growing population of unemployed Mexicans could damage their nation's image in New Orleans. When indigent Mexicans in the rural South asked for financial help repatriating, the consul responded that no funds were available, though he occasionally offered shipboard repatriation if the petitioner could come to New Orleans at his or her own expense. In one case, consulate officials suggested that penniless Mississippi Delta cotton worker Francisco Gomes work his way to the border "little by little" in order to return home.[193] But when poor New Orleanean immigrants wrote for help returning home, they received it. New Orleans resident Alejandro Colar C., for example, sought repatriation when he became unemployed. The consul secured him free passage on a Pan-American Petroleum boat, and Colar returned to his home in Mexico via the port of Tampico.[194] These different responses reflect consular workers' perceptions that Mexicans' privileged position in New Orleans needed constant fortification, as well as their indifference to rural Mexican compatriots who found themselves in a far more abject situation.[195]

The Depression years created uncertainty and insecurity in the lives and racial position of New Orleans's Mexicans but ultimately did not dislodge them from their place alongside European immigrants in the local white imagination. The concerted deportation and repatriation campaigns and open racial hostilities seen elsewhere never materialized. Rumors of New Orleans's less punitive environment spread during the Depression years. "Are we going to Louisiana?" asked the singer in the narrative ballad or *corrido* "Los Enganchados" (The Contracted Ones). "We arrived at Laguna without any hope," the stanza concluded.[196] The corrido "Los Betabeleros" (The Beet Pickers) began with the same inquiry, "Are we going to Louisiana?" and concluded unhappily in the Midwest.[197] Consular officials lamented that Mexicans flocked to New Orleans from other parts of the United States during the Depression, certain that they would find work even when "the situation is completely adverse for them here, without any possibility of improving."[198] In September 1930, Alfonso and Vicente Sánchez contacted the consulate for help. They were unemployed in New York and wanted to repatriate to Mexico but were afraid they would be racially harassed if they returned through Texas. Louisiana seemed like a safer option: could the consulate help them get back to Mexico by ship? A few weeks later, the brothers returned to cancel their request. There would be no need for repatriation to Mexico—they had found work in New Orleans.[199]

And so, hostile deportation and repatriation campaigns, the defining experience that instigated the transition from the Mexican generation to the Mexican American one in the Southwest, passed New Orleans by. Mexicanness in New Orleans would not be defined as a degraded racial stereotype, a burden on society, or a threat to white Americans. Rather, an elite, Europeanized Mexican culture dominated popular views of Mexicanness even as hundreds of darker and poorer Mexicans made their way in the city as laborers, peddlers, and longshoremen. For their part, these working-class Mexicans showed little interest in forging a communal Mexican identity. Quietly reaping the benefits of their elite compatriots' cultural work, they assimilated into white New Orleans geographically, socially, and economically. When a Catholic archdiocese official visited Our Lady of Guadalupe, the parish designated for Mexicans, in 1934, he scribbled on a report, "The Spanish-speaking Catholic population of this city is around 7 to 8 thousands [sic]. Come to this chapel for confession or call in case of sickness only those who do not speak any other language than Spanish—about 1500."[200] Our Lady of Guadalupe, an icon of Mexican religious cultural expression throughout the United States, attracted just a small minority of New Orleans's Mexican immigrants. Most had the option to worship with white, English-speaking New Orleaneans—and took it. The parish held its last Spanish mass in 1939, by which time visions of New Orleans's Mexican immigrants following in the path of San Antonio were clearly expired.[201] As Mexican Americans around the country enlisted in the U.S. army to prove their patriotism, the assimilation of Mexicans into white New Orleans was all but complete.

The story of Mexicans' incorporation as white ethnics in New Orleans fundamentally departs from the regional and national stories of Mexicans' racialization between 1910 and 1939.[202] It is the first case historians have yet uncovered in which Mexicans' experiences paralleled those of European immigrants much more closely than that of their Mexican counterparts elsewhere in the United States. Since the histories of Mexican immigrants and Mexican Americans are still being written, scholars may yet find other similar cases. In some ways, the New Orleans story was unique because of the southern regional obsession with the binary of black and white. Yet midwestern cities had similar binaries, and the imperative of imposing Jim Crow on this or any city of racial complexity could easily have led to a harsh othering of all groups considered potentially threatening to white supremacy. In the case of New Orleans's Mexicanos, the opposite happened. The biological racism espoused in the *Plessy* decision proved not to fully structure the implementation of Jim Crow.

Local and international power holders shaped the terms of racial segregation in New Orleans, allowing Mexicans to enjoy the privileges of whiteness without having to prove their genetic bona fides. Local politicians and businessmen envisioned their port city as a gateway to Latin American trade opportunities and used the city's Mexican immigrants as symbols of this Pan-American future. The Mexican consulate and the middle-class Mexican families who surrounded it emphasized Mexicans' cultural compatibility with white New Orleans. And Mexican immigrants themselves seized the opportunity to assimilate with the city's whites, thereby opening their own doors to social mobility. Segregation in New Orleans was harsh and real, but its biological underpinnings proved a pretense that served the needs of migrants and elites on both sides of the border.

Mexicans' advantageous social position in New Orleans had ramifications beyond the Crescent City itself. The South had no significant Mexican American community east of Texas at this time; thus, New Orleans's Mexico-oriented community served as the main touchstone of political power for the thousands of Mexicans scattered on plantations throughout the rural South during the 1920s and 1930s. Mexicans upriver in the Mississippi Delta faced considerable barriers in their own quest for social and racial mobility. When they needed political support, they turned to the Mexican consulate in New Orleans.

CHAPTER TWO

Different from That Which Is Intended for the Colored Race
Mexicans and Mexico in Jim Crow Mississippi, 1918–1939

More than two decades into the black exodus from the rural South, a U.S. federal government photographer captured images of African Americans bending over to pick cotton in the Mississippi heat (fig. 4). For this photographer and other liberals in the 1930s, the image of black people toiling in cotton fields evoked hundreds of years of racial oppression, from slavery through the failures of Reconstruction and the horrors of lynching and Jim Crow.[1] These photos and hundreds like them entered the official U.S. archival record through the Farm Security Administration (FSA) photography project, alongside a few dozen others that depicted a different group at work in the same Mississippi fields: "Mexican seasonal labor, contracted for by planters" (fig. 5). Though just one photograph, taken in a plantation store, included blacks and Mexicans in the same frame (fig. 6), images of the two groups in the fields echoed each other, depicting workers chopping and picking cotton, then loading it onto large flatbed trucks.[2]

Taken for a national audience, the photos were meant to evoke white viewers' sympathy for poor black agricultural laborers in the South, a region notoriously abusive to them. The limited visual evidence of Mexicans' lives showed them in the same predicament as blacks, and had the photos been taken in the 1910s or 1920s, the impression would have been largely correct. But at the time of their creation in 1939, the photos' similarities were misleading: though they picked cotton in the same fields, by that year Mexicanos in the Mississippi Delta were well on their way to a fate distinct from that of African Americans.

From the 1910s through the 1930s, tens of thousands of Mexicans and Mexican Americans who initially lived in Texas moved on to the rural black–white South. Unlike their counterparts in New Orleans, who hailed from a range of economic backgrounds, Mexican migrants to the rural South had only their physical labor to sell to crew leaders, plantation managers, and companies.

To see a selection of original historical sources from this chapter, go to http://corazondedixie .org/chapter-2 (http://dx.doi.org/10.7264/N39K48H5).

FIGURE 4 "Day laborers picking cotton on Marcella Plantation, Mileston, Mississippi Delta, Mississippi, 1939." Marion Post Wolcott, Farm Security Administration Photography Project, 1939. Library of Congress, Prints and Photographs Division, FSA-OWI Collection, LC-USF33-030553-M3.

FIGURE 5 "Mexican seasonal labor, contracted for by planters, emptying bags of cotton on Knowlton Plantation, Perthshire, Mississippi Delta, Mississippi." Marion Post Wolcott, Farm Security Administration Photography Project, 1939. Library of Congress, Prints and Photographs Division, FSA-OWI Collection, LC-USF33-030538-M4.

FIGURE 6 "Mexican and Negro cotton pickers inside plantation store, Knowlton Plantation, Perthshire, Mississippi Delta, Mississippi. This transient labor is contracted for and brought in from Texas each season." Marion Post Wolcott, Farm Security Administration Photography Project, 1939, Library of Congress, Prints and Photographs Division, FSA-OWI Collection, LC-USF34-052248-D.

They mined aluminum in Bauxite, Arkansas, worked in the lumber industries of rural Mississippi and Louisiana, and loaded coal in Floyd County, Kentucky.[3] By far the largest group traveled to pick the cotton that grew from the rich soils of the Yazoo-Mississippi River Delta: some to Louisiana and Arkansas but most to the Mississippi River's eastern banks in the state of Mississippi (see map 3).

The migration started in the 1910s and grew quickly in the early 1920s, peaking in 1925; most who came in those early years stayed for just a few months at a time, arriving in early fall to pick cotton and returning to Texas or Mexico by winter. Yet throughout those years, some Mexicanos pursued social and economic progress by staying in the Delta year-round or nearly year-round as sharecroppers who worked the full cotton cycle from planting in the spring through chopping in the summer and picking in the fall. Newspapers and word of mouth soon exposed Texas's Mexicanos to the exploitative potential of laboring in the Delta on a short-term contract, and those who traveled there after 1925 were much more likely to insist on a sharecropping arrangement

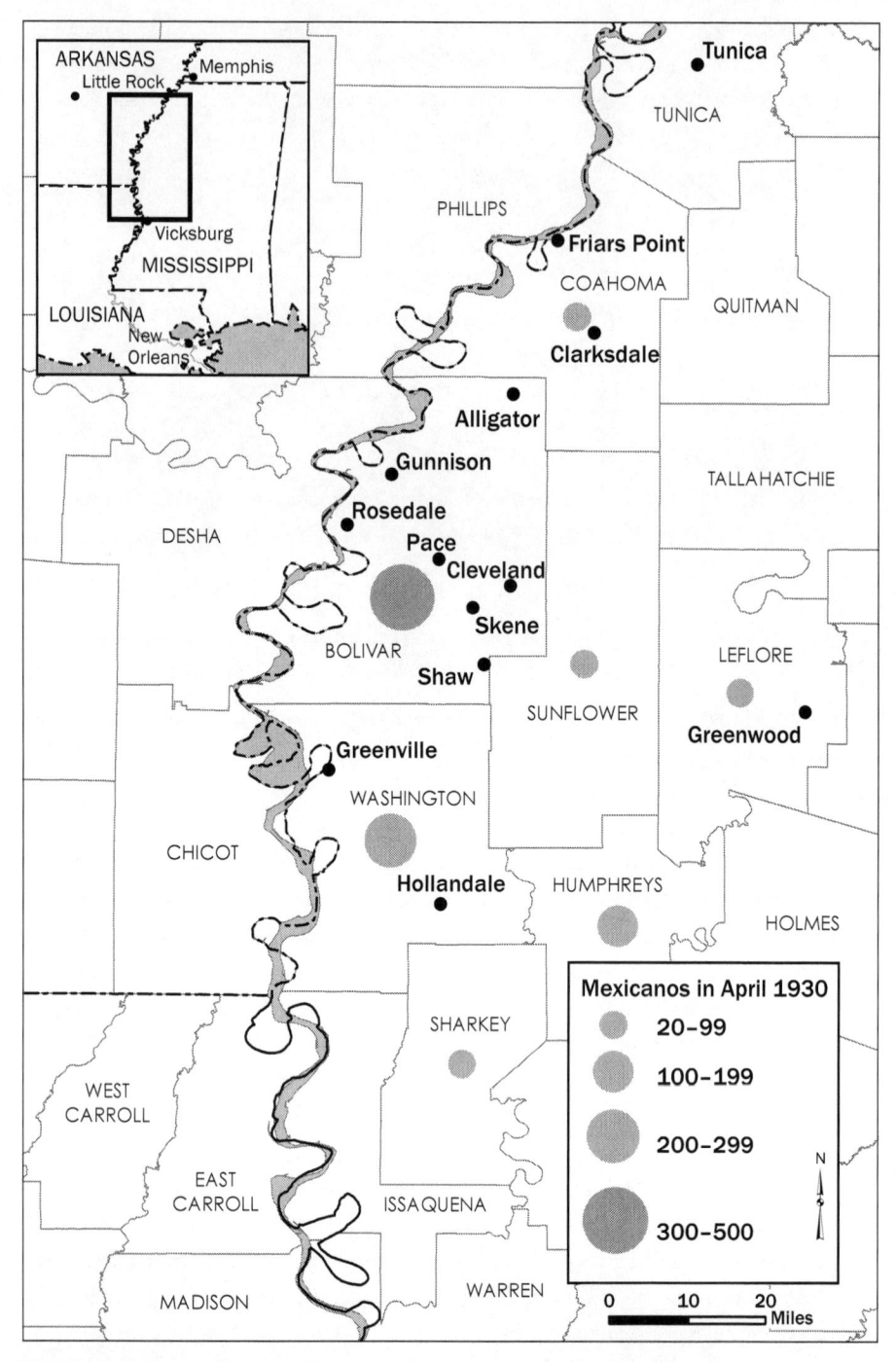

MAP 3 Mexicanos in Mississippi Delta counties, 1930. Data from Truesdell, *Fifteenth Census of the United States: 1930*, vol. 3, pt. 1. Map by the author.

and remain year-round with their families. But for the Depression, in fact, Mississippi might have become a significant destination for Mexicano families to settle in the 1930s–60s, the period between the start of large-scale African American out-migration and the widespread adoption of the mechanical cotton picker. Even during the economically difficult 1930s, small numbers of Mexicans and Mexican Americans remained in the Delta or continued to travel there seasonally from Texas, as the FSA photographs showed.

While Mexican immigrants to New Orleans occupied a racial position alongside European immigrants in the 1910s and successfully clung to it thereafter, those who worked just a few hundred miles away in the Delta arrived to the opposite side of the color line. From the moment recruiters' trucks delivered them to their new work sites, Mexicanos in Mississippi tasted the brutality and exclusion that the region's white planters had used to segregate, terrorize, and control African Americans; many Mexicanos had experienced similar abuses in South Texas. Like African Americans, and like Mexicanos in the Southwest, Mississippi's Mexicanos found refuge in their families and religious practices and forged community however they could. They fought against racial and economic oppression in their daily lives or fled to new places. But they also used a political and legal strategy unique among these groups: they appealed first and foremost to the cross-border and cross-class nationalism of the Mexican government and its consulate in New Orleans, rather than the institutions, lawyers, and liberal discourses of U.S. citizenship. They battled most intensely from 1925 through 1930, the period when many envisioned a future in the Delta. And though most left the area during the Depression, those who remained at long last reaped the fruits of these labors: they forced local officials to admit them to the privileges of whiteness, decisively separating their futures from those of the region's African Americans and paving the way for their families' advancement into the white middle class.

Solving the "Question of Common Labor in the South"

From the moment of blacks' emancipation and particularly in times of their out-migration, rural southern plantation owners and managers had fantasized about importing immigrants to their fields. As they watched their human property become free people, southern planters sought out Chinese workers rather than confront the newfound need to actually negotiate the terms of employment with blacks. "To bring coolie labor in competition with negro labor—to let the negroes see that laborers can be had without them—is the main feature of the plan," explained a reporter in 1865.[4] But Chinese were unwilling to work on planters' terms and quickly left the plantations; those that remained in the area opened small grocery stores rather than pick cotton.[5] In the 1880s–90s, southern planters, still unable to exert total control over the lives of African American laborers, tried to attract Italian immigrants. The Italians did arrive, but once again, the "experiment" with immigrant labor yielded conflict and controversy.[6] Planters' hopes of attracting a permanent and pliant immigrant workforce remained mere fantasies, leaving them dependent on poor African American and white cotton pickers.[7]

Mexicans briefly took their place as desired immigrants in the cotton fields in 1904–5 and worked in the lumber industry in south-central Mississippi as early as 1908.[8] They, too, proved unwilling to tolerate the region's abusive conditions, and nearly all left the area.[9] The small handful that remained in Mississippi or came there in the early years of the Mexican Revolution attracted little attention and encouraged few in Mexican America to follow their routes.[10] The Los Angeles newspaper published in Spanish by exiled Mexican revolutionary Ricardo Flores Magón pointed to the plight of Mexican immigrants in the South as evidence of the evils of "Yankee capitalism." "How have Mexican workers been treated in the United States?" asked a 1912 article in *Regeneración*. "Worse than the blacks. . . . It pierces the heart and makes the blood boil to see the lives of our brothers in Texas, Louisiana and Mississippi. Seeing the treatment that is given to Mexican workers in the South and witnessing how they are humiliated and degraded makes us shed tears and yearn for vengeance."[11] While this image of "the South" helped *Regeneración* critique U.S. exploitation of Mexican workers, in practice the Mexican Revolution led Louisiana and Mississippi planters to briefly lose interest in Mexican worker recruitment. Meanwhile, Mexicanos in Texas faced extreme retaliatory violence at the hands of Anglos.[12]

Though white planters had complained of "labor shortages" since Emancipation, World War I gave their anxieties renewed urgency. Cotton production in the Delta had increased dramatically in the years preceding the war, just as African Americans headed north.[13] To resist the flight of their black labor force to military posts and northern industrial jobs, planters pressured draft officials, attacked northbound African Americans at train stations, and, in one case, closed down pool halls in an attempt to force black workers back into the fields.[14] The federal government intermittently supported their efforts, approving of "work-or-fight" orders that all men not enlisted in the army pick cotton or go to jail and creating the U.S. Employment Service to ensure that adequate labor was available in rural areas.[15] Soon, planters appealed to the U.S. federal government to help them secure a new labor source: Mexican immigrants. Like the Louisiana sugar planters described in Chapter 1, Yazoo-Mississippi Delta cotton planters asked the federal government to foot the bill for the importation of Mexican laborers during World War I. With hopes that up to 5,000 Mexican workers could "Solve [the] Question of Common Labor in the South," a federal labor official invited 300 Arkansas farmers to attend a New Orleans meeting about the promise of Mexican labor for the region's rural areas in 1918.[16] The federal government, however, would not contract Mexicans to the Delta in large numbers until the late 1940s under the auspices of the bracero program, as the next chapter will detail.

The end of World War I did not bring an end to Delta planters' desperation for labor. High wartime cotton prices allowed many African Americans to buy cars, increasing their mobility and control over their own lives and labors. They continued streaming north and west to industrial jobs while those who stayed behind had more leverage negotiating the terms of work. Agricultural managers on larger plantations preferred to hire wage laborers whom they could supervise closely, but African Americans usually insisted on sharecropping, an arrangement in which the workers lived on a plot of land that they also planted, tended, and harvested. Their payment was half the crop at the end of the season. Forced to buy their goods and sell their cotton on the plantation rather than the open market, most sharecroppers barely subsisted after paying back their annual debts. Still, they preferred this arrangement to wage labor because it gave them marginally more autonomy, and plantation owners found themselves forced to accept it.[17] When African Americans organized to improve the terms of sharecropping in the 1920s, white planters and vigilantes responded with violence. Others turned to illegal debt peonage and convict leasing, in which real or trumped-up debts and fines were used to force men to work against their will. This violence in turn made African Americans more determined to leave the area.[18] Planters who abused their workers might wake up one morning in January to find that "their Negroes" had left for a different plantation after cashing out the season's crop.[19] Thus, though the federal government did not sponsor a major Mexican labor importation program in these years, Delta planters continued their quest for a more "cooperative" labor force and tried again to recruit Mexicans.

Out of Texas: The Meanings of Mexicano Mobility in the 1910s–1920s

In the 1910s and 1920s, Mississippi planters followed the lead of agricultural bosses elsewhere in the United States: they hired enganchadores, labor recruitment agencies that operated in Texas and along the Mexican border. These agents promised Mexican and Mexican American workers set wages and transported them to the agricultural fields of California, Arizona, the Midwest, and now the South. Whatever the destination, wages and conditions of work often bore little resemblance to those promised.[20]

Still, Mexicanos followed enganchadores, friends, and family members to faraway work sites in the 1910s and 1920s because, like African Americans in the Yazoo-Mississippi Delta, Mexicanos in South Texas held little hope of autonomy or advancement in their current location. While the northern side of the border may have appeared a safer alternative to the violence of the revolution and the economic havoc it wrought on Mexico's countryside, the 1920s was precisely the period when systematized segregation, violence, and labor exploitation of Mexicanos hardened in South Texas. When a small group of Tejanos, Texas-born Mexican Americans, took inspiration from the Mexican Revolution in 1915 and plotted to throw out the Anglos who had conquered them seventy years before, white Texans responded with extreme vigilante violence that all but eliminated the last vestiges of political power Mexican-origin people held.[21] Then, as both immigration from Mexico and the scale of Texas agriculture increased, Texas planters became increasingly committed to forcing Mexicanos into a permanent laboring underclass, policing their movements, suppressing their wages, and deliberately creating inadequate Mexican schools to ensure that agricultural work was their only option.[22] Anglos also used mob violence to assert control, lynching dozens of Mexicans in the 1910s.[23] In the 1920s, agents of the newly established U.S. Border Patrol harassed, assaulted, and sometimes killed those in the borderlands who appeared to be Mexican.[24] As Mexico birthed a new regime and U.S. economic prosperity grew, Mexicanos in Texas felt themselves pounded by ever-thickening layers of economic and political repression, their lives getting worse, not better.

Some Mexicans and Mexican Americans responded by forming organizations emphasizing loyalty to the United States, while others organized *sociedades mutualistas*, mutual aid societies, and Comisiones Honoríficas, consulate-affiliated Honorary Commissions, to draw on the strength of the Revolution-era Mexican government in demanding rights.[25] Still others decided to leave, zigzagging their trucks northward by night to avoid detection by state officials or Border Patrol agents charged with ensuring that the Mexican labor force went nowhere. The secrecy surrounding their journeys was, in the words of one observer, akin to an "underground railroad."[26] Some maintained homes in Texas and followed harvests seasonally to the Midwest or California, while others settled in these new places. Wherever they went, they maintained relationships with their Texas communities through letters, hometown clubs, and the Spanish-language press, even as the violence and poverty they had experienced in Texas haunted their memories and provided the major point of comparison to conditions in their new locations.[27]

While a few Mexicans settled in the Mississippi Delta as early as World War I, planters renewed their recruitment efforts in the early 1920s.[28] Appeals for federal help with recruitment failed again; instead, private enganchadores brought Mexicano men and families from South Texas to work for wages in the cotton fields of Mississippi.[29] As their trucks crossed the river from Arkansas into Mississippi, they wended their way on country roads, past the lakes and riverbeds of the Mississippi River's natural and man-made diversions. Stately plantation houses, gins, and commissaries sat at the edges of vast cotton fields, far from the dilapidated bunkhouses and sharecroppers' cabins Mexicans would occupy.[30] Willow and cypress trees, browning as the fall wore on, provided meager shade from the September sun in what had once been tree-filled swampland. Mexicanos dispersed among the plantations in groups, from a handful to 200–300; when rains fell, roads became impassible by car, leaving them almost completely isolated.[31] This isolation limited but did not foreclose Mexicans' possibilities for community and resistance.

Most of Mississippi's Mexicano laborers had experienced exploitative cotton work in South Texas and expected that the Delta would be an improvement in wages, conditions, or both. They quickly found otherwise.[32] In early 1924, thirty Mexican families signed up with Laredo enganchadores to sharecrop on Richard Neelly's plantation near Rolling Fork, Mississippi. Like their black counterparts, the Mexican sharecroppers were forced to purchase their food on credit at the plantation store, which they would then repay when they sold their cotton, also to the plantation, at the close of the season. In response to "simply intolerable" conditions, the newfound sharecroppers refused to work, and Neelly retaliated by cutting their food rations. On August 1, twenty-three of the plantation's thirty Mexican families protested, staging "a small revolution in Camp . . . taking up their belongings and leaving."[33] Among them was Fidel Serja, who wrote of the experience in a letter to his sister in Laredo. The sister alerted Laredo's Mexican consulate, who wrote to his counterpart in New Orleans, who in turn asked the U.S. Department of Justice to launch an investigation into possible peonage on Neelly's farm.[34] When investigators arrived at the farm, the seven Mexican families remaining there reported they were not being held by force, and thus the case was closed. But Neelly's hope that Mexicans would solve his labor woes were still dashed, as all seven families "stated that they would leave when they sold their crop."[35]

Another group of Mexicanos arrived to chop cotton in Issaquena County, Mississippi, in the spring of 1924 and quickly found themselves even worse off than their compatriots on the Neelly plantation: far from home, working sunup to sundown in mortal fear of their foremen. There, white planters immediately used the violent tactics they had employed on African Americans to extract as much labor as Mexican workers' bodies could bear for as low a cost as possible. Wages bore no relationship to those promised by enganchadores, and workers who protested were liable to be punished. Many tried to leave the plantations, but search parties tracked them down, heading them off at train stations and on roads, beating them and forcibly returning them to work. One dissatisfied Mexican couple tried to flee along the Mississippi River but were quickly caught. A search party shot the man to death and returned his wife to the fields, leaving her husband's dead body at the side of the road. Appealing to their families or the Mexican consulate for help was impossible, as foremen inspected Mexican workers' letters before mailing. A few letters did make it back to Texas, and San Antonio's largest Spanish-language newspaper, *La Prensa*, publicized their story.[36]

"A Thousand Punishments" in 1925

Still, most of Texas's Mexicanos did not hear these tales. The following year, a record number traversed the same routes to Mississippi, some with promises of $8 daily wages—several times higher than those offered in Texas.[37] The San Antonio office of the U.S. Employment Service added Mississippi to its list of destinations for available Mexican workers, while Mexico's Houston consulate supervised the signing of contracts between workers and their future employers.[38] Labor-hungry planters in western Arkansas watched helplessly as trucks of Mexican workers passed their fields by en route from Texas to the Delta.[39] "Never in the history of the states of Louisiana and Mississippi has there been such a large quantity of Mexicans as there are today," marveled a Los Angeles Spanish-language newspaper that September. "The planters are very satisfied with the work entrusted to our compatriots, and they are continuously praising them as wonderful farmhands."[40]

Mexicanos' presence was indeed ubiquitous in the Delta's fields in the fall of 1925. The Catholic priest in Clarksdale, Nelius Downing, claimed that 5,000 "Mexicans," and presumably Mexican Americans, were picking cotton on plantations throughout the region, in Clarksdale, Greenwood, Greenville, Cleveland, Tunica, and Hollandale. And, he wrote in October of 1925, "more are coming every day."[41] By the end of the 1925 picking season, Downing would pay a visit to every plantation in his Clarksdale parish, finding Mexicanos on all of them.[42] He estimated that one-eighth would remain in the Delta, while the rest would move on or return to Texas.[43] "Not a few planters," he explained, "are very well pleased with them and will do all they can to have them remain."[44]

Planters indeed did all they could to keep Mexicanos in their fields, including the familiar resort to violence. Families in Weslaco, Texas, received letters from kin in Mississippi decrying the "thousand punishments" and injustices to which they had been subjected there.[45] Rather than earning high wages, Mexicanos were not even paid enough to eat.[46] Contracts signed with enganchadores were worthless and provided no protection.[47] When four Mexicanos tried to leave the cotton fields near Clarksdale, they were apprehended as they tried to board a New Orleans–bound train and imprisoned in the town jail.[48] One crew leader reported that Mexicanos in Greenville and Cleveland had been killed by their foremen; the crimes went unpunished.[49] The abuse Mexicanos decried would have been intimately familiar to the African Americans picking cotton a few rows away in the same fields and plantations.

In turn, Mexicanos recognized the echo of African Americans' oppression in their own treatment in Mississippi, and this increased their feelings of humiliation and exploitation. One woman wrote in horror to her Texas family that local officials in Mississippi attempted to force the burial of a Mexican man, Santiago Castillo, in the black cemetery. His compatriots refused to comply, and for three days the man's body lay exposed as they sought permission to bury him somewhere, anywhere not set aside for the area's most degraded residents. Castillo's friends from Weslaco finally received permission to inter him in a riverbed, rather than the black cemetery.[50] Though few African Americans lived in South Texas, Mexicano migrants had lived in the United States long enough to understand the consequences of being classed with blacks. So woeful was the experience of desperately saving her compatriot's body from the black cemetery that the woman recounting it concluded her letter, "From what I have written, you will realize the crisis we are experiencing and the fact that we have lost all hope."[51]

The woman's hopelessness reflected, in large part, isolation: Mississippi's newly arrived Mexicano workforce had few places to turn for help. Those who were U.S.-citizen Tejanos had no way to use their citizenship to claim rights. During this period, their southwestern counterparts formed mutual aid societies and the civil rights organization League of United Latin American Citizens (LULAC). The Delta's African Americans joined civil rights organizations NAACP and United Negro Improvement Association, and both groups sometimes became members of the few labor unions that were not hostile to them.[52] But Mississippi had no Mexican American middle class, and early attempts at cross-racial cotton labor organizing in the Delta had been violently crushed. While the historical record offers little insight into African American discussions of their Mexicano neighbors in Mississippi, national black publications of the time presented Mexicanos as both allies and competitors.[53] Either way, Mississippi's black organizations ignored them. The Delta's Mexican nationals had the right to call on New Orleans's consulate, but its staff did not conduct routine visits to Mississippi plantations and usually took greater interest in "protecting" their compatriots in New Orleans. Writing a letter in hopes of getting a reaction from the consulate or *La Prensa* in San Antonio—something only literate workers could do—provided Mexicanos' only lifeline to external institutions with power.

The Catholic Church provided spiritual but not political support for the Delta's Mexicanos. Catholic priests visited Mexicanos at their scattered plantation work sites throughout the 1920s, but the local bishop was ardently pro-segregation, and his priests saw themselves as peacekeepers and soul savers, not advocates.[54] They were invited to the plantations by labor managers eager retain their Mexican workforce.[55] This, too, would have been familiar to African Americans, as during this period some Delta plantations encouraged the growth of black churches on their premises. Those churches' pastors, in turn, supported the bosses against any "agitators or foreign elements."[56]

Catholic priests ministering to Mexicans similarly dismissed labor conflict as the result of outside meddling. Clarksdale's Father Downing explained to his superiors that when Mexicans first arrived in the area in September 1925, they "were getting into trouble with outsiders and were not being paid enough also."[57] So Downing printed and distributed a pamphlet in English and poorly translated Spanish, advising workers to adhere strictly to their contracts, to never refuse to work, and to always avoid any contact with organizers. The pamphlet described these work contracts as expressions not only of U.S. law but also of "the laws of almighty God." It continued, "Violations of the contract, such as agitating, refusing to work, or running away to other places, make you subject to a fine, imprisonment or both. Unfortunately, there are people already in prison for these offenses."[58] Sanctifying the local racial and economic order, Downing attempted to aid planters in maintaining that order with their new workforce. The following month, the priest proudly claimed, "I have succeeded in getting practically all the Planters to give them [Mexican workers] a general increase of 25 cents a hundred [pounds of cotton]; better sleeping and living quarters; an assurance of trainfare home; plenty to eat if they fail to make enough, and many other considerations." Furthermore, "Those who got in jail, I got out and restored to work."[59] In this decidedly local negotiation, the priest may also have been motivated by a desire to save Mexicans from retaliation for their acts of protest. Yet even if planters could threaten Mexicans with violence or have them thrown in jail, their utter desperation for labor meant that sometimes they also had to pay more to keep their workforce on site.

Still, with stories of abuse more widespread than those of twenty-five-cent raises, at the end of the 1925 picking season San Antonio's *La Prensa* called on the Mexican consulate to open an investigation into Mexicans' conditions of work in the Mississippi Delta.[60] Days later, the consul reported that workers there indeed faced "humiliating" conditions, though it is not clear that he actually traveled to the Delta to see those conditions for himself. He filed a formal complaint with the governor of Arkansas and alerted the Mexican embassy in Washington, D.C., who in turn asked the U.S. secretary of state to request a Department of Justice investigation. The Arkansas complaint went nowhere and the results of the Justice investigation are unclear.[61] Even as the consul pressed U.S. authorities, he told his countrymen: "Mexicans should not go to the plantations of Mississippi; the blacks left them because of the poor treatment they were receiving."[62] For hundreds of compatriots, the warning came too late: farmers who had agreed to pay their transportation back to Texas now refused, leaving these workers in Mississippi, abandoned in terrible housing with little food during the winter.[63]

While planters wanted Mexicanos to stay in the area and many used force to ensure they would, other white observers in the Delta shared the consul's sentiments that Mexicans would best avoid Mississippi. Prioritizing the area's racial order over its labor needs, Sunflower County's newspaper opined, "If the Mexican cotton pickers are ever needed here again, it will mean the beginning of another race problem. These fellows butt into exclusive white places and make themselves at home in negro places. They marry negro women and try to marry among the lower class of whites. We hope they will all leave this part of the Delta and never come back here."[64] Once again, it seemed, concerted efforts to recruit immigrant laborers had failed to secure a workforce fully compliant with the demands of Delta planters and the white supremacist society they inhabited.

Settling into Mississippi

Despite the concerns of both Mexican and white leaders, planters remained desperate for labor, and the racial humiliations of Texas kept Mexicanos there looking for an alternative. Even as word of abuses in Mississippi spread in the Río Grande Valley's Spanish-speaking communities, thousands of Mexicanos continued to seek work in the Delta's cotton fields, albeit in somewhat smaller numbers after 1925. Now their intentions were different. Mexicanos may have been exploited by their enganchadores in the early 1920s, but they used the enganchadores, too—to acquire the familiarity with Mississippi that allowed them to return, this time as sharecroppers. Sharecropping allowed workers more control over their own labor and a sense of social ascendance. If conditions were abusive in both Texas and Mississippi, at least the latter offered them the opportunity to sharecrop rather than being permanently relegated to wage labor.[65] Now living in the Delta at least nine months a year, Mississippi's more settled Mexicano newcomers would eventually use the limited power within their reach to claw their way to the white side of the color line.

The demographic profile of the Delta's Mexicano residents in the late 1920s mirrored that of the era's Mexican and Tejano migrants in the United States overall. When census enumerators traveled down the Mississippi Delta's country roads to survey families in April of 1930, the nearly 1,200 Mexicanos they encountered there were almost exclusively sharecropping families—after all, April was the planting season, not the more labor-intensive picking time when short-term hired hands were brought in.[66] In Bolivar County, which had the most Mexicanos of any (see map 3), five-sixths of Mexicano household heads, wives, and boarders counted that year were Mexican born, while one-sixth were Tejanos.[67] A quarter had first crossed the border before the Mexican Revolution, some as early as the 1880s; half crossed during the revolution (1910–17), and a quarter had crossed since its end.[68] Overall, these workers' backgrounds and migration histories made them typical of the era's Mexican and Mexican American labor migrants overall.

Regardless of their original intentions, Mississippi's Mexican sharecroppers between 1925 and the Depression were not migrant but had settled into Mississippi for at least a few years. Records of their children's births and baptisms reveal this stability. Among Mexican sharecroppers in Bolivar County surveyed for the census in April 1930, most children born in 1925 or earlier had been born in Texas and a few in Mexico. Half of the five-year-olds, those born in 1925, were born in Texas and the other half in Mississippi. But the littlest children, those born after 1926, were majority Mississippi born.[69] Furthermore, while the Delta's Catholic priests baptized a few Mexican children in 1922–25, usually during the picking season in the fall, they baptized many more at all times of year from 1926 through 1932.[70] In other words, most of the Mexican and Mexican American sharecropping families present in the Delta in 1930 were not mere sojourners on a one-off trip. They had laid roots in the Delta, most for more than five years and some for up to a decade.

For much of the year, their lives were similar to those of black sharecroppers. Their labors began in late winter, when they plowed under the last of the old season's cotton plants and broke up the land with the help of tools, preparing rows for a new crop. In April, they walked along the rows to plant the new year's seeds, which they had purchased on credit from the plantation. Late spring and early summer was the time to thin out the cotton plants and remove the weeds by chopping. It was also the time when their crop was at greatest risk. They could not control the rain: too little and some of the plants would not make it, too much and the stalk would shoot up to the sky, stealing energy from the growth sharecroppers really needed, the bolls of cotton lint lying within the plant's blooms. When those bolls burst open in the fall, entire families and children as young as five took to the rows to pick out the lint and deposit it in large sacks that trailed behind them. When the sacks were full, they dumped the cotton into a wagon or truck and brought it to the plantation's gin, which separated the lint from the seeds. Prohibited from taking their cotton lint to the open market, sharecroppers then sold it to the plantation. If all went well, the sharecropper's half of the proceeds would pay off the debts he had incurred at the start of the season, leaving his family a bit of money to make it through the winter until the next year's crop. And if it did not, all they would have to show for the season was debt.[71]

Mexicans and Mexican Americans had strong roots elsewhere and might use the start of winter to return to Texas or Mexico if they had the funds to get there. Some bought a few livestock such as chickens, hogs, and cows and survived the winter in Mississippi on meager meat and eggs.[72] Others, like A. González, left their wives and children in Mississippi and migrated elsewhere for temporary work at the end of the cotton harvest. Living even more precariously than he had in Mississippi, González's tertiary migration ended in tragedy. He was accidentally run over while asleep on the railroad tracks in Middlesboro, Kentucky, in November 1930.[73]

In the late 1920s, Mexicanos' hopes that the Delta would afford them more economic progress than South Texas were not entirely misplaced. As settled sharecroppers, they had at least eliminated the *enganchador* middleman and could negotiate the terms of work directly with planters. Like African Americans, Mexicanos knew that while bosses might use violence to keep them from leaving, the area's labor market favored workers. After the last of the crop had been sold each winter, "January was 'movin' month' for sharecroppers in the Delta," explained one historian.[74] Mexican sharecroppers were no exception, as they sought the best conditions and compensation wherever in the area they might be. Sara and José Esparza, for example, lived on plantations in Skene, Pace, and then Cleveland—each location less than ten miles from the other—between 1923 and 1934. Carmen and Herminio Lucio moved a dozen miles from Skene to Shaw in 1929, then relocated again, to a plantation forty miles upriver in Gunnison, in the early 1930s. Their children's godparents, Antonio and Aurelia Conteras, moved with their children the few miles from Gunnison to Waxhaw and then back again over a ten-year period.[75] With both Mexicanos and African Americans willing to move around in search of the best wages and conditions, most planters eventually had to accept that violence alone would not get their labor needs met.

The Mississippi River flood of 1927 further destabilized the area's labor force, to planters' chagrin and, eventually, Mexicans' benefit. An estimated 5,000 Mexicans numbered among the half-million people displaced in the fourteen million acres of flooded land during the planting season that April.[76] The Red Cross brought relief programs to the area, but local planters controlled their disbursement to ensure that every poor person who remained in the Delta, particularly African Americans, would still have to pick cotton in order to eat.[77] The Red Cross did establish a special camp for Mexican refugees from the flood, and about 250 Mexicans took shelter there.[78] One Mexican woman "lost her husband and two children in the flood and she is in the hospital very sick," wrote a priest who visited the distraught woman in the hospital.[79] As the flood made national news in both English and Spanish, working- and middle-class Mexican immigrants throughout the country, in South Texas, Los Angeles, New Orleans, and Oklahoma, donated money to aid the flood's Mexican victims.[80] The Mexican consul in New Orleans appropriated funds for the cause as well.[81] "Entire settlements of Mexicans have disappeared before the impetuous advance of the waters," decried Los Angeles's *El Heraldo de México*. "For several years, our compatriots have lived there, fighting tenaciously and ardently in the cotton fields, saving up their little inheritances and hoping to gather a bit of capital with which to return to the land of their ancestors."[82] Aid from compatriots may have placed Mexicano immigrant flood survivors in a marginally better position than their African American counterparts. Either way, the flood caused many African

Americans to redouble their efforts to leave, increasing Mexicanos' bargaining power in the coming cotton season.

The case of the Mexicano workers on the area's largest plantation, British-owned Delta & Pine Land (D&PL), shows that particularly after the flood, even Mississippi's most powerful planters were not immune to the laws of supply and demand. In 1924, a plantation manager there had tried to secure federal help in transporting Mexicano workers from Texas to its vast cotton fields in Mississippi.[83] Though bureaucrats did not respond, D&PL managers still drew Mexican sharecroppers to their fields in 1926 or 1927, and in the fall following the flood they asked Catholic officials to help them recruit more from Texas.[84] In exchange, plantation president Oscar Johnston offered to build a permanent school and church for Mexicans on the plantation and pay a Spanish-speaking priest's salary. Like the federal government, church officials declined to act as labor recruiters, and so Johnston's managers tried to lure Mexican workers by offering them better treatment than the competition.[85] At the close of the picking season in 1927, fifteen Mexicans working at D&PL bought cars with the money they had earned "and were not cheated out of," observed the local priest.[86] Through their willingness to move and awareness of their own bargaining power, these workers successfully leveraged planters' hunger for labor to achieve the economic progress they had been unable to secure in Mexico or Texas.

Recognizing the economic opportunity that the flood had presented to those who survived it, a small group of immigrants founded Mississippi's first Mexican community organization weeks after the waters receded. These local leaders, including Manuel Solís and Telesforo Robledo, emulated organizing they had witnessed in Texas when they founded the Mexican Honorary Commission at Alligator, Mississippi.[87] Honorary Commissions, known in Spanish as Comisiones Honoríficas, were meant to function as volunteer extensions of Mexican consulates who would promote Mexican culture and nationalism among the immigrants in their communities. They were often bearers of a Mexican middle-class progressive tradition, middlemen who had some voice before both the consulate and white power holders on behalf of working-class Mexicans.[88] Alligator's Commission, led by poor sharecroppers with middle-class aspirations, soon moved twenty miles south to Gunnison, perhaps because its members relocated there to send their children to the Mary Ann School established just for Mexican children on the plantation of J. G. McGehee.[89]

Embracing their charge to promote Mexican nationalism in the Delta, the sharecroppers at the Commission's helm invited all the Mexicans they knew to their celebration of the Cinco de Mayo holiday in 1928. Immigrant sharecroppers found their way to the plantation school that Saturday, perhaps with the help of the few compatriots who had cars. For several hours that evening, they were not poor racialized laborers but rather patriots in the service of a larger cause. The program began with a chorus of children singing the Mexican national anthem, while sharecroppers accompanied them in a makeshift orchestra. A teen then read aloud an account of the battle of Puebla, when Mexican troops drove out French would-be conquerors on May 5, 1862. Commission president Manuel Solís addressed the attendees, and then a dozen children individually read poems or other recitations. Carving out a space for community life in a society that saw them only as workers, the families then danced together to Mexican music into the wee hours of the night.[90]

Confronting the Color Line

By 1928, then, a small group of Mexicans and Mexican Americans had tried to forge a future in the Mississippi Delta, believing they had greater opportunities there than in South Texas or on the migrant trail in the Midwest. Yet Mexicanos plainly saw that African Americans had little possibility for social mobility besides leaving the Delta entirely.[91] As the 1925 struggle over Santiago Castillo's corpse attested, Mexicanos remained vigilant to signs that they would be classed alongside African Americans in the area's racial hierarchy. Before long, Gunnison's Mexican Honorary Commission would turn its attention from encouraging Mexican patriotism to fighting for Mexicanos' improved racial status.

Mexicanos waged this struggle to achieve their own goals for social mobility, and there is little evidence that it reflected their private attitudes toward African Americans.[92] While Mexicanos and African Americans generally worked in distinct crews and family groups, they encountered each other by circumstance and by choice. Residential segregation by race was a feature of cities and towns rather than plantation back roads, and Mexicanos lived among both black and white sharecroppers, though most often among blacks. Nine out of ten Mexicanos in Bolivar County had at least some black neighbors in April 1930, while four out of ten had at least some white neighbors.[93] Though the historical record leaves few clues as to poor black and white sharecroppers' views of their Mexicano neighbors during this period, members of both groups, though African Americans more often, did form intimate relationships with the newcomers. African Americans Lula and Kit

Mason took their daughter's new Mexican-born husband, Manuel Sifuentez, into their home, and Mexican-born Antonio Martínez settled down with his African American wife, Sarah.[94] Other black families housed Mexican men for a fee, in one case assigning the nickname "Mexican Sam" to a Mexican-born boarder. The consequences of living with blacks were suggested by the notation of a census enumerator, who in 1930 listed Mexican Sam's race as Negro, rather than Mexican.[95] Though less common, some Mexican men married white women as well. Maggie Mackenzie was a Mississippi-born white woman alone in her thirties with six children to support. She married Frank Torres, a Texas-born Mexican American man nine years her junior.[96] While marrying a black man in the 1920s would have brought banishment or even death to an impoverished white woman in the Delta, marrying a Mexican American man apparently was more acceptable.[97] Having grown up in Texas, Frank Torres knew well the benefits of marrying "up" in the racial hierarchy, which may have motivated him to do so despite Maggie's more advanced age and the financial burden of supporting her six children.

While planters and white officials initially used violence on Mexican workers as severely as they had on African Americans, many locals entertained the possibility that their racial classification could be distinct from that of blacks. The region's white leaders had experience creating new racial categories beyond just black and white, most notably in their responses to the Italian and Chinese immigrants who first came to the region in the late nineteenth century. Just across the Mississippi River from Vicksburg, in Tallulah, Louisiana, Sicilians were lynched in the late 1890s; Chinese, too, were initially considered nonwhite.[98] As the largest influx of Mexicanos arrived at Mississippi's fields in 1925, the Mississippi Supreme Court ruled in the case *Gong Lum v. Rice* that a Mississippi-born Chinese girl, Martha Lum, could not attend the white school in Rosedale, Bolivar County. The court reasoned that while the Mississippi state constitution may have referred specifically to "whites" and "Negroes" in its sanction of segregation, its intent was to preserve the purity of the Caucasian race from all other races, not only blacks. While "Negroes" were the only threat to this purity at the time of the constitution's writing, surely it intended for all non-Caucasian races to be schooled separately. In defining these "colored" races, the court followed the lead of a Washington state court that utilized the categorization of racial groups first generated by German physiologist Johann Friedrich Blumenbach in 1776:[99] "(1) The Caucasian, or white race, to which belong the greater part of the European nations and those of Western Asia; (2) the Mongolian, or yellow race, occupying Tartary, China, Japan, etc.; (3) the Ethiopian, or negro (black) race, occupying all

Africa, except the North; (4) the American, or red race, containing the Indian of North and South America; and (5) the Malay, or brown race, occupying the islands of the Indian Archipelago."[100] Since Chinese fell into the "Mongolian" category, they could be excluded from the white school. A third school for Chinese students opened as a result and operated intermittently in Bolivar County during the 1930s.[101] The ruling and its consequences set a precedent for racial compromise: white leaders could exclude new racial groups from their own schools and spaces but would also stop short of relegating them to those of blacks.

Though Mexicanos also lived in Bolivar County at the time, the *Gong Lum* decision, later affirmed by the U.S. Supreme Court, did not explicitly mention them nor did it indicate into which of these five categories they might fall. The Treaty of Guadalupe Hidalgo, which brought an end to the U.S.-Mexican War of 1846–48, implicitly guaranteed Mexicanos' status as Caucasian by promising them "the enjoyment of all the rights of citizens of the United States." But subsequent legal opinions citing the treaty left room for interpretation, and white officials in Mississippi may not have known about them in any case.[102] They thus interpreted *Gong Lum* as a license to exclude all undesirable immigrants from white schools. In 1926, a year after both the *Gong Lum* decision and the large-scale arrival of Mexican workers, the Bolivar County Schools Board of Trustees voted to prohibit Mexicans from attending the Gunnison Consolidated School with white children. Instead, the county paid Mexican Honorary Commission president Manuel Solís to offer instruction at the Mary Ann School, a separate Mexican school on the Gunnison plantation of J. G. McGehee.[103] In so doing, local authorities sent a clear message to Mexicanos that they were not welcome in white society. Mexicano community leaders seem to have found the school a tolerable compromise, sending their children there and using its building as a home base for their patriotic celebrations.

Yet just a few months after being reelected president of Gunnison's Honorary Commission, teacher Manuel Solís left town, creating a crisis for his compatriots. Authorities were unable to convince a young Tejana woman to assume the role of teacher, and the number of Mexicano children in the area had dwindled.[104] Honorary Commission treasurer Telesforo Robledo and his wife, María, along with a couple newly arrived from Mississippi's Lake Cormorant, Rafael and Martha Landrove, managed to enroll their children in the local white school in 1928.[105] It is not clear whether the decision to admit them came from a high-level administrator or a secretary unaware of the controversy their admission might cause. Pupils eleven-year-old Hortensia

Landrove and her fourteen-year-old uncle George thus attended the white school for a few weeks during the winter of 1928–29. The following year, the Robledo children enrolled in the white second-grade class once the cotton was picked. While the Robledos pulled their son Freddo out in February to help prepare for the next cotton crop, their daughter Jubertina finished out the school year, struggling with English but otherwise earning As and Bs. She was promoted to the third grade at the end of the year even as many of her peers were left behind.[106] She became the first Mexican child to complete the academic year in the white elementary school of Gunnison, Mississippi.

In early 1930, school officials began to enforce the 1926 school board ruling and told the Mexican families their children could not attend the white school.[107] The Landroves and Robledos thus confronted the possibility of sending their children to the black school or to no school at all. In addition to the racial stigma that attached to them, the Delta's black schools made little real attempt to educate students, with some enrolling 100 pupils for every teacher and offering barely four months of annual instruction to ensure that black children were on hand for the planting and picking of cotton.[108] Of course, the Landroves and Robledos could have left the Delta altogether as thousands of other Mexicano families had done over the course of a decade, but they chose instead to find a way to challenge the ruling. In so doing, they participated in a national movement, probably unknowingly. That same year, Mexican families in Lemon Grove, California, and Del Rio, Texas, mounted challenges to Mexicanos' exclusion from white schools.[109] Yet unlike Mexicano activists in the Southwest, the Delta's Mexicans had neither Mexican American organizations nor white liberal lawyers on whom to rely.

The Delta's Mexican leaders were trying to shift their position in the area's Jim Crow system, and to do so they would have to pick their allies carefully. The most powerful people with whom they had frequent contact were the area's Catholic priests, yet the immigrants wisely decided not to appeal to the church for assistance. Whatever their views on long-standing church–state conflicts in north-central Mexico, both the Landroves and Robledos had baptized their children and godparented others at Our Lady of Victory in Cleveland.[110] Still, they correctly perceived that in Mississippi, church officials viewed "Mexican" as a separate and distinct race. Priests spoke about "Mexicans" as a homogenous group without regard to citizenship, recorded them separately from whites on church censuses even before the U.S. census offered a separate category, and arranged specific services and religious education for Mexicans.[111] There is little evidence that they sought to minister to Mexicans alongside the Delta's other main Catholic group, Italians. While

Mexicans in New Orleans had used white Catholic churches as a vehicle for their assimilation into white New Orleans, Mississippi's Mexicanos saw no such potential in the Delta.

Though they did not adopt all southwestern stereotypes of Mexicans, priests did espouse one repeatedly: the image of Mexicans as poor, docile, and "childlike."[112] Clarksdale's Catholic priest described them as "poor . . . struggling to keep body and soul together and illiterate at that."[113] Later, he mused, "when our Blessed Lord said 'Unless you become as little children you cannot enter the Kingdom of God' He could have had in mind those poor faithful children, the Mexicans."[114] Whatever their paternalistic intentions to help Mexicans, priests remained entrenched in the U.S. American system of fixed racial categories, seeing Mexicanos as inherently unfit for self-determination and political personhood.

The Mexican Strategy

Local priests were unable to imagine Mexicans playing a different role in the Delta's racial hierarchy; the area had no Mexican American middle class, white liberals, or active tenant organizing; and African Americans were preoccupied with survival and their own abundant political struggles. Conversely, the Landroves and Robledos had established contact with the Mexican consulate thanks to their involvement with the local Honorary Commission. Their most proximate advocate was actually hundreds of miles away in New Orleans. Mexicans in the Southwest also petitioned Mexican consulates for assistance in their school desegregation struggles, but there these consulates in turn engaged local liberal advocates. The Mississippi case played out differently. Because there were no political partners in the South who could make claims on U.S. citizenship, Mexicans' racial politics in the South were just that—Mexican.

The life history of the man who ultimately succeeded in reversing the Mississippi schools' decision provides one window onto the interaction between two seemingly opposed racial ideologies: the Mexican system, favoring race mixing and positivist cultural "improvement," and the South's Jim Crow, a binary system ostensibly based on biological definitions of race. Rafael Landrove was born in northern Mexico, probably Nuevo León or Coahuila, in 1893. Since at least the 1870s, the Landrove family had migrated within Mexico to better their circumstances. His parents and siblings moved between Zaragoza, Coahuila, and several towns in Nuevo León, among them Lampazos de Naranjo, where his father, Rafael, and mother, Petra Jayme, married in 1879.[115]

In an area dominated by ranching and agriculture, the Landrove siblings were small-town urbanites, members of the aspiring middle classes that emerged under the regime of Porfirio Díaz, Mexico's dictator almost without interruption from 1876 to 1911. In his early decades of rule, Díaz had succeeded in growing Mexico's economy and developing its infrastructure, particularly in the north. For the first time, for example, railroads connected the Lampazos area to both Mexico City and the U.S.-Mexico border, giving its residents and agricultural capitalists access to new markets, goods, and work sites throughout both countries. The climate of economic prosperity in the north led to greater social mobility there than elsewhere, making it "the land of the self-made man" as a small middle class began to develop in its towns and cities.[116]

As the Landroves moved from town to town, they employed entrepreneurial strategies in their attempts to become "self-made"—attempts that never quite succeeded, at least in Mexico. Rafael's brother Constancio made his living between Lampazos and San Antonio, Texas, where he moved and married in 1913 and worked as a blacksmith. By 1930, he owned a home.[117] Despite settling in Texas, Constancio renewed his ties to Lampazos, registering his Texas-born children with the municipality there and even opening a liquor store in the town in 1916.[118] Brothers Melchor and José worked as musicians.[119] Sisters Margarita and María owned a restaurant in Lampazos but did not find the economic stability of marriage. Both gave birth to "illegitimate" children and supported them on their own; in María's case, that meant moving a few hundred miles north to the border town of Laredo, Texas, where she worked as a cook and servant for a middle-class Tejano family.[120] Margarita, too, eventually moved to the United States, settling in Oklahoma.[121]

The Landrove siblings were not alone in their frustration at a stifled social ascent. Indeed, Rafael Landrove was about seventeen years old in 1910 when his generation of middling northern Mexicans rebelled against the late Porfiriato's social inequalities, though not necessarily against its promises of individual and national improvement, progress, and modernization. The north's rising middle class saw itself reflected in this positivist vision during the early years of the Porfiriato. Yet particularly after the economic downturn of 1905, the lower and middle classes were increasingly squeezed, and the contrast between expectation and reality led the region to become a hotbed of opposition to the Díaz regime.[122] Though Díaz and his conservative followers were politically defeated by 1914, the new elite inherited many of the old guard's ideological legacies.[123]

Revolution, however, still did not allow Landrove to realize his ambition of class ascendance, so he journeyed to the U.S.-Mexico border in his midtwenties, around 1916. He lived for a few years between Piedras Negras, Mexico, and Eagle Pass, Texas, across the border, and fathered a daughter, Hortensia, in 1919.[124] Though his brother Constancio had found a measure of economic stability in San Antonio, Rafael's failure to do so parallels the declining fortunes of most Mexicans in South Texas during the 1920s. Like his sister Margarita and countless other Mexican immigrants, Rafael Landrove's journey north began in South Texas but did not end in that place of racial oppression. By 1924, Landrove was traveling to work in the rapidly expanding cotton industry of East-Central Texas, and there he wed Martha Perry (or possibly Pérez), a Tejana from the East Texas town of Nacogdoches.[125] Within three years, the couple had moved yet again, to Lake Cormorant at the far northern end of the Mississippi Delta.[126]

Once Landrove was there, his strategy for racial and economic "progress" did not draw on the biological understanding of race then dominant in the United States, in which "one drop" of African blood made a person black and some argued that "one drop" of Indian blood could make Mexicans Indian.[127] Rather, Landrove's understandings of race and class emerged from his social position in Mexico. He told the census enumerator in 1930 that although he was born in Mexico, his parents were Cuban and his Texas-born wife, Martha, had Spanish parentage.[128] Yet records in Lampazos, some of which describe Rafael's mother, Petra Jayme, as a native of the town, reveal that his claim on the census was a lie.[129] A photograph of the couple (fig. 7) shows Rafael's skin to be very dark, too dark to claim biological European parentage. Landrove presumably sought through Cubanness to extricate himself from the denigrated "Mexican" racial category he and his wife had known so well during their time in Texas.

This early 1928 family photograph of Rafael and Martha Landrove reveals their middle-class aspirations, framed in both Mexican and U.S. terms. The photo survived, loose and unframed, in the personal collection of his friends, the Enriquez family.[130] Thus, there is no way to know how the Landroves themselves used this photo. Was it in an album or, more likely, framed on a wall?[131] Either way, its visual conventions fell squarely within scholars' consensus about family photographs: they were typically idealized versions of domestic life.[132] By the end of the nineteenth century, the posed family photograph had emerged in the United States as a representation of the middle-class ideal: an economically independent husband, nonworking domestic wife, and a baby inheriting the legacy of race and class privilege bestowed by her parents.[133] The Porfirian positivist tradition encouraged the creation

FIGURE 7 Landrove family photograph, Mississippi Delta, ca. 1930. Courtesy of Nick Enriquez and family.

of such images for a complementary reason: as symbols of Mexico's modernity.[134] Mexican migrants themselves valued such self-portraits in middle-class dress as reminders that they were more than the racialized laborers white U.S. observers believed them to be.[135]

All of these traditions are visible in the Landroves' posed family photo. The pen in Rafael Landrove's pocket implied that he was a professional, which, in Mississippi, he was not; Martha's fur coat and pearl necklace suggested a wealth the couple did not possess. The bench on which they sat certainly did not belong in their sharecroppers' cabins in the northern Mississippi Delta. By the time this photograph was taken, the Landroves may have conformed nominally to the type represented: Rafael Landrove was indeed literate, the couple's more formal clothing suggests at least a modicum of economic progress, and like half of Mexican families in the Delta, they claimed Martha did not work.[136] Yet the image nonetheless exaggerates these qualities, depicting an aspiration more than a reality. It helps explain why the Mexican government, not the Catholic Church, was Landrove's advocate of choice. The photograph depicts a modern middle-class family, not a family of "poor" and "simple" Mexicans.

Yet two years after commissioning this middle-class image of his family, Landrove had nowhere to send his children to school. The black school was unacceptable to him, the Mexican school had closed, and the white school now rejected his children. Unlike his counterparts in Texas, Landrove could appeal to no U.S. citizen middle class to pursue his children's readmission to the white school through a "Caucasian" legal strategy.[137] Rather, like his counterparts in Lemon Grove, California, he sought help from the nearest Mexican consulate.[138] In so doing, he drew on the social and political status that New Orleans's Mexican bureaucrats like Armando Amador and upper-class families like that of Hortensia Horcasitas, discussed in Chapter 1, had amassed through their cultural representations of Mexicanness to white New Orleans.

The Mexican government's paternalistic concept of *protección*, protection of emigrants, obligated it to respond somehow to the appeal of a poor, dark-skinned Mexican like Landrove. Though records suggest that the consulate looked less favorably on appeals from Mississippi than on those from its backyard of New Orleans, its officials sometimes intervened directly on behalf of poor Mexicans in the Delta in the case of wage disputes and criminal matters.[139] In fall 1930, for example, the consulate successfully helped Tomás Vielma recover the $30 that Greenville farmer T. P. Ranes underpaid him for his labor planting and picking cotton.[140] When it came to intervening in the race politics of Jim Crow, however, the "protection" mission came into direct conflict with another aspect of the nascent Mexican nationalist agenda: the promotion of the "cosmic race," or *raza cósmica*, ideology that celebrated race mixing in direct opposition to the white supremacy of Mexico's northern neighbor. But in Mississippi, "protection" meant cooperation with white supremacy by securing Mexicans' recognition as white, or at least not black.

Though contemporaneous with the "Mexican school" court cases in Lemon Grove, California, and Del Rio, Texas, Landrove's Mexican strategy to achieve educational desegregation departed from the strategy deployed in the Southwest, which emphasized the promises of U.S. citizenship and relied on Mexicans' legal classification as Caucasian. LULAC, an organization that restricted its membership to U.S. citizens, argued the case in Texas.[141] The Lemon Grove, California, case started like Mississippi's, with distressed parents appealing to the Mexican consulate there. But in California, that Mexican consul contracted a liberal white lawyer who presented Mexican parents' petition stating that their children were almost all U.S. born and therefore entitled to all the rights and privileges of U.S. citizens."[142] This argument, too, relied on the presumption that Mexicans were legally Caucasian. The Mexican and Mexican American plaintiffs in Lemon Grove succeeded while those in Del Rio lost their case.[143] Either way, the so-called Caucasian strategy, which also emphasized U.S. citizenship, failed to end the segregation of Mexican children, who now were kept apart based on alleged linguistic or cultural deficiencies.[144] Furthermore, many historians have criticized this "Caucasian" strategy, contending that its "pact" with white supremacy hindered the civil rights struggles of both Mexicanos and African Americans.[145]

In Mississippi, however, the consul did not appeal to U.S. legal precedents about Mexicans' citizenship status or racial categorization. Rather, he wrote to Mississippi's governor, Theodore Bilbo, asking for Mexicans' admission to the white school based on a presumed mutual "desire to strengthen the cordial relations that fortunately now exist between both countries," the United States and Mexico.[146] The argument depended not on the racial qualifications of Mexicans nor on U.S. legal precedent but rather on the influence of a foreign government. Indeed, though the Mexican government sought to retain the loyalty of its citizens abroad by intervening on their behalf, in these years it had scant leverage in its dealings with the U.S. federal government.[147] Bureaucrats thus relied on the persuasion of stateness—the respect Mexico could command from local authorities, if not necessarily federal ones, by virtue of being its own sovereign nation-state.

The strategy worked. Governor Bilbo responded to the consul's request, and by April, Landrove won the dispute. The following school year Hortensia Landrove, her young uncle George Pérez, and Telesforo Robledo's son Trinidad once again enrolled in the white school after they had finished helping their families pick that season's cotton. All three finished out the academic year and were passed on to the next grade.[148] Rafael Landrove had gained his children's admission to the white school solely under the banner of Mexican nationalism. Though Landrove's original petition to the consulate did not enter the archival record, nowhere in the consulate's letters to Landrove or Bilbo did Mexican officials use the word "Caucasian," nor did they appeal to liberal ideas of U.S. citizenship. Rather, Landrove and the Mexican consulate were allied under the banner of an inclusive, modernizing Mexican nationalism. In turn, the consulate utilized the political capital generated through its advantageous position in New Orleans, making good, at least this time, on the Mexican government's postrevolutionary promise of national homogeneity and equality. The racial position of Mexicanos in the Mississippi Delta thus hinged not only on the logic of U.S. white supremacy but also on the Mexican government's power to influence local officials' application of that logic.

The victory in the Gunnison schools was crucial for Rafael Landrove. His children's education alongside white children, something that would not have occurred in Texas, seemed to introduce the possibility of his family's eventual ascendance into the Delta's white middle class. Yet the Landroves' transformation from poor Mexicans to poor whites began at a moment when the latter identity's utility was rapidly declining. Indeed, Mexicanos had entered sharecropping in the Delta at the beginning of its end. As the Depression caused cotton prices to crash from seventeen cents per pound in 1929 to six cents per pound in 1931, sharecroppers, white, black, and Mexicano, found themselves unable to pay the debts they had incurred by purchasing seed and equipment, let alone turn any profit.[149] For most of the Delta's Mexicanos, the experiment with Mississippi was over.

The Depression brought federal relief into a region that had long resisted it, and that relief held the potential to shape the social order. In many parts of the United States, social workers dispensing charity in the 1930s became de facto immigration agents, encouraging the deportation and repatriation of unemployed immigrants and their families.[150] Mississippi relief agencies had a different charge: even in the Depression, powerful planters worried that they would not have enough labor come cotton-picking time.[151] Absent white-driven deportation and repatriation efforts, destitute Mexican sharecroppers begged the consulate in New Orleans for financial assistance returning to Mexico. Though the consulate typically arranged for free or discounted shipboard repatriation for its compatriots in New Orleans, it denied each claim that came from the cotton fields. These decisions reflected Mexican bureaucrats' priorities in the Depression: they used their limited resources to preserve Mexicans' good image in the commercially important city of New Orleans. Poor Delta sharecroppers like Timotea Arroyo were on their own. Arroyo wrote from Estill, near Greenville, in November 1930. Her husband was sick with no medical care, and she was unable to support her children. Drawing on their experiences with repatriation efforts elsewhere, consulate officials suggested that Arroyo find a charitable organization to transport her family to the border, at which time the Mexican government would fund the rest of their journey. Arroyo replied that Estill had no such group, and so like hundreds of her compatriots in 1930, she remained destitute and abandoned in the Delta.[152]

The Depression had wiped out the meager financial gains, hopes for social mobility, and communal institutions of the Delta's more settled Mexicanos. Many Mexicano families who came to Mississippi in the 1920s and 1930s ended up returning to the Southwest, but others continued the search for an alternative. When the Mexicano children baptized in Mississippi in the 1920s and 1930s eventually married in the 1940s, 1950s, and 1960s, many wed other Mexicans and Mexican Americans in the rural Midwest. Their nuptials took place in towns like Waukegan, Illinois; Albion, Michigan; Kenosha, Wisconsin; and Fostoria, Ohio—though it is difficult to know if they had settled in these places or were passing through as migrant workers.[153]

Rafael Landrove, however, was not to give up so easily on Mississippi. In August 1931, he wrote to the consulate to reestablish Gunnison's Honorary Commission. While the group hoped to celebrate Mexican Independence Day, its real goal was to organize the Mexicans in the area to "regulate the cotton market and prevent a disaster in the next harvest."[154] Landrove again turned to the Mexican government for help gaining economic stability in Mississippi. By 1932, however, he had apparently lost hope and petitioned the consulate for repatriation assistance, which was denied.[155] But he remained in Mississippi at least eight years beyond this appeal, continuing to add children to his and Martha's family and applying for naturalization in Mississippi courts in 1940.[156] On his petition for naturalization, he listed his color as "white," his complexion as "natural," and his race, once again, as "Cuban." Records do not indicate how the Landroves left Mississippi, only that they eventually divorced and made their homes in more traditional areas of Mexican American settlement. Rafael Landrove moved to Sacramento in 1949 and died there in 1976, while Martha died three years later in Houston.[157]

Though the Landroves left the Mississippi Delta, their middle-class self-conception and Mexican strategy—expectations forged in the positivist tradition of Mexico's nineteenth century and politics born in the revolution of the twentieth—succeeded in winning new rights for their family and their compatriots. The revolution had not fulfilled its promises for Rafael Landrove in Mexico, but in Mississippi it did create more social mobility for his and other Mexican immigrant families. His successful strategy was one inaccessible to his Tejano counterparts in Mississippi, who were citizens of the United States but did not have any means to realize the rights that citizenship technically conferred. After all, even the Southwest's Mexican American middle class spent three decades pursuing civil rights through claims to U.S. citizenship and "Caucasian" identities, yet most Mexican and Mexican American children there continued to attend segregated schools.

For their part, Mexican government representatives well understood the realities of their "protective" role in the U.S. South, not only in cosmopolitan New Orleans but also in the more challenging environment of the Mississippi Delta. Their choices show that while Mexican nationalist bureaucrats' celebration of race mixing may have been unpalatable to U.S. sensibilities, their parallel emphasis on cultural, political, and economic whitening—the Porfiriato's legacy—could serve as a wedge into the winning side of U.S.-style white supremacy. That both Mexican government representatives and individual Mexican immigrants so readily dispensed with mestizaje reveals the thin penetration of "cosmic race" nationalism a decade after the revolution's close, as well as the influence of U.S. white supremacy on the development of Mexican racial ideologies. Furthermore, it shows that the Jim Crow system incorporated cultural and political understandings of race into its ostensibly eugenic system decades before segregation's demise forced a change to more veiled forms of cultural racism. This happened because southern Jim Crow did not stand alone—not in the nation and not in the world. By recruiting Mexican workers to their plantations, the Delta's white farmers unwittingly recruited international influences into a notoriously closed racial system.

Delta Legacies

The more settled community of Mexicano sharecroppers from the late 1920s mostly left the area in the early 1930s, but the Depression changed the region's agricultural systems in ways that would eventually encourage more Mexicanos to arrive. From 1933 to 1939, the federal government's Agricultural Adjustment Administration (AAA) paid planters to let their lands lie fallow in order to reduce the commodity's oversupply and arrest its downward price spiral. Planters were supposed to split these payments with their sharecroppers, but most evicted them instead. Armed with more capital and facing an ample supply of labor, planters now insisted on working with wage laborers rather than sharecroppers.[158] The shift would prove permanent. Some of the Delta's long-standing Mexicano families managed to return to sharecropping, but a larger number of Mexicanos began to arrive as wage laborers from the mid-1930s onward.[159]

Though Mississippi farmers were comparatively slow to take advantage of the guest worker program that would come to be known as the bracero program, the influx of Mexican laborers into Texas after 1942 made it easier for them to recruit Tejanos for the picking season. Tejanos and a small number of braceros picked cotton in Mississippi alongside African Americans and German prisoners during the war years. During the 1950s, hundreds of Tejano families settled in Mississippi, where they performed agricultural labor until mechanical cotton pickers slowly replaced them in the fields.[160]

For decades, these Mexican and Mexican American newcomers faced an uneven process of racialization. Local authorities continued to bury Mexicanos in Clarksdale's black cemetery in the early 1930s. When the area's Mexicans asked the New Orleans consulate to intervene, they received no advocacy, only instructions to take up a collection themselves to ensure their compatriots' burial "in a different place from that which is intended for the colored race."[161] Two years later, Baptist ministers held a service for Mexicanos in a black church, presuming perhaps with cause that at least some would be willing to attend in that location.[162] When Mexicanos returned to the area in larger numbers during the 1940s, their admission to white schools remained contested. A priest reported in 1946, "Some of the white schools here in the Delta will admit the children of these Mexican families, and other white schools will not admit them. For instance, Friars Point School will admit them but the Clarksdale City Schools will not admit them." White privilege, however, still had its limits for poor Delta cotton pickers. "Practically all the children of the King & Anderson plantation could attend the Friars Point School if the Plantation Manager would cooperate," observed the priest. "The children have to work in the fields just like the adults and very few of them go to school."[163]

Over time, however, recognition as white did bring material rewards and the possibility of social mobility to the Delta's Mexicans and Mexican Americans. The few families that continued to sharecrop—the Enriquezes, Vargases, Palacioses, and others—maintained a distinctly Mexican communal life in private, staying friends with each other and with newer Mexican arrivals, socializing at country dances with Mexican bands, and often speaking Spanish at home.[164] But from the 1930s through the demise of segregation, most of the Delta's Mexican Americans sent their children to white schools, and from the 1940s they married white people in substantial numbers.[165] Stories from the 1960s and beyond suggest that Mississippi's Mexican Americans deliberately avoided public discussions of their ethnic heritage, the cost for their admission to the Delta's white middle class.[166] That group has had its own hardships, suffering periods of unemployment and economic downturn, and Mexican Americans have been along for the ride. Many of them, the descendants of Rafael Landrove's friends and compatriots, remain in the Delta to this day.

CHAPTER THREE

Citizens of Somewhere
Braceros, Tejanos, Dixiecrats, and Mexican Bureaucrats in the Arkansas Delta, 1939–1964

"Wike's Drive Inn (Restaurant)," reads the photograph's caption (fig. 8). "It is at the outskirts of Marked Tree, Arkansas, heading towards Harrisburg, Arkansas. A well constructed and nice-looking establishment." It was November 1949 when Mexican consul Rubén Gaxiola traveled to Marked Tree, Arkansas, to investigate alleged discrimination against Mexicans. He recorded his findings with a camera: "No Mexicans" signs prominently displayed in front of eleven establishments. Additionally, one of the town's two movie theaters seated Mexican patrons only in the area reserved for blacks.[1] Attaching the photos as evidence in his report to Mexico City, Gaxiola immediately recommended that Marked Tree's employers, most prominently its largest planter, E. Ritter, have their bracero contracts canceled. Gaxiola hoped that swift action would set an example for the rest of Arkansas, "as an energetic protest against these discriminatory acts against Mexicans."[2]

The signs would not remain for long. During the decade following their arrival in the Arkansas Delta, Mexican cotton workers successfully resisted Jim Crow–style exclusion through strategies this chapter will explain. The victory was ambiguous and gave way to a new, more fluid separation in which Mexicans had access to white public space but felt more comfortable socializing with African Americans. The first-class citizenship that Mexicans demanded with an end to their formal segregation never extended into the economic realm, where they fought for, but failed to win, broad guarantees of economic security.

Braceros' tenure in the Arkansas Delta included the years of Jim Crow's fall. Five years after Consul Gaxiola captured the "No Mexicans" sign, the U.S. Supreme Court negated the doctrine of "separate but equal" through its ruling in *Brown v. Board of Education*; the following year, the nearby town of Hoxie became a national flashpoint for school integration, and two years after that, the federal government forced the desegregation of Little Rock

---

To see a selection of original historical sources from this chapter, go to http://corazondedixie.org/chapter-3 (http://dx.doi.org/10.7264/N35T3HR0).

FIGURE 8 "Wike's Drive Inn (Restaurant). It is at the outskirts of Marked Tree, Arkansas, heading towards Harrisburg, Arkansas. A well constructed and nice-looking establishment." Attachments to letter from Consul Rubén Gaxiola, Memphis, to Ministry of Foreign Relations, Mexico City, November 19, 1949, TM-26-32, Archivo Histórico de la Secretaría de Relaciones Exteriores, Mexico City.

Central High School.[3] As the legal structures of racial segregation crumbled in the face of black political organizing and federal government interventions, battles over race and rights moved increasingly into cultural and economic territory. The New Deal's two-decades-old liberal promise, that U.S. American workers would enjoy basic economic security and regulated labor conditions, had still not been extended to rural workers thanks to the efforts of white southern conservative elites.[4] Growers across the country lauded the arrival of the bracero program in 1942, which promised to deliver them Mexican workers on temporary visas to alleviate wartime labor shortages and the attendant upward pressure on agricultural wages. But the program continued for two decades beyond World War II, bringing more than four million Mexican men to perform agricultural labor in the country before it ended in 1964.[5] In Arkansas (map 4), around 300,000 braceros worked the cotton fields between 1948 and 1964, in some years comprising more than a third of all laborers there.[6] For Arkansas planters, the promise of the bracero program was the promise of continued access to cheap and available labor

Braceros in the Arkansas Delta 83

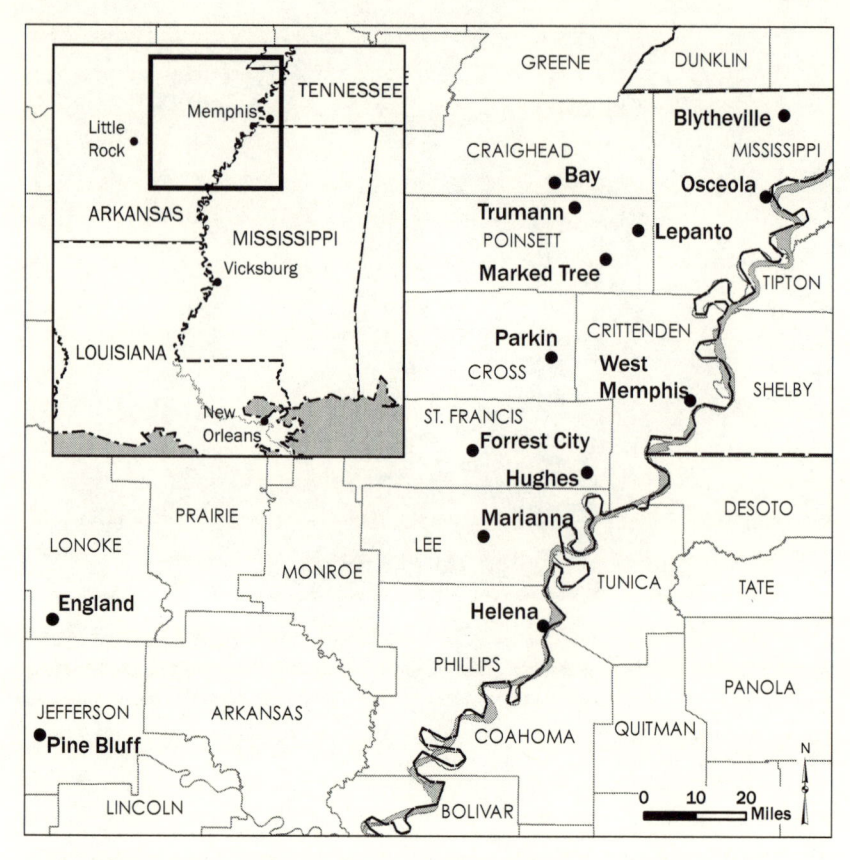

MAP 4 Arkansas Delta counties and towns. Map by the author.

even as the postwar boom drew workers to cities and white elites' control over African Americans deteriorated.

That promise, however, went largely unfulfilled. Mexico's expanding economy and nationalist protective economic policies ushered in its "golden age" of economic growth and national cohesion during the World War II years, and this led ordinary citizens to have rising expectations for their material well-being and political recognition. Furthermore, braceros felt strongly compelled to maximize the remittances they delivered to the families that had endured painful separations for the sake of their labor in the United States.[7] Once in Arkansas, braceros demanded the social and economic rights they felt were due them as workers, Mexican citizens, and patriarchs, setting off a battle in the Arkansas Delta among Tejano crew leaders, Mexican consuls, white planters, and white and African American tenants and laborers. At

84   *Braceros in the Arkansas Delta*

stake were not just Mexicans' social and economic rights but the fates of all of Arkansas's cotton workers. The twin demands of racial equality and improved economic security for rural workers dogged white southern conservatives facing down New Deal liberals at midcentury, and braceros challenged them on both fronts. They rejected both poor labor conditions and social discrimination in Arkansas. White conservatives responded by steadfastly protecting their economic and political advantages over labor, even if this meant compromise in the area of race.

Though the U.S. federal government attempted to regulate the comings and goings of Mexican agricultural workers for the first time through the bracero program, a different federal government—the Mexican government— played a much more decisive role in negotiating the terms of braceros' work and lives with the planters who employed them in Arkansas. Historians have painted 1948–53 as the period in which the Mexican government steadily lost control and bargaining power in the bracero program, or they have discounted the effectiveness of Mexican consuls entirely; but the case study of Arkansas reveals a more complicated story that varied greatly in different bracero destinations.[8] During the late 1940s and early 1950s in the Arkansas Delta, the targeted local efforts of activist Mexican bureaucrats effectively curtailed white farmers' unfettered access to low-cost Mexican labor. In so doing, Mexican migrants and bureaucrats placed a transnational weight on the Delta's political scale, promoting the equivalent of New Deal liberalism to the dismay of farmers who had seen Mexican labor as a way to circumvent it.

When workers and their consulates pushed back, these local authorities used every means at their disposal—law, culture, and practice—to ensure Mexicans' nominal access to white public spaces and to defuse racially charged conflicts as they emerged. In so doing, they appeased the Mexican consulate to ensure their continued ability to contract workers but fought braceros and their government on matters of economic consequence. As conservative white elites forced local residents, shop owners, and policemen to treat Mexicans differently from African Americans and nominally accept their presence in white public space, they further paved the way for increased contracting of braceros to the area, which in turn kept wages low. The social, cultural, and economic history of the Arkansas Delta's "Mexicanization" in response to a transnational battle over New Deal liberalism thus set the stage for the future trajectory of race relations in the rural South, even if its implications would not be obvious until the largest influx of Latino workers to the region thirty years hence.

"Place Your Order": Recruiting Mexicano Labor

Delta planters had complained of labor shortages since Emancipation, but during the Depression their actions ultimately forced thousands of workers out of the area. The federal government began in 1933 to pay planters to keep their fields out of production, in a successful bid to boost cotton prices. As in Mississippi, most Arkansas planters ignored requirements to share these payments with their sharecroppers, instead evicting them and using the cash influx to hire them back as wage laborers. Many white and black cotton workers left the Delta, and when World War II brought a newfound demand for cotton, planters could not count on the worker surplus they had long enjoyed.[9] Long-standing forms of violent labor control were no match for the opportunities of a wartime economy, a mobilized society, and an increasingly powerful civil rights movement.[10] Some Arkansas Delta planters held meetings with African American laborers and employed black preachers to convince workers to remain on their farms.[11] But after decades of discrimination, abuse, and violence, black workers ignored their bosses' pleas and once again left the rural South, in even larger numbers during World War II than they had during the "Great Migration" of the 1910s and 1920s.[12] Cotton-picking contests and public relations materials marketed at white workers touted the economic and moral benefits of cotton picking, but these efforts also failed to stem the tide of white people out of rural Arkansas.[13]

Though Arkansas planters had not recruited Mexicanos as aggressively as their Mississippi counterparts in the 1920s–30s, their turn to Mexican labor during the war had some precedent. Small numbers of Mexicans and Mexican Americans had worked in the Arkansas Delta for decades, and sometimes their presence was specifically sought to discipline African Americans.[14] When black wage laborers in Phillips County refused to pick cotton for abysmally low wages in 1931, planters responded by recruiting 500 Mexican workers to their farms.[15] By 1940, some Mexican immigrants had established a Mexican Patriotic Committee on the Sycamore Bend Plantation in Hughes, where their children attended a separate Mexican school even as many Mexicanos across the river in Mississippi attended white schools thanks to the efforts of Rafael Landrove and his circle.[16]

When World War II began, Arkansas planters first redoubled their efforts to secure German prisoners of war and "negroes from the Bahama Islands" to pick their cotton.[17] They also offered the highest wages in memory, $3 per hundred pounds of cotton, to recruit white workers from the hills of Arkansas and black workers from Memphis.[18] Determined to find a cheaper alternative, they quickly turned their sights to Texas, where large numbers of Tejanos sought an escape from low wages and racial oppression. The Texas Farm Placement Service (TFPS) had used violence to stifle Tejano mobility since the 1920s, prompting one Louisiana official to state matter-of-factly in 1950 that "Texas-Mexican[s] . . . are not allowed to leave Texas."[19] Yet as more Tejanos acquired trucks of their own and labor controls weakened because of wartime mobility, Arkansas planters advertised for workers in Texas's Spanish-language newspapers and worked through middleman contractors.[20] TFPS eventually cooperated with Arkansas's agricultural extension service to regulate Tejano migration to the state, enabling an Arkansas county agent to offer triumphantly in 1946, "If you want some Mexican cotton pickers this fall, please come to my office and place your order."[21] Yet TFPS could hardly control Mexicano workers by this point: the 1947 harvest in one Arkansas county employed six times more privately than officially recruited Tejanos, in addition to nearly a thousand undocumented Mexican workers.[22]

Texas authorities' willingness to send at least some laborers to Arkansas also reflected the border state's newfound access to Mexican labor via the bracero program. Delta farmers resented their southwestern competitors' easy access to Mexican workers, complaining that "these wetbacks come over and pick the cotton over in southern California and Arizona and New Mexico," giving those states the unfair advantage of lower labor costs.[23] Circumventing official channels, some Arkansas planters hired contractors to bring them braceros who had been sent to work in Texas. When Texas and U.S. authorities caught four busloads of braceros headed out on an unauthorized journey to Arkansas, they fined the contractors in charge.[24]

Tired of haggling with Texas authorities, Arkansas farmers large and small launched efforts to recruit their own braceros in 1948. In Crittenden County, for example, more than a hundred farmers attended an initial meeting about bracero recruitment and between them placed requests for 500 workers. Near the end of the 1948 picking season, the county's extension agent wrote, "The farmers, as a whole, are very well pleased, and it looks as if there will be a demand for 5,000 such workers next year. This program is working out like a lot of others—once we get involved in a program, it is difficult to get away from it."[25] Smaller farmers placed orders for as few as five braceros while larger planters like Lee Wilson employed up to 1,600, with the median in 1952–53 around thirty braceros per farm.[26] Soon, county seats like Osceola became the sites of unfamiliar scenes: Tejano crew leaders and bracero crews, newly arrived from Texas, parked in the center of town, awaiting direction to farms from county extension agents.[27] Most arrived in the fall, often from summer contracts in the Midwest or elsewhere, and remained in Arkansas for less than three months, the duration of the picking season.[28]

"Golden Age" Mexicans Encounter Jim Crow Arkansas

Poor black and white cotton workers had resisted low wages through the Southern Tenant Farmers' Union (STFU), out-migration, and a thousand acts of daily resistance. If Arkansas's cotton farmers were "well pleased" with their initial experiences with bracero workers, it was because they saw braceros as uniquely willing to get the job done at low wages and with minimal resistance. Yet unlike migrant Tejanos, who effectively had no political power far from their Texas homes, braceros had more meaningful citizenship rights because of their connection to the newly robust Mexican state. Though that state's bracero management efforts could lead to disillusionment, particularly among the women and children braceros left behind, its claim to be the authentic protector and representative of the Mexican people at home and abroad emboldened braceros to petition for the guarantee of their rights in Arkansas.[29]

Workers signing up for the bracero program, whether for money to begin or support a family, as an independent adventure of masculine modernization, or both, likely knew something of the Mexican migrant experience in the United States from friends and relatives who had already journeyed to work there.[30] Particularly in the early years of the program, most had not heard about Arkansas. In 1948 at the age of twenty, Gabino Solís Aguilera rode three buses from his hometown of Pueblo Nuevo, Guanajuato, to the bracero contracting center in Monterrey. There he waited more than a week, all the while watching his precious pesos disappear to lodging costs. When he finally was called for a contract to Arkansas, he knew that "I was one of the first braceros who went there."[31] The two-day journey from bracero contracting sites along the U.S.-Mexico border in southeastern Texas to the cotton fields of the Arkansas Delta gave workers their first taste of the poor conditions to come. While bracero contracts enumerated very specific rules for transport vehicles, sleeping arrangements, and food along the way, Tejano crew leaders often remained ignorant of these rules, were instructed by Arkansas farmers to ignore them, or flouted them of their own accord. I. G. García and J. P. Yepes reported that they were given nowhere to sleep overnight, no restroom facilities, and nowhere to sit during the long ride.[32] Antonio Vega Aguiniga and the braceros in his group were given only three sandwiches to eat during the 800-mile journey from Laredo to Pine Bluff.[33] On the other hand, Tejano crew leader Pedro Villarreal Jr. was instructed by farmers to feed braceros only bread, but he pitied the workers and bought them canned sardines in addition.[34]

On arrival in Arkansas, braceros were distressed to see that they would stay in abandoned sharecropper cabins, "extremely old houses which were abandoned by the blacks," as many described them. In the program's later years, some were housed in barracks.[35] Miguel Jáquez López recalled that the Arkansas town where he worked in the mid-1950s was very beautiful, "but the only thing that was not beautiful was the barracks where we lived." They lacked indoor plumbing, so he and other braceros bathed in a nearby river—something Jáquez López had not had to do in the three other states where he had worked as a bracero.[36] Documentary evidence suggests the lack of bathroom facilities was typical among Arkansas bracero work sites.[37] Workers routinely cited problems including "grass filled mattresses, insufficient tables and benches, and insufficient cooking utensils."[38] One worker told of being made to sleep in the farm's garage alongside its tractors.[39] In another case, workers on C. E. Scott's plantation in England, Arkansas, lost all of their possessions and barely escaped with their lives when their cabin caught fire from a heating stove that had been installed "to avoid the furnishing of blankets and mattresses to the workers."[40] With long distances from field to town and no public transport, braceros' mobility was limited and varied. Employers would offer them rides into town on weekends, sometimes charging handsomely for the service, but braceros had little access to transportation on their own.[41] While some braceros recalled in later interviews that they did not mind conditions in Arkansas, more felt that their living environments mocked the bracero program's promise of a modern agricultural work experience in the United States.

Braceros knew that their contracts required planters to bring them to the doctor when sick, cover them with medical insurance, and pay them a minimum salary, but in practice bosses often ignored these mandates. Jack McNeil recalled serving as an interpreter at doctors' visits during his days as head of the Parkin Farmers' Association, but many braceros requesting medical attention were "completely ignored."[42] And whether or not they received medical attention, many, if not most, laborers in these early years of bracero contracting were denied the subsistence pay guaranteed to them in the event that sickness or poor weather prevented them from picking on a particular day.

Perhaps the most important clause in bracero contracts, however, was their wage guarantee—something that black and white wage laborers did not have. Indeed, in the era before the minimum wage in agriculture, braceros were the first of any class of workers in southern fields to have any economic rights at all. These internationally negotiated rights upended planters' fantasies about braceros. "The only item of cost of production ... which may be reduced is that of harvesting," explained one planter to his sympathetic congressman. "This can only be reduced if the labor supply of Mexico is available."[43] From planters' perspectives, the purpose of Mexican labor importation was to avoid bidding for white and black labor on the open market, competing with higher urban wages in Memphis and beyond.

Yet in their public discourses, white planters proclaimed that local laborers were not too expensive but rather too lazy.[44] "The higher the wage, the less a Delta Negro picks," alleged one official in a 1950 congressional hearing. But other witnesses at the hearing disagreed.[45] A Tennessee official noted that during periods when cotton picking paid more, "you can't get a maid in Memphis" because African American women preferred to earn more money cotton picking. African American truck drivers who drove workers from Memphis to the Delta to work for the day insisted that these workers "pick hard every day" and that if the wage were $3 per hundred pounds of cotton, there would be no trouble filling their trucks with workers before dawn.[46] The problem, then, was not black laborers' willingness to pick cotton but rather their willingness to do so when wages for cotton picking were lower than those for urban work in Memphis.

To compete with wages in Memphis and the Delta's cities, Arkansas planters often paid African Americans more than braceros during the first years of the bracero program there. This violated the bracero contract, which guaranteed Mexicans the prevailing wage in the area—a flawed premise to begin with, as the availability of braceros discouraged farmers from raising wages for locals. Nonetheless, braceros knew about these guarantees and were determined to receive them. Gabino Solís Aguilera recalled earning $3.00 per hundred pounds of cotton in Arkansas in 1948 and believed his earnings were the same as those of black workers.[47] Yet countless braceros, among them José Aldama, Dagoberto Caballero, and Heriberto Salas Ochoa, alleged that they were earning $2.50 per hundred pounds of cotton picked, while local labor, presumably white hillbillies and African Americans who lived in the area or came in from Memphis, earned $3. Additionally, braceros claimed that they were consigned to the second or third pickings, while locals were given the prized first picking.[48] Left unchecked, farmers hoped to pay Mexicans less than blacks earned and therefore to save money by transitioning from a predominantly black to a predominantly Mexican labor force. Indeed, M. C. Baumann conceded in 1952 that, while he had been paying black workers $3 per hundred pounds, "he has employed no domestic labor since the arrival of the Mexican workers." Baumann paid those Mexican workers $2.50.[49]

Planters believed that Mexicans could chop and pick cotton not only cheaper but also faster. Several white observers recalled that many Mexicans picked at least a hundred pounds more per day than whites and blacks: 500–700 a day rather than 350–500.[50] Some African Americans also adopted this view of Mexicans' efficiency. "Man, they could chop a lot of cotton," was the word around town, remembered Calvin King, the son of black farmers.[51] White and black workers had been fighting dismal wages in Arkansas's fields for a generation; while hundreds of Mexicans, too, would protest low pay, a larger number calculated that dollars, which could become the foundation of their economic and therefore personal lives, were worth exerting themselves to the limits of their physical capacity.[52] Jesús Ortíz Torres explained that he pursued bracero contracts in Arkansas and other work sites because of "the obligation one has" as a married man; those unwilling to work as hard as he did "won't have anything, not a family or a wife, nothing."[53] Reflecting on men like Ortíz Torres, farmer John Gray concluded, "After the Mexicans came in, nobody could compare with the kind of help they were."[54] As Gray's statement so plainly showed, braceros did not step into a labor vacuum in rural Arkansas; rather, their arrival altered the economic possibilities for white and black wage laborers.

Interpreting Race

Black and particularly white Arkansans probably had some awareness of anti-Mexican stereotypes originating in the U.S. Southwest, and at least one Arkansas Delta community educated Mexican children at their own plantation school in 1940.[55] Across the river in Mississippi, most but not all Mexicans could attend white schools by this time, having fought for and won that right a decade earlier. Still, Mexicans' and Tejanos' numbers in Arkansas were small by the end of the Depression, and no single stereotype or racial definition of "Mexican" dominated thinking there. The Tejanos and then braceros who arrived in large numbers in the 1940s found that relationships with the white and black people they encountered were ambiguous, contingent not only on race but also on class. Some Arkansans found Mexicans to be harmless or exotic, others perceived them as an economic threat, and still others adopted outdated Texan stereotypes, separating poor, working-class "peons" from upper-class Mexicans.

By the late 1940s, most of the Arkansas Delta's African Americans envisioned a future away from its cotton fields and did not begrudge Mexicans' arrival. Many of their families might have left the fields in the 1910s–20s if not for planters' violence and intimidation. During the sharecropper evictions of the 1930s, African Americans who still believed agriculture was their best or only option organized for better wages and security through the interracial STFU. But by the end of that decade, the union was severely weakened, offering African Americans little hope to improve their lives within the Delta just as new opportunities opened up in the war industries of the North and West. Wartime spikes in cotton wages notwithstanding, African Americans streamed out of the area in the 1940s.[56] One African American former STFU organizer spoke out publicly against the bracero program in 1950, but by that time he represented a rapidly shrinking number of black Arkansans who sought futures in agriculture.[57]

Recalling her upbringing in an African American sharecropping family, Delores Atkins said that her parents "always wanted us to do something different because this was hard work, and we knew we were working for nothing." Accordingly, she remembered, "We were trying to get something to eat and get some clothes to wear, so we didn't worry about anybody else," least of all Mexicans coming to do a job they despised.[58] Indeed, when the NAACP's *The Crisis* reported on Mexicans abandoning a Delta plantation in 1952, its coverage pitied rather than envied workers "forced to accept whatever the farmer chooses to pay" and subject to arrest, "as often happens," when they defied planters' wishes.[59] Though Calvin King's family owned its own land, he recalled that "there was plenty of chopping to go around, plenty of picking to go around," and noted that Mexicans "were coming in as a lot of African Americans were trying to get out."[60] For them, the pain of cotton picking extended beyond the physical effects of bloodied hands and hungry stomachs, to include a longer history of slavery and violence that they hoped to escape—in the words of one historian, "un-freedom."[61]

In contrast, some poor white people still envisioned a future for themselves farming in the Delta, clinging to the myth of white male upward mobility within cotton production even as agricultural land became concentrated in the hands of fewer and fewer owners.[62] Braceros seemed to threaten these white men's aspirations. James O. Scarlett wrote to his congressman in 1952, "I am a very poor man with a family of seven including myself. . . . How can the thousands of sharecroppers, renters and laborers carry on and face Mexican peonage?"[63] By referring to peonage, unfree labor, in an area that used this practice primarily on immigrants and African Americans, Scarlett mourned the end of agriculture as a way of life for nonelite southern white men.[64] Braceros, he believed, had dealt his dreams their final blow.

For those who did not envision cotton picking as a long-term livelihood—that is, most African Americans and middle-class white people—the influx of Mexican workers sometimes resembled an international or intercultural exchange, rather than a race or economic threat. Bobby Wood, whose family owned a filling station and store, recalled that as a teen in the mid-1940s, "I learned a lot of Spanish words.... I enjoyed [serving Mexican patrons] very much."[65] Delores Atkins recalled that feelings of excitement and curiosity at the newcomers' arrival also affected black children. She remembered laughing with her friends as she listened to braceros' Spanish, "excited because I hadn't heard anybody speak that kind of language before."[66] For both Wood and Atkins, Tejanos and braceros added a touch of cosmopolitanism to an otherwise black-and-white small-town existence.

Texan stereotypes from a previous century, which separated Indian and mestizo "peons" from European-descended upper-class Mexicans, influenced the views some white farmers and authorities had of Mexicans during the first few years of their presence. A lawyer for the Mexican consulate expressed outrage at a white farmer's presumption that "we, the lawyers and consular representatives of the Government of Mexico, should understand the situation because like bosses, we belong to a 'superior' class which is predestined to exploit the masses, whose only goal in life should be completing the tasks of beasts of burden."[67] Still, at times even consular officials could be treated with racial suspicion. When a Mexican official arrived in Pine Bluff to conduct an investigation of bracero conditions there, local officials at first tried to direct him away from the town's one hotel and toward a campground, presumably because the all-white hotel did not want to accommodate him. Only once the Mexican consul insisted and the Arkansas officials conferred among themselves was the consul given a room at the hotel.[68]

Perhaps white residents' most consequential view of Mexicans in the first years of their presence, however, was farmers' sense of being "very much satisfied" with Mexican labor.[69] "They thought of them as, 'That was labor.' That wasn't a buddy," explained Bernard Lipsey, whose Jewish family's grocery store in Lepanto depended heavily on Mexican consumers during the 1950s.[70] Both smaller farmers who picked cotton alongside braceros and larger planters who viewed them as "input factors" fantasized that Mexicans represented the ideal labor source to replace more troublesome and expensive whites and blacks.[71] They were soon to find out otherwise.

Racialized Laborers or Citizens with Rights?

Having already invested their money and personal credibility in a bracero journey, many braceros were willing to tolerate Arkansas's poor living and working conditions in exchange for the dollars they could earn there.[72] But thousands of others were not. When Gabino Solís Aguilera first arrived in Arkansas in 1948, he found the area to be "peaceful. . . . I ended up there and I was happy with it."[73] But that same year, a bracero in Pine Bluff found the conditions so depressing that he attempted suicide.[74] Charting a course in between these two responses, thousands of braceros employed varied resistance strategies to improve their lives and earnings in Arkansas. Indeed, just two years after the first braceros were contracted to Arkansas, a growers' spokesman observed, "In 1948 . . . we thought our labor problem was solved, but we soon found that instead of having a seasonal labor supply we had a year-round headache."[75] This comment referred specifically to the interventions of the Mexican and U.S. federal governments, but braceros themselves were the original source of planters' woes. Unlike Solís Aguilera, a steadfast minority of braceros actively pushed for greater economic and social rights. Their challenges to farmers and authorities were entwined with both the financial and cultural expectations they had brought into the program. Braceros needed to maximize their earnings to meet familial obligations, but they also petitioned for modern living and equal social conditions to reaffirm their sense of themselves as modern men and rights-bearing citizens of Mexico.[76] These braceros appealed directly to farmers for improved wages and conditions, organized their own strikes, fled farms altogether, and went to great lengths to appeal to the Mexican consulate for help.

Braceros dissatisfied with their wages and working conditions sometimes began by lodging their demands directly with farmers. Tejano crew leader Joe García recalled braceros demanding a raise from their contracted rate of $2.50 per hundred pounds of cotton. García brought the concern to farmer E. D. McKnight, who approved a twenty-five-cent raise.[77] Others communicated directly to employers. A group of braceros who had worked for Royce Stubblefield in Monette wrote a letter to Stubblefield once they were back in Mexico, stating that the truck driver who transported them to the border was supposed to disburse money for transit from the border to their home towns in Mexico but did not do so.[78] Pablo Soto Amaya and Cristóbal Vázquez Martínez asked farmer C. E. Hardin to bring medical attention to some sick compatriots; when Hardin did not comply at first, the braceros continued to ask "an infinite number of times."[79] These braceros perceived farmers' dependence on their labor and believed they had enough bargaining power to demand their compliance with the bracero contract.

Even repeated an "infinite" number of times, however, simple requests from small groups of braceros usually were insufficient to win change. In escalating their efforts, braceros drew on a nationalist Mexican consciousness that promised, and in some ways delivered, modernity and improvement. Most young male braceros in the late 1940s and early 1950s were products entirely of Mexico's liberal postrevolutionary regime but not the years of actual violent revolution. Solís Aguilera, of typical bracero age, was born in 1928 after the regime's consolidation of rule.[80] He was reared during the populist land redistributions and oil nationalization of the 1930s and educated, if only for a few years, in schools that had become deliberate parts of the nationalist project.[81] He came of age in the 1940s, a decade marked by uneven economic expansion and the growth of the state apparatus, and signed on to the bracero program, which promised to be an engine of both.[82] Whereas Mississippi's Rafael Landrove had developed his expectations during the Porfiriato and revolution, Solís Aguilera and his fellow braceros were products of a populist, nationalist, and statist era in Mexican history.

Braceros' collective actions drew on these nationalistic expectations in ways both subtle and overt. On an Arkansas farm during the picking season of 1948, braceros were disgusted by poor housing "once inhabited by blacks" and pay of $2 per hundred pounds of cotton when the contract guaranteed $3. They elected two of their own, José Luís Landa and Manuel Gallegos, to lead them in a work stoppage. This internal, informal selection of one or two spokespeople—probably those who spoke some English—was typical of bracero politics in Arkansas.[83] On September 16, Mexican Independence Day, Landa, Gallegos, and their group of sixty-five workers went on strike. They returned to the fields for a brief time after a Tejano interpreter insisted that $2 was the most the boss would pay. But soon, they "[knew] that there had been strikes in other fields," declared Landa and Gallegos, "and there was a visit from the Consul of Mexico in New Orleans, and it was then that they started to pay us $3."[84] The braceros' choice of Mexican Independence Day for their strike reflected their use of Mexican nationalism as an internal rallying cry for resistance to abuse even when official Mexican government representatives were nowhere in sight. While their counterparts in New Orleans and Mississippi twenty years earlier tended to rely on Mexican nationalism mostly as a strategy to create middle-class identities and make claims on consulates, by the late 1940s at least some Arkansas braceros had come to think of themselves as full citizens of this modernizing nation, linked through this identity to diverse compatriots.[85]

Braceros struck to maximize the wages they could earn but also to demand dignified treatment, more control over their labor, and acceptable food and cooking arrangements. On one Phillips County farm, 300 workers wanted to replace their Tejano crew leader with a leader from their own ranks. To make their point, they "mutinied and were engaged in throwing their bunks and bed clothes through the windows and doors of the barracks in which they were lodged."[86] Braceros employed by the Miller Lumber Company in Marianna were upset that they were forced to buy food at the company restaurant, wanting instead to be provided with cooking utensils to make their own food at lower cost. They went on strike and refused to eat in the restaurant. Afraid of losing the workforce altogether, the company caved and provided cooking utensils and facilities.[87] In at least some cases, Arkansas planters succeeded in requesting the deportation of braceros, like Esteban Saldaña, who had led their compatriots in strikes.[88]

Other braceros—by some estimates, at least one in seven—resisted their conditions in Arkansas by leaving the farms altogether.[89] Though farmers sought Mexicans to replace a black labor force that had moved north, they found themselves confronting the same problem with braceros. One planter complained that some braceros never had any intention of working in agriculture and would quickly disappear, while others vanished as soon as they learned how much they could earn in cities.[90] Still smarting over the exodus of their black workers, planters reacted strongly to indications that braceros planned to leave their farms. In 1953, Mississippi Delta farmer E. J. Ganier asked the local sheriff to arrest bracero José Dionisio Sosa because Sosa had threatened "to influence other workers so that they would leave the place."[91] Unlike braceros in California and Texas, who tended to desert the program for the Southwest's urban centers, Arkansas's braceros left the farms for a destination to which planters had already lost countless racialized laborers: Chicago. And as in the case of blacks, local authorities openly served planters' needs by arresting workers who tried to leave their jobs.

The escape plans of Juán Braya Carlos, Angel Ramírez López, and Eduardo Gracios Mora particularly provoked the wrath of white authorities in 1953. The men arrived to pick cotton on the farm of A. H. Barnhill in Bay, Arkansas, and immediately rejected the dilapidated housing they were provided. Barnhill asked the local sheriff to arrest the departing workers and return them to him. When the patrolman found the workers, he asked them if they wanted to go back to Mexico, to which they responded, "No." Asked if they wanted to go to Chicago, the workers shrugged their shoulders and said, "Maybe."[92] Yet an inspection of the braceros' living quarters suggested that their intentions had been firmer; a map of Illinois lay in the run-down house, "with the City of Chicago face up." The workers claimed the map was not theirs but was already in the house when they arrived, allegedly left behind by earlier groups of braceros or the African Americans who had previously fled the objectionable conditions on Barnhill's farm.[93]

As this story also illustrates, local law enforcement joined with federal immigration officials to restrict braceros' mobility, keeping them on their Arkansas farms by force if possible.[94] After all, these local police officers had long used their authority to keep black workers on the job.[95] When Feliciano Parano Chávez demanded payment for forty-six pounds of cotton he had picked, employer M. C. Jenkins first threatened him with a knife and then got him thrown in jail.[96] Similarly, more than 200 braceros left their plantations for Forrest City when a surplus of labor meant they were receiving neither work nor pay. Local Border Patrol agents arrested them, and the group was held in jail while officials determined who would pay for their return to Mexico.[97] As with a previous labor force trying to head "north," law enforcement authorities readily used their power to help planters control their workers.

Building the Mexican Nation—in Arkansas

Yet unlike Arkansas's African Americans and Tejanos, who were U.S. citizens in name only, Mexican braceros had meaningful citizenship rights in Mexico that allowed them to turn to a government filled with officials of their own.[98] Beginning immediately with their arrival in 1948, braceros began lodging complaints with the nearest Mexican consulates, at the time in New Orleans and San Antonio, through extreme means if necessary. Before long, the Secretariat of Foreign Relations opened a consulate in Memphis specifically to oversee the Delta's bracero contracting. Though growers usually insisted that workers were happy and only the consuls themselves wanted to create trouble, in fact workers reached out to involve their consulates in their struggles. "No sooner" had Mexican workers arrived in Arkansas, noted Mexican officials, than "they began to present themselves to our consulate in New Orleans as well as this consul general" in San Antonio, decrying mostly wages and living conditions in violation of the bracero contract.[99] The complaints arrived via both phone and letter and represented not just individual workers but also groups.[100]

While braceros resisted their conditions in Arkansas by making demands of crew leaders and farmers, staging ad hoc strikes, and fleeing to Chicago, they believed that whatever its limitations and shortcomings, the Mexican government represented their greatest source of political power. Indeed, black and white workers had utilized all of the former strategies, even organizing the STFU, but faced brutal repression. The liberal ideas of the United States and those of Mexico had long influenced and echoed one another, and Mexican workers in pursuit of greater rights could have appealed to either liberal tradition.[101] Potential U.S. allies, however, did not provide the type of advocacy they sought. Though the STFU enjoyed a brief resurgence in the 1940s, the organization and its affiliates in the national Congress of Industrial Organizations wanted to end the bracero program, not represent braceros.[102] Outside the U.S. liberal tradition, churches eagerly sought out braceros, with Baptists at one point employing seventeen Spanish-speaking preachers in Arkansas and Catholics doing their best to compete.[103] But there is no evidence that Catholic or Protestant clerics advocated on braceros' behalf.[104]

Independent, nonstate organizations in the Mexican liberal tradition also could have helped the braceros, if those efforts had gained any traction in the first place. Activist Ernesto Galarza's independent National Farm Labor Union and its Mexican sister organization, La Alianza de Braceros, focused their efforts in California and Mexico, enjoyed little success, and by the mid-1950s also aimed primarily to end the bracero program entirely.[105] Through repression of the Alianza, Mexican bureaucrats succeeded in preserving their paternalistic role as braceros' best hope for change in the Arkansas Delta.[106]

In the post–World War II period, during Mexico's so-called golden age of nationalist protective economic policies and cultural production, Mexican workers in Arkansas resisted poor economic and social conditions by appealing to local Mexican consulates, which in turn took up both the racial and economic arguments with southern white planters and their political allies. Consul Angel Cano del Castillo first responded to Arkansas braceros' petitions from his post in the Dallas consulate but in 1950 moved to Memphis to open his government's office there.[107] Though a thirty-year veteran of Mexico's Foreign Service, Cano often eschewed diplomacy in his strident defense of braceros even as his government slowly ceded control of the program as a whole.[108]

Cano rapidly developed a reputation among planters and braceros for his willingness to take up even the smallest of workers' petitions, and some braceros went to extreme lengths to call their plight to his attention. While some braceros could simply write the consulate and receive responses in care of the farms where they were employed, others had to circumvent planters' attempts to monitor their phone conversations.[109] In another case, a hundred Mexican men set out for a hundred-mile walk to see the consulate in Memphis when they refused the bad food and low salaries on Terry Jamison's plantation; forty-nine made it while the other fifty-one got stuck along the way.[110] These men trudged for hours through the chilly Arkansas fall because they believed they could find meaningful help in their country's Memphis outpost.[111] Far more than their counterparts decades earlier in the Mississippi Delta, these men believed that as full citizens in a modern nation, Mexico, they were due better wages and working and living conditions in the United States; they hoped and expected that Mexican consular representatives would use their political power to enforce superior conditions.

Cross-Border Liberalism and the Fate of the New Deal

In this moment of expanding national states, braceros' choice to work through the Mexican federal government touched a nerve in rural Arkansas. For nearly two decades, New Dealers in Washington, D.C., had engaged in a political balancing act: fomenting a class-based coalition on the basis of federally guaranteed economic security, while doing so in the context of white supremacy and the need to keep white southern Democrats, known as Dixiecrats, in the fold. Economic security, then, could not extend also to African American agricultural and domestic workers. Democrats thus excluded those industries from the labor rights legislation that gave industrial workers a minimum wage and work condition guarantees.[112] Meanwhile, the federal government allowed other aspects of the New Deal, notably the AAA crop reduction payments, to benefit white southern elites at the expense of their workers. Evicted Delta sharecroppers formed the STFU in 1934, organizing across race lines to demand "decent contracts and higher wages," organizing rights and improved housing conditions, and overall security—in other words, many of the rights that had been granted to industrial workers over the previous two decades.[113]

To planters' chagrin, the postwar period's liberal ideals had gained currency in Mexico, too, inspiring braceros to lodge demands notably similar to those of displaced local cotton workers. Between 1948 and 1953, braceros filed at least 400 complaints with their consulate. Each complaint represented an average of two to three men, with some representing dozens of braceros. About a third focused on unpaid wages, with transportation, lodging, discrimination (usually wage discrimination), and medical care each representing a significant share as well.[114] Mexican workers were petitioning, in effect, for economic security. Miguel Santiago complained that he had been forced to pay for his own medicine, when it should have been the farmer's responsibility.[115] Braceros demanded that Byron Landres pay them for additional days of work they lost when the labor contractor's truck broke down on its way to Arkansas. Others demanded pay, as stipulated in the contract, when poor weather made it impossible to pick cotton.[116] In all, braceros advocated for shifting the burden of risk from workers to employers.

These demands emerged from a liberal worldview deeply opposed to that of planters—a view in which states and employers, not workers, absorbed the economic risks of markets, weather, and other unforeseen factors. When Esteban Saldaña convinced his fellow braceros to go on strike because a poor cotton crop made it impossible to earn decent wages, he framed the struggle as a "fight for our rights."[117] A U.S. Labor Department official acknowledged this liberal worldview in a private conversation with Arkansas's representative E. C. Gathings in 1953. Decrying Memphis consul Angel Cano's "megalomaniac" actions on behalf of Mexican workers, the official noted that neither drought nor economic conditions would sway the consul into accepting less for Mexican workers. "Cano takes the position that these things have no bearing," complained the official. "He says we gamble on the weather."[118] A Mississippi Delta official, testifying before Congress in 1950, expressed farmers' fundamental concern: that organized labor would say, "All right, you have entered into an agreement with the Mexican Government to furnish certain facilities, bedding, housing, insurance, a guaranty of minimum work hours.... We feel that we want that for our domestic workers as well."[119] The question of who would "gamble" on unforeseen circumstances and make a "guaranty" struck at the heart of the New Deal reforms and welfare capitalism that urban industrial workers had already begun to enjoy.

Though southern planters had thus far resisted U.S. government attempts to bring a minimum wage to agriculture, they proved unable to defeat the Mexican government's advocacy: in 1952–53, Mexicans became the first agricultural workers in Arkansas to earn a minimum wage. Bracero agreements stated that braceros should be paid the local prevailing wage or an amount "necessary to cover their living needs," whichever was higher. But during the early 1950s, consulates also set a floor for the bracero wage scale: $0.50 per hour or $2.50 per hundred pounds of cotton.[120] During the 1953–54 picking season, farm jobs in other bracero-receiving areas had prevailing wages as low as $0.45–$0.60 per hour in Texas and as high as $1–$1.25 per hour in Oregon. In Arkansas, however, prevailing hourly wages were $0.30–$0.40.[121] Only in Arkansas was the prevailing hourly wage substantially below the bracero program's $0.50 floor. Thus, only in Arkansas did the Mexican government effectively set a minimum wage for its workers.

The minimum wage for Mexicans threatened the economic advantage over all laborers that Arkansas planters had fought so hard to maintain. Farmer Earl Beck Jr. worried that "if we would all start paying 50 cents an hour to the Mexicans our common day labor would expect the same, no matter if they are worth it or not."[122] The head of the Parkin Farmers' Association declared, "I do not believe that our farmers or our government should be put in the position so that Mexico can dictate the wage for our farm workers."[123] Planters had recruited braceros specifically to keep labor costs down, yet they now faced the prospect that Mexican government intervention would erode the regulation-free work environment they had so desperately fought to maintain.

A bizarre dispute between Consul Cano and U.S. Employment Service (USES) representative Ed McDonald in 1953 well illustrated planters' fears that the bracero program would cause all cotton workers to demand higher wages. To resolve an earlier conflict with the consulate in advance of the 1953 picking season, A. H. Barnhill, a farmer from Bay, Arkansas, signed an affidavit promising to pay Mexican workers $3 per hundred pounds of cotton and to provide them with improved insurance. Cano was satisfied and acted to remove Barnhill from the contracting blacklist for the upcoming season. McDonald protested, however, arguing that Barnhill was offering too much on both counts and that his largesse would force all the area's planters to pay more for labor that season. Ironically, he wanted Barnhill to remain on the ineligible list because he was offering too much to braceros. Cano insisted that he could not keep employers on the blacklist for treating braceros too well. If an employer offered to house workers in a hotel, Cano mused, would McDonald deny him workers because this was more than other farmers offered? "I cannot justify being placed in the position of asserting the rights and privileges of your country-men under the Migrant Labor Agreement," Cano concluded.[124] With prevailing wages in Arkansas lower than minimum bracero wages, however, Cano's actions ultimately gave white and black workers fodder for demanding improved wages and working conditions for themselves.

In their attempts to intervene on behalf of Mexican workers, consular officials sought to bolster their image as champions of their countrymen in the United States. To retain legitimacy as Mexicans' representatives and stave off independent strikes, consular officials would have to deliver on at least some of their promises, and evidence suggests that they did. No matter, it seemed, was too small to merit "protection" and attention from Consul Cano and his office's bureaucrats. The office regularly collected unpaid wages in amounts as low as $1—the equivalent of two to three hours of work—per bracero and distributed them via check to braceros' homes in rural Mexico.[125] Consul Cano demanded a $2.50 refund from farmer R. S. Bretherick for braceros who were inappropriately charged for their kitchen utensils.[126] He followed up on bounced checks.[127] He contacted insurance companies directly to ensure they made good on their bracero policies.[128] By the early 1950s, Arkansas planters had experienced confrontations with sharecroppers, the departure of unsatisfied workers, and even organized labor strikes.[129] But this was the first time they had to answer to any government for the routine abuse and theft to which they had subjected their workers for decades.

Though interventions on small matters provided a constant nuisance to farmers, the consulate's most significant tool for battle was the threat of blacklisting, which could threaten farmers' labor source, often after the crop had been planted. At various points, entire states, including Texas and Idaho, were prohibited from employing braceros due to widespread discrimination.[130] But historians have noted that the Mexican government's bargaining power in the bracero program slipped away after 1948, in part because the U.S. government undermined it by allowing undocumented workers to enter the country.[131] In 1949, the Mexican government lost the right to blacklist entire areas and could blacklist only individual employers. By 1954, the Mexican government had relinquished the right to unilaterally blacklist altogether.[132] Yet while Texas farmers had easier recourse to Tejano or undocumented labor, the threat of blacklisting carried more weight in Arkansas and other states far from the border and established Mexican American communities even as the Mexican government's control over the process slipped away.[133] Indeed, the Arkansas case presents a different narrative, in which specific conditions and an activist consul decisively enabled the Mexican government to exert control over the local racial and, to a lesser extent, economic order.

Outraged by the conditions braceros endured in Arkansas, consulate officials first attempted to blacklist the town of Pine Bluff, in the Delta's southwestern reaches. Mexican officials wanted to exercise their paternal authority, cancel the area's contracts, and send all braceros out of the area regardless of whether they wanted to leave. The only exception would be the one farm that had agreed to correct all of its contract violations. U.S. federal officials, in contrast, wanted only to make "voluntary departure" available to Mexican workers, letting those who wished to stay remain on the farms.[134] The U.S. officials prevailed, and the consulate prepared a form that each bracero would sign to indicate his preference: to return to Mexico or to stay in Arkansas until the contract's end.[135] The distinction proved decisive in undermining the Mexican government's ability to follow through on its promise to represent its workers. Out of nearly 2,000 braceros in the area, only 285 chose to leave. Consular officials attributed this to "improved conditions," but given the time lapse of mere weeks, more likely the majority of the workers preferred to tolerate poor living and working conditions rather than return to Mexico empty-handed.[136] Mexican men's determination—often depicted as desperation—to bring dollars home undermined the Mexican government's nationalist bargaining stance in 1948.[137]

In subsequent years, however, the Mexican consulate in Memphis did succeed in blacklisting employers and went to extreme means to do so even when U.S. officials did not cooperate. Cano refused to renew contracts for employers who had matters such as unpaid wages pending with the consulate.[138] Longview Farms' bracero request in 1950 was rejected because of contract noncompliance the year before.[139] John B. Luckie owed back wages to braceros from 1951, and he remained unable to contract for at least the following five years since he had refused to pay up.[140] A. H. Barnhill, the farmer who had his workers arrested when they attempted to leave for Chicago, remained on the ineligible list four years later as a result of the incident, despite appeals to be removed.[141] Though not successful every time, the consulate's threat of blacklisting in Arkansas posed a real threat to planters' access to Mexican workers.

Those planters had fought off U.S. federal intervention into the labor conditions on their farms for decades, only to face this intervention from a different federal government during the bracero program. When J. S. Cecil found himself on the ineligible list, he threw up his hands and declared that he did not want any more Mexican workers anyway.[142] But consular interventions and contractual obligations notwithstanding, most farmers desperately wanted to continue employing Mexicans, and they fought hard to do so. They made their case to Representative Gathings, Senators John McClellan and J. William Fulbright, the Mexican embassy in Washington, the consul himself, or USES representatives. Leo Powell tried to circumvent his blacklist status by contracting braceros under his father's name.[143] Convinced that the only real problem with the bracero arrangement was Consul Cano's "personality problem," planters conspired with Gathings and Fulbright to have Cano removed from his post. They portrayed Cano as an outside agitator, suggesting that braceros themselves had no problem with their living and working conditions in Arkansas. A. H. Barnhill, for example, complained, "It was not until after they talked to the consul that they complained of the blankets being wet."[144] His comment, of course, ignored the fact that bracero complaints brought Cano to his farm in the first place.

The Mexican government's "protection" of Mexican workers more effectively promoted the New Deal's ideals in rural Arkansas than did New Dealers themselves. Federal Labor Department bureaucrats tried to use regulation of the bracero program to insert federal oversight into the backwaters of rural Arkansas, the fiefdom of white conservative Dixiecrats, but their representatives on the ground in Arkansas were sympathetic to farmers, not workers.[145] For example, Labor Department officials based in Pine Bluff told Mexican officials that their only job was to ensure that planters had enough labor, not to regulate wages or conditions.[146] Ultimately, liberal federal bureaucrats in Washington, D.C., were still more than a decade away from forcing any type of labor regulation on the white southern planters who, in the 1950s, remained key constituents in the Democratic Party.

Mexican citizens and the Mexican state, in contrast, ultimately did succeed in exerting some of the authority given to them in the bracero contract. Under pressure from two federal governments, planters felt that their long-held monopoly on rights in the employer–employee relationship was under assault. This was not what they had in mind when they first began to contract braceros.

Against "Discriminatory Acts against Mexicans"

While the vast majority of issues raised by braceros and consuls related to wages and working, living, and transport conditions—concerns that echoed the STFU and the New Deal's economic agenda—others took on matters of race. Contrary to farmers' frequent assertions, braceros themselves, not consular interlopers, initiated battles over discrimination. Both braceros and their consular officials were acutely aware of blacks' inferior position in the Delta, and they were committed to ensuring that Mexicans, as citizens of somewhere, not suffer the same fate. Just as Mexicans sought to influence their treatment on the farms, so too did they work to control it in the Jim Crow landscape of the Delta's towns.

Mexican bureaucrats in this period advanced a version of Mexicanidad that had evolved somewhat from earlier expressions in New Orleans and Mississippi. Mexico's New Orleans consulate in the 1920s and 1930s did not control the supply of Mexican labor into the region and thus relied on whitened cultural representations and calls for international cooperation to influence the treatment of Mexicans. Now consular officials utilized power—the imperfect yet real power to control current and future bracero contracting—to defend a cultural nationalism claiming that since the region's blacks were poor citizens of nowhere, seemingly without rights, Mexicans should not stand to be treated like blacks. "This region still exists in a semi-feudal state," wrote one official in 1948. "All you see is, on the one hand, bosses living like princes in the Middle Ages, and on the other, 'servants,' in general black Americans, existing in a state of extreme poverty." Another official wrote that the area's blacks "dedicate themselves to the agricultural work of the region and to the servitude of the so-called 'whites.'" The official thus expressed skepticism of the white racial category's validity in the first place.[147] Mexicans were not white in the consuls' discourses, but they also did not have to be. They were modern, first-class citizens.

Like their counterparts in 1920s Mississippi, Arkansas's Mexicans and Mexican Americans remained alert to signs they would be treated like African Americans and lodged complaints with consuls when they were. The most severe and overt acts of discrimination were reported in the majority-white counties on the northern end of the Arkansas Delta, particularly Poinsett and Mississippi counties, rather than the majority-black counties to the south.[148] In the middle of the 1949 cotton-picking season, Tejano Nick C. Amador and two Mexican nationals approached the Mexican consulate in Memphis. The workers were picking cotton near Marked Tree, in Poinsett County, and reported that anti-Mexican discrimination there was rife. As described at the start of this chapter, Consul Rubén Gaxiola initiated a joint investigation together with the U.S. Labor Department and recommended the cancellation of the area's contracts.[149] A week later, Gaxiola traveled to the town to gather information. He took photos of eleven establishments that bore "No Mexicans" signs (figs. 8 and 9). Mexicans tended to be served in establishments open to blacks (see fig. 1). Though Gaxiola did not interview proprietors in Marked Tree, the words of a restaurant owner in nearby Osceola suggest a likely reason for Mexicans' exclusion: "We have a very high class trade that would leave if my place was filled up with Mexicans. I would close up before I would serve them."[150] The Arkansas Delta's white people, in other words, simply considered Mexicans to be below their station racially and economically. Himself conscious of class, Consul Gaxiola noted details of the establishment's construction and appearance with each photo of an offending sign, explaining whether it was a "nice" establishment or more shabby. He also noted that in the town's movie theater, run by the son of its largest employer, E. Ritter, Mexicans were consigned to the seats reserved for

FIGURE 9 "Come In Café (restaurant and bar)—A well constructed and average establishment." Attachments to letter from Consul Rubén Gaxiola, Memphis, to Ministry of Foreign Relations, Mexico City, November 19, 1949, TM-26-32, Archivo Histórico de la Secretaría de Relaciones Exteriores, Mexico City.

blacks. Gaxiola did not express outrage at the conditions African Americans endured in Arkansas. Rather, he remained silent about Jim Crow as a whole, decrying only "discriminatory acts against Mexicans."[151]

Though they had openly and mightily resisted bracero minimum wages, work guarantees, and the monitoring of their housing and transportation conditions, local officials and farmers immediately agreed to bring social discrimination against Mexicans to an end. Little Rock–based members of the Farm Placement Service explained to Ritter that failure to do so could lead to the cancellation of Marked Tree's contracts by mutual agreement of the U.S. and Mexican governments.[152] After a decade of rural out-migration and battles with the STFU, the area's planters were determined to hold onto their new labor force. So Marked Tree's mayor personally approached the offending businesses, as did Ritter, and by Christmas of 1949, all of the signs were down.[153] Regardless of Mexicans' racialization and exclusion in the southwestern United States, local officials in Arkansas responded to transnational political pressure by immediately admitting Mexicans to white establishments. In exchange, the town remained off the blacklist.

Yet a few months later, Mexican workers in Marked Tree again wrote their consul to report discrimination. The very same "No Mexicans" sign was back up on Wike's Drive Inn (see fig. 8). Many other businesses had taken down signs to appease the consulate, but they still refused to serve Mexicans or Tejanos.[154] Despite farmers' desire to have continued access to Mexican labor, many white Arkansans were not prepared to begin admitting Mexicans and Mexican Americans to their establishments. Over the next year, the consul repeatedly pushed to have the Marked Tree area contracts canceled. Local officials signed affidavits promising to afford Mexicans the same rights "as the local citizens."[155] Business owners wrote declarations affirming their intention to treat Mexicans equally.[156] Local officials showed movies "favorable to Mexico" in town.[157] Still, the discrimination continued.

To assess the validity of the allegations, consular and USES officials met up in Marked Tree to conduct an "experiment," sending a bracero "dressed in clean work clothes" to order a cup of coffee in several establishments. Bryant's Cafe refused him service. At Knott Hole Cafe, the bartender as well as several customers pointed the bracero to the back of the establishment, where a separate bar was available for Mexicans.[158] The following month, the consul learned that Marked Tree police waited outside of bars in an area now dubbed "Little Mexico" to arrest Mexicans whether or not they were drunk.[159] As Mexican and U.S. officials plainly saw, anti-Mexican practices in Marked Tree were reflective of both official policy and popular sentiment. In neighboring Trumann, too, the chief of police admitted that discrimination against Mexicans persisted. There, four Tejanos told USES and Mexican consular officials of widespread discrimination in local restaurants.[160]

During battles over discrimination in Arkansas, Consul Cano occasionally made explicit arguments that Mexicans should be classified as white in all instances, a stance at odds with Mexico's national celebration of mestizaje. For example, he cried "insult" when Marked Tree's police chief used the phrase "whites and Mexicans" four times in conversation.[161] Cano recognized that this semantic distinction between whites and Mexicans connoted an intended racial distinction between the groups and insisted that they be discussed as one racial group, not two. The plea departed from the vast majority of consular action and discourse, which focused on Mexicans' claim to equal treatment as a result of their citizenship in a modern nation, thus supporting rather than contradicting Mexican nationalist ideologies of the time.

In Marked Tree, the consulate received USES agreement late in the picking season of 1951 to blacklist Ritter, though they did not succeed in withdrawing labor from the area's other farmers and associations, nor were they able to cancel Ritter's contract at midseason.[162] Yet even this partial victory placed enormous pressure on Ritter and other town leaders. Making a last-ditch attempt to secure workers for the 1952 picking season, local officials employed new and inventive means to stymie discrimination. The Marked Tree City Council published an ordinance in the *Marked Tree Tribune*, stating that any person or business discriminating against Mexicans would be fined between $10 and $50, "and each act of discrimination shall constitute a separate offense."[163] The police department removed incentives that previously encouraged officers to make superfluous arrests of Mexican workers.[164] The farmers' association even purchased outright two restaurants that refused to comply with the mandate against discrimination.[165] The full weight of local officialdom came down on the side of ending anti-Mexican discrimination in white establishments.

While the steps were extensive, the measures' very severity offended the consulate. If Marked Tree's white residents had to be pushed that hard not to discriminate against Mexicans, he reasoned, surely their racism was too deeply ingrained and "the anti-Mexican sentiment still prevails."[166] Marked Tree remained unable to contract workers in 1952, and farmers contracting braceros to neighboring towns had to affirm that they would not put them to work in the Marked Tree area.[167] Finally bending to pressure and the stack of antidiscrimination affidavits signed by Marked Tree officials, Mexican government officials agreed late in the 1952 picking season to once again permit contracting to Marked Tree.[168] A year later, officials from nearby Trumann submitted their own sheaf of affidavits vowing not to discriminate against Mexicans, in the hopes of being removed from the blacklist as well.[169]

Though the consulate was not able to enforce every threat of blacklisting and contract cancellation, by 1953 it had flexed enough power to have most white establishments in the Arkansas Delta admit Mexicans. Consulate documentary records show that discrimination complaints after 1953 were few, far between, and far less severe than they had been previously. More important, oral history interviews suggest that while the long-term results of these political battles over anti-Mexican discrimination were uneven, overall Mexicans in Arkansas did gain admission to white establishments in Arkansas by the mid-1950s. Claude Kennedy, an African American man whose father owned a small farm near Marianna, recalled how Mexicans' superior access to public space only stoked his indignation at the Jim Crow system.[170] "They could go to the movies with whites, where black people still had to go upstairs," Kennedy said. "That was something that black people could not understand." He remembered his mother, a schoolteacher, explaining to him why Mexicans were not subject to the painful discrimination of Jim Crow. "Their government would not allow them to be treated that way," he recalled. "That was the agreement. It was common knowledge that you can use them, but you've got to give them the respect of being equal to the white man. They could go anywhere they wanted to go."[171] Bernard Lipsey, the son of Jewish store owners, remembered a Mexican American boy attending the white school with him around 1957, before Lepanto's schools had desegregated. Though Mexicanos had attended a separate school in at least one Arkansas town in 1940, the boy's assignment to the white school in the late 1950s had seemed natural to Lipsey at the time, suggesting that within the binary world of the Arkansas Delta, locals had come to accept that Mexicanos would nominally fall into the white category.[172]

Accepting Mexicans as white for Jim Crow purposes, however, did not mean local white people accepted them socially; conversely, Mexicans' access to white public space did not connote a feeling of affinity with white Arkansans. Both white and African American observers also remembered that, like poor white cotton workers, Mexicans certainly were not made to feel welcome in every town establishment; unlike most poor white people, Mexicans often favored black sides of town in their leisure time. The son of a white farmer, John Collier, remembered that when he rounded up braceros in Parkin to return to the farm on Saturday nights, those who did not report for the ride were most likely to be found in black "honky-tonks," beer joints, or seeking the services of black prostitutes.[173] Some white employers encouraged these relationships. Bracero José Gutiérrez, who worked near West Memphis, recalled that his white supervisor brought black prostitutes directly to braceros on the plantations and took Mexicans to gamble in black casinos in West Memphis. "I don't know anything," Gutiérrez would insist to the boss's wife when she asked what they had done there.[174]

In subsequent recollections, both braceros and African Americans reminisced about genial relations between the two groups. "We got along well with [blacks], they were very friendly," said Gutiérrez.[175] Harrison Locke, an African American man raised near Brinkley, recalled local authorities forbidding Mexicans from black establishments, even though they felt "more comfortable" in them.[176] And though Claude Kennedy resented Mexicans' ability to sit in the white section of the local movie theater, he also remembered that Mexicans' racial position in that theater did not fully encompass their lives in Arkansas. Once, Kennedy was getting a haircut at a black barbershop when a Mexican man who spoke no English came in. From the man's attempts to communicate, Kennedy understood that he had been a barber in Mexico who missed practicing his trade. Kennedy and the barber let the man cut Kennedy's hair, even though the result left his locks a bit longer than they would have liked.[177] The bracero likely felt grateful to this black man for helping him reconnect with his identity as a man with a trade rather than a farm laborer like any other. As the stories show, Mexicans in 1950s Arkansas fought for access to white establishments because they rejected discrimination, not because they disdained African Americans or considered themselves white in the Jim Crow sense of the word.[178]

The Limits of Ending "Discrimination"

In economic matters as opposed to racial ones, braceros achieved fewer and more inconsistent gains. Though most continued to be housed in former sharecroppers' cabins, in some areas they successfully pressured farmers to find more "modern" accommodations, such as an old Air Force hangar in Blytheville.[179] Many planters and planters' associations did begrudgingly comply with bracero contract stipulations that they be paid the prevailing wage or $2.50 per hundred pounds of cotton, whichever was higher, though others did not. And just as white elites had feared, this sometimes meant raising wages for local workers. "We have approximately 150 domestic workers living on the place," said officials from a plantation in Helena in 1953, and "we started the season paying them $2.00 but on arrival of the Mexican workers we raised the domestics to $2.50."[180] In these cases, the Mexican federal government effected changes that the U.S. federal government still had not: regulating the wages and conditions of southern agricultural workers. Yet in many more cases over the course of the 1950s, planters responded minimally or not at all to bracero and consulate demands for compliance with the economic components of the contract.

As planters relied increasingly on braceros to pick their cotton over the course of the 1950s, local wage laborers suffered more than sharecroppers and tenants.[181] Delta planters benefited from having at least some stable year-round workers, and there is no evidence that the bracero program caused them to massively evict the white and black sharecroppers and tenants who remained on their land.[182] Some tenant farmers, among them African Americans, even hired braceros on a casual basis from the plantation owners who had contracted them.[183] But local white and black wage laborers correctly perceived that planters had hired braceros to replace them. In 1958, E. Z. Hensen, presumably a white man, complained to Arkansas's governor that, as a result of the influx of Mexican labor, he and his neighbors were now unable to find employment as cotton pickers.[184] Employers' statements corroborate his story. "The minute the Mexicans arrived I fired my domestic labor," said one employer. The employer speculated that those workers had moved to Tennessee, Mississippi, or Oklahoma in search of work.[185] Another planter admitted in 1956 that he had the opportunity to hire domestic workers but refused them in favor of braceros.[186] Indeed, while 13,000 predominantly African American day laborers from Memphis picked cotton in Arkansas in 1949, half as many did so in 1959.[187] The arrival of braceros combined with the slow advance of the mechanical cotton picker to put black and white wage laborers out of work.[188]

Like their white counterparts, and unlike rural black sharecroppers, black cotton day laborers in Memphis were angry at their displacement by braceros. Though unwilling to live on the farms where their families had suffered generations of exploitation, they counted on the ability to ride buses to the fields to earn extra money when they needed it.[189] Furthermore, as more braceros became available, planters refused to raise day-haul wages to parity with bracero contracted wages. In 1954, African American truck drivers in Memphis complained to Memphis black community leader George W. Lee that Mexicans were earning more than blacks for cotton labor in the Arkansas Delta. A Republican, Lee lodged a formal protest with Memphis's Republican congressman, Carroll Reece, claiming that African American laborers were paid thirty cents per hour for cotton chopping while Mexicans were paid fifty cents.[190] Black day-haul laborers felt outraged, and Lee addressed their concerns as he tried to build political power in a city dominated by a white Democratic machine.[191]

On July 14, 1954, Lee staged a huge picnic in Memphis's Lincoln Park for the workers to present an "Appreciation Petition" to himself and Reece for their attempts to bring blacks' wages to parity with those of Mexicans (fig. 10). Drawing on these workers' immediate personal and family histories of rural labor, the petition decried foreigners' superior treatment over those whose "fore-parents have toiled in the hot and chilly rains from season to season to plant, cultivate and harvest cotton." More than 1,000 black workers ate barbecue and watermelon, singing songs and playing games with their children before piling into crew leaders' buses to go register to vote.[192] In the midst of a surge in black voter registration in the early 1950s, black day laborers sought to counteract Mexicans' labor competition by forcefully claiming their own long-denied citizenship rights.[193] Yet, though rich in meaning, there is little evidence that the picnic and petition led to any substantive change. Neither NAACP nor Urban League chapters in Little Rock, the Arkansas Delta, or

FIGURE 10 African American cotton day laborers in Memphis attending an "appreciation picnic" on July 14, 1954, for George W. Lee and Representative Carroll Reece, after Lee and Reece decried wage disparities between black and Mexican cotton laborers in Arkansas. Photo proofs, the George W. Lee Collection, Memphis and Shelby County Room, Memphis Public Library.

Memphis ever noted or addressed the effect of Mexican labor on the fates of African American day laborers.[194]

As newly urban African Americans couched their protests in the language and symbols of emancipation and citizenship, rural white wage laborers embraced the populist rhetoric of the STFU in demanding the same rights as braceros. Like their black counterparts, they gained little political traction in their appeals. "This year they got their cotton choppers out of Old Mexico," wrote Lee Beegle of Trumann to Gathings in longhand. "There is rottener stuff going on here than anywhere else in the world. . . . I think that no man should have more land than he can make and gather."[195] Wrote another white man six years later in 1961, "Why should the Mexicans that are brought into Arkansas for farm work be treated better than a United States Citizen? . . . His living quarters must meet specifications. His electricity, gas, dishes, bedding, etc. are furnished. There is a minimum wage paid him, if weather does not permit him to work. . . . I would rather be a citizen of Mexico, so I could be sent here to work on their kind of terms." Unlike industrial workers who had similar guarantees, he contended, American agricultural workers were the "lost sheep of the employment world."[196] Poor white and black workers in the mid-South struggled to use the bracero program as a wedge to demand greater employment security and higher wages for themselves. These were the very things they had sought but not acquired through the STFU.

Meanwhile, powerful white conservative Democrats like Representative Gathings and Senators Fulbright and McClellan treated the transnational struggle over the rights of Mexican workers as one front in a larger battle to resist the imposition of labor and civil rights in the mid-South. These elected officials pressured the U.S. Department of Labor to keep the program running but bracero wages and guarantees at a minimum.[197] Their constituents' primary motivation was getting their crops out of the ground at the lowest possible price, as the mechanical cotton picker still had not obviated the need for hand labor.[198] And at the same time, as they watched the battles over integration in the Delta and Little Rock, these white men knew an old order was slipping away.[199] They were determined to not see the bracero program transformed into yet another liberal assault on their racial and economic dominance. In 1958, for example, in a signed letter to Gathings, 150 planters protested new housing requirements for braceros.[200] Tying bracero rights to two bogeymen of the New Deal coalition, one grower blamed unfavorable changes in the program on the "Hebrews and Africans" who had supposedly taken over the federal government.[201] Planters had recruited braceros to help preserve their economic and political advantages under white supremacy, yet they now feared the program would undermine them.

As hundreds of growers wrote their senators and representatives to demand the program's continuation and protest attempts to regulate wages and housing conditions, they continued to face charges of discrimination that threatened their ability to contract Mexican labor. The consulate had largely succeeded in ensuring Mexicans had access to white Jim Crow establishments by 1953. But now in several towns, Mexicans complained to their consulate of rampant abuse by police officers who had arrested and fined them on accusations of being drunk. Indeed, police logs in Blytheville showed more Mexicans arrested than white and black residents combined during a sample week in October 1956.[202] Similar complaints emerged from Trumann, Lepanto, Joiner, and Auverge.[203] Some observers conflated Mexicans' drunkenness with their innate racial qualities, explaining that these men from "the lower strata of Mexican society . . . got their Indian blood inflamed by alcohol and ended up in jail."[204] Rather than fight back as they

FIGURE 11 Bracero reception center in Arkansas, probably Phillips County, exact date unknown. Photograph by Ivey Gladin, courtesy of the Gladin Collection, Archives and Special Collections, University of Mississippi Libraries.

did on economic matters, Arkansas authorities acknowledged, "We have no defense against such charges if found to be based on fact."[205] Though many Tejanos and undocumented Mexicans worked in the area throughout the 1950s, planters remained sufficiently dependent on contracted braceros that the threat of blacklisting still pressured them to act.[206]

Though white elites could not ensure that no braceros complained of discrimination to their consulate, they could attempt to preserve their labor access by fostering improved "community relations." Such efforts seemed particularly urgent since braceros were unaccompanied men. African American men had long been subject to violence and lynching when accused of sexual advances or worse, sexual assaults on white women.[207] Just across the river in the Mississippi Delta, a black teenager, Emmett Till, was beaten and murdered for supposedly whistling at a white woman in 1955. The racial threat of black masculinity was never far below the surface in this region, and farmers could not risk allowing locals to feel threatened by thousands of Mexican men with their "Indian blood inflamed," as violence against the men could create additional troubles in recruiting a now-crucial labor source.

114   *Braceros in the Arkansas Delta*

FIGURE 12 Bracero reception center in Arkansas, probably Phillips County, exact date unknown. Photograph by Ivey Gladin, courtesy of the Gladin Collection, Archives and Special Collections, University of Mississippi Libraries.

Local authorities and farmers in several Delta towns thus promoted the opening of special recreational centers "to help alleviate the differences between the mixture of cultures," in the words of one county agricultural agent. These centers in church basements provided Mexican men with "harmless entertainment," luring them into socializing separately from both whites and blacks to avoid conflicts that might draw the consulate's attention.[208] A local photographer documenting the Phillips County center depicted Mexican men playing guitar, putting together puzzles, drawing, and singing under the watchful tutelage of dark-haired, light-skinned women—possibly local whites, possibly Tejanas—who appear to be in charge of the activities (figs. 11 and 12). Similar centers opened in Lepanto and Forrest City. A local white woman in charge of the Forrest City center claimed proudly that volunteers working at the center had a "heart warming experience."[209] Still fastidious about ensuring that braceros were not treated overtly like second-class citizens, Mexican officials approved of the facilities, so long as their existence did not "impede [workers'] access to other public centers."[210] Ultimately, both consular officials and local white elites accepted the racial accommodation

Braceros in the Arkansas Delta   115

that the centers represented: Mexicans would be permitted to access white establishments but in practice would be discouraged from doing so.

Overall, farmers' rush to bracero contracting in the early 1950s and subsequent negotiations between local and international actors over economic and racial matters directly shaped local labor markets, social relations, and even racial thinking. Farmers deliberately pushed black and white families out of cotton wage labor, local ordinances outlawed a type of discrimination, and new social spaces designated as Mexican emerged in towns once defined by black and white. Yet by the years of the bracero program's demise in the early 1960s, planters naturalized the changes that had occurred over the course of the previous decade. Like growers in the Southwest, they attributed their newfound dependence on braceros to the laborers' essential racial qualities.[211]

In Arkansas these discourses specifically compared braceros to the mid-South's poor white and African American day laborers, their most obvious alternatives. Though they had deliberately displaced these groups by recruiting braceros and paying them higher wages, farmers blamed poor southerners, particularly African Americans, for their own disappearance from the cotton fields. "This [day-haul] labor is not dependable," lamented one farmer in 1964. "Our Government's efforts to provide a portion of the basic necessities of life to these people results in their having a greater indifference to work."[212] Complained another in 1965, "The state and gov[ernment] are feeding and supplying too many people's needs. . . . What are the white people sitting by and saying nothing for."[213] Fifteen years after farmers dispatched black preachers to convince African Americans to stay on their farms, the farmers now discounted blacks as potential laborers altogether.

While cotton planters from Texas to Mississippi relied increasingly on mechanical cotton pickers and reduced their dependence on hand labor over the course of the 1950s, Arkansas planters, flush with bracero arms but holding less capital than their Texas counterparts, did not make this change until the early 1960s.[214] Where nearly 40,000 Mexican men labored under contract in Arkansas's fields in the peak year of 1959, just over 2,000 did in the program's penultimate year, 1963.[215] Under pressure from the labor movement, the United States ended the bracero program in 1964. The following year, the Voting Rights Act made a surplus of black workers a political liability more than an economic advantage; those workers could now vote.[216] Mechanization seemed more attractive than ever, and by 1967, 93 percent of Arkansas cotton was harvested by machine.[217] While the bracero program brought long-term Mexican settlement to other regions of recruitment, a stunningly low number of braceros—probably fewer than ten, out of hundreds of thousands that had passed through—remained in Arkansas.[218]

In the Shadow of Jim Crow

The major decade of bracero contracting to Arkansas was the one in which legalized de jure segregation fell. Braceros arrived in Arkansas in the wake of a war fought in segregated battalions; they left just before the passage of the Civil Rights Act. In the intervening years, the Supreme Court struck down the doctrine of separate but equal and Arkansas Dixiecrats lost the battle over school integration with civil rights leaders and the federal government. Having spent decades fighting against both racial integration and agricultural employees' demands for labor rights, planters sought temporary Mexican workers, who seemed the ideal solution to meet labor needs without further threatening a crumbling social order. Unfortunately for planters, the racialized workers who arrived had—in many ways, like their Memphis- and Chicago-bound black counterparts—come to see themselves as modern citizens with rights and, in Mexicans' case, as citizens of a nation that championed the cause of working people.[219] Unlike their rural black counterparts, Mexicans had access to a transnational source of power strong enough to effect rapid change: the emigration-minded Mexican government and its local activist consulate.

Race and class overlapped imperfectly in battles over the New Deal, and only in the Arkansas Delta, with its majority-black population and exceedingly low wages, did Mexican activism abet both strands of the liberal agenda: economic security and an end to de jure racial discrimination. Mexican workers, appealing to their consulate for support, succeeded in forcing farmers to reject overt anti-Mexican discrimination and to admit dark-skinned foreigners into white establishments as early as 1948. By all accounts, this gain stood, if imperfectly, throughout braceros' tenure in the Arkansas Delta. In the economic arena, where farmers resisted the consulate more vehemently, Mexicans' gains were more inconsistent. Notably, however, Arkansas was the only state where bracero minimum wages exceeded the local prevailing wage. Thus, at key moments in the early 1950s, braceros did force white planters to pay a minimum wage in agriculture—the first in the state's history—not only to braceros but, inadvertently, also to black and white workers.

Mexican workers—Guanajuato's Ignacio Canchola García, Durango's Cristóbal Vásquez Martínez, Zacatecas's Margarito Reyna Torres, Veracruz's Angel Ramírez López, and thousands of others—raised these demands.[220]

The success of their challenges to Jim Crow and their sometime ability to claim higher and fairer pay depended directly on the intervention of a robust Mexican government retaining real control over farmers' access to labor. After all, as Mexicans' initial exclusion from white spaces and preference for frequenting black bars and businesses showed, the race and class politics of the Arkansas Delta did not "naturally" afford Mexicans rights or acceptance of any sort. The Mexican government's control over contracting declined substantially in the early 1960s, leaving in its wake a region where locals were generally willing to view Mexicans favorably and tolerate their presence in white establishments but where Mexicans' wages were stagnant and working conditions were deplorable. Bracero Juan Loza, who worked near Helena in 1962, recalled once but not always being asked to leave a white lunch counter there. He also remembered one Sunday that year when he and other braceros went to Helena's Catholic church. They sat together in a pew, and a white couple joined them at the other end of the bench. "When the mass was over, it was only us there," he said. "I don't even know when they moved."[221] Rejected but not ejected by the church's white members, Loza's predicament encapsulated that of braceros in Arkansas in the early 1960s. These men eluded the rigid structures of Jim Crow but did not escape the economic, social, and cultural caste system it had created.

Mexican workers and their consular allies had succeeded for more than a decade in bringing piecemeal reform to the Delta. They gained recognition as not black and sometimes secured improved housing, better food in their labor camps, wage floors, and full payment of the wages due them. Braceros valued these victories for their own dignity as workers, men, and Mexican citizens. Yet while planters' victories were also incomplete, they proved to be more durable. The bracero program allowed the Arkansas Delta to rely on a cheap, racialized cotton labor force longer than anywhere else in the Delta region.[222] By the time civil rights and labor activists pushed President Lyndon Johnson to sacrifice the once-"solid" Democratic South, sign the Civil Rights Act, expand federal protections to black agricultural workers, and begin an agricultural minimum wage during the mid- to late 1960s, Arkansas planters had already pioneered a new model to circumvent these changes. Their violent efforts to preserve white supremacy had driven away the very African American workforce on which they once depended.[223] Now they worked hard at the local level to tamp down overt anti-Mexican discrimination, thus ensuring a continued supply of Mexican laborers. This supply of laborers would enable them to keep wages low, minimizing the impact of liberal reforms on their bottom line.

The specific nature of this social, economic, and cultural transformation in the Arkansas Delta established a logic that would shape the rural South's "Mexicanization" in subsequent decades. For the rest of the twentieth century, the agents of this Mexicanization were largely undocumented immigrants without the limited protections of an internationally negotiated work contract. Local southern authorities after the bracero program thus sought improved relations between whites and Mexicanos not to please a foreign government but rather to make their communities attractive to Mexicano workers.

Though Arkansas was the only state in the black–white South to recruit large numbers of braceros, Florida and Georgia also recruited them occasionally, though never in numbers larger than 5,000 per year.[224] As the next chapter will discuss, the Arkansas experience, bridging the Jim Crow and post–Jim Crow eras, portended the future struggles of white, black, and Mexicano workers in those states and throughout the rural South during the 1960s–90s.

CHAPTER FOUR

Mexicano Stories and Rural White Narratives
Creating Pro-immigrant Conservatism in Rural Georgia, 1965–2004

Some farmworkers double over; others rest a full body's weight on their knees. A few inches above the ground, cabbage peeks from the soil. The workers' job is to pick it, whatever the physical toll on their backs or joints. It is the early 1970s in southern Georgia, most likely spring or fall when most cabbage there is harvested. The photo is black and white, but the sky has the milky look of so many warm and muggy mornings in the U.S. South's most fertile agricultural areas (fig. 13).

The images seem to echo those blared to the public a decade earlier in the documentary *Harvest of Shame*. The documentary, hosted by journalist Edward R. Murrow and broadcast on CBS, brought the plight of agricultural migrant workers into contemporary popular culture for the first time since the Depression. Released in the middle of the civil rights movement, it focused largely on black workers in Florida and Mexican American farmworkers in California, seeking to generate national outrage that such working conditions could exist "in the United States, in 1960."[1] The program helped generate sympathy for farmworkers among middle-class viewers, contributing to the successes of the subsequent decade's farmworker movements.

The subjects of these photographs, however, did not participate in any such movement. Upon closer examination, the black-and-white photos do not echo the documentary's message; instead, they subvert it. *Harvest of Shame* presented farmworkers as American society's greatest victims, utterly left behind by the postwar economic expansion and American narrative of progress that so many others were enjoying. Recounting the same labor, the photographs tell a different story. Rather than a white public, these photographs were produced by and for a family of farmworkers. They are preserved in a family photo album of Bernardo and Andrea Avalos, among the first Mexican Americans to move to southern Georgia in the 1960s. The Avalos family saw participation in farm labor as a choice, not a last resort; for them,

---

To see a selection of original historical sources from this chapter, go to http://corazondedixie .org/chapter-4 (http://dx.doi.org/10.7264/N3222S10).

FIGURE 13 A page from an Avalos family album: picking cabbage in Georgia in the 1970s. Courtesy of Andrea and Slim Avalos, Omega, Ga.

stooping over to pick cabbages was hard and sometimes damaging work, but it was also an integral part of their family story of self-sufficiency and upward mobility. Rather than undermine the American narrative of progress, for the Avalos family these photographs fit squarely into it.

From the 1960s through the 1990s, millions of Mexican immigrants and Mexican Americans journeyed through the rural U.S. South as agricultural migrant laborers and tens of thousands settled there. Like their predecessors in rural Mississippi and Arkansas, these newcomers were initially greeted as objects of curiosity that did not fit neatly into the binary racial organization of economic, social, and political life. As their numbers grew rapidly in the 1980s and they became visible in the largest swath of the South to date, they often faced hostility.

Yet the post–civil rights South and postnationalist Mexico created new possibilities and constraints for the South's Mexicanos in the second half of the twentieth century. Migrants' experiences in Texas, Florida, and particularly Mexico, where political consensus unraveled in the 1960s and the economy declined sharply in the 1980s, shaped their expectations of citizenship, states, and society. Unlike their bracero counterparts during previous decades, these Mexican agricultural laborers did not arrive expecting that any government would guarantee their rights and economic security. Thus, they did not focus their energies on claiming these things. Rather, they sought to exercise control over their own economic futures through wage labor strategies and to live free from violence and harassment. While organizers in Florida and a few other places in the South successfully presented unionization as a tool for Mexicanos' upward economic mobility, in Georgia migrants pursued their goals through different means.

Mexicans and Mexican Americans in rural Georgia in the 1960s, 1970s, and 1980s (map 5) confronted a region in transition from legal racial segregation to an evolved conservative ideology that framed social issues in terms of individual rights and responsibilities; the neoliberal ideology ascendant in Mexico also emphasized individuals and free markets rather than collective rights or state protections. In the U.S. South, this celebration of self-sufficiency eschewed group claims for redress of historical injustices as well as government "handouts," such as welfare and food stamps. Though African Americans were the primary targets of disdain within this framework, poor white people could run afoul of its taboos as well. Mexicanos defied their difficult living and working conditions in indirect or individual ways, but the local political culture provided little encouragement or reward for open protest or organizing along lines of race or workplace. Meanwhile

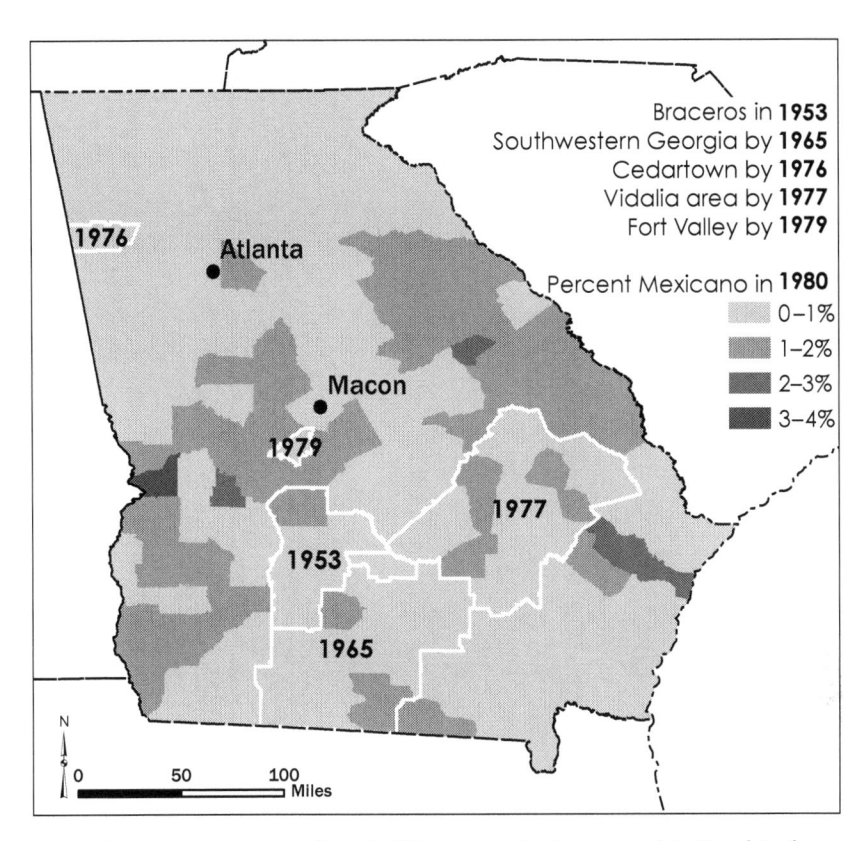

MAP 5 Mexicanos' presence in Georgia. U.S. census 1980 data accessed via Social Explorer; historical data from author's primary research as cited in this chapter. Map by the author.

in Mexico, a massive decline in the resources and power of consulates and the betrayal many Mexicans came to feel vis-à-vis their national state effectively removed the option of pursuing political action through trans-state appeals for protection.[2] As both federal governments reduced spending on their poorest citizens in keeping with neoliberal ideology, corporations and churches—ironically, often subsidized by those same federal governments—now played a more prominent role in ordinary people's lives than they had in the mid-twentieth century.[3]

Thus, rather than labor or political movements, southern Georgia's Mexicanos seized a different set of opportunities for social and economic progress in their new environments. In southern Georgia, both farmer employers and charity- and mission-minded white church leaders—representatives of the area's two most powerful interests—sought personal and spiritual relationships with migrant workers. In their public discourses, these influential white people framed Mexican migrants' lifestyles as archetypical examples of upright working poor who merited the opportunity to stay in town, earn wages, attend school, and receive charity despite their foreign accents and racial difference. Mexican and Mexican American workers reciprocated the interest and did not become involved in labor or political organizing, albeit for their own reasons. Their seeming acquiescence to local mores allowed white elites' pro-immigrant conservatism to permeate white society far beyond the ranks of labor-hungry growers. For their part, middle- and lower-middle-class African Americans trumpeted Mexicans' arrival into the agricultural fields as proof that black people had moved up in the world; those who remained in farm labor had little power to protest their newfound competition. In this way, a fragile peace around immigration issues settled over southern Georgia and much of the rural agricultural South through the end of the 1990s, even as farmworker organizing and populist anti-immigrant backlash took hold elsewhere in the country during the same period.[4]

The Mexicanization of Southern Agricultural Labor

Though Mexican labor migration to Georgia did not reach the national radar until the 1990s, in fact it had begun in the 1950s (see map 5). In the fall of 1953, approximately 1,300 braceros entered southwestern Georgia to pick cotton in Crisp, Dooly, Turner, Wilcox, and Worth counties. Their stay was short, a mere six weeks to reach their hands into cotton plants to gather lint for the gin.[5] That same year, observers noted that Tejanos had joined the majority-black labor force in the vegetable fields and citrus groves of Florida.[6] While a decade would pass before Mexican-origin laborers again worked Georgia's fields, the stream of workers from Texas to Florida continued unabated. By the late 1970s, Florida would join Texas as a home base for many of Georgia's Mexican and Mexican American migrant workers.

Andrea and Bernardo Avalos were among the first Tejanos to power southern Georgia's agricultural industries. Bernardo was a World War II veteran who had worked for a time in aluminum plants in South Texas. But the couple soon determined that migrant agricultural labor would allow them to make faster, not slower, economic progress than Bernardo's industrial job. And so Bernardo, Andrea, and their young children joined the postwar Tejano diaspora of migrant laborers, journeying seasonally to New Mexico and eventually settling for a time in Oklahoma.[7] Just as they had hoped, wages from agricultural labor allowed them to buy a home there. Now based in Oklahoma, the family continued traveling to the Midwest and Florida to pick crops seasonally, and Bernardo was able to increase his earnings by using grower relationships to contract work for other laborers.

Around 1965, the Avaloses received a tip from a Tejano friend who had found his way to southern Georgia a few years earlier: work was plentiful in Georgia. Bernardo soon began bringing work crews to Hank Dodson, a prominent white farmer in the Tifton–Omega area. Dodson had previously relied on local workers, mostly African Americans, to plant, cultivate, and harvest his crops. But the civil rights movement and postwar economic expansion had begun to open up new opportunities for black agricultural workers away from the fields.[8] Besides, like his grower contemporaries in the Arkansas Delta, Dodson may have felt that those black and white workers who remained were not sufficiently dependable and obedient. To encourage more migrant Mexicano crews to come in, Dodson built barracks to house this new seasonal workforce. Within five years, the Avalos family settled in Georgia. Bernardo, who came to be known as "Slim" for his tall stature, organized work crews locally, including not only Mexicano workers but also whites and blacks.[9]

Dodson was not alone in his desire to find a new source of seasonal farmworkers, nor was the Avalos family alone in its search for new farm labor opportunities in territory previously uncharted by Mexicans and Tejanos. By the 1970s, Mexicanos had begun to join Atlantic Coast migrant labor streams, with reports of their appearance surfacing in North Carolina, South Carolina, and Virginia.[10] They joined white and African American workers who had been following these routes since at least World War I, when Florida, the coastal Carolinas, and the Chesapeake areas first turned to seasonal vegetable and fruit farming.[11]

Meanwhile, Georgia remained a land of cotton and sharecroppers much later than other parts of the South.[12] By the 1960s, the changes that had fundamentally restructured the business of agriculture elsewhere began to catch up with farmers in the state. Family farms declined while corporate agriculture rose in prominence. Growers mechanized parts but not all of the harvest cycle for crops such as tobacco. And King Cotton was pushed aside, replaced by seasonally intensive vegetable and fruit farming. These developments all caused an increase in demand for hired (as opposed to family or tenant) and highly seasonal (as opposed to nearly year-round) labor in Georgia during the 1960s, 1970s, and 1980s.[13]

Initially, Georgia growers depended mostly on local laborers, particularly school-age children, black women, and older blacks and whites, to perform this new class of waged, seasonal labor.[14] Yet in the wake of bracero-era discourses that denigrated domestic farmworkers, growers were perpetually unsatisfied, grumbling that welfare checks made locals unwilling to put in an honest day's work.[15] Despite the ubiquity of this claim in public pronouncements, Georgia farmers admitted to researchers in the mid-1970s that the manufacturing and textile industries, not welfare, were their biggest competitors for labor.[16] One grower acknowledged as much several years later, saying, "The local labor went to the factories, and the migrants came in to take their place."[17] In addition to higher wages, the manufacturing and textile industries could offer year-round steady employment—something increasingly scarce in farm work.

Texas- and Florida-based Mexicanos, however, had already developed strategies of seasonal migration and family labor that enabled them to see the potential for economic gain in the very arrangements that local white and black people had begun to reject. Vegetables in southwestern Georgia required intense harvest labor over the summer—exactly the time of year that farm work in Florida slackened.[18] Since the 1920s, many Mexicans and Tejanos had spent their summers harvesting crops in the Northwest or Midwest; now, with the help of crew leaders, those working in Florida had to travel only a few hundred miles north to find summer employment.[19] And so, by the mid-1970s each summer brought a noticeable influx of Mexican-origin workers—mostly Tejano families like the Avaloses but also some Mexican men and women—into southwestern Georgia.[20] In 1975, they comprised 40 percent of the agricultural workforce there alongside an equal proportion of African Americans and half as many whites.[21] The INS noticed them, too, raiding Tifton's fields in June 1976 and deporting dozens of Mexican workers.[22] Yet despite such intermittent immigration enforcement, the presence of Mexicans in Southwest Georgia continued to grow.

Experienced farmworkers, particularly bilingual Tejanos, fashioned themselves as crew leaders who used connections in Florida and Texas to provide Georgia farmers with a seemingly endless supply of workers. The Cortez family was among them. In 1980, shortly after Israel Cortez finished the sixth grade in Bejucos, State of Mexico, his parents gathered their eight children. The next morning before dawn, they would leave for the United States. "We [kids] didn't know where we were going, where America was," Cortez recalled.[23] After crossing into Texas with the help of a smuggler, the Cortezes joined an aunt in Oklahoma, where they began picking cotton. But soon Florida beckoned with higher wages, and the family relocated once more. They spent winters picking oranges. While U.S. citizen or legal permanent resident farmworkers could draw unemployment during the slack summer months and remain in Florida or return to families in Texas, the Cortez family was undocumented and had no such safety net.[24] So when the orange picking wound down in late spring, the Cortezes joined thousands of other Mexicans and Mexicans Americans on the road to Michigan and the upper Midwest for the summer harvest.

That changed around 1984, when a Tejano crew leader approached Cortez's father in Florida, offering his family the opportunity to work in Tifton, Georgia. Mr. Cortez was delighted. "There's no need for us to go to Michigan or any of those states," Israel Cortez recalls his father reasoning, "because by the time you get up there, you've spent everything you've saved."[25] The family could now pick cucumbers, peppers, squash, and tomatoes in Tifton from April through December, then return to Florida each year for the orange season.[26] Florida-based José and Anselma Gómez also saw Georgia as an appealing alternative to spending summers in the Midwest. "We got tired of traveling so far," Anselma said, and in 1982 the family replaced summer destinations in Michigan and Ohio with Douglas, Georgia.[27] Migrants who once journeyed between Florida and the Midwest formed the first large group of Mexicano laborers in southern Georgia: Spanish-surnamed children baptized in Vidalia in the 1980s were most likely to have been born in Lansing, Michigan; Fremont, Ohio; or Dade City, Florida.[28]

The sudden availability of a seasonal workforce—there when you need them, not when you don't—allowed farmers to form new business plans. Previously, investing in crops that were seasonally labor-intensive posed a risk: if a grower could not recruit sufficient harvest labor locally, his high-value crops might rot in the field. Georgia farmers' relationships with Tejano crew leaders enabled them to take their businesses in new, lucrative directions with the help of seasonal laborers. Between 1982 and 1987, the value of Georgia's vegetable crop increased by 60 percent, and growers' use of "contract labor"—as opposed to tenant farmers or permanent employees—tripled.[29] These were the years in which the migrant labor stream turned over almost entirely to become majority Mexicano.

For example, southeastern Georgia's local onions, now branded as Vidalia sweet onions, required a ready army of agricultural labor to pick the crop during a six-week window in the spring; farmers could not plant the crop unless they knew workers would be waiting.[30] Thus, Vidalia onion production grew in lockstep with Mexican and Mexican American labor migration to Southeast Georgia. The area's largest packinghouse, New Brothers in Toombs County, saw a twenty-five-fold increase in onion production from 1978 to 1983.[31] New Brothers utilized Mexican and Tejano migrant labor recruited by presumably Tejano crew leaders, Benny Rodríguez and Román Flores.[32] Their reliance on Mexicano labor to power the rapid increase in Vidalia production was typical of the region's farmers.[33] Though the onion season was short, lasting May to June at most, workers in Southeast Georgia could remain in the area from March through November by traveling to nearby vegetable farms.[34] Others supplemented their income by collecting pine straw on local forest land and selling it to businesses like Georgia Pine Straw.[35]

Like Vidalia farmers, peach growers in middle Georgia also had summertime labor needs, and in 1981 they began recruiting Mexican workers with the help of brothers Abel and Albert Aguilar. The Aguilars were born on an *ejido*, or communal land grant, in Michoacán. Their migrant path was typical for the 1970s, beginning in the fields of California and Texas and wending toward Florida by the end of that decade.[36] There, they and their wives purchased homes in 1979. Like other experienced migrants, the Aguilars soon started organizing work crews. In 1981, they stopped in Peach County on their way to the Midwest and quickly found growers eager to work with them.[37] "If you bring me more Mexicans," grower Chop Evans told Aguilar as he gestured toward the black workers nearby, "I'll let *them* go." Aguilar did, and so did Evans. In 1989 the Aguilars and their families settled in Peach County for good.[38]

As the stories show, in the early 1980s Georgia's fruit and vegetable growers took their place among generations of white southern farmers who purposefully sought alternatives to black laborers. Georgia's farmers experimented with an array of migrant workers in addition to Mexicanos—Puerto Ricans, Cubans, and Haitians recruited through a combination of federally run programs and informal relationships with labor contractors.[39] Yet Haitian workers quickly fell out of favor, perhaps due to race.[40] While Cubans and Puerto Ricans would remain in Georgia's fields in small numbers, Mexicanos outnumbered them by far.

When the Immigration Reform and Control Act (IRCA) of 1986 allowed undocumented seasonal agricultural workers (SAW) to legalize their status, families like the Cortezes rejoiced while farmers worried, "Now that people are legal aliens, are they going to change professions?"[41] Nearly six in ten of the Southeast's foreign-born agricultural workers were part of the SAW legalization process in 1989, the highest percentage of any region besides the northwestern United States.[42] Growers told of cucumbers rotting in the ground and labor shortages that year.[43] But what IRCA took from southern Georgia's labor supply, it ultimately gave back with interest. Thousands of migrant laborers in traditional destinations like California and Texas used their newfound legal status to settle down, saturating low-end labor markets in those places.[44] As one economic crisis after the next rocked Mexico, a new generation of undocumented workers would find Georgia even more attractive by comparison.

By 1989, the ethnic composition of Georgia's agricultural labor force had turned over almost entirely. The same was true throughout the southeastern United States. While "Hispanics" comprised just 2 percent of the region's agricultural workforce in 1977, in 1989 seven of every ten farmworkers in the Southeast was foreign born—of these, the vast majority from Mexico.[45] The state's black farmworkers—mostly young, elderly, and/or female—entered poultry plants or service jobs or left the local workforce.[46] Since Emancipation, white farmers had dreamed of replacing their black labor force with immigrants. Time and again they targeted Mexican workers, but the Depression, the end of the bracero program, or the workers themselves foiled these plans.[47] Now more than a century after Emancipation, African Americans' modestly rising fortunes combined with Mexico's declining circumstances during the same period to make farmers' dreams of an immigrant agricultural labor force come true.

"Strange Animals" in Georgia

While southern Georgia ultimately proved an attractive or tolerable location for hundreds of thousands of Mexicanos, employers' satisfaction with their labor hardly translated into dreamy living conditions. In the 1960s and early 1970s, Mexicanos living in camps or trailers near agricultural work sites were invisible inhabitants of sparse rural landscapes. Miles of country roads separated them from their nearest neighbors, and few attended church in those early years.[48] "We had migrant camps," recalled Texas-born Javier González, whose family first came to southern Georgia in 1978, "and we didn't really interact much with the larger population, mainly because we didn't speak the language."[49] Since the influx of workers peaked during summertime, the few children who benefited from migrant education programs did not meet local kids in schools.[50]

But the number of Tejano and Mexican workers steadily increased through the 1970s, and so did their ranks who settled locally, as the Avalos family did. Families of Mexican workers had settled in Tifton and Vidalia by 1983; others, like the Cortez family, stayed in town most of the year, from April through December.[51] Migrant education teams fanned out into the fields, recruiting Mexican and Mexican American children to enroll in programs run out of local schools.[52] There they spent at least part of the day in classes with local white and black children. In 1983, "when we started coming on our own," without a crew leader, "and when we started extending our stays into the school year, that is when we were forced to go into this foreign environment," González recalled.[53]

González and other children who entered southern Georgia's schools in the early 1980s remembered being treated as objects of fascination, disgust, or confusion. When González first enrolled in school in the Vidalia area in 1983, people would poke their heads into the classroom just "to look and stare and to see the novelty."[54] Classmates asked a Mexican American girl in the Vidalia area if she was Indian. "And I would tell them no, I'm a Mexican American.... I come from Texas."[55] Robert Marín spent a few months attending school in Lyons in 1981 and recalled classmates gathering around to see how he ate.[56] Peers taunted Israel Cortez when he entered the seventh grade in Omega around 1984. "My school years were rough, tough, and frustrating," he remembered. Cortez craved academic success but felt confused and alienated by assignments in a language he barely understood. And then there was the relentless teasing. "I never took any food from home because I couldn't stand [the teasing]," he said. "If I was to bring a rolled taco to school, were they going to make fun of me? Laugh at me? Think that it was gross and nasty?"[57] In contrast, Tejana Diana Mendieta (née Avalos) enjoyed the extra attention that classmates paid her when she entered the sixth grade near Tifton in the early 1970s. When teachers and friends asked her to speak Spanish on command or answer questions about Mexico, "that always made me feel welcome, like I knew something and could be part of the class."[58] In general, high school years were the worst to be a newly arrived Mexican American student; González's high school–age brothers got into fights when classmates called them derogatory names.[59]

Intense attention, whether violent, mocking, or merely curious, pained or pleased Mexicano children in different ways. Yet on a social level, classmates' actions were all of a piece. The South's rural schools had just emerged from battles over desegregation, and youths—particularly as they neared high school years—were in the midst of drawing and redrawing boundaries of race within integrated school environments. Singling out Mexicanos constituted yet another way—along with cliques and lunch tables—to draw the lines between "us" and "them."[60] Indeed, Mendieta remembered disputes during the early years of integration when black and white friends would ask her, "Whose side are you on?"[61]

Newly arrived Mexican and Mexican American adults had far less contact with locals than their children did during the 1970s and 1980s. Their strongest memories of these interactions are somewhat more positive than those of their kids: mostly curiosity, some exclusion, all a bit uncomfortable. Anselma Gómez remembered being looked at as a "strange animal" when she first arrived in Douglas in 1982. A curious passerby asked her husband, "Are you an Indian?" Quick-witted Anselma responded for him, "We might be, I can't lie. What I do know is that we are Mexicans."[62] In the 1970s in Tifton, members of the Avalos family remembered a few businesses that said, "We don't serve Hispanics," and a few landlords who suddenly said the apartment had been rented when they met their potential tenants in person.[63] Yet discrimination did not define their memories. Robert Marín and his mother, Teodora, remembered that in the mid-1980s, they were not invited into white people's homes but were not subjected to hostility either. Teodora felt the situation was an improvement on Texas, where one of her sons had been beaten up by white kids.[64]

Expanding opportunities for African Americans meant that the majority of blacks, who had already left agriculture, seldom expressed open resistance to Mexicanos' arrival in those early years. "Back then" in the 1980s, recalled Tejana Andrea Hinojosa of the Vidalia area, "I don't even remember hearing [from African Americans] that 'We were taking their jobs.'"[65] If anything, middle-class blacks usefully pointed to Mexicanos' arrival as evidence that their own community had finally risen above the low stature of agricultural labor. "We were never really concerned with the Hispanic community," explained Jerome Woody, a former African American city councilman and poultry plant administrator in Claxton. "It's not a lifelong dream" to work in the fields or on the line in a poultry plant, he added with a hint of sarcasm. "It's difficult work, and they do it with a smile."[66] John Raymond Turner, an African American city councilman in Vidalia who also worked as a hotel manager, echoed the sentiment. "Why complain about the Mexicans doing the farm work when we're not doing the farm work anyway?" he mused.[67] Middle-class African Americans like Turner and Woody also did not perceive Mexicanos as a threat to their political power.[68]

Documentary evidence offers mostly silence on the question of how black agricultural workers felt about their Mexican counterparts in the 1970s and 1980s. But what evidence is available suggests the groups had extensive contact with each other in the fields, leading to relations of tension, cooperation, and everything in between.[69] In Georgia, Tejano crew leaders Slim Avalos as well as Flores, Hernández, and Galván led mixed crews of both Mexicanos and blacks. African American crew leaders Clayton Clark, Charles Bank, and L. D. and Wanita Walker had Mexicanos in their crews.[70] Workers affiliated with particular crews by choice, and the mixing suggests that blacks and Mexicanos facilitated each other's employment and shared space in migrant camps even as Mexicanos slowly displaced blacks over time. Even when the displacement was obvious, as in Chop Evans's peach orchard, there is no evidence that black agricultural workers—highly marginalized, with little political power, and often near the end of their working lives—publicly voiced their opposition to the Mexican influx.

In all, documentary evidence confirms migrant workers' memories of cordial relations with underlying unease in the 1970s and early 1980s. A nun working in southeast Georgia wrote in a 1982 report that "last year 2000 migrant farmworkers came into the area and there was a great deal of tension between them and local residents." Yet, she continued, "there were no serious incidents."[71]

Majority-White Industrial Towns

The same could not be said of northern Georgia's majority-white factory towns, which began recruiting Mexican labor in the late 1970s. Cedartown, a mostly white town in northern Georgia, recruited Mexican immigrants to work at its Zartic meatpacking plant in 1976.[72] Mexicans began working in the carpet mills of Dalton, Dayton Steel Company in Rome, and the poultry plants of Gainesville around the same time.[73] Similar plants throughout the South also turned to Latino workers in the 1970s and 1980s.[74] While negative responses to Mexican immigration were largely muted in the agricultural southern part of the state, Mexicans in majority-white factory towns in northern Georgia suffered open hostility from the Ku Klux Klan as well as violence. The Klan long had a stronghold in the entire state of Georgia and was most active among blue-collar white men in majority-white industrial towns.[75]

Ramiro López was the first to lose his life to Klan-supported violence. Like many of the Zartic plant's Mexican workers, López hailed from Cuaracurio, Michoacán. He crossed the border illegally in 1979 when he heard about opportunities at the Zartic plant.[76] López, then twenty-nine, took up residence in a Cedartown trailer park, where he began dating a fellow trailer park resident, fourteen-year-old Theresa Ann Ballew, whom newspapers later described as a "pallid blonde." Like a growing number of white–Mexican couples in town, Ballew and López planned to marry.[77] On Labor Day in 1981, a drunk López lost control of his car and got into an accident. A car of white men stopped, ostensibly to help López and his three Mexican companions. But soon one man, construction worker David Wayne Richardson, shot and killed López. Richardson had openly expressed resentment toward Mexicans prior to the shooting.

A textile plant in Cedartown had recently shut down, leaving hundreds out of work and clearing the path for a revival of Klan activity among demoralized white workers; these Klan members now directed their anger at Mexicans.[78] Signs appeared around town proclaiming, "KKK. Mexicans get out." Another, placed in front of the trailer park where the Mexican men lived, read, "Mexican Border. Do Not Cross." Someone fired guns at the men's trailers.[79] The Mexican witnesses fled Cedartown, and an all-white jury affirmed Richardson's argument that he had shot López in self-defense. He was acquitted.[80]

Two years later, the story seemed to repeat itself. In 1983, Dwayne Pruitt, a white man, killed Mexican immigrant Casiano Zamudio, who was married to a local white woman.[81] The assailant said he killed Zamudio because his stepdaughter was being sexually harassed by Mexican immigrants.[82] He had called the sheriff the prior week to say that if the situation continued, "he was going to kill him a Mexican."[83] In the weeks leading up to Pruitt's murder trial, the Klan intimidated Mexican witnesses with shotguns, broke into the home of Zamudio's white widow, and solicited money for Pruitt's defense. Once the trial began, members sat in the audience wearing Klan buttons.[84] One told a reporter that Pruitt "just did what any American would do, protect his home and family."[85] Pruitt was acquitted by an all-white jury, which accepted his argument of self-defense. Mexican American organizations active in the Southwest at the time, such as the Mexican American Legal Defense and Education Fund, had no involvement in the case; rather, white liberal organizations like Catholic Social Services, the American Civil Liberties Union (ACLU), and the *Atlanta Journal-Constitution* called for a federal investigation after the acquittal.[86]

Anti-Mexican hostility in Gainesville was less violent than in Cedartown but still differed sharply from the uneasy coexistence of southern Georgia. In Gainesville, police notoriously harassed Mexicans. And when poultry plant owner Ron Gress praised the new workers in a local newspaper, a Ku Klux Klan leader called for a boycott of his products.[87] Though less dramatic than the Cedartown murders, anti-immigrant Klan activity in Gainesville signaled a political climate in northern Georgia's majority-white factory towns wherein open expression of hostility toward Mexican immigrants was the norm even as Mexican men quietly integrated themselves into trailer park communities and dated and married white women. The only significant exception to this trend in Georgia's majority-white industrial towns was the carpet manufacturing center of Dalton. There local carpet mill owners used their outsize influence to calm fears, foster pro-immigrant sentiment, and encourage local initiatives to help immigrants integrate into the community.[88]

Absent the countervailing voices of powerful local employers like Dalton's mill owners, the Klan typically led the response to Mexican workers in northern Georgia's industrial towns. While anti-Mexican reaction remained isolated in these communities and did not spread throughout the state or region just yet, it marked the first major spate of anti-Mexican violence in the U.S. South. Mexicans and Mexican Americans in the region had suffered labor exploitation, Jim Crow segregation, and political disenfranchisement. But not until the 1980s did a powerful and violent anti-Mexican discourse rise to the public sphere, nor did anti-Mexican violence previously threaten the region's immigrants in a systematic way.

Suffering and Resistance in the Fields of Southern Georgia

Though community relations were tenuously manageable for Mexicanos in the agricultural areas of southern Georgia, working and living conditions were abject. In the 1970s and 1980s, workers spent the season living in trailers, houses, barracks, motels, or hotels.[89] While some farmers funded workers' housing, others charged workers for it or left them to find a place to stay on their own.[90] Mexicanos in migrant camps often lived with "rats, snakes, exposed electrical wiring, open sewage, broken windows, windows without screens, excessive uncollected trash, leaking roofs, dangerous steps, toilets and showers not working properly," wrote a state government observer in 1981.[91] One camp had twelve people living in one room with no indoor plumbing but plenty of insects; at another, children played with carelessly discarded pesticide cans as though they were toys, "and the migrants informed us that when they were working in the fields and the crops were dusted with pesticides, they were dusted also."[92] At another farm, a nun observed, worker housing consisted of "2 long narrow (6 to 8 ft wide) corrugated metal buildings with walls unfinished to the top leaving an empty space between the wall and roof. . . . Piles of burning trash between the units . . . no separate toilet facilities for women . . . earthen floors."[93]

State and federal government officials visited the camps, inspecting about half of migrant labor camps in 1981, for example, but did little to force change.[94] If anything, local Department of Labor bureaucrats, in a pattern set by generations of southern government officials, supported planters over laborers; in this case, that meant warning farmers in advance of inspections and defending them in the media when their practices came under fire.[95] One state labor official told a reporter that workers, not farmers, were to blame for poor housing conditions. "Keep in mind, you can take the nicest place in the world and put a certain class of people in it and it's going to look bad," she explained.[96] At a site that a federal labor official had called one of the "best camps in the state," a nun found workers living in a converted chicken coop.[97] With no meaningful oversight from state or federal officials, migrant housing remained hazardous to workers' health.

Like their living conditions, migrants' agricultural work routines presented daily perils. Their jobs were back-breaking, terribly paid, and physically dangerous.[98] Between 1993 and 1997, at least three children lost legs, arms, or hands in packing shed accidents in southern Georgia.[99] An average of one Latino farmworker died each year in the state of Georgia during the 1990s and 2000s, usually in accidents with automobiles or large machinery or from heat exposure.[100] Most children suffered from malnutrition because of their families' poverty wages, and a disproportionately high number died as infants. They were routinely cheated out of wages, as when a grower was convicted of pocketing their Social Security deductions in the mid-1990s.[101]

But Georgia's fields still generated less scandal than others nearby. Death rates were twice as high among Latino agricultural workers in Florida.[102] There the federal government successfully prosecuted slavery cases in relation to migrant agricultural workers at least six times. Crew leaders in Florida were known for being particularly abusive, berating, beating up, and in one case routinely murdering workers who did not cooperate to their satisfaction.[103] While such bondage and physical violence may have taken place in the agricultural fields of Georgia, there is scant evidence of it in oral history interviews, newspaper accounts, or Mexican consulate records. It is difficult to know if this means such things did not transpire or that workers did not have anywhere to take their grievances. It is possible, however, that Georgia's considerably smaller farms meant crew leaders had a less powerful role there than in Florida, where growers running gigantic operations gave tacit permission for middlemen to extract more productivity by whatever means necessary. Physical intimidation in Georgia could be more restrained. One social services staffer recalled a farmer quietly placing his gun on the table during discussions with a worker about unpaid wages; the worker did not get hurt, but he also did not get paid.[104]

While some Mexicanos achieved substantial financial progress through migrant labor, others barely subsisted. Most would start at the bottom as laborers subject to the whims of both farmers and crew leaders. In that situation, crew leaders' cut and housing and food deductions often left migrants with little take-home pay. At one camp, for example, migrants earning $25 a day were spending $21 per day for room and the remaining $4 for board.[105] In other words, their take-home pay was zero. Food stamps could have mitigated the poverty of many, but farmers insisted that workers did not need them and blocked access when government employees attempted to sign them up.[106] Like their Mississippi Delta counterparts in the 1930s, Georgia's growers wanted to ensure that farm labor was local workers' only means for subsistence.[107]

Yet for countless Mexicanos, life on the road with a crew leader was a worthwhile investment because it could be the first step toward family autonomy. As workers became more experienced, learned some English, and acquired their own car or truck, they could develop direct relationships with farmers.[108] Israel Cortez remembers that as a boy, his translation skills enabled his father to communicate with farmers and get out from under the crew leader system. "That's when we realized how the business worked and how much some of the crew leaders made," he said. "We realized that what we were getting paid was pennies" of what their labor actually was worth.[109] Dealing directly with farmers, an entire family at work in the fields could earn enough money to save for the eventual purchase of a house or trailer that would, in turn, free them from the need to live in run-down farmworker housing under the constant surveillance of farmers.[110]

While the promise of such advancement kept many workers silent in the face of abuses, others found ways to push back. Enrique Flores Ortiz, an undocumented worker, and his companions in the Vidalia area used county courts to sue their boss for unpaid wages in 1986.[111] In subsequent years, more migrants used the courts to claim their rights as once-undocumented workers legalized their status through the IRCA, thus becoming eligible for Legal Aid's help and less afraid to come forward.[112] Others, like the Contreras family in Byromville, sold their labor freely, to the dismay of crew leaders who had already contracted it out to a particular farmer.[113] Indeed, leaving one farm or crew for another was likely the most common way that Mexicano agricultural workers throughout the rural South asserted what little power they had.[114]

No union, workers' center, or other form of collective protest took root among Georgia's Mexicano agricultural workers during the 1960s through 1990s. There is no evidence that even small groups of Mexicano agricultural workers walked off the job or staged a protest together anywhere in Georgia during that period, though it is possible, if not likely, that such actions occasionally transpired but escaped the written historical record. Still, reluctance to take collective action made Georgia's Mexicano farmworkers exceptions among their peers in those decades. In nearly every other region where Mexicanos worked in farm labor, these were years of strikes, boycotts, and collective movements for justice. From the fields of California, the Mexican American–led farmworker movement spread to Oregon, Texas, Wisconsin, Illinois, and Ohio.[115] Though the 1971 farmworkers' unionization effort in nearby Florida was powered by black migrants, in 1976 a majority-Mexican labor force in Immokalee went on strike for higher wages.[116] By the 1990s, Latino farm labor organizing even reached one agricultural community in eastern North Carolina.[117] During that decade, Latino agricultural workers in Immokalee, Florida, and poultry workers in Morganton, North Carolina, organized themselves without the agitation or resources of any formal union, ultimately conducting successful strikes and boycotts for higher wages and a greater say in the conditions of their own workplaces.[118] Mexican and other Latino workers in this period certainly were not "un-organizable" just because they were poor, migrant, indigenous, undocumented, or did not speak English.[119]

Furthermore, Mexicano workers in the Mississippi and Arkansas Deltas had sporadically organized coordinated actions to protest conditions in the U.S. South earlier in the twentieth century. They decamped together from their work sites to protest subpar conditions, fought for educational rights, and won admission to white public spaces.[120] The binary racial organization, anti-labor environment, and stark inequalities of the South's agricultural areas did not inherently foreclose all possibility for Mexicanos to take collective political action in their own interest. Tejanos and Mexicans working the fields of southern Georgia in the 1970s, 1980s, and 1990s could well have organized themselves, or been organized, into a collective political unit.

But they did not. Both evidence and logic suggest that Mexicano workers in southern Georgia knew about contemporary farmworker movements elsewhere, connected as they were to communities in Texas, Florida, and the Midwest.[121] Furthermore, those who hailed from Mexico's *ejidos*, communal land grants, had experienced the wave of peasant organizing that swept the Mexican countryside during the 1970s.[122] In Georgia, however, they chose not to emulate the oppositional strategies of their peers elsewhere. True, they were never the target of a concerted organizing campaign by an established farmworkers' union as, say, cucumber pickers in Mount Olive, North Carolina, were.[123] But they also did not initiate walkouts or protests on their own like their historical antecedents in Mississippi and Arkansas or their Latino contemporaries in Morganton and Immokalee. Structurally, Immokalee farmworkers were at least as disempowered as southern Georgia farmworkers; oppression alone cannot explain the different paths these migrant communities chose.

Rather, these disparate strategies reflect the contingencies of the migrant experience itself. Workers who came of age in Central Mexico in the 1960s, 1970s, and 1980s had different expectations of citizenship and ideas about labor than earlier Mexican immigrants, immigrants from southern Mexico, or workers like those in Immokalee and Morganton who had resisted oppressive regimes in Haiti or Guatemala. Work regimens and paternalistic growers on Georgia's comparatively smaller farms subjected Mexicanos to some forms of exploitation but not others that their compatriots protested elsewhere. And Georgia's charity-minded white church people alleviated the worst of migrants' poverty and isolation, brokering Mexicanos' relationships with local authorities and creating opportunities for them to recreate away from farm labor camps—opportunities that were attractive, yet not conducive to organizing.

Citizenship after Mexico's Golden Age

When José Luís Landa and Manuel Gallegos led sixty-five of their fellow braceros in a work stoppage on an Arkansas farm in 1948, they chose September 16, Mexican Independence Day, to begin the strike.[124] These men had come to the United States with both the Mexican state's promise of protection and the Mexican nation's mandate for the individual and collective improvement of rural men like themselves.[125] But much had changed in the following thirty years. Mexican migrants of the 1970s–90s, families like Israel Cortez's, had come of age during and after the decline of the Mexican state's economic and rhetorical support for social justice and the poor.[126] Leaders of the long-ruling Institutional Revolutionary Party (Partido Revolucionario Institucional, or PRI) increasingly used violence on their own people over the course of the 1960s, culminating in the massacre of student protesters in Mexico City's Tlatelolco district in 1968. The massacre highlighted the state's loss of control over the narrative of Mexican political development, exposing severe internal fissures both nationally and internationally.[127] The economic crisis of the 1980s, known as Mexico's "lost decade," cemented the loss of public faith in the PRI while depriving the state of the resources needed to fund its huge apparatus. It also accelerated the ruling party's withdrawal from the policies of economic protectivism, state intervention in the economy, and rural land redistribution that had marked Mexico's golden age. By 1992, two-thirds of rural Mexicans were laborers, not landowners.[128] Presidents and party leaders now promoted the notion that Mexican nationalism and sovereignty would be best advanced not through cross-class solidarity but rather by assuring Mexico's competitiveness in the global market.[129]

Raised in this new historical moment, most Mexican immigrants looked to the United States not as a beacon of modernization and improvement but rather as a place where they could earn enough money to halt or at least slow the steady decline in their standard of living. Teodora Marín, for example, was landless in Guerrero while Petra Soto and her children were poor in Coahuila; both migrated to Texas and eventually to Georgia in the 1980s.[130] The Sotos, Maríns, and other families like them expected that, over time, their sacrifices would pay off in dollars. They also believed that agricultural labor was a respectable vocation and that they should be able to live and work in the United States without suffering physical violence or harassment.

Developments in Mexico not only shaped Mexican immigrants' expectations of citizenship and labor; they also neutralized what had once been their most important ally in the U.S. South: Mexican consulates. The demise of the bracero program constituted one element of the Mexican state's retreat between 1960 and 1990. U.S. employers were still hungry for labor but unwilling to negotiate bilateral contracts with Mexico because of both liberal criticism and agribusiness greediness, so migration streams from Mexico to the United States became increasingly undocumented. The new undocumented immigration eliminated Mexican bureaucrats' erstwhile role as middlemen with the power to cut off the labor supply from uncooperative farmers. Though Mexico opened a consulate in Atlanta during the late 1970s, it dealt with business and trade matters, not migrant protection, in its early years.[131] Even once the Atlanta consular staff began visiting migrant work sites in the mid-1980s, they involved themselves only in individuals' legal matters, mostly supporting criminal defendants or workers trying to collect unpaid wages.[132] The consular corps' retreat from its onetime role as defender of Mexicans' collective rights in the U.S. South reflected the new emphasis on individual over group claims in Mexican political discourse as well as a lack of sufficient budget and personnel to meaningfully complete the work of *protección*.[133]

From the perspectives of migrants, the disaffection was mutual. Having lived through "the end of faith in the Leviathan" of the Mexican state, Georgia's Mexican immigrants mistrusted and evaded consular officials rather than turning to them for support.[134] When Mexican officials visited Cedartown in 1985, for example, Mexican workers at the Zartic plant reported that they had not "been harassed by any group or person in this town"—a finding belied by the anti-Mexican violence surrounding the murder case just two years earlier.[135] Similarly, when officials responded to a newspaper article about anti-Mexican discrimination in Gainesville, they were told by immigrants there that "at the moment they did not have any problem with authorities or civilians in this community."[136] While the South's Mexican immigrants three decades before walked dozens of miles and risked employer retribution to involve consuls in their struggles, by the 1980s they no longer believed that Mexican citizenship gave them, poor emigrants, the ability to make claims on the Mexican state.

Migrant Labor, Migrant Life

Mexican immigrants to the United States in the 1970s–90s, including those in Georgia, largely hailed from rural areas in Mexico. But by the 1980s, most did not have their own land and a quarter had first migrated to Mexico City or the border region in search of wages.[137] Both their lived experiences and the Mexican government's new discourse of individual self-sufficiency and global competitiveness had already exposed them to the restrictive and thankless qualities of low-wage labor.

Yet for all of its privations, migrant farmwork offered certain advantages over other forms of low-wage labor. Rather than dispersing to different factories or parts of the assembly line, families could spend all day in the fields together.[138] Many preferred outdoor work to indoor and believed in the inherent worth of farm labor. "I preferred the field to a factory because I was in the open air," explained Anselma Gómez, who had previously worked in a shrimp-processing plant in Texas.[139] And perhaps most important, Mexicanos expected that once they got a foothold in the region, they would be able to contract their own work directly with farmers or even become crew leaders themselves.[140]

While documentary evidence from journalists and government officials has allowed for a reconstruction of migrants' routes and work routines, they reveal little about migrants' own understandings of life and labor in the 1970s and 1980s. Diaries and other written records from their perspectives are not available, nor did scholars conduct interviews with migrant workers in Georgia during that time. Oral histories recorded two or three decades later provide insight but may be colored by nostalgia, particularly among those who have since "made it" into the middle class.[141]

Yet there is one type of enduring document that Mexican Americans and Mexican migrants produced constantly as they labored in the fields of Georgia in the 1970s, 1980s, and 1990s: family snapshots and photo albums.

Mexicanos had used family photographs to assert their own identities against U.S. society's racialization of them since the 1920s.[142] By the late 1970s, access to cameras had expanded dramatically on both sides of the border, as U.S. Americans of all income levels purchased them in equal shares and the market for cameras in Mexico grew by double-digit percentage points each year.[143] For this generation of Mexican migrant workers—indeed, for most of the hemisphere's families in the twentieth century—personal photographs rather than written records thus constitute the most extensive archive of daily experiences available to historians. They document the stories that families created and passed down about themselves, revealing the ways migrants saw the world, rather than just how the world saw them.[144] Migrant photographers' choices of what to include and exclude, migrant subjects' choices of which expression to wear when facing the camera, and migrant family historians' decisions about which photos to keep and how to arrange them in albums all reinforced particular ideas about the meaning of family and the place of migrant labor within it.[145]

The personal photo collections of three migrant families who settled in Georgia, two Mexican and one Mexican American, show that family togetherness, self-sufficiency, and most of all independence were prized components of these families' narratives both during their years of farm labor and in subsequent decades. To be sure, these families represent the subset of the migrant population that was successful enough to remain in the area, though not all rose to be crew leaders. Furthermore, it is difficult to account for the ways each member of each family understood each album.

Yet considered alongside oral history interviews, the albums as a whole provide a precious window into the ways migrant parents conceptualized the relationship between their labors and their lives. Photo albums of white middle-class families have usually excluded images of employment or housework, thus erasing labor from the family story and reinforcing a divide between labor and leisure.[146] An earlier generation of Mexican farmworkers also shied away from sharing images of themselves performing degrading agricultural labor.[147] In contrast, Mexicanos who migrated and labored together with their families in 1970s–90s Georgia snapped, developed, and preserved copious photographs of themselves working in the fields. Albums made no separation between farmwork, on the one hand, and family or leisure time, on the other.[148] For the two families who hailed from Mexico, the message was doubly clear: unlike the braceros and male migrants who had once departed their villages alone, these families traveled and worked as a unit.

The economic structure and work routines of migrant agricultural labor bore little resemblance to those of smallholder production in rural Mexico. Yet once families owned their own cars and began to arrange work directly with farmers, they retained a sense of independence and control over their own time and labor. Teodora Marín recalled in an oral history interview that she did not like moving around so much; she hoped her family's years of constant migration would be few.[149] Yet she still devoted an entire page from her family's album to photos of their station wagon, the trailer of possessions they carried behind them, and the view from the windshield of the highway stretched out ahead (fig. 14). The photos demonstrate a conscious attempt to document the Marín family's travels as they were taking place and to incorporate those travels, however difficult, into the family story. Three photos depict the station wagon and trailer at the side of the road, indicating that a family member paused amid the driving routine to capture the moment for future reflection. Seemingly out of place among the photos taken of and from the family station wagon in outdoor settings, the album maker included an interior shot of a toddler sitting on a leather couch. The photo's place on a page of car and road shots might have elicited sadness in Mrs. Marín, who regretted the need to travel for work.[150] Yet it also highlighted the mundane pleasures of family life, which the Marín family could enjoy in part because of the wages and independence that migrant labor afforded them.

The pages of the Gómez family album from the 1970s also blend images of migrant labor with those of family and leisure time. Having cars "in good condition" was always important for the family, Anselma said, and their albums show this.[151] As in the Marín album, one page of the Gómez album includes a Polaroid of the orange-and-white family station wagon alongside one of a baby (fig. 15). Below sits an image of a family trip to Busch Gardens in Florida. Again, the story of each photo depends on the others that surround it: the mobility of the station wagon enabled the nurturing of the baby and the leisure of the theme park. The album pages confirm Anselma's recollection that she appreciated farm labor's seasonality because it allowed the family to visit relatives for weeks at a time—unlike the shrimp-packing plant where she got only one week of vacation per year.[152] The family's use of a more expensive Polaroid camera rather than a traditional film camera signaled their investment in viewing these images of themselves instantaneously.[153]

The orange-and-white family station wagon appears again on a subsequent album page (fig. 16). Here it sits in the cucumber fields of Georgia a few feet from Gómez family members as they perform stoop labor in 1984. "I always taught my kids . . . that farm labor is not denigrating, but something to help you get a better life," said Anselma Gómez in an interview; the album page

FIGURE 14 A page from a Marín family album depicting the family's journeys north from Florida in the 1970s. Courtesy of Teodora Marín, Cedar Crossing, Georgia.

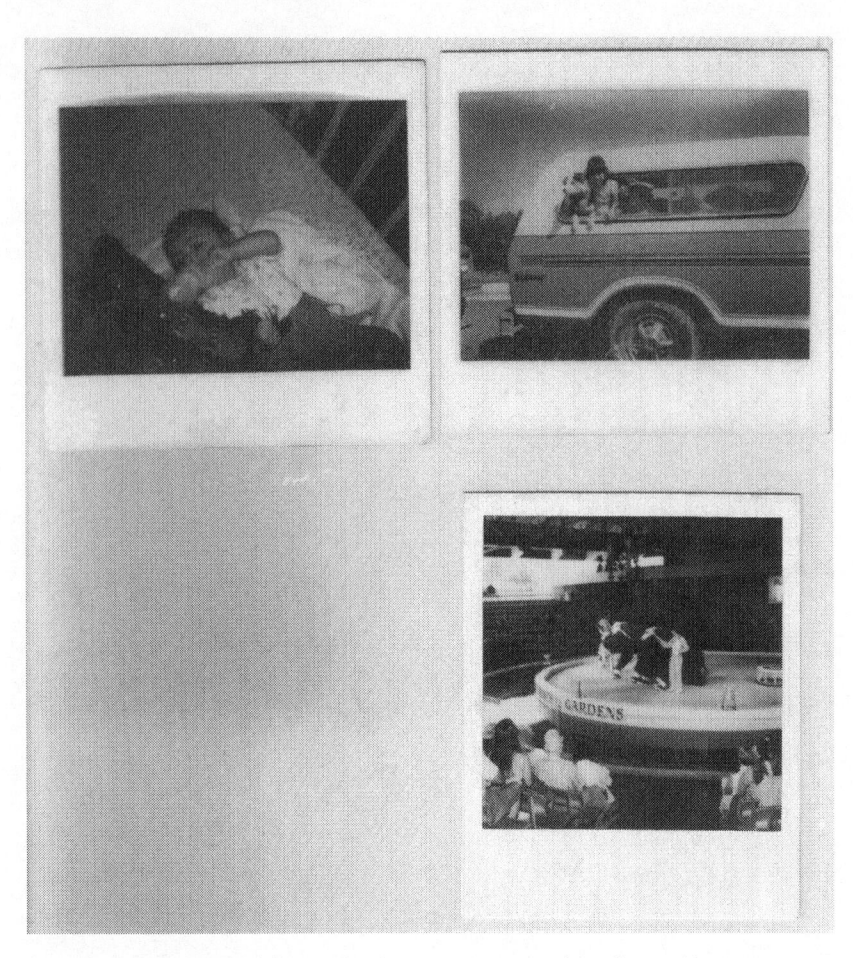

FIGURE 15 Gómez family album, Florida, 1970s. Courtesy of Anselma and José Gómez, Nicholls, Georgia.

shows that her children at least nominally agreed. Two family members in the photo ignore the camera, perhaps unaware that they are being photographed as they focus on the task at hand. But two others smile at the photographer, offering their agreement that agricultural labor was a worthy subject for a picture. The presence of the station wagon at the edge of the frame and the exclusion of other laborers who may have been present in the fields that day helped the Gómezes remind themselves that, however difficult their actual work, they performed agricultural labor on their own terms, moved about in their own car, worked together as a unit, and exerted some control over their own financial progress. Anselma did not want "someone looking over me to say what I do or don't do," and the photo's framing conveys that she achieved

FIGURE 16 Gómez family album, Georgia, 1980s. Courtesy of Anselma and José Gómez, Nicholls, Georgia.

just that in the fields of Georgia.[154] Again, the album page further joined the joys of family to the hardships of wage labor by placing the photo in an album alongside one depicting the family life cycle—in this case, a wedding.

In one case, the Gómez family utilized a photo caption to explicitly transmit their values to their offspring.[155] A loose Polaroid of farm labor (fig. 17),

Pro-immigrant Conservatism in Rural Georgia   145

FIGURE 17 Gómez family photograph of agricultural labor in Georgia, ca. 1983; inscription on back reads, "At Work." Courtesy of Anselma and José Gómez, Nicholls, Georgia.

taken in Georgia in 1983, has written on the back, in English, "At Work." It depicts four male farm laborers, indeed at work, an overseer observing and directing from a tractor, and a woman riding in the tractor's rear flatbed. The Gómezes' English skills were limited; why would they have captioned the photo in English, "At Work"? Most likely, the choice invited their descendants at some future date to see the photograph and marvel at how far the family had come from its humble beginnings in the United States. After all, once their grandchildren were born, the Gómezes would take them out to pick tobacco for a few hours in order to instill an appreciation for the grueling nature of farm labor. The message was, in Anselma's words, "Study, and God will bring the reward."[156]

Historians have shown that factories run according to Fordist principles of welfare capitalism enabled workers, including Mexican American workers, to view their workplaces as positive sites of identity formation in the postwar years.[157] While it may be more difficult to imagine that racialized low-wage agricultural workers viewed their places of work with similar pride and loyalty, the interviews and photo albums show that many of those traveling in family groups did see it this way. Such a perspective certainly would not have precluded labor organizing, as indeed it did not for industrial workers.[158] Yet if Mexicano agricultural workers were receptive to the analyses of farmworker organizers in Ohio, labor progressives in Wisconsin, Chicano movement veterans in Oregon, and Haitian farmworker activists in Florida, so too were they able to view their work life within the metaphors of self-help that southern Georgia's white farmers and church people would ultimately offer them.[159] While Mexicanos never denied the exploitative dimensions of farm labor or erased them from their memories and accounts, it was this latter story of independence, self-sufficiency, togetherness, and progress that most ultimately chose to tell themselves.[160]

Postwar Liberalism and Migrants' Brief Great Society

Of course, more critical analyses of poverty did circulate in the United States in the 1960s through 1980s, and these ideas had a long history in southern Georgia as well. African Americans in the area had flocked to black nationalist Garveyism in the 1920s and participated in interracial packinghouse unionization drives in the 1940s. Yet over the subsequent twenty years, the area's white residents recommitted themselves to preserving segregation through any means necessary, including violence.[161] As a result, the civil rights movement struggled mightily to make gains in southern Georgia.[162] Still, events on the national stage in the 1950s–70s familiarized African Americans and Mexican Americans nearly everywhere with the era's ideologies of rights, citizenship, and redress of historical inequalities. Scholars have shown how Mexican Americans seized this historical moment to claim their place as Americans with the full rights of any other citizen, most notably in South Texas, where they were the demographic majority, and in places with more progressive political traditions, like California and Wisconsin.[163]

Though black agricultural workers in Florida had led a unionization drive in 1971, no such activity took place among black workers in Georgia.[164] The area's African American working class had forged earlier movements for justice, but black students and professionals led southern Georgia's most prominent postwar civil rights struggle, in the city of Albany.[165] While black farmworkers in nearby states were largely interstate migrants, those in southern Georgia were cut off from that circuit; they were locals, many elderly, who enjoyed little political support from the rising black middle class.[166] Their work devalued on a communal level, they had little incentive to organize an industry they hoped to soon leave behind.[167] As the movement's gains opened new opportunities for African Americans' economic and physical mobility in the 1970s, those who remained in farm labor did have extensive contact with Mexicano migrants but did not engage them in cultivating an alternative politics. José and Anselma Gómez remembered having wide-ranging discussions of politics and society with their black fellow farmworkers. These men and women suggested that the Gómezes were foolish to work so hard for so little money when they could receive government support instead. Anselma insisted back, "I want something that's my own."[168] Though such conversations allowed blacks and Mexicanos to compare notes about work, wages, and strategies for survival, they did not lead Mexicanos to adopt an openly critical stance toward the area's race and labor relations. If anything, these interactions helped Mexicanos strengthen their own family narratives of independence and hard work by contrasting themselves with African Americans, echoing the public discourse of local white elites.[169]

In Georgia, Mexicanos did benefit from the political legacy of the civil rights era through participation in War on Poverty programs as clients and, occasionally, as administrators. Yet both timing and geography caused their participation to be much more limited there than elsewhere. In southern Georgia, social service programs such as Head Start, food stamps, and migrant health clinics started reaching out to Mexicanos in the 1980s, nearly two decades after Lyndon Johnson first declared the "War on Poverty"—and at precisely the moment that President Ronald Reagan's administration declared that war "lost" and began to attack its foot soldiers.[170] For example, the first Migrant Head Start program in the Vidalia area opened in 1982—the same year a local migrant health program that had "worked very well" was defunded.[171]

Furthermore, federal programs distributed resources via local agencies, and these agencies' interest in serving Mexicano migrants was decidedly mixed. Migrant Education, for example, was indirectly beholden to local power holders, including farmers; thus social services workers were dissuaded from challenging labor and political relations.[172] Though the food stamps program did not rigorously monitor immigration status at that time, only 163 of the thousands of migrant farmworkers in Georgia were enrolled in the program in 1980. Two college interns at the Women, Infants, and Children (WIC) social program noted that public health services were vastly underutilized by migrant women because of language barriers and transportation problems. "More unwillingness to cooperate existed among the WIC staff than among the migrants," they wrote.[173]

Legal Aid, which served as an important means for farmworkers to redress grievances in other parts of the country, was also pushed into retreat just as it began to serve Mexicano clients in Georgia. In 1983, Ronald Reagan's administration forbade federally funded legal aid programs from representing undocumented immigrants; shortly thereafter, the Georgia Legal Services

Program tried to transfer several undocumented workers' cases to the under-resourced Mexican consulate.[174] Growers who had paid major judgments to farmworkers with legal aid representation pressured politicians to crack down on "troublemaking" lawyers. In nearby North Carolina, Farmworkers Legal Services won several judgments against growers and soon found itself under investigation at the urging of Senator Jesse Helms. Though no violations were found, legal aid agencies in states where growers held substantial power knew that they had been put on notice.[175]

If Mexicanos in southern Georgia had little opportunity to benefit from Great Society programs, they had even less opportunity to lead them. Struggles over community control of Great Society social service agencies served as a catalyst for pro-migrant political activism in more liberal environments such as Milwaukee.[176] But local conservative politics notoriously hampered the implementation of antipoverty programs in rural southern communities.[177] In Georgia, participation in Great Society institutions as clients did bring Mexicanos into contact with sympathetic middle-class African Americans, some of whom had experienced the region's civil rights struggles. These social service workers quickly came to regard Mexicanos as their primary clients, learning a bit of Spanish to communicate with them.[178] But they too had learned to tread lightly in the overall conservative climate of southern Georgia. While some local NAACP chapters attempted to register eligible Mexicans and Mexican Americans to vote, middle-class blacks in southern Georgia never adopted the immigrants' cause as their own.[179]

Of course, those Mexican Americans who moved to Georgia from Texas or Florida as young adults had come of age in places where the liberal ideologies of the civil rights era manifested differently. One person with such migrant experiences, Andrea Hinojosa, would eventually use the tattered remains of the Great Society—dwindling federal antipoverty funds—to challenge southern Georgia's political order as so many Mexican Americans elsewhere in the United States had done.[180] Florida's more developed migrant education program gave Hinojosa her first job away from the fields around 1980.[181] She returned to farm labor for a few years thereafter, joining her sister who had settled in Lyons, Georgia. There she joined the newly opened Head Start as a paraprofessional and went on to social services and organizing positions funded by various antipoverty federal grants. Such a grant helped Hinojosa found the Southeast Georgia Communities Project (SEGCP) in 1995. SEGCP initially targeted migrant camps for health education outreach. But as the only Latino-run agency in the area, the project quickly expanded beyond social services to challenge local officials on matters including migrant education and racial profiling by the local sheriff's deputies. For years the area's first major Latino organization received hate mail from locals unconvinced by the public consensus that Latinos were good for the rural economy.[182]

Attuned to the risks of challenging the status quo, the vast majority of Mexican and Mexican American workers used antipoverty programs primarily for basic subsistence needs, if at all, rather than as springboards for political empowerment. Coming of age as migrants and immigrants a half-generation later than their counterparts elsewhere who were active in the 1970s, these workers missed the heyday of such programs' influence in the lives of minority communities—an influence that had been always been more limited in the rural South. As a whole, the liberal ideologies of the civil rights era and the Great Society did not have much opportunity to shape the lives, politics, and expectations of Mexican and Mexican American migrant workers in Georgia.

Pro-God, Pro-business, Pro-Mexican

Yet if Georgia's Mexicano migrant workers arrived a bit late for the liberal ascendance of the 1960s and 1970s, they came just in time for the conservative resurgence of the 1980s. By that decade, white people in the rural South were actively rebuilding their worldviews after the civil rights movement discredited their previous conservative ideology, white supremacy.[183] The arrival of Mexicans and Mexican Americans at this moment provided local whites with an ideal building block for their celebration of color-blind conservatism, individual self-help, and Christian values. Soon, a pro-immigrant, pro-"Hispanic" stance became an integral part of the area's new conservative belief system.

The moral power of evangelical Protestantism increasingly aligned itself with the economic power of large business during this period, and southern Georgia was no exception.[184] Growers and churches had separate motivations to prevent a populist backlash against Mexicano and other Latino workers, but those motivations were grounded in a common ideological sensibility. Though neither group alone had the power to shape public discourse, the two worked on parallel tracks to achieve a common goal: for more than three decades after the arrival of the immigrants, no movement opposing their presence took root in rural southern Georgia.

More so than their counterparts in Florida or California, Georgia's fruit and vegetable farmers had personal contact with their labor force on a regular basis. Though southern Georgia's farms expanded in size over the course of the 1960s and 1970s, the vast majority were still owned by local individuals and families through the 1990s.[185] Comparatively, they remained small. In 1987, most of the harvested crop land in Georgia was in farms of 500 acres or less, while in Florida most was in farms of 2,000 acres or more.[186] Growers in southern Georgia still generally lived on or near the farm property and were intimately involved in its daily operations. They were acutely aware of their increasing dependence on Mexicano labor. And they were powerful voices in local communities, affecting local politics, culture, and institutions, including law enforcement.[187]

Growers' choices about how to relate to their Mexicano workers thus encompassed multiple considerations. They sought to maximize profit by spending as little money as possible on labor. They sought to retain access to Mexicano workers by actively promoting positive images of them in the community and discouraging police harassment. And for some farmers, this relationship held an additional possibility. For them, being good Christians and good people meant that obviously poor employees should also be objects of charity and goodwill across boundaries of race and nation. The terms of this imagining had evolved from previous forms of paternalism in southern agricultural labor relations.

Certainly, farmers' first priority was to earn a profit. Increasingly squeezed by competition from cheap imported fruits and vegetables, they turned to high-value specialty crops like Vidalia onions but needed reliable, seasonal, and inexpensive labor to make their investment worthwhile. As such, they assiduously resisted each round of implemented or proposed U.S. Labor Department regulations that would require them to provide toilets, water, hand-washing facilities, or child care to workers, referring to such measures as "just another government regulation that . . . adds to the cost."[188] Even more odious to farmers were proposals to make it easier for farmworkers to sue them or to hold growers accountable for the labor violations of their crew leaders.[189] To justify their opposition to regulation of their fields, powerful growers publicly praised Mexican laborers for their apparent willingness to work hard under unfavorable conditions.[190] They made it known to local officials that their economy depended on Mexicanos' willingness to work in the area, curtailing police harassment in some times and places.[191]

For some growers, however, Mexicano laborers were not just productivity machines whose praises needed to be sung in public. In a local culture with strong Evangelical influence, Mexicano workers comprised so many souls who could be saved and poor people who could be uplifted. In this way, growers could conceive of Mexicano workers as physically and spiritually needy members of the human family who could be grateful recipients of charity and love rather than low-wage laborers with interests opposed to those of their bosses. This attitude grew in part from the newly ubiquitous idea in Christian circles that service, not domination, should guide missionary work now that colonialism was no longer defensible.[192] After four Mexican workers in Fort Valley died in an auto accident in 1994, for example, Jeff Wainright, the owner of the orchard where the deceased migrants worked, explained why he was paying for the funeral and expenses to transport the bodies back to Mexico. "I cared about them," he said. "And not just as employees."[193] There is no reason to doubt Wainright's sincerity; for him, Mexican workers were "not just" employees who enhanced his bottom line. They were also human beings who he believed could connect with him emotionally across barriers of race, nation, and power.

White church leaders, too, sought to transcend boundaries in their relationships with migrant workers. Most of the white churchgoers who became active in migrant ministry were middle-class professionals or business owners, not farmers, and so had fewer competing prerogatives in their work with migrants. Yet like farmers, they had to mind their own reputations in small-town life; church leaders showed little appetite for conflict. They did, however, show a voracious appetite for charity work with Mexican migrants. One Catholic Church official assessing the parish in Vidalia mused in 1985, "One wonders if the interest in migrants were as much as in the negro and white natives, if evangelization among blacks and white natives would not be significantly higher."[194]

But for both Catholic and Protestant church leaders, Mexicano migrants offered an attraction that black and white Americans could not. White Christian southerners' belief in the universalism of humanity demanded "bridge building" and reconciliation across racial and national lines, particularly in the wake of segregation.[195] They trusted that individual acts of racial reconciliation and Christian love, rather than structural changes, would help redeem black communities from poverty and "dysfunction."[196] Yet white churchgoers in the post–civil rights era found that charitable work with African Americans was fraught with pitfalls. Their worldviews were shaped by a post-1960s conservatism that emphasized the individual not only in spiritual matters but also in matters of political and economic justice. Rural white Evangelicals thus recoiled against black Protestants' insistence that reconciliation required structural change, antidiscrimination legislation, and a robust welfare state.[197] And besides, the simple act of venturing into black parts of town could provoke fear in even the most well-intentioned middle-class white churchgoers.[198]

With Mexicanos, in contrast, white church leaders could fulfill their moral ambitions to forge personal charitable relationships across racial boundaries without encountering objectionable political ideologies or menacing black neighborhoods.[199] Charity with Mexicano migrants did not bear the taint of longtime racial struggles. Rather, it inspired the same idealism, adventurousness, and volunteers as foreign mission work.[200] For Mary Ann Thurman, work with Mexican men was "the fulfillment of a childhood dream, to be a missionary."[201] Baptists Sonny and Ruth Bridges did not notice Moultrie's Mexican migrants until they returned from a mission trip to Honduras in 1996. Sonny bought two Spanish dictionaries and used them to start teaching himself Spanish; on the weekends, he would hang out in the local Walmart to practice with the Spanish-speaking customers. Over the coming years, Sonny and Ruth Bridges would take more than twenty missionary trips to Mexico and Central America while also throwing themselves into Baptist migrant ministry efforts in Moultrie. "I just enjoy being involved in a different culture," Sonny Bridges explained.[202]

Nearly all Mexicanos were Catholic on arrival in Georgia, but most were nonetheless reluctant to attend Catholic churches there in the early 1980s.[203] By the mid-1980s, however, Mexican men who were single or migrating without families began filling the pews of Catholic churches. The Thurmans noticed the newcomers at St. Juliana Catholic Church in Fort Valley and soon organized dozens of volunteers to teach English, provide refreshments, donate clothes, and, in one case, offer free weekly free haircuts to the men. The Thurmans were distressed to learn that some workers were so hungry that they ate the chrysanthemums near the orchard where they worked. So the couple engaged local Protestant churches, Kiwanis clubs, and stores to start a food bank for the migrant workers.[204] Soon Mary Ann Thurman found herself driving Mexican young men from migrant labor camps to church each Sunday, unable to understand the Spanish-language sounds that filled her car.[205]

Protestant denominations, particularly Baptists, seized the opportunity to extend the mission work they had conducted for decades in Latin America.[206] Baptist schoolteacher Carolyn Flowers came to migrant ministry after a series of personal encounters with Mexican migrants near Tifton. Around 1983, Flowers saw a young Mexican woman talking on a public telephone, distraught that her husband had been jailed. Flowers helped the woman place her call and recounted the incident to her missionary women's group, which began paying visits to migrant camps. One day shortly thereafter, a truck of Mexican migrant workers drove past Flowers, and she flashed on the biblical instruction to entertain strangers because they might be angels in disguise.[207] For Flowers, outreach to Mexicans in migrant labor camps was an ideal opportunity to put her devout Christian beliefs into action. One Baptist minister in Oglethorpe wanted to construct a cinderblock church near the migrant camps since "his congregation is not in favor of welcoming Mexican-Americans into their own building," but many more churches took the opposite tack, encouraging contact between white and Mexican parishioners.[208] Growers Wendell and Janis Roberson's Victory Tabernacle Church of God, for example, offered Spanish classes for English-speaking parishioners, arranged simultaneous translation of worship services, and conducted fundraisers to help finance migrants' transportation to the main church.[209]

Concerned white church leaders who sought out Mexicano migrants all had to start their efforts at the same place: with local growers. Most migrant workers still lived in housing provided by growers or crew leaders, and there could be no access to migrants without their employers' consent. Protestant churches had the advantage that many growers, such as the Robersons, sat in their own pews on Sundays. Sonny and Ruth Bridges received permission from Kent Hamilton to visit workers on his produce farm near Moultrie.[210] Catholics, a sometimes-suspect minority in these parts, could have a more difficult time. Sister Patricia Brown was at first rebuffed by some farmers who she surmised were "wary of any outsiders who might criticize the work conditions, housing or wages." Still, other farmers were "very cooperative" in pointing out their camps to Brown and introducing her to crew leaders.[211]

If growers initially feared that church volunteers would decry their labor practices, their qualms were fast allayed. In the public sphere, farmers' discourses and church leaders' were of a piece—and occasionally were coordinated. Rather than criticize farm labor conditions, church volunteers became trusted local voices insisting that Mexicano migrant workers were good people whose values mirrored those of local communities. White church leaders in rural Georgia self-consciously pursued a role as mediators between Mexicano migrant workers, growers, and would-be instigators of anti-immigrant backlash. Ruth Bridges drew on her missionary experiences to admonish skeptics, "If you would go to their country you would understand why they're here. You would understand that they come here to work and they send most of their money home."[212] One hundred miles north in Fort Valley in 1988, Mary Ann Thurman met privately with peach grower Duke Lane and pushed him, gently, to improve migrants' housing conditions. "I want to help you, too," she offered in a follow-up letter. "As you must know, many people are very opposed to the migrants being in our area. . . . I think that if the people in

FIGURE 18 Westfield School students and migrant children at an Easter egg hunt, 1990. Courtesy of Mary Ann and Howdy Thurman, Fort Valley, Georgia.

this community share in helping the Mexicans, it will help them to become more tolerant."[213] Church leaders like Ruth Bridges and Mary Ann Thurman worked self-consciously and deliberately to prevent private anti-immigrant grumblings from rising to the level of prominent public discourse.

They also indirectly protected growers from criticism by providing for the basic needs of migrants who otherwise did not earn enough to subsist. Mary Ann Thurman openly acknowledged the inadequacy of migrants' pay in her appeals to fellow church people for funds. The appeals naturalized this shortfall, rather than questioning it. "At the present, the Mexicans are thinning the young peaches," Thurman wrote in April 1991. "We expect another lull in the work between the thinning and the picking of the peaches. Supplementary food will probably be needed then, too."[214] Church volunteers and officials thus described Mexican workers as charity cases, both eliding the basic fact that the workers *worked* and carefully avoiding any implication that farmers might bear some responsibility for their poverty. Whatever church volunteers' personal views, their public actions strategically touted the migrant cause in ways that accepted the local status quo.

Given the ubiquitous influence of churches in rural Georgia, charity projects directed at Mexican migrants quickly spread to other quarters. In 1990, a Spanish teacher at the Westfield Christian private school in Perry brought high school students to visit with Mexican migrant kids at a local camp and sponsored an Easter egg hunt and lunch for them. Several of the high school students had already been going to the camp regularly to serve as Big Brothers and Big Sisters to the migrant kids (fig. 18).[215] The Westfield School had been founded in 1969, a year that saw a boom in new Christian private schools as the Supreme Court and Internal Revenue Service moved to deny tax-exempt status to private schools explicitly defined as whites only.[216] In a county that was nearly half black, this school founded to avoid integration eagerly pursued charity toward the Mexicans who comprised just 1 percent of the local population. What the Mexican poor offered that the black poor could not was an experience that highlighted international exchange rather than the legacy of segregation.

Envisioning Pro-immigrant Conservatism

The actions and attitudes of white growers and middle-class Christians in rural Georgia opened a new phase of paternalism in the history of southern labor and race relations. Historically, paternalism—as practiced under the slavery or sharecropping systems—was the opposite of free-market capitalism. Growers would (at least theoretically) provide for the basic needs of "their" workers in exchange for labor. Little, if any, money changed hands between the parties, denying workers the ability to sell their labor or cotton to the highest bidder.[217] Paternalism could also be political, as when white progressives claimed themselves to be adequate advocates for blacks' "uplift" but created no space for blacks to forge their own political movements on their own terms.[218] Such paternalism was often associated with the efforts of religious, particularly Protestant, denominations.

Now the paternalistic expressions of southern Georgia's white leaders offered Christian, universalistic, and humanistic responses to post-1960s concerns about local and global inequality. Planters were not economically paternalistic, as they preferred not to be responsible for workers' housing and food if they could avoid it.[219] Rather, they and their church-based allies espoused a belief that although Mexicans were poor because Mexico was backward, their poverty demanded a loving response from good Christians.[220] Mexicans were assuredly human beings just like white growers and church leaders, equal in the eyes of God. Christians should thus respond to their poverty by creating bonds of intimacy and charity. Absent from this view was an acknowledgment of the vast gulf in power between migrants and their white patrons. While earlier white progressives believed that their way of life was superior to that of blacks and immigrants, the post-1960s version insisted on the parties' equality against all evidence of a profound power imbalance.[221]

Among growers, Tifton's Janis Roberson best exemplifies this attitude toward the Mexican men who worked for her and her husband, Wendell, throughout the 1980s and 1990s. Roberson recalled that the first Mexicans and Mexican Americans to plant, cultivate, and harvest greens on her farm arrived in the mid-1980s. In 1989, she and her husband were among the first farmers in the area to contract Mexican workers under the H2A agricultural guest worker program. The program brought foreign workers to labor in the fields of the United States on contracts that limited their stays and effectively tied them down to one employer.[222] While employers were technically required to provide workers with a minimum wage and meet certain standards for their housing, they had the ability not only to fire men who called for enforcement of the contract but also to jeopardize their ability to remain in the United States altogether. "We never had any trouble with any of them," Roberson remembered. "If any of them caused any trouble, we would just ask them to leave."[223] Structurally, then, the Robersons held an enormous amount of power over their workers.[224]

Yet Janis Roberson chose to perceive her relationship to the workers as more intimate and charitable than economic. She would greet returning workers with a hug as they disembarked from their buses (fig. 19). "And whenever they got off the bus, they'd become my children." In an interview, Roberson consistently referred to the farmworkers as "the children" or "the kids." She made a point of celebrating each worker's birthday—or, at least, "the birthday they told us they had" on their immigration documents. Hearing stories of the purchases workers made back in Mexico using their wages from Georgia, Roberson came to believe that her employment of Mexican workers was akin to an act of benevolence. "We felt good about it," she explained, "that we were helping." As evidence that the feeling was mutual, Roberson warmly recalled the sight of H2A workers vying to be pallbearers at Wendell's funeral and filling the church beyond capacity for his memorial service.[225] Fundamentalist Christians, the Robersons also facilitated workers' attendance at Victory Tabernacle Church of God by donating a bus to the church for the purpose of transporting Mexican workers to worship services.[226]

There is indeed some evidence that Roberson might have afforded workers more amenities than other farmers in the area. When other growers complained about new requirements for drinking water, toilets, and handwashing facilities in 1987, Roberson told a reporter that she already provided

FIGURE 19 Janis Roberson hugs H2A workers arriving at her farm, ca. 1990. Courtesy of Janis Roberson, Tifton, Georgia.

those things for her workers and had no problem with the new regulations. "These are human beings," she explained. "We're not going to treat them like animals."[227] Roberson prided herself on having more than just a financial interest in the Mexican immigrant workers who made her farm profitable.

What explains the gap between Roberson's worldview and that of larger-scale growers in nearby Florida? For white growers and church leaders as for migrant workers in southern Georgia, photo albums can provide a window into a worldview unlikely to be recorded in a written journal. White people who interacted with Mexicans as employees or charity cases extensively documented these relationships with cameras. In so doing, they joined a global trend of the late twentieth century. Because it could supposedly be understood across barriers of language and nation, photography promoted the idea, rooted in liberal humanism, that those societal differences did not matter because all people belonged to the same human family.[228]

Many of Roberson's photos, such as those of her greeting migrant workers with a hug, depict togetherness across divides of race and nation. For example, one album page is dedicated to a quinceañera that took place on the farm.

158   *Pro-immigrant Conservatism in Rural Georgia*

FIGURE 20 Wendell Roberson and migrant workers at a quinceañera on the Robersons' farm. Courtesy of Janis Roberson, Tifton, Georgia.

In three photos on the page, Wendell Roberson is featured alongside young Mexican women in taffeta dresses and three white children, presumably Roberson's grandkids. The resultant image echoes a multigenerational family photo, in this case interspersing the grower's generations with the workers' (fig. 20).[229] Other album pages include photographs of the Robersons and their workers enjoying social and recreational events together: Christmas and birthday parties, hunting and fishing trips, and a July 4 barbecue.

Pro-immigrant Conservatism in Rural Georgia

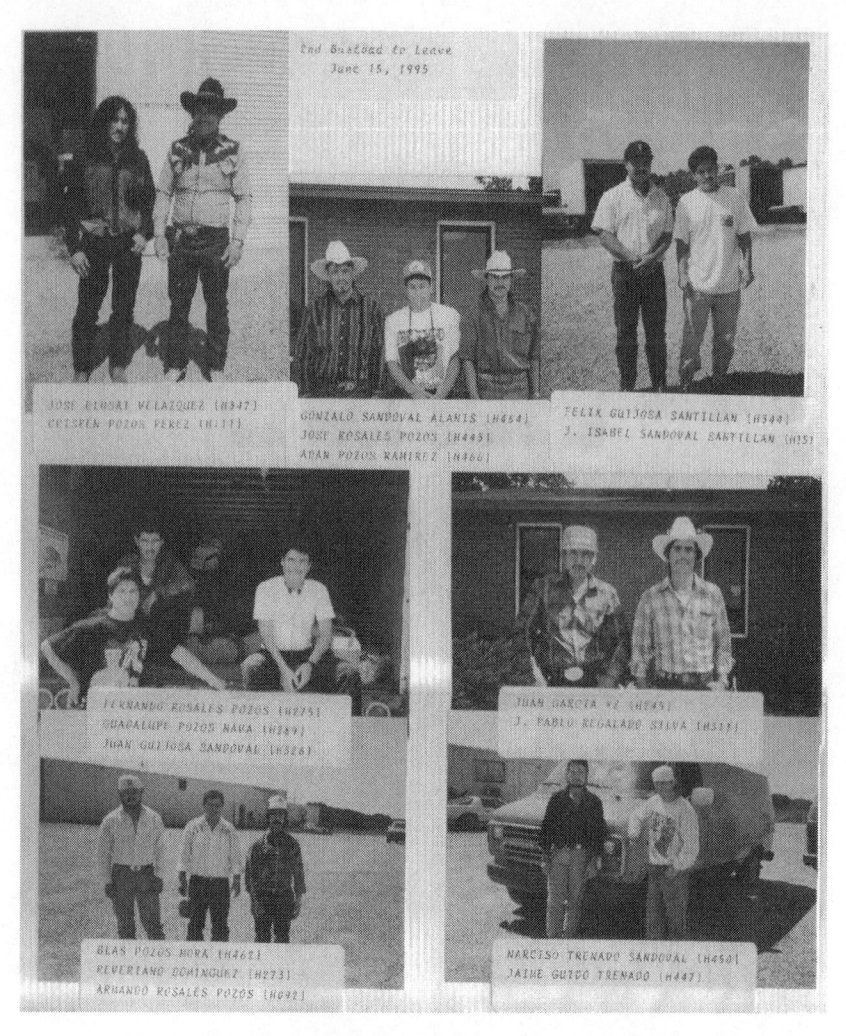

FIGURE 21 H2A workers' photos in the albums of employer Janis Roberson, 1995. Courtesy of Janis Roberson, Tifton, Georgia.

But in other ways, the albums surely reminded Roberson that Mexican migrant workers were just that to her—workers. The bulk of the three albums' pages were filled with simple posed portraits of two to three men at a time (figs. 21 and 22). The purpose of the photographic records, Roberson explained, was to help her learn the men's names and remember them from one year to the next.[230] Roberson created a total of sixty-three pages of labeled worker portraits within three photo albums dedicated to documenting the Mexican workers on her farm. In the photos, the men stare at the camera; while a few smile, the vast majority do not. They appear to have dressed for

160   *Pro-immigrant Conservatism in Rural Georgia*

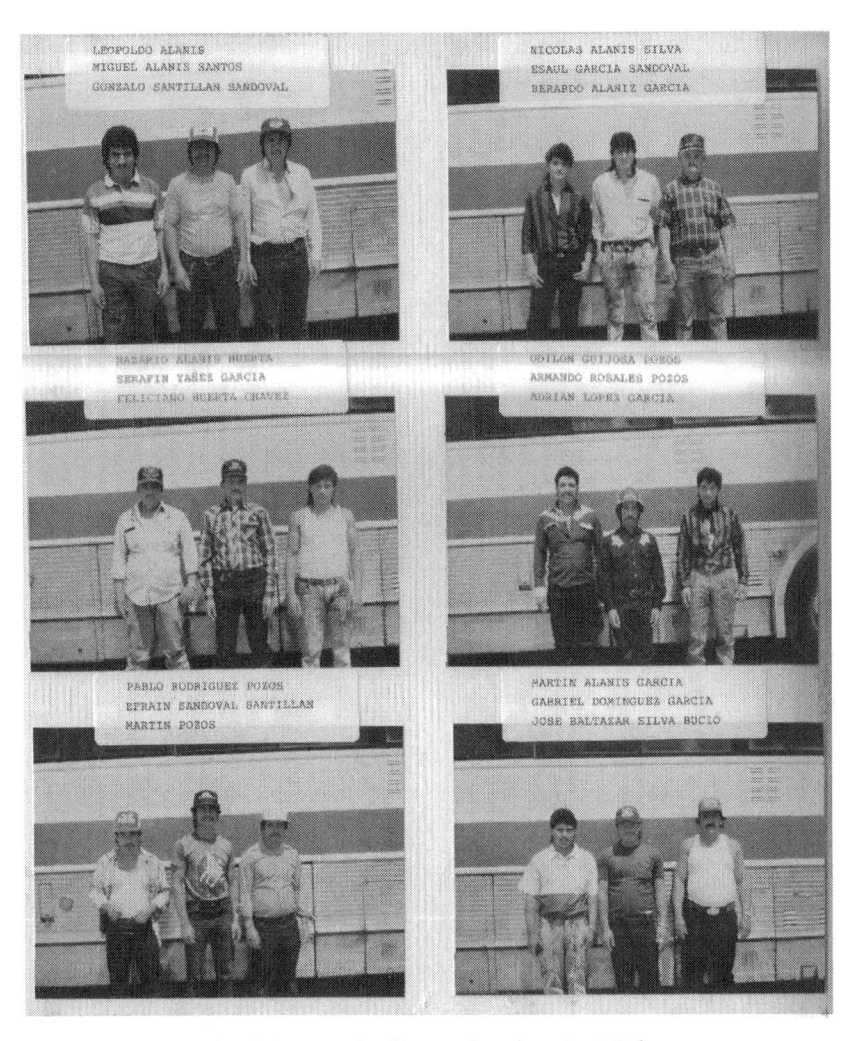

FIGURE 22 H2A workers' photos in the albums of employer Janis Roberson, 1991. Courtesy of Janis Roberson, Tifton, Georgia.

the occasion: most are wearing impeccably clean shirts, some button-down, that do not bear dirt, sweat, or other evidence of farm labor. Under each photograph, a typed label notes each man's name as well as his internal control number for the Robersons' payroll system. The men were human beings, as Roberson liked to emphasize. But they were also employees, identified by number for the purposes of labor management. The contradiction irked at least some of the men. Roberson recalled that some workers would run away and try to avoid being snapped. She believed they wanted to test her memory of their names.[231] Another possibility, perhaps more likely, is that H2A guest workers, unlike their family migrant counterparts, did not view Georgia farm labor in emotional terms. The request to pose for these photos came from a boss, not a wife or brother.[232] Having been hired to harvest vegetables, not pose for photographs, these men may have resisted Roberson's attempts to literally capture the employer–employee relationship and reconfigure it as somehow familial.

Like local growers, white church volunteers developed intimate emotions about the Mexicano migrant workers they got to know. Mary Ann Thurman did keep a written testimony of her experiences working with Mexican migrants, in which she wrote of how "helping" them also helped her recover from the trauma of her son's recent death in a car accident. One night shortly after she began teaching English classes, "I woke up realizing that I had been praying in my sleep. It was a prayer of Thanksgiving for these men and boys that the Lord had sent to me.... It was [as] if after losing one son, the Lord had given me 100 more to love."[233] Though both Thurman and Janis Roberson used metaphors of family to discuss their relationships with Mexican workers, church leaders were far less compromised than growers in their ability to develop mutually satisfying relationships with migrants. While farmers' economic ambitions (maximizing profit) conflicted directly with workers' economic ambitions (maximizing wages), church leaders' moral ambition to serve God and the needy was largely compatible with Mexicans' desire for a life away from the farms, connections in local communities, and a sense of themselves as striving, upwardly mobile workers.[234]

The photos taken by Mary Ann and Howdy Thurman and by Ruth and Sonny Bridges emphasized the crossing of boundaries and the integration of Mexican migrant workers into white families and church communities. Rather than liberal realist images of poverty and desperation in the tradition of *Harvest of Shame*, they showed the values of Christian universalism and liberal humanism in action. For example, a photo of an English class at St. Juliana in Fort Valley depicted a casual camaraderie among whites and Mexicans sitting around a table like any group of peers (fig. 23). Ruth Bridges invited a camp full of Mexican migrant workers to a few of her birthday parties in the late 1990s and captured the moments on film (fig. 24). Both couples preserved photographs of migrant workers celebrating Christmas in their homes (fig. 25). Sonny Bridges enjoyed teaching Mexican men to make ice cream and also enjoyed looking back at photos of the lessons (fig. 26). In all, the church volunteers' photographs came to serve as visual proof that, in Sonny's words, "they want our friendship ... they're human beings just like I am."[235]

FIGURE 23 English class at St. Juliana Catholic Church, Fort Valley, Georgia, ca. 1988. Courtesy of Mary Ann and Howdy Thurman, Fort Valley.

FIGURE 24 Ruth and Sonny Bridges invited Mexican workers to Ruth's birthday party in the early 2000s. Courtesy of Ruth and Sonny Bridges, Moultrie, Georgia.

FIGURE 25 Mary Ann Thurman in her home with migrant workers at Christmas, 1988. Courtesy of Mary Ann and Howdy Thurman, Fort Valley, Georgia.

FIGURE 26 Sonny Bridges teaching a Mexican agricultural worker how to make ice cream. Courtesy of Ruth and Sonny Bridges, Moultrie, Georgia.

FIGURE 27 Mexican migrant family, Fort Valley, Georgia, ca. 1988. Courtesy of Mary Ann and Howdy Thurman, Fort Valley.

Mexicans' Views of White Employers and Church Volunteers

Examined closely, church leaders' photos can also reveal something else: that Mexicano migrant workers reciprocated church leaders' interest in personal relationships, if not in exactly the ways that church leaders hoped. Mexican migrant workers look far more at ease in the photos by Sonny and Ruth Bridges and those by the Thurmans than in Roberson's. One man pictured at Ruth Bridges's birthday party raised his pointer finger in the back of the group, grinning as he called attention to himself (see fig. 24). In a photograph from around 1988, a migrant family prepared themselves for the Thurmans to take their picture (fig. 27). They posed in the style of U.S. middle-class family portraits: groomed for the occasion and gathered together to smile directly at the camera. Journalists never captured them this way, and the family likely appreciated the respect that the Thurmans' approach conveyed.

Most Mexicano migrant workers did not concern themselves with the underlying ideologies of pro-immigrant conservatism. Rather, they understood that white people had more power than they did. Relationships with white volunteers gave Mexicano workers social connections in otherwise alienating places.[236] Middle-class white volunteers in church vans could negotiate with growers to whisk migrants away from isolated farms to English classes, field trips, and worship services, and they could intervene in sticky situations with local authorities.[237] After a Baptist-sponsored event to introduce Mexicanos to white community members in Douglas, Anselma Gómez recalled that "people didn't look at me so distrustfully. It was a change."[238] Mexicanos also knew that growers were among the most powerful men in rural Georgia—successful and respected people whose opinions mattered. White growers and church volunteers sought relationships with Mexicanos to reaffirm their beliefs that borders of race and nation did not matter; Mexicanos sought relationships with these white people because they knew that they did. The disconnect could occasionally lead to disappointment, as when Mary Ann Thurman was "just heartbroken" that a particular migrant family left town without saying goodbye.[239] But mostly the different worldviews underlying the mutually pleasing activities were never spoken. Albeit for their own reasons, Mexicanos' interest in their white admirers was real.

For the majority of workers who did not have their own transportation, a church service, a party at the home of Sonny and Ruth Bridges, or English class at St. Juliana provided a space for something that migrant camps and work sites did not: a spiritual life—a communal life—a life away from the farm and as something other than a worker. Mexicans flocked to the Thurmans' English classes not only to improve their skills but also to actively claim their own full humanity in a space over which they had more control.[240] In migrant camps, "they had rooms, but no meeting place," explained Mary Ann Thurman. "So, church became their meeting place." After English class, the men could socialize with cookies, donuts, coffee, and Kool-Aid in hand. Between forty and ninety men attended each class.[241] One scholar has asserted that "the defense and recovery of community may be the most unrelenting of all challenges faced by poor and marginalized peoples around the world."[242] In white churches, Mexicano workers found a space outside the direct control of farmers and crew leaders where they could gather at least partly on their own terms.[243]

While the reactions of migrants to the outreach of Carolyn Flowers and Ruth and Sonny Bridges must be interpreted from those volunteers' interviews and photos, the Thurmans preserved written evidence of migrants' interest in them—letters that migrant workers had sent them from Texas, Florida, and Mexico. The letters convey emotions of love, respect, and gratitude for the Thurmans and in some cases share intimate details of family life. Margarita, who did not sign her last name, wrote the Thurmans in Spanish from Malinalco, State of Mexico, in December 1988. In her letter, she echoed the familial metaphors that white church volunteers favored. "My dear family,"

FIGURE 28 Funeral program of former employer Roscoe Meeks, 2006, which sat framed on the television in the Gómez household in 2008. Courtesy of Anselma and José Gómez, Nicholls, Georgia.

she wrote, "I miss you and remember you so much." Margarita confided that she was worried about her husband as she had not heard from him and was afraid he did not understand that her delay in returning to Georgia was under doctor's orders due to her pregnancy. If the Thurmans saw Mario around, could they communicate the message?[244] Jesús and María sent a postcard from Guadalajara, saying, "The very nice treatment you gave us has remained in our memories."[245] Eujenio Moreno wrote from McAlpin, Florida, in 1990, asking Howdy and Mary Ann to send him a Spanish-language Bible "or something with the word of God to read" since there was no Spanish mass in his current location.[246] Bernice Gallegos, daughter in a migrant family, wrote Mary Ann from Nixon, Texas, that same year. "We always remember everybody. I hope we can see you again one day."[247] Long gone from Georgia, with no more coffee to drink or donuts to eat, Gallegos and her family affirmed the emotional bond they felt with the Thurmans.

Mexicano migrant families who worked directly with growers or contracted work for others also affirmed personal bonds with their employers. They did this not just for growers' benefit but also for their own. For example, the Gómezes placed a framed photograph above their television depicting grower Roscoe Meeks, to whom they brought labor crews for more than a decade (fig. 28). "The man in this picture, he was my boss," Anselma Gómez

Pro-immigrant Conservatism in Rural Georgia 167

FIGURE 29 Angelina Marín and supervisors, Toombs Manufacturing, 1989. Courtesy of Teodora Marín, Cedar Crossing, Georgia.

explained in 2008. "This man saw us as people, like a part of himself."[248] The Marín family in the Vidalia area took several photographs of Angelina Marín, one of the first Vidalia-area Mexicanos to leave the fields for a factory, with her bosses from that factory (fig. 29). And the Avalos family preserved a photographic Christmas card sent to them by longtime boss Hank Dodson (fig. 30). "He was a good boss," recalled Andrea Avalos. "He thought well of us."[249] In their oral narratives, both Avalos and Gómez explained that beloved employers pictured in their photos had shown them respect and kindness. Those sentiments acquired their meaning in the power imbalance between migrants and growers: the growers had treated Mexicano migrants well even though their superior power meant they did not have to. Workers not only reciprocated the friendship directly to farmers; they preserved these images in their personal albums, evoking the men who had respected them as people, not just low-wage workers.

Ultimately, those Mexicans and Mexican Americans who settled in southern Georgia drew on the approval of white people to reinforce the narratives of perseverance and independence that had brought them there in the first place. "I've told my story a hundred times" to Georgians, said former migrant worker Israel Cortez in an interview. "This country opened its arms to my family, and we're all proud." When his family gathers, Cortez told an inter-

FIGURE 30 Christmas card sent from employer Hank Dodson to crew leader Slim Avalos and his wife, Andrea. Courtesy of Andrea and Slim Avalos, Omega, Georgia.

viewer, they talk about "the things we accomplished in this country that we could not have accomplished if we'd stayed in Mexico." The early years were hard: "We had people call us bad names, people throw us out of houses, people not giving us work, people telling us to leave." But ultimately those things were not the most important part of the family story. "We don't dwell on those things," Cortez explained. "We just keep going forward.... We have progressed."[250] Javier González also described growing up in a migrant family as "difficult," yet insisted, "It wasn't a typical American childhood but it was great because I learned a lot of valuable lessons. I have a six-year-old son now that is never going to experience cold or wet, or smelly, and any of that."[251] Photo albums show that the first generation of Mexican migrant families told themselves such stories not only in hindsight but also during their early years of agricultural labor in Georgia.

Yet their recollections of poverty and discrimination show that even the most successful Mexicanos in southern Georgia were under no illusion that whites' approval had alleviated the potency of race and difference there. "Whites have always treated me well," insisted former migrant worker Petra

Soto. Still, Soto knew she was not one of them. "I have done my best not to get too involved with the people here," she explained. "Because you know where you will be accepted, and where you won't be."[252] For Israel Cortez, fitting in in southern Georgia was a constant and Herculean effort. "I have made some drastic changes through the years," including learning English and converting to Protestantism, he explained. "I have adapted myself, assimilated myself to the system and the culture. I have a Georgia accent. I have tried ... to fit in."[253] Soto, González, Cortez; the Avalos, Marín, and Gómez families; the Aguilar brothers; the workers who wrote to the Thurmans and smiled for Sonny and Ruth Bridges's photos; and other Mexicano compatriots were proud of their accomplishments in Georgia and grateful to the white growers and volunteers who had given them opportunities to work, recreate, and pray. Their own pride in independence, family togetherness, and self-sufficiency perfectly mirrored white conservatives' post–civil rights emphasis on those traits. But Mexicanos could not reflect back their white admirers' underlying pro-immigrant conservatism: that both Jesus and the civil rights movement had erased the salience of racial, national, and economic barriers, making all people one and the same.

Nonetheless, the contingencies of the migrant experience in Georgia set migrant workers there apart from their compatriots in California, Florida, the Northwest, the Midwest, and the few unionized Latino workplaces in nearby North Carolina. In those places, Mexicanos' pride in lives dedicated to farm labor made them receptive to the critical analyses of labor organizers, Chicano movement veterans, and immigrants with histories of resistance in Haiti, Central America, and the indigenous communities of southern Mexico. In Florida, growers with huge farms delegated all labor management to unscrupulous and violent crew leaders, while in Georgia they retained more intimate control themselves. Georgia's church volunteers and other middle-class white people found in Mexicano migrants seemingly perfect recipients of charity who could reinforce their Christian commitment to serving the poor across lines of race and nation without threatening their conservative positions on welfare and color-blindness. And in church vans, pews, social halls, and volunteers' living rooms, migrants found places to build valuable social relationships, pray, recreate, and forge community—but not organize.[254]

And so, southern Georgia in the 1970s through 1990s was a place neither of anti-immigrant violence and backlash nor of pro-immigrant or pro-labor activism. White people there once suspiciously regarded migrants as "strange animals," but through time they forged a pro-immigrant conservative consensus that spared Mexicanos the worst fates of their compatriots elsewhere.

Rather than labor organizers, Mexican and Mexican American migrant workers met church volunteers who praised their values, alleviated their hunger, and offered them spaces to re-create themselves and each other away from growers and crew leaders. In these spaces, migrant workers also found affirmation for their inclinations to narrate their stories as tales of self-help and progress rather than poverty and discrimination. One scholar has observed that "Mexican Americans adapted their lives to the many identities and ideologies in the United States."[255] Mexicanos did not adopt rural Georgia's conservative ideologies and identities wholesale, but adapt to them they did.

"Bullying Tactics": Georgians versus Federal Immigration Enforcement

The locally rooted accommodation between Mexicanos and area white and black communities ensured that as other parts of the country turned to anti-immigrant politics in the 1990s, southern Georgia continued to accommodate a conservative pro-immigrant sensibility. White power holders lauded Mexicans' role in local economies and communities while middle-class African Americans used them as evidence of their own social mobility. As Republican-led anti-immigrant movements pushed President Bill Clinton to vastly increase enforcement efforts in the 1990s, conservatives in rural southern Georgia resisted immigration enforcement as an unwanted intrusion of federal outsiders.[256] Like their counterparts everywhere, southern Georgia's farmers openly resented federal immigration raids in their fields; one Echols County man reportedly claimed that the INS had violated his farm's airspace by flying its helicopters overhead.[257] But the South's rural agricultural areas were unique in an important way: thanks to the pro-immigrant conservative consensus, prominent white and black leaders, including politicians, openly supported farmers' positions with little apparent fear of a populist anti-immigrant backlash.

As during the bracero years, a major goal of immigration enforcement in the 1990s was to push farmers into government-sanctioned temporary migration programs, in this case the H2A farmworker visa program.[258] The IRCA reforms of 1986 had established fines for employers who hired undocumented workers, and a few Georgia growers, including the Robersons, petitioned for H2A workers shortly thereafter. But like their counterparts in Arkansas fifty years before, southern Georgia's growers found that government-managed migration created additional hassles and expenses. They also had little incentive to abandon their now-routine practice of hiring undocumented immigrants. While the INS had sporadically raided Georgia's fields since the 1970s, officials often told farmers exactly where and when to expect enforcement actions. Diana Mendieta remembered growers instructing her father Bernardo "Slim" Avalos to keep undocumented crew members out of the fields on those days.[259]

That changed in the late 1990s when a new southern INS district director began fighting for resources to step up enforcement and warned the region's farmers and politicians that action in Georgia's fields was imminent. Growers, he advised, should pursue legal H2A workers rather than continue to rely on undocumented farm laborers.[260] But when growers looked into the process, what they saw was "the epitome of a bureaucratic nightmare" that failed to offer the benefits they had derived from migrant labor in the first place: flexibility and rock-bottom labor costs.[261]

Turning to their congressional representatives for help, growers found support not only among their fellow white Republicans or conservative Democrats but also in the offices of liberal black Democrats. In 1997, Representative Sanford Bishop Jr. and civil rights hero Representative John Lewis worked with Republican representative Saxby Chambliss to ease the path for Georgia's growers to import guest workers with minimal regulations and oversight.[262] In lobbying on growers' behalf, Bishop directly undermined the black farmworkers in his vast agricultural district, yet nowhere in his written communications did he mention the effects that H2A contracting would have on them.[263] Powerless and ever smaller in number, Georgia's black farmworkers were still invisible to middle-class African Americans and other potential advocates. Their public silence contributed to southern Georgia's consensus that Mexican immigrants were good for business and communities while strict federal immigration policies and enforcement were unwelcome intrusions.

The local-versus-federal struggle over immigration reached its apex in 1998. Early that year, Vidalia growers did petition for H2A workers, but their application was rejected because they did not promise to pay the local prevailing wage, demonstrate a good-faith attempt to employ domestic workers, or submit an adequate housing plan. Rather than reapply for guest workers, Vidalia farmers decided to rely again on undocumented laborers that year.[264] The INS struck back, launching the raid "Operation Southern Denial," on May 13, 1998, in Toombs and Tattnall counties. Mexican consul Teodoro Maus quietly gave the raid his go-ahead because he believed the H2A program was a better deal for workers and afforded his own government more leverage to protect its citizens abroad—leverage it had lost since the decline of the bracero program.²⁶⁵ Some local police chiefs offered logistical support to the INS, but others said they were too "busy"—or, more likely, too sympathetic to labor-hungry growers—to help.²⁶⁶ By design, the raid's effect was more psychological than practical: it resulted in the detention of just twenty-one workers, though the overall estimated Vidalia harvest workforce was 3,500–5,000. But many workers, legal or not, were reluctant to come to work in the days that followed, angering farmers who feared their highly valuable Vidalia onions would rot in the fields.²⁶⁷

White Republicans defended farmers' interests apparently without fear of an anti-immigrant constituent backlash. Senator Paul Coverdell chastised the INS for its "indiscriminate and inappropriate use of extreme enforcement tactics against Vidalia area onion growers . . . [interfering with] honest farmers who are simply trying to get their products from the field to the marketplace" while Chambliss referred to INS "bullying tactics."²⁶⁸ Coverdell strong-armed the local INS into suspending enforcement during the picking season, a move some called a "temporary amnesty." Though the truce stipulated that farmers must seek H2A visas the following year, they once again deemed them too expensive.²⁶⁹ As the struggle between growers and the INS continued through the 1990s and early 2000s, the battle lines remained clear: southern Georgia's white political leaders, with the acquiescence of their black counterparts, wanted the Mexicans to stay with or without the federal government's blessing.

Pro-immigrant Conservatism under Pressure

Yet while rural politicians displayed a united front of pro-immigrant conservatism in 1998, the seeds of Georgia's later turn to statewide anti-immigrant politics were beginning to take root hundreds of miles away from the onion fields. In 1995, home owners in the majority-white Atlanta suburb of Smyrna mounted a small anti-immigration letter-writing campaign. One man, identifying himself as a "property owner" in his letter to Georgia's governor, protested that "the growing tidal wave of illegal immigration threatens to drain our economy dry."²⁷⁰ An ex-Californian wrote that the Los Angeles suburb where he was raised "has been invaded by people from Mexico and all points south. . . . Can you imagine Smyrna looking like Mexico City? Well, drive done [sic] parts of Buford Highway and you will see it starting to happen."²⁷¹ Like the man distressed by the sight of Buford Highway, this campaign was an import from suburban California, where voters overwhelmingly approved a statewide anti-immigrant initiative, Proposition 187, the year before.²⁷² As allegations of an immigrant "invasion" spread outward from the West, southern Georgia's pro-immigrant conservative consensus came under pressure from all sides. The state's coming legislative battle over immigration would pit suburban Republicans against rural pro-immigrant conservatives while inspiring rural Mexican American and Latino youths to break with their parents' strategic political silence.

Though there is little evidence of organized anti-immigrant politics in southern Georgia during the 1970s, 1980s, and early 1990s, by the end of that decade those who did not subscribe to the pro-immigrant bent of local conservatism began to make their views known publicly.[273] In 1997, Omega police officers harassed attendees at the hugely popular La Fiesta del Pueblo, and the following year its city council wavered on permitting the event again.[274] This agricultural community needed Mexican workers in the fields but quickly tired of seeing them in central public spaces. Yet if La Fiesta del Pueblo was unwelcome in Omega, it did not have to look far for a new home; in 1999 it took its place downtown in nearby Tifton, drawing support from local politicians as well as thousands of fiesta-goers. Embarrassed by the negative publicity and missing the economic boon of the fiesta, Omega officials called the event's organizer and asked her to return the fiesta to Omega. She declined.[275]

Over the following five years, Mexican guest workers and Mexican American youths violated the unspoken terms of rural Georgia's pro-immigrant conservatism by publicly challenging local power holders. These efforts relied on U.S. federally funded antipoverty agencies—a mirror image of the bracero era when Mexican government support was pivotal for emigrants and even some Mexican American workers in the U.S. South. Throughout the early 2000s, H2A workers with the help of the federally funded Georgia Legal Services Program repeatedly sued local growers and almost always won their suits.[276] Blas Pozos Mora and Armando Rosales Pozos, pictured at the bottom of Janis Roberson's album page, "2nd Busload to Leave, June 15, 1995" (see fig. 21), joined with other H2A workers and legal aid lawyers to sue Roberson in 2004 for violation of the Fair Labor Standards Act and again in 2010 for retaliating against the workers who had pursued the original suit.[277] For Roberson, the lawsuits felt "like somebody just stuck you in the heart.... We just thought we were all one big happy family," she said sadly in a 2010 interview. After the lawsuits began, she said, "We quit doing a lot of things," like throwing birthday parties for workers.[278] These workers challenged a power structure whose very existence Roberson had once denied.

Two years later and a hundred miles away in the Vidalia area, Mexican American youths, joined by the children of Central American immigrants, offended pro-immigrant conservatives in a different arena. Even after the area's Toombs High School had integrated, black and white seniors there continued to hold separate proms. In 2004, Latina girls were allowed to buy tickets to the white prom, but a white girl buying a ticket for her Latino boyfriend was told that he could not attend. Distressed, the students turned to Andrea Hinojosa, the Tejana former migrant worker who had formed southern Georgia's answer to a Latino community-based organization, the Southeast Georgia Communities Project. With Hinojosa's help, the students set about planning a third, "Latino," prom, which welcomed all students.[279] Asked about the segregated proms, African American school principal Ralph Hardy said that while one prom for all students would be preferable, "I don't think that tradition right now, and history, would allow that to happen. . . . I think I'm going to leave it alone."[280] Television cameras and journalists from around the world arrived to Toombs County to cover the seeming throwback to an earlier era, embarrassing local elites who blamed Hinojosa and the students for creating a problem.[281]

These suburban activists, guest workers, and second-generation youths disturbed the myths of pro-immigrant conservatism but did not unseat the ideology from southern Georgia. When the U.S. Senate introduced a bipartisan immigration reform bill in 2005 and House Republicans countered it with a punitive anti-immigrant proposal, HR4437, rural Republican sentiment in the South was far more contested than national party politics suggested.[282] Journalists and pundits noted that "big business" and "law-and-order" Republicans were on opposite sides of the measure, but few saw the regional dynamics at play: while suburban and exurban Republicans led the anti-immigrant faction (including the House bill's primary sponsor, Representative James Sensenbrenner, who represented the outskirts of Milwaukee), those in rural agricultural areas, particularly in the South, staked out more moderate positions or followed behind their suburban counterparts in the name of party discipline.[283] Now a senator answering to suburban as well as rural conservatives, Saxby Chambliss, who called the INS a "bully" during Operation Southern Denial, suddenly supported tough anti-immigrant measures. But South Carolina's conservative Republican senator Lindsey Graham became an "absolute hero" to the National Council of La Raza (NCLR) thanks to his "practical" approach to immigration reform.[284]

A microcosm of the national battle raged in the Georgia statehouse. No sooner did Republicans gain a majority there than state senators from the Atlanta exurbs and a majority-white upstate district joined with one southern Georgia state senator to cosponsor get-tough-on-immigrants legislation,

SB529. It passed almost exactly on party lines and awaited the governor's signature. "People are always calling me and saying, 'Greg, what are you going to do about immigration?'" explained cosponsor Greg Goggans, an orthodontist whose southern Georgia district included heavily agricultural Coffee and Echols counties.[285]

When Mexican and other Latino immigrants filled the nation's streets to protest the federal anti-immigrant bill in April 2006, southern cities including Atlanta saw massive demonstrations, but Latinos in Tifton were among the few to march in an agricultural area. There an estimated 2,000 people joined the protest, holding signs that opposed not only the national HR4437 but also the statewide anti-immigrant bill, SB529. The march ended at a park with a festival of Hispanic culture, allowing the protest to blend with the area's more cautious tradition of public "fiestas."[286] Unmoved by the protests, Republican governor Sonny Perdue signed SB529 the following week.

Southern Georgia's Latino youths heeded national calls for a Latino economic boycott that May 1 even as their parents proceeded with caution.[287] Playing by the rules of pro-immigrant conservatism, more established Mexican immigrants and Mexican Americans had long emphasized individual hard work and had not built independent political power. The next generation had other ideas; some Latino schoolchildren wore white T-shirts to school that day and expressed disappointment that their community's adults did not take to the streets as urban immigrants had done. Other southern Georgia youths—in some cases more than a third of Latino pupils—skipped school to show their solidarity with the "Day without an Immigrant" action.[288] As pro-immigrant conservatism came under assault from the Atlanta suburbs, so too did Mexican American and Latino youths cast off their own parents' version of that conservatism, which had eschewed collective action in favor of individual effort.

The polarizing national debate of 2005–6 challenged but did not overwhelm the ethos of pro-immigrant conservatism in southern Georgia.[289] There anti-immigrant voices still competed for airspace with those who hewed to the terms of the conservative pro-immigrant consensus. Even as suburban Republicans drafted anti-immigrant legislation in the statehouse, Tifton mayor Paul Johnson, a former agricultural extension agent, flew the Mexican flag outside city hall for six days to honor six local Mexican men who had been killed in a robbery. When distressed listeners called a popular local talk radio show to protest, the host was unmoved. "We have to have [the Mexicans] here," he insisted. A popular white barber well known for his political prognostications concurred, "I think everybody realizes the farmers got to have them."[290] The flag remained in place for the full six days. The following year, an immigration raid on a Stillmore chicken plant prompted the town's mayor to openly compare immigration agents to the Gestapo. A white mother told a reporter that she worried about the psychological effects on her adopted Mexican American son. A mobile home park owner flew the American flag upside down for several days as an act of protest. And an African American shoe saleswoman insisted that the poultry plant could not attract local workers anyway—"not to cut no chickens up."[291]

Even once the national Republican Party fully coalesced around an anti-immigration agenda in 2010, many rural conservative whites in Georgia remained unmoved. Though he supported the conservative agenda on most issues, Sonny Bridges did not subscribe to that movement's views of "illegal immigrants." "I've got no problem with them," he said simply in a 2010 interview. "They accept me, and I accept them."[292] Faced with the idea that immigrants use up too many social services, Carolyn Flowers, a staunch Evangelical conservative, begged to differ. "If a person is hungry," she said, also in 2010, "if they don't have food for their kids, you feed them."[293] White or black, elite or middle class, many southern Georgians continued to hold a different kind of conservative position on the increasingly divisive immigration issue.

In 2011, suburban Atlanta state senators once again joined with those from majority-white northern Georgia areas to propose get-tough anti-immigrant legislation, this time called HB87. Once again, Republicans from southern Georgia followed along to approve the measure and a Republican governor signed it into law. And once again, many conservatives on the ground in southern Georgia remained unconvinced. The *Valdosta Daily Times* editorialized, "Georgia needs [immigrants], relies on them, and cannot successfully support the state's No. 1 economic engine without them," and went on to suggest that legislators caught up in "anti-immigrant fever" come to southern Georgia to pick the crops themselves.[294] When the ACLU challenged the law in court, a Republican mayor, Paul Bridges of Uvalda, in the Vidalia area, was a plaintiff. "Everything about HB87 is not Republican," he insisted. "They title this bill anti-immigration but they should have titled it anti-business. They should have titled that bill, let's grow the government." Like farmers and church volunteers before him, Bridges employed images of family to erase differences between whites and Latinos. So many Latinos had married whites in his town that "they have become a part of our societal network," he explained.[295] Bridges noted that he himself could be branded a criminal for "taking fellow parishioners to church" under the law's harsh terms.[296] The press called Bridges an "unlikely" ally in the fight for immigrants' rights, but the long history of pro-immigrant conservatism in southern Georgia shows that his public stance was decades in the making.[297]

When Bridges held a roundtable on immigration at the Uvalda Community Center in May 2011, local Republican state legislators had to defend their support for the law in the face of community members and farmers who used Nazi comparisons and decried the law's effect on children. Halfheartedly defending their votes, one protested, "I did not write the bill," while another said he'd like to change the law in the future to "lessen the blow."[298] A third legislator lamented of his party's anti-immigrant wing: "They've got the votes."[299] These representatives had cast votes on behalf of party discipline or their own future political careers, not their constituents in southern Georgia.

In the end, the conservative consensus fostered by southern Georgia growers, church volunteers, and Mexicanos succeeded in staving off the national anti-immigrant movement for more than three decades—but not forever. Though that movement still failed to win the hearts and minds of many white conservatives in southern Georgia in the early twenty-first century, the state-level legislation it spawned radically disrupted life for the region's immigrants anyway. In Atlanta and the college town Athens, advocacy groups such as the Georgia Association of Latino Elected Officials, the Georgia Latino Alliance for Human Rights, Freedom University, and NCLR's new Atlanta office challenged anti-immigrant laws and policies on the state level.[300] But southern Georgia's Mexicanos had built no infrastructure to raise a political voice. Instead they voted with their feet, abandoning the area's agricultural jobs in droves.

Why did white suburban Republicans spew such vitriol against the immigrants who plainly powered swaths of the state's economy, and how did their movement acquire enough power to politically steamroll the more varied local cultures around immigration in the U.S. South? What options did the Mexican immigrants and Mexican Americans in those politicians' backyards have in the midst of this assault? The next chapter explores the experiences of Mexicanos in the South's suburbs and exurbs, telling the story of their encounters with a new politics of exclusion.

CHAPTER FIVE

Skyscrapers and Chicken Plants
Mexicans, Latinos, and Exurban Immigration Politics in Greater Charlotte, 1990–2012

Like so many school classes captured by photographers in Charlotte, North Carolina, during the 1970s–90s, the 1994 Berryhill Elementary School kindergarten included eleven black and twelve white students smiling at the camera or looking askance (fig. 31). In a country where the racial integration of schools has rarely been achieved even after the fall of legal segregation, the photograph commemorated not just its subjects' first year of schooling but also Charlotte's role as a national leader in a social and political experiment: using two-way busing to achieve meaningful school desegregation. In 1965, Charlotte black parents filed a lawsuit, *Swann v. Charlotte-Mecklenburg Board of Education*, which eventually reached the Supreme Court. There, in 1971, it drew a landmark ruling that told school districts around the country they must achieve racial balance in public schools even if that meant putting both white and black kids on buses to faraway neighborhoods. The controversy brought anti-busing white parents' groups into conflict not only with black and white liberals but also with a mostly white business elite that eschewed open racial conflict, preferring the "Charlotte Way" of closed negotiation to preserve racial peace. The Charlotte Way and its liberal allies triumphed, defeating anti-busing boycotts and successfully integrating the Charlotte-Mecklenburg schools. Proud businesspeople, civic boosters, and ordinary citizens celebrated the achievement as proof of their city's racial progressivism and forward-looking ethos.[1]

To parents admiring the Berryhill class picture, the presence of kindergartener Eréndira Molina in the second row might have seemed a novel curiosity that did not fit into Charlotte's usual two racial categories. Still, civic-minded Charlotteans could easily envision smiling Molina as a next logical step in the city's journey from its southern past toward a more cosmopolitan future. There stood evidence that Charlotte's booming economy was drawing ambitious new arrivals, in this case the California-born daughter of Mexican

---

To see a selection of original historical sources from this chapter, go to http://corazondedixie .org/chapter-5 (http://dx.doi.org/10.7264/N3X928K4).

FIGURE 31 Kindergarten class picture from Berryhill Elementary School, Charlotte, 1994. Courtesy of Laura Mendoza and Eréndira Molina, Charlotte, North Carolina.

immigrants. Eréndira Molina's mother, Laura, found steady work immediately on arrival in the Queen City in 1992, first as a maid, then as a machine operator, and eventually as a bank teller. She purchased a home within two years, something she had not achieved in her six years in the suburban barrios of Los Angeles's San Fernando Valley. Young Eréndira completed her education in this increasingly diverse middle-ring suburb southwest of downtown, thriving in the racially progressive environment on which many of the city's businessmen and citizens prided themselves.[2]

The spatial and temporal limits of that progressivism were soon to become obvious. A school photograph taken thirty miles away and fifteen years later confirmed what Berryhill parents may have suspected by 1994: that Charlotte civic leaders' resolve to lift the weight of southern history in the late twentieth century would not hold sway once the city outgrew its original boundaries and regional identity in the twenty-first. At brand-new Poplin Elementary School in Union County's Indian Trail just east of the city, Jacqueline R. and her fellow third graders smiled at the camera in 2010 (fig. 32). Indian Trail was a classic commuter exurb, an area undergoing rapid transformation from a rural character to a suburban one.[3] Like commuter exurbs elsewhere in the country, Indian Trail grew explosively in the 1980s and 1990s as upwardly mobile young parents, mostly white and middle class, fled cities for places

FIGURE 32 Third-grade class picture from Poplin Elementary School, Indian Trail, Union County, North Carolina, an exurb of Charlotte, 2010. Courtesy of Mercedes R.

not under busing orders, with "better" public schools, less crowded public services, and more house for their money. Many were themselves raised in suburbs following the first wave of "white flight" in the 1950s–60s, while others came from rural areas.[4] But as inner suburbs grew increasingly diverse both ethnically and economically, a new generation of middle-class white families now created largely homogenous communities in freshly built housing developments beyond county borders.[5] For these families, the Charlotte Way was not the only way to partake of the metro region's growing economy.

The presence of Jacqueline R. and other Latino students in the Poplin class picture threatened the area's homogeneity, and with it white parents' narratives of upward mobility in the exurbs (see map 6). The trailer park where they lived marred Indian Trail's neat landscape of recently constructed single-family homes (see map 7). Their employment in chicken plants, factories, and low-end service jobs disturbed visions of a singularly middle-class community. Their racial difference disrupted spaces imagined to be nearly all white. And their consumption of public services, particularly seats in school classrooms, undermined the very political underpinnings of exurban development: that white middle-class families had an exclusive claim to partake of the services their tax dollars funded. No wonder Jacqueline's mother, Mercedes R., recalled feelings of alienation and racism from teach-

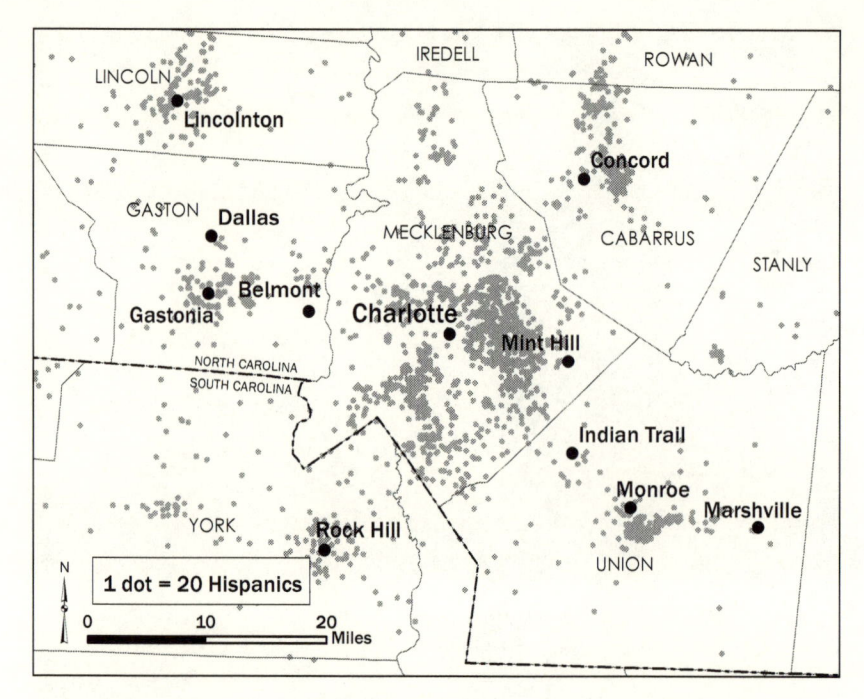

MAP 6 "Hispanic" population in Charlotte, Mecklenburg County, and surrounding area, 2000. U.S. Census data accessed via NC OneMap GeoSpatial Portal, http://nconemap.gov. Map by the author.

ers and wealthier white parents at Poplin. The family soon left the Indian Trail trailer park and moved to an apartment complex in the county seat of Monroe, where they enrolled their children at a majority-minority school that felt more comfortable.[6]

This chapter traces the dreams, migrations, and eventual collision of two groups: middle-class white exurban home owners and immigrant families from a globalized Mexico. It sets the stage by discussing the 1990s boom in Mexican immigration to Charlotte, showing how the Charlotte Way moderated white and black reaction to the arrival of a mostly male workforce. But soon, manufacturing and chicken-processing plants remaining from the area's rural past drew entire Mexican families to Charlotte's fringe, while a more affordable middle-class lifestyle attracted white home owners to those same spaces. A globalized consumer culture and middle-class ideal shaped both groups in related ways, causing both to make their homes in the exurbs. While one group freely navigated the exurban landscape and set its political agenda, the other found mostly isolation. They struggled to travel its roads, access its social services, and connect with political allies. They lacked U.S. citizenship

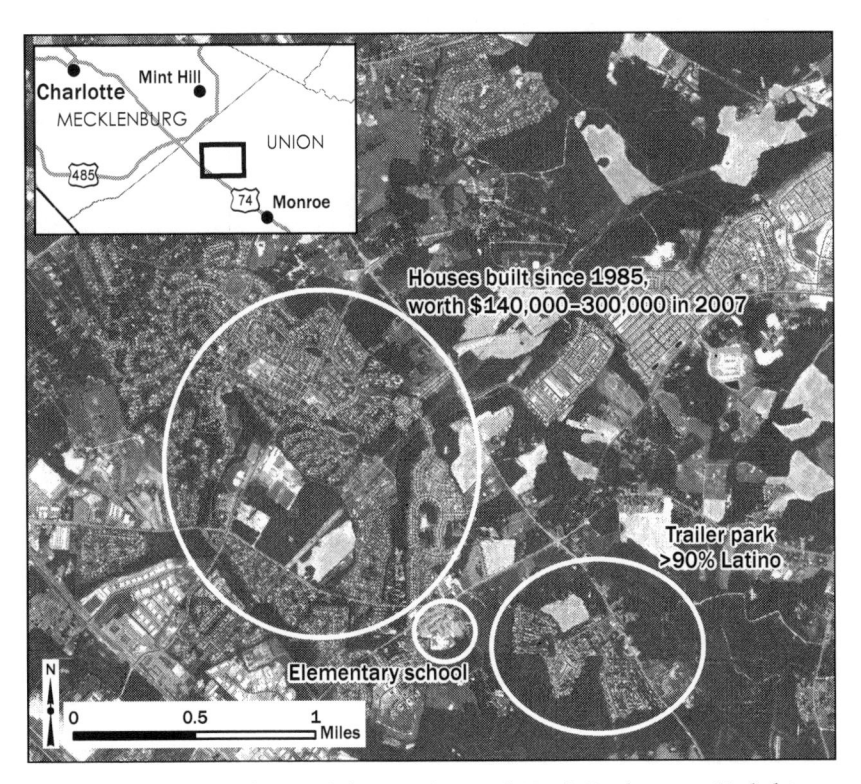

MAP 7 The geography of race and class in Indian Trail, North Carolina, 2012. Underlying image from U.S. Geological Survey, www.usgs.gov; real estate values from Zillow.com; trailer park population estimation from author's interviews and observations. Map by the author.

and often legal immigration status even as their Mexican citizenship was of little political use. From 2005 onward, tens of thousands of immigrants in Charlotte and other southern cities marched through diverse urban spaces to defend their human rights. But those in more hostile and privatized exurbs like Union County remained on the sidelines. Rather than march, they created community and pursued their own families' upward mobility as quietly as possible.

The collision between Mercedes R.'s middle-class dreams and those of white Poplin parents ended the South's history of tenuous accommodation to Mexican immigrants and Mexican Americans. English- and Spanish-language newspapers, government reports, and interviews with politicians and community leaders can tell the larger social and political story of Mexican migration to the suburbanizing counties surrounding Charlotte and other fast-growing southern cities. But to understand how immigrants experienced

Exurban Immigration Politics in Greater Charlotte 183

these locations and why the immigrants' rights movement of the mid-2000s passed them by, this chapter also draws on oral history interviews with Mexican immigrant women in Charlotte's most mature exurb, Union County, where since 1990, majority-white bedroom communities like Indian Trail have exploded along Route 74 between Charlotte's eastern reaches and the poor, industrial, majority-minority county seat of Monroe.

These sources show that between 2005 and 2012, a host of southern cities, counties, and states considered or approved legislation designed to make day-to-day life difficult for undocumented immigrants.[7] National stereotypes about the region would suggest that these moves have been logical outcomes of the South's racially unsavory history. Yet the previous chapters of this book show that aside from pockets of Klan activity in northern Georgia in the early 1980s, anti-immigrant movements targeted at Mexicans did not gain traction in the twentieth-century U.S. South even in areas where those immigrants' presence was highly visible. In the twenty-first century, middle-class white residents of the region's least southern spaces—exurbs that developed more than a decade after the fall of Jim Crow—took their lead from the West's exurban anti-immigrant movements as they mounted the South's first major anti-immigrant movement targeted at Latinos. While the general political conservatism of white exurbanites is well established, scholars know little about the politics, expectations, and lives of exurban Latino immigrants. Indeed, though exurbs have largely escaped the notice of immigration scholars, they—not particularities of southern history—provide the key to understanding the region's recent anti-immigrant turn.[8]

New South Origins, Queen City Migrants

The flourishing of anti-immigrant movements and legislation throughout the South would have been difficult to predict in the early years of Latino migration to Charlotte and other central cities, when these newcomers were either professionals or, like Eréndira Molina's mother, welcome laborers in a growing city. While Mexicano migrant workers had journeyed to rural North Carolina since at least the 1960s, the state's urban Latino population, mostly educated Cubans and South Americans, identified as "Latin Americans" and had little interaction with rural workers.[9] As in other Sunbelt South areas like Atlanta, Raleigh, and northern Virginia, the very knowledge-based jobs that Charlotte's business elite hoped to attract with their New-New South rhetoric and politics brought with them demand for vast new construction projects as well as more services to clean these new office buildings, feed their professionals, and house their business travelers. Economic mobility for white and black southerners created demand for low-wage workers, and as they had for decades in the rural South, from the 1980s onward Mexican immigrants arrived in southern cities en masse to fill the gap.[10]

Mexican men recruited by the construction industry were among the first working-class Latinos to arrive in large numbers in Charlotte. They came on trucks driven by Texan subcontractors or migrated to cities when a series of droughts dried up North Carolina's rural job market in the mid-1980s. In 1986, a state labor official said he had "received reports from virtually every urban area in the state of Spanish-speaking migrant workers in construction crews."[11] Arriving just prior to the implementation of widespread amnesty under the IRCA, it is likely that many of these earliest Spanish-speaking workers were undocumented. As Latino workers in the Southwest gained legal status and settled down in the late 1980s, they saturated low-skilled urban labor markets, prompting others to seek new opportunities in cities throughout the South.[12] By 2000, nearly 20,000 Mexican-born people—more than two-thirds of them male—lived in Mecklenburg County, and Hispanics comprised more than a quarter of the construction workforce there.[13] The industry employed more Hispanics than any other, but significant numbers also worked in the service industry, providing low-skilled labor for restaurants, hotels, landscaping services, temp agencies, and office buildings.[14] The cost of living was comparatively low and job opportunity seemed limitless. Alicia E. traveled to Charlotte on a tourist visa around 2000 to visit her brothers and their families for one month. Expressing a sentiment that Eréndira Molina's mother, Laura, and many other southern Latino immigrants shared, the brothers told her that they were "making more progress here than in other states."[15]

For many immigrants, Charlotte offered not only economic progress but also a comparatively favorable racial climate. As California's anti-immigrant movement reached its apex in the mid-1990s, North Carolina seemed downright hospitable by comparison.[16] Mexico's honorary consul in Charlotte recalled telling a young Mexican girl, "'Look, you came from California, and probably the people out there didn't treat Mexicans very well.' You could see that I was hitting home. I said, 'Here, people will say, "Oh, you're from Mexico? Tell me about it!"'"[17] Mexican immigrant activist Angeles Ortega-Moore had a more sober perspective on Charlotte white elites' comparatively "welcoming" attitude in the mid-1990s. Their praise was code for "We'd rather have you than African Americans," she believed. "Somehow, we became the lesser of two evils. 'You're closer to our liking. You represent more of our values.'"[18] Most of the city's immigrants in this period were single men whom native-born Charlotteans probably glimpsed only at work sites, as they tended to live in groups in nondescript suburban apartment complexes. Like in rural case studies from earlier in this book, employers publicly praised Mexicans' and Latinos' "work ethic" most of all. Indeed, one temp agency saw fit to market itself as a specialist in Latino labor because, in a spokesperson's words, "Employers request Latinos since they're not lazy and they come here to work."[19]

The descriptor "not lazy," when applied to an ethnic minority, had a well-understood racial connotation in the late 1990s United States. The country and its Congress had passionately debated the merits of welfare benefits in the years before and in 1996 reached bipartisan consensus to, in President Bill Clinton's words, "end welfare as we know it."[20] In the Southwest, media and politicians focused the controversy on welfare recipients' allegedly questionable immigration status.[21] They extended a discourse earlier espoused by proponents of California's 1994 ballot initiative, Proposition 187, which sought to deny public services to undocumented immigrants, including those such as emergency health care and primary education, that were mandated by the U.S. Supreme Court. Though its unconstitutionality prevented the law from taking effect, 187 gave voice to anti-immigrant sentiments in California's suburbs, winning a stunning 59 percent of the vote.[22] The message reached Washington, leading the 1996 welfare reform bill to severely restrict legal immigrants' access to the public safety net.[23] Meanwhile in the southern states where a majority of welfare recipients were African American, mid-1990s debates tended to paint those recipients as "lazy" members of "pathological families."[24] So when a Charlotte staffing agency spokesman said in 1998 that Latinos were "not lazy," American listeners knew he was comparing them to black people.

Indeed, stereotypes of blacks, not southwestern stereotypes of Latinos, set the tone for early discussions of Latino immigration in Charlotte, giving both Democrats and Republicans a useful point of contrast as they tried to give their new workforce a good name. The prominence of Republican pro-Latino voices was particularly notable. Describing Latinos as "very happy" people, Republican city council candidate Don Reid told *La Noticia* in 1997, "I represent people with qualities that I see in Latinos: hard working people, family oriented, loyal, patriots and people who don't expect the government to give them money to live. . . . Many of them don't speak English, and nonetheless they make the effort to come here and get a job when other minorities are complaining that they can't find work."[25] Reid's comment a year after welfare reform left little doubt which "other minorities" he was referencing. Republican mayor Pat McCrory, suburban Republican congresswoman Sue Myrick, and Senator Elizabeth Dole, each of whom would embrace anti-immigrant politics in the 2000s, all expressed open pro-Latino sentiment during the late 1990s.[26]

Polls showed mixed views on immigration during this time, and many Charlotteans undoubtedly grumbled about Latino newcomers under their breath.[27] But the legacy of the Charlotte Way provided a moderating framework for immigration discussions in the public sphere. Civic, philanthropic, and educational organizations responded to the Latino influx with characteristic pragmatism in the late 1990s. The University of North Carolina at Charlotte sponsored a conference on "Serving the Hispanic Population"; a foundation underwrote a Spanish-speaking social worker for Mecklenburg County; the International House offered citizenship classes in Spanish; a private elementary school sponsored a "Mexico Day" to learn about Mexican culture; and the Mayor's International Cabinet sent representatives to a Latino-oriented health fair to survey the needs of the Latino population.[28] Well aware of the economic benefits this new labor force was bringing to the region, Charlotte's biracial civic leadership reflexively turned to the city's political culture of business-driven pragmatism in the face of divisive racial issues. In the process, they created real opportunities for Latino immigrants to access vital public services and find points of connection with more established Charlotteans; in many other new immigrant destinations, doors to these services remained shut.[29]

The African Americans among Charlotte's civic and political leaders explored a range of relationships with newly arrived Latinos even though on-the-ground interactions ranged from warm to tense in the 1990s and early 2000s. Members of the two groups often competed for jobs in construction, housing in the same neighborhoods, and attention in the same schools.[30] While statewide polls showed black North Carolinians were slightly more supportive than their white counterparts of Latino newcomers, scholars conducting intensive research in Durham and rural eastern North Carolina during those years found negative attitudes between blacks and Latinos, with Latinos more fixed in their negative views of blacks than vice versa.[31] Still, in Charlotte the African American business and political class never chastised the newcomers publicly. Instead, some sought Latino clients for their businesses and students for their universities while others benignly ignored Latinos, at least for a time.[32] Over the following decade, black politicians would eventually embrace liberal coalition politics, defending immigrants from hostile legislation on the local level.

During the 1990s, the pragmatic Charlotte Way complemented progressive and business-friendly traditions in North Carolina to shape state-level policy, too. That decade, North Carolina was among a shrinking number of states to let undocumented immigrants obtain driver's licenses. The ability to drive legally had wide-ranging effects in the lives of immigrants. It allowed them to forge personal, political, and economic relationships throughout the sprawling metropolitan area. With driver's licenses, immigrants could report crimes to the police, drive to faraway job sites, attend the Latin American festival, take a trip to the zoo, or vacation at the shore without the constant fear of arrest and possible deportation. Undocumented teens could join their peers in the Department of Motor Vehicles (DMV) rite of passage at age sixteen. "You feel calmer with an ID," explained Mercedes R. of the years when undocumented immigrants freely obtained them.[33] The state's practice not only provided myriad practical benefits to immigrants; it also sent a message of inclusiveness that gave North Carolina a good name among immigrants throughout the country.[34]

Yet the very DMV offices that offered undocumented immigrants an entry point to American society ignited the state's first major fracas over its fast-growing Latino population. As out-of-state immigrants flocked to North Carolina DMV offices to obtain licenses, lines of families speaking foreign tongues snaked out the doors. Allocation of DMV resources had not kept pace with the state's urbanization in any event, and cities—particularly Charlotte—saw wait times skyrocket.[35] The then-director of the DMV Wayne Hurder later reflected that "arguments for highway safety find few takers when you are waiting in line for a service you don't really want, and which may have taken you 30 minutes to transact five years ago, but now takes 90 minutes."[36] In response to a public outcry, state legislators tightened requirements to prove in-state residence (but not immigration status) in 2001, but this did not alter perceptions that immigrants were the cause of rapidly declining customer service at the DMV.[37] Scarcity of government resources, not national security concerns, thus prompted the beginnings of public disgruntlement with the state's immigrant-friendly driver's license policies. Even as North Carolina continued to issue the licenses well past the national security uproar of 9/11, the underlying debate over who was entitled to public services presaged changes in immigration politics to come.

Middle-Class Dreams, Migrant Families

Were Latino immigrants hard-working laborers or unworthy consumers of government amenities who crowded out U.S. citizens in an era of shrinking resources? The question ricocheted throughout the United States in the 1990s, dominating the immigration debate and the racial boundaries it drew.[38] Yet despite their limited political power in all but a few U.S. cities, Latinos' own life choices swayed the outcomes of these debates in unexpected ways. Greater Charlotte's Mexican migrants fueled and followed two larger trends in human migration during that decade: increasing numbers of female migrants to low-wage service and domestic jobs on a global scale and suburbanization of immigrant settlement throughout the United States.[39] Scholars have documented the political and economic bases of these developments but have seldom asked how migrants' own beliefs and desires shaped them.[40]

Mercedes R. wanted different things out of migration than her mother had, and she and other Mexican women pursued those particular ideas of progress in exurban Charlotte.[41] Men, viewed by the public as workers, had received a warm welcome from the elite businesspeople and politicians of both political parties who dominated Charlotte's public discussions during the 1990s. But cultural, economic, and policy changes spurred increased migration of women and children during that same decade. And when those Mexican women and children settled in the exurbs, their presence elicited a reaction among their new white middle-class neighbors. The exurbs became fertile ground for the rhetoric and strategies of national anti-immigrant politics.

To understand the desires that brought Mexican families to the Charlotte exurbs, this chapter relies heavily on thirteen oral history interviews with undocumented Mexican women in the area's most mature exurb, Union County. The immigrant women who granted these interviews are representative in their origins but distinct in their life experiences. Like greater Charlotte's Mexican immigrants as a whole, interviewees were young, born between 1966 and 1990.[42] Their regions of origin were typical among Charlotte's Mexican immigrants in this period, with half hailing from states such as Guerrero that did not have extensive out-migration earlier in the century and half coming from traditional sending regions such as Michoacán.[43] Eight of the interviewees lived their entire premigration lives in rural contexts, while five had lived in Mexican cities at some point; this reflected larger trends of the late twentieth century in which at least a third of rural Mexican migrants first tried to work and live in cities before deciding to move across the international border.[44] The women agreed to interviews after I met them either through a social service agency or at a gathering for Mexican women who bought and sold Herbalife nutritional products. So while the women's origins were typical of those in greater Charlotte, the method of reaching them identified only those who had cultivated a life outside the home.

By definition, then, the women whose stories appear in this chapter had personal qualities, marriages, or both that allowed them to connect with friends and social services despite their limited economic resources; after the DMV stopped renewing undocumented immigrant driver's licenses in 2007, they also had to overcome transportation difficulties.[45] Whether they were single or married, rural or urban, or lived in Mexico or the United States, Mexican women as a whole had increased autonomy during the late twentieth century, though this emerging cultural norm was not universal.[46] Yet it is precisely women with some autonomy—those whose voices enter this chapter—who would have been the most likely to take political action in the public sphere. By understanding the larger trajectory of these women's lives and migrations, we can understand the meaning behind their decisions to sit out the activist moment of the mid-2000s. Half of the interviewees agreed in 2011 to having their full names used in this book, but the rapid proliferation of e-books now means their names would be Web searchable in the context of their undocumented status, a possibility of which I had not advised them.[47] They are named here with their real first names but only a last initial, so that they may recognize themselves in the text without a form of public exposure whose long-term ramifications are still unknown.

Angelica C.'s ideas about economics, gender, and marriage—ideas developed in a fast-changing rural Mexico—spurred her journey from Guerrero to the Charlotte exurbs and shaped her expectations once there. Angelica C. was born in Copalá, a coastal Guerrero town, in 1977. Her family of nine worked together in agriculture, and Angelica C. did not see herself as poor. "We never lacked for anything," she explained. Though Copalá and Guerrero in general did not have decades-long traditions of U.S.-bound migration, Angelica C.'s cousins were experienced migrants, and she spent six months in Texas with her father as a teen in the early 1990s. The stint was short, and after her return, Angelica C. followed in the footsteps of generations of Mexican women: she married a man from a nearby *rancho* before her twentieth birthday.[48]

Yet traditional village married life did not suit the couple. Angelica C. and her husband joined his parents' household, exchanging labor for food and shelter. But once their two children arrived, Angelica C. wanted cash to care for her kids in modern style, with store-bought milk and disposable diapers.

Still, though her husband had spent time in North Carolina as a single man, he was reluctant to extricate his new family from his parents' home. His wife was the one to push the issue. "I was always telling him, 'Let's go, let's go, let's go,'" Angelica C. recalled. And so in 2000, the couple set off for the United States together, walking for three days across the desert spanning Sonora and Arizona. From there, they joined her husband's brothers in Union County. Three years later they sent for their son, and two years after that, Angelica returned to Mexico and, against her husband's wishes, crossed the desert with their daughter. The family was now together, building a life under a single roof on the outskirts of Charlotte. Reflecting on the decision years later, Angelica C. explained, "I was better off here than in Mexico. Here I worked and at the end of the week I had money. In Mexico, I worked and didn't end up with money."[49]

While the pursuit of dollars had fueled Mexico-U.S. migration since its inception, the desires that brought Angelica C.'s family into its fold were specific to their historical moment. Fifty years before, braceros acquired sewing machines from a Singer factory in Arkansas and brought them home to impress their wives; their dollars fueled the purchase of American-made clothes, hats, guns, or exciting new appliances such as radios.[50] In the rural areas from which most braceros hailed, goods manufactured by U.S. companies were comparatively expensive, and they symbolized the progress and sophistication of that northern neighbor.[51] For braceros, migration began with Mexican men's desire for status, adventure, service to country, or capital to establish and support young families—desires fostered in part by official rhetoric of the Mexican state. Migration continued in large part because migradollars from just one or two trips to the United States were seldom sufficient to fund the foreign goods, home and business improvements, and hometown fiestas that would allow these men to fulfill well-defined roles as patriarchs.[52]

In contrast, by the time Angelica C. convinced her husband to head for North Carolina in 2000, consumer culture in Mexico much more closely resembled that of the United States, even as purchasing power did not. From city to country and border to border, twenty-first-century Mexico was awash in foreign goods that were cheaper to purchase than their locally made counterparts. The North American Free Trade Agreement (NAFTA) of 1994 was followed by agreements for free trade between Mexico and the European Union, Japan, Israel, and most other Latin American countries, solidifying the country's neoliberal economic trajectory. Mexico's retail industry exploded in the fifteen years after NAFTA, with stores selling the same products that could be found in supermarkets and shopping malls everywhere: baby formula and disposable diapers, Nescafé and packaged tortillas, Nike shoes and Walmart blue jeans, Motorola cellular phones and Sony DVD players.[53] The options were endless, the goods were largely disposable, and the purchasing power of millions of Mexicans was frustratingly limited. The same free trade agreements that lowered the price of imported finished goods made it nearly impossible for rural Mexicans to compete in newly international agricultural markets, especially when it came to products such as grain, whose import prices were artificially low thanks to U.S. government subsidies.[54] A quarter of Mexico's agricultural jobs disappeared in the years following NAFTA, while others moved from family-based to industrial-scale farms.[55] As ten million Mexicans rose out of poverty between 1990 and 2006, twenty million others watched them from a different circumstance: neither destitute nor comfortable, they were able to afford food, school, and health care, but not much else.[56]

As it had since Rafael Landrove's journeys from Nuevo León to Mississippi in the 1920s, this gap between expectation and reality drove migration. María N., who joined her brothers in Union County as a single nineteen-year-old, explained that in Mexico, "You could just have the basics, food and clothes to wear. . . . There was no possibility of acquiring other things."[57] Edith H. concurred: "It's possible to support yourself in Mexico, but it's difficult. There are things you can't buy," not because those things were unavailable but because they were unaffordable for her. In Union County, by contrast, she knew that after a hard week at work, she could enjoy a vacation in Myrtle Beach or dinner out at a restaurant.[58] Angelica C., Edith H., María N., and countless others felt that migration to the United States was the surest way to gain the purchasing power of the middle class.[59]

Angelica C.'s decisive role in spurring her family's migration also reflected uneven yet widespread shifts in ideas about gender and family in Mexico—shifts that made it increasingly likely that women and children would join men in the United States.[60] Mercedes R., who felt unwelcome at Indian Trail's Poplin Elementary, was born in the village of Villa Madero, Michoacán, to parents in a typical midcentury migrant marriage: her father worked seasonally in the United States while her mother used his remitted dollars to raise their nine children in Mexico. Like so many others, Mercedes R. suffered the painful familial dislocations that these arrangements too often brought.[61] Her parents divorced, and her father moved permanently to the United States, abandoning his financial commitment to the family.[62] Eventually her mother, too, moved north, and Mercedes R. grew up with her grandmother, seeing her mom only every few years. For all of its sound economic logic, the traditional cross-border division of labor—wages in the United States, reproduction in Mexico—held little appeal for Mercedes R. and women like her as they grew into adulthood.[63] When five years of domestic work in the nearby state capital failed to yield a steady relationship or a compelling path toward financial progress, Mercedes R. crossed the border as a single woman with a group of friends and joined her brother in Union County. She would spend days in a wood factory and nights at Charlotte's dance clubs. Soon, she met and married a man from Guerrero and started a family in the exurbs of Charlotte.[64] Women's increasing participation in wage labor, experiences like Mercedes R.'s with cross-border family separation, and images of "modern" marriage available in global and particularly U.S. popular culture fostered a newly dominant ideal of emotionally intimate, companionate marriage in many rural and urban Mexican communities.[65] Being separated from their husbands had long pained migrants' wives in private, but changes in gender roles and local cultures now emboldened Mexican women to refuse such separations outright.[66]

Meanwhile, a new U.S. border enforcement policy, Operation Gatekeeper, made cross-border marriages increasingly difficult to sustain. Angelica C. had twice crossed the blazing Sonoran desert on foot; like most migrants of the late 1990s, she knew firsthand the life-threatening dangers that the journey presented. During those years, increased enforcement in urban areas such as San Diego and El Paso began to push undocumented border crossers like Angelica C. into harsh deserts. Operation Gatekeeper discouraged frequent border crossing and disrupted century-old patterns of circular male migration.[67] Loosened family control over women's movements and increased attention to their desires in marriage combined with stepped-up U.S. border enforcement to inspire single women to migrate alone and married women to insist that any family separation be temporary rather than a long-term economic strategy.[68] María F., who followed her husband to the United States at his insistence, in turn insisted herself that their children come not far behind. "I said, if we can't bring my daughters, I'm going back to Mexico," María F. told her husband. "Otherwise, we will lose everything. If I don't go back for seven or eight years, my daughter is not going to love me."[69] María F.'s forthright discussion of her family's psychological well-being and relationships differed from the discussions that typically took place in midcentury migrant households, where women were discouraged from talking openly about the emotional tolls of transborder family life.[70] It also reflected her different economic position: María F. felt that her family would not starve in Mexico, even if it might not advance there.

Finally, though Mercedes R., Angelica C., and María F. hailed from large families who made ends meet through agricultural work, their decision to have just two or three children was emblematic of their generation and its understanding of the changed economic landscape in which they lived. From the 1960s to 2010, the number of children per woman in Mexico dropped from seven to two. These smaller families both contributed to and resulted from the belief that each child required a significant investment of time and resources for education.[71] As these women's stories demonstrate, the growth of low-wage service and caretaking jobs in the United States encouraged women to migrate, but so too did women's assertion of their own evolving ideas about the kinds of marriages, families, and lifestyles they themselves wanted.

Unlike earlier migrants, Mexican migrants at the turn of the twenty-first century prioritized the formation of nuclear families with companionate marriages and two or three children, all living together under one roof. They valued access to the full range of consumer goods that the global marketplace churned out, from baby clothes to high-end electronics. For them, the good life meant not only work but also leisure and enough money left over for an annual vacation. And they saw education, starting with "good" elementary schools, as the undisputed key to their children's futures. Thus, while Latinos' differences perturbed Indian Trail parents, families like Jacqueline R.'s became exurban neighbors in large part because their migrant dreams overlapped substantially with those of the white exurban middle class.

Exurban Collision

Though they developed in distinct contexts, the plans and desires of greater Charlotte's white and Mexican residents drew them to similar spaces: fast-growing exurbs beyond the borders of Mecklenburg County. County seats Lincolnton, Concord, Monroe, and Gastonia entered the late twentieth century as small Piedmont towns, each with their own independent sense of place, politics, and local memory oriented around textile mills, light manufacturing, and eventually poultry production. Fruit orchards and strawberry and tobacco fields lay just beyond town centers. Yet as Charlotte grew during the 1990s, subdivisions replaced crops and edges of mill towns began to function as bedroom communities for growing numbers of mostly white residents. By 2000, a quarter of Gaston County's workers, a third of Cabarrus's, and more than 40 percent of Union County's workers commuted into Mecklenburg.[72] These commuters made Union a top-ten growth county nationwide and the fastest-growing county in North Carolina for much of the 1990s and early 2000s.[73] In exchange for their congested fifteen-mile drives, residents of these exurbs found larger houses for less money, an escape from the busing politics of Mecklenburg, and lower property taxes.[74] Jill Reed, a mother of three who moved from Ohio to a Union County subdivision in 2000, explained to a reporter, "Union County had really good schools.... The neighborhoods were beautiful and the taxes were cheaper."[75] In other words, Reed was attracted to a seemingly idyllic middle-class lifestyle that would allow her children to get the best education possible with the least amount of taxes paid.

The exurban parts of Union County were filled with newcomers like Reed. A third of Indian Trail's white people in 2000 had arrived there in just the preceding five years.[76] Like Reed, a substantial minority came from the Northwest or Midwest, but unlike in comparable exurbs such as Atlanta's Cobb County, three-quarters of Indian Trail's white residents over the age of five in 2000 had been born in North Carolina or elsewhere in the South, though many of these were children.[77] Furthermore, three of every seven domestic newcomers to Union County between 1995 and 2000 had moved out from Mecklenburg, though one in seven arrived from farther afield, New York or Florida.[78] Whatever their origins, Union County's new residents lived a life connected to cosmopolitan Charlotte, not the poorer county seat of Monroe.

Class and race bound Union County's newcomers. While poorer white and African American residents continued to live in the county seat of Monroe and more rural areas to its east, subdivisions like Indian Trail closer to Charlotte were overwhelmingly middle class and white at the turn of the twenty-first century. White people comprised 96 percent of Indian Trail's residents in 1990 and still 90 percent in 2000.[79] Their educational profile was average among white people nationwide: in 2000, nearly 90 percent of Indian Trail's white adults had graduated high school or earned a general equivalency diploma, just over half had attended at least some college, and one-fifth had a college or graduate degree.[80] Indian Trail's workers as a whole tended to occupy middling white-collar positions in management, insurance, finance, and sales.[81] Median household income among Union County's white people in 1999 was just over $53,000, lower than Mecklenburg's but higher than the other counties in its metropolitan area.[82] The white people moving into suburbanizing Union County housing tracts were thus members of a middle class whose share of the national income had been in decline since the 1960s.

These white newcomers further sidelined already-weak African American political voices in exurban counties. Poorer black residents lived in Union and other Charlotte-adjacent counties' rural areas and aging county seats but had little political clout to begin with; they comprised no more than 16 percent of the population in any of Charlotte's fringe counties in 1990, as compared with 26 percent in Mecklenburg.[83] But as Mecklenburg blacks' share of the population and political representation grew modestly over the subsequent decade, in fringe counties the wave of new white arrivals further cemented blacks' political marginality.[84] A few middle-class African Americans did move to new subdivisions, and in 2000, 6 percent of Indian Trail's residents were black. Though these new black exurbanites were on average more educated than their white neighbors, they did not have the votes to elect their own to office.[85] As African Americans played an increasingly prominent role in Charlotte's politics, black politics in exurban counties consisted of a few small NAACP chapters but almost no elected officials.

Rather than political rights or economic inequalities, exurban politics revolved around "growth, growth, growth" and persistent worry that local public services—the very things that had drawn exurbanites in the first place—were becoming overburdened.[86] Like middle-class voters throughout the country, Charlotte's exurbanites regarded these public services as goods to be purchased and consumed, like iPods or tract houses. Unable to afford private schools and amenities like their wealthier Mecklenburg counterparts, the main question they asked of government was, "Am I getting my money's worth?"[87] In this context, newcomers were assessed by the extent to which they contributed to, or drew down, the area's tax base.

As the twentieth century turned to the twenty-first, more and more newcomers were Latino, of those the majority Mexican. In the 1990s, Charlotte's predominantly male Mexican workforce had settled mostly in rental apartments in Charlotte's middle suburbs, close to work sites in construction.[88] In this sense, they were typical of immigrants generally during that period, who made their homes in suburbs more frequently than ever before.[89] But in greater Charlotte, the industrial jobs that remained from the twentieth-century Piedmont economy pulled Mexican immigrants still farther from the center of town and into neighboring counties. Shogren Hosiery Manufacturing in Concord, a sewing machine company in Gaston and Mount Holly, the Wagner Knitting Factory in Gaston County's Lowell, and Tyson chicken plants in Union County all recruited Latino workers through ads in Charlotte's Spanish-language newspaper in the late 1990s.[90] These industries were on the decline in North Carolina during those years as companies began to move production offshore, often to Latin America. Despite the anti-NAFTA rhetoric about the importance of saving "American" jobs, in practice immigrants from Mexico and Latin America, many of them undocumented, more than doubled their presence in North Carolina's industrial sector over the 1990s, as white and black workers assumed better-paid service jobs.[91]

Indeed, as observers marveled at the rapid growth of Charlotte's Latino population during the 1990s, growth in the metropolitan area's exurban counties was even more dramatic, particularly for Latino women and children. Mecklenburg County saw nearly sixfold Hispanic growth during the 1990s. But all of the exurban counties grew at least as quickly, while Cabarrus and Union, the most exurban of the bunch, saw more than tenfold growth in Hispanic population during the 1990s.[92] In 1991, a journalist in Union County noted an increasing presence of Mexican workers, most of them single men, living in crowded apartments in the county's majority-minority industrial center of Monroe.[93] His impression was accurate: statistics from 1989 showed just two Latino children born in the county that year, an indication that few Latina women lived there. But as women like Mercedes R. and Angelica C. sought social mobility through the migration of entire nuclear families during the 1990s, they increasingly directed those families—wives, children, and all—to trailer parks and single-family homes in Charlotte-adjacent bedroom communities. By the first years of the twenty-first century, half of the Hispanics in metro Charlotte lived outside city limits and Latina women outnumbered Latino men in the subdivisions and trailer parks of fast-growing Indian Trail (see map 6).[94] Unlike single men, women and children were viewed not just as workers but also as consumers of educational and health care services.

Newly settled exurban Mexican men and women did difficult jobs in nearby factories and chicken-processing plants but also in work tied to the metro area's booming service economy: construction and gardening for men and housekeeping for women.[95] Both María N. and Ana Hernández came to Union County to join relatives who worked in plastics and clothing factories, while Rosa Elba Gutiérrez monogrammed golf towels alongside elderly white women near Monroe.[96] Mercedes R. recalled the physical toll that factory work took on her body: when placing wood in a machine that sliced it, her hands would burn from the friction heat. By the time she came home at the end of the day, they were so blackened she would clean them with bleach. Women who cleaned houses typically commuted to work in Charlotte; Union County's new white residents were more middle class than wealthy and did not hire domestics as commonly as their city counterparts. Edith H. and María F. cleaned homes and offices; Mercedes R. preferred housecleaning to working in a factory and being "closed in eight hours a day."[97] Men whose work supported Charlotte's service economy as gardeners or construction workers, like the husbands of Alicia E. and Elvia H., worked in crews that traveled throughout the metro area. There was minimal overlap between the blue-collar jobs Mexicans did and the middling white-collar occupations of their white neighbors.

Yet though they occupied distinct economic classes, Union County's white and Mexican residents shared a common cultural orientation toward middle-class consumption and intensive child rearing and education. If the drive to live like the Mexican or U.S. middle classes had brought many of this generation's Mexican immigrants across the border in the first place, the desire to give their children a stable upbringing and the best shot at success in the neoliberal knowledge economy attracted them to the exurbs. Alicia E., for example, moved to a trailer park in Indian Trail in the early 2000s. She appreciated the "calm" environment, with almost no crime to speak of, where her two children could play with friends from nearby trailers. Though plenty of Mexican immigrants in Charlotte and elsewhere settled in black neighborhoods during this period, Alicia E.'s reference to "crime" may have alluded to her fear of such neighborhoods.[98] Echoing Ohio transplant Jill Reed and the white neighbors who lived in single-family homes just outside the trailer park's entrance, Alicia E. proudly claimed, "My kids are in one of the best schools in Union County. It's very clean, very pleasant. I am here for the kids, because they can have a better education here."[99] Though both she and her husband hailed from large families who worked in agriculture in a small Durango town, their decision to have just two children and orient their lives around these children's well-being and education reflected their belief that focused and thoughtful parenting could give their offspring the best possible future.

In addition to reputable schools, the promise of more living space for less money appealed to Mexican newcomers, albeit in ways different from the way it did to their white counterparts. Alicia E. said that her family "still fit" in its Indian Trail trailer as long as the kids were young, hinting that like other immigrant families, she believed good parenting meant providing adequate physical space for her nuclear family. Indeed, while neighbors criticized Mexicans for packing multiple families into one house or apartment, immigrants hailed from a country decades into its own suburbanization—a place where the number of residents per household was rapidly shrinking and multiple-family living arrangements were in decline.[100] The suburbanization and exurbanization of immigrant settlement thus reflected not only the availability of housing but, at least as important, Mexicans' changing attitudes toward the ideal composition of a household.

As white would-be home owners rushed to the exurbs in the 1990s and

2000s, developers wooed Latin American immigrants to some of those same subdivisions with promises of space and financial independence. One developer promised "Spacious living rooms, large bedrooms, big closets, grassy backyards, two-car garages, more than 2800 square feet" in a Spanish-language advertisement for its exurban tracts.[101] Fleetwood Homes hired a special Spanish-speaking sales agent and noted that she could work with potential buyers who had no Social Security number.[102] An advertisement for Adams Homes in Cabarrus, Gaston, and outer Mecklenburg counties summed up the aspiration: "The good life deserves a marvelous house."[103] And they had takers. From 1996 through around 2003, "everybody was buying a home," including undocumented immigrants, recalled Doris Cevallos, an Ecuadorean-born real estate agent who served Latino customers.[104] Peruvian-born real estate agent Celia Estrada recalled that in the late 1990s, the typical Latino home buyer was "Mexican, seeking a three-bedroom brick home on a big piece of land."[105] Like their white counterparts, many of these purchasers were buying homes beyond their means, as Latinos nationally were at least twice as likely to be talked into predatory subprime loans in those years and to later lose those homes in the economic crash of 2008.[106] Cevallos recalled that good schools, followed by "space," were the top priority for Mexican immigrant home buyers. Feeling a bit apprehensive about moving into largely white neighborhoods, Mexicans sought "a little bit of privacy" on larger parcels of land, separated from their new neighbors.[107] As Cevallos's observation suggested, Mexican newcomers tried to reap the benefits of exurban living while shielding themselves from the disapproval they felt from white exurbanites.

For Mexicans who could not afford a newly constructed single-family home, trailer parks nestled between pricier subdivisions provided many of the same advantages. When Alicia E. purchased a trailer in Indian Trail's Suburban Trailer Park in 2003, she was among the first Latinos there, but within ten years the trailer park became nearly all Latino, the vast majority of these Mexicans. By making ambitious middle-class white parents their neighbors, Mexicans secured their children spots in schools known for high achievement. Yet rather than the large lots and privacy that white and some Latino home owners wanted, immigrants in trailer parks enjoyed a communal environment in which their children could play in the street with other Latino kids, far from the eyes of critical white onlookers. That many felt quite satisfied with trailer park living showed that while Mexican immigrants shared some of the same ambitions as the white home owners who lived around the corner, they did not adopt them all. For them as for many of the South's

Mexicanos over the twentieth century, creating the physical and political space for community was, in itself, a valued act of resistance to economic and racial subjugation.[108]

Unworthy Consumers in Years of Plenty

As the U.S. economy boomed in the late 1990s and again from 2003 to 2007, Mexican immigrants rode the rising tide in greater Charlotte, finding plentiful employment in factories, private homes, and construction sites; taking vacations on the coast; shopping in malls and big-box stores; starting families of two or three children; purchasing homes and trailers in carefully selected school districts; and driving with state-issued licenses even if they were undocumented. These very choices made them more visible to white exurbanites than the single Mexican men who had once appeared only at construction sites. The Suburban Trailer Park in Indian Trail, for example, sat around the corner from a subdivision of middle-class tract homes built between 1985 and 2010; homes there sold for $140,000–300,000 in the mid-2000s.[109] The trailer park was just up the street from Poplin Elementary, the highly regarded school where Mercedes R. felt hostility from white families during the years her children attended (see map 7). No longer a hidden workforce, these nonwhite, working-class families were newly apparent consumers of middle-class public services.

While popular and scholarly discussions assume that anti-immigrant sentiment has typically flared during economic downturns in U.S. history, the mid-2000s present a counterpoint. It was during these years of plenty that southern communities, including exurban Charlotte, became home to influential Mexican-directed anti-immigrant movements for the first time in the history of the U.S. South. These movements did not spring from those who feared employment competition from immigrants, as in Cedartown and Gainesville, Georgia, in the early 1980s. Rather, they emerged from middle-class white home owners who decried the ways that Mexican immigrants used their newfound purchasing power to gain access to the very same things white families had sought in the exurbs: affordable homes, low-crime neighborhoods, highways for commuting, large stores for shopping, and, most of all, good schools. Mexican immigrants sought and acquired access to all of these things in exurban Charlotte. But because white families did not see Mexicans as one of "us," they targeted "them" as unworthy consumers of private and particularly public goods.[110] Advocating an increase in tax revenues for local coffers was fraught; advocating a decrease in the number of Mexicans drawing on those coffers became increasingly easy.

Still, labeling the problem as such—Mexicans—would have run counter to the dominant strand of suburban conservatism, which eschewed overt racism.[111] Instead, local activists and politicians began to attack "illegal" immigrants, a rhetorically raceless category of people that California activists had christened a decade before.[112] And as in California, discussions of illegal immigration in Charlotte drew almost always on observations and examples of those who were brown-skinned and spoke Spanish.[113]

Greater Charlotte's mid-2000s anti-immigrant movement found its rhetoric in national discussions but its political base in the exurbs. State legislator Wil Neumann, a primary sponsor of early anti-immigrant legislation in the North Carolina House of Representatives, shared many of the characteristics of his exurban neighbors in Gaston County's Cramerton. Neumann was a home owner, husband, and father of two. He had a graduate degree in business and worked in the health care and technology industries. In an interview, he recalled spending time and money enrolling his young son in a special program to prepare him for kindergarten. The Neumanns were frustrated to see who sat next to their child on the first day of elementary school: a Spanish-speaking girl who had recently arrived in the United States with no English skills. The Neumanns watched, deflated, as the girl took up resources they believed were rightfully their son's. "It's not only a matter of how much money this child is costing the school," Neumann explained, "but where does your attention as a teacher go?" In the era of high-stakes testing, Neumann knew the teacher had no choice but to give more of her time to the immigrant student.[114] Educated in background, middle class in resources, color-blind in discourse, Neumann's comments captured the sentiments of white middle-class home owners worried that their family's economic progress was stunted when resources for which they had paid instead became diverted to Latino immigrants. He discussed the incident in the context of his anti-"illegal" immigration activism, though he would have had no way to know the immigration status of the young girl in his son's class.

The connection Neumann drew between Gaston County's changing demographics and his son's life chances developed in a context well beyond that first-grade classroom. Rhetoric like his first developed in California's suburban Orange County during the 1990s Proposition 187 debate. It then traveled throughout the country during the following decade. From 2006 through 2008, a wave of anti-immigrant state legislation, local ordinances, and mandates for police cooperation with federal immigration authorities swept through the United States.[115] The movement combined grassroots energies with national politics, often advocating that model legislation from national conservative organizations be implemented on a local or state level.[116] It traveled from California through Long Island, from Hazleton, Pennsylvania, to suburban Milwaukee, and found strong traction in the South, particularly its suburban and exurban areas.[117]

Indeed, rather than a southern "rogue political culture," suburban and now exurban "color-blind" white entitlement best explains this anti-immigrant movement.[118] Within the South, anti-immigrant organizations, ordinances, and politicians emerged from those most generic of southern landscapes: suburbs and particularly exurbs grappling with the early or middle years of demographic changes. Georgia's Dustin Inman Society was founded in 2005 by D. A. King, a lifelong resident of Cobb County, an Atlanta suburb that had become increasingly diverse during the decades he lived there.[119] The group was named after a Cobb County teenager killed in a car crash by an allegedly undocumented Latino immigrant. In Virginia, the Save the Old Dominion coalition included seven anti-immigrant groups: Help Save Loudoun, Vienna Citizens Coalition, Help Save Hampton Roads, Centreville Citizens Coalition, Help Protect Culpeper, Save Stafford, and Help Save Manassas.[120] All seven groups aimed to "save" communities on the fringe of Washington, D.C., or Norfolk, Virginia, from Latino immigrant influxes. And in North Carolina, Americans for Legal Immigration Political Action Committee (ALIPAC) was born of its founder William Gheen's experience with rapid Latino growth in Union County. Believing the mainstream media were not sufficiently outraged by the immigrant influx to the state, Gheen became consumed by the issue of illegal immigration and formed ALIPAC in 2004.[121] Another anti-immigrant organization founded around the same time, NCListen, was headquartered in Cary, a rapidly growing suburb in the Raleigh–Durham–Chapel Hill triangle.[122]

California-bred discourses circulating nationally offered a "ready-made framework" for southern exurbanites worried about changes in their communities.[123] In turn, southern organizations' activists moved in a decidedly national space thanks to Internet-based networks and frequent interviews with the mainstream media. Though based in North Carolina, ALIPAC claimed its strongest support in California, Texas, Florida, and Colorado.[124] The Dustin Inman Society maintained national networks even as it focused on preventing the coming of "Georgifornia," by which founder King meant the immigrant-induced "chaos that has befallen the once wealthy and desirable state of California."[125] Spokespeople, usually group founders, traveled to speak at anti-immigrant rallies across the country, weaving together a loose national network in which suburban white southerners played a prominent role.

Some of the movement's more extreme grassroots supporters linked overtly racial rhetoric with their objections to undocumented immigrants' consumption of public services.[126] Spokespeople for ALIPAC and the Dustin Inman Society painted Latinos as "drunk drivers, gang members, invaders, murderers, and disease-carriers."[127] Further along the political spectrum, self-proclaimed members of the Aryan Nation wrote occasionally to Charlotte's Latin American Coalition, in one case asserting that "the U.S. taxpaying citizen will not have to spend one penny" deporting "wetbacks" because they would be "delivered across the border free of charge, by the Aryan Nation in a body bag."[128] The writer overtly melded white supremacy with a discourse of taxpayers' individual rights.

But such openly racial rhetoric was rare in these discussions. In both public and private communications, greater Charlotte's anti-immigration grassroots activists hewed to the terms of color-blindness, emphasizing their identities as taxpayers above all.[129] Dotti Jenkins of Mint Hill, an independent town on the eastern edge of Mecklenburg County, wrote to Representative Neumann that at her daughter's nearby community college, "there were many days when there were no parking spots.... I believe all children should have an opportunity to get an education because it is the way to ensure a brighter future, but we cannot support illegals at the expense of our own children."[130] Though Jenkins did not report that these parking spots were taken by Latinos, let alone undocumented immigrants, she focused on the scarcity of this all-important public resource—higher education—in her political rhetoric about immigration. John Love, an information technology consultant based in the Raleigh suburb of Cary, shared Jenkins's sentiments about community colleges. "Let the illegals pay their own way," he wrote in opposition to those who would grant them in-state tuition rates. "I would prefer they not be allowed to attend at all."[131] Terry Lewis thanked Neumann for his efforts to reduce immigrants' presumed overconsumption of public services: "Why don't we cut their free medical that my children that were born here can't even receive?"[132] However inaccurate, Lewis's allegation drew on the consumer and taxpayer identities at the heart of the first anti-Mexican immigrant political movement to gain widespread traction in the South.

In many cases, Charlotte's white middle-class exurban activists utilized Internet activism to participate in the immigration debate nationally as well as locally. Tish Huss of Mooresville, thirty miles north of Charlotte in Iredell County, wrote Neumann, "Illegals are breaking state budgets across the country. We've HAD IT, folks ... we have absolutely HAD IT."[133] Two years later, she signed an online petition in support of Arizona's tough-on-immigrants Sheriff Joe Arpaio.[134] Monte Monteleone, a research and database manager, wrote to praise state representatives who opposed the admission of "illegals" to North Carolina's community colleges. "In the words of Sean Hannity," he wrote, referencing the national conservative commentator, "You are a great American."[135] Though they resided in greater Charlotte, Huss and Monteleone, like so many other Charlotte exurbanites who championed the anti-immigrant cause, drew their rhetoric and politics from a national milieu linked to the ascendance of a national conservative media on air and online.

The movement's first successes in the South were anti-immigrant ordinances passed in suburban and exurban landscapes that were politically independent from cities and heavily urban counties: in North Carolina, in the independent town of Landis in Rowan County, and on the county level in Lincoln and Gaston counties, as well as in Winston-Salem-area counties Davidson and Forsythe. In Georgia, ordinances appeared exclusively in the area surrounding Atlanta: Cherokee, Cobb, and Gwinnett counties, as well as the cities of Coweta and Canton. In Virginia, all but two ordinances appeared in suburban Washington and Norfolk.[136] These proposals enjoyed success because they emerged from suburban or exurban counties and independent cities that did not include urban or rural areas within their boundaries. While many rural areas still hewed to forms of pro-immigrant conservatism described in the previous chapter, urban areas like Charlotte were home to liberal and business-driven coalitions that acted as a bulwark against anti-immigrant policy making.

A comparison of anti-immigrant ordinance debates in Mecklenburg and Gaston counties shows how the Charlotte Way and a Democratic majority kept the movement at bay in the city even as politically independent exurbs passed anti-immigrant legislation. Gaston's ordinance was proposed in 2006, a time of economic prosperity and rapid exurban growth, by Commissioner John Torbett. Torbett represented a comparatively wealthy slice of Gaston County, where just 1 percent of the population was classified as Hispanic in 2000, as opposed to 3 percent countywide.[137] The commissioner representing the old industrial county seat of Gastonia, a poorer area where most of the county's Latinos actually lived, was absent from the meeting altogether. Poor whites and African Americans—those most directly competing with Latinos for jobs—were not the base of Gaston's anti-immigrant movement.

The Gaston County ordinance's text affirmed federal immigration law and linked Latino immigrants to criminality and inferior lifestyles in ways echoing the extremist rhetoric of some national anti-immigrant spokespeople. The ordinance called for the county to fund only federally mandated services for "illegal" immigrants; to forbid contracting with businesses hiring them; to restrict the number of people who could live in one rental unit; to establish a partnership between local law enforcement and Immigration and Customs Enforcement; and to encourage county law enforcement to "diligently battle the ever increasing criminal element which is growing daily with the influx of the illegal population and to consistently check the immigration status of each undocumented resident."[138] The link between "illegals," criminality, and the negative effects of "Latino" living practices on suburban neighborhoods projected concerns about Latinos' class status and purported racial qualities onto the "legal"–"illegal" axis. Indeed, when supporter Commissioner Tom Keigher was asked why a rental housing ordinance would be tied into an illegal immigration measure, he responded uncertainly, "It is attached to this because that is one of the major issues facing . . . ummm . . . the access for illegal aliens."[139] Keigher was not alone: throughout the country, zealous enforcement of single-family zoning laws was a primary means through which localities sought to discourage immigrant settlement in the mid-2000s.[140] His stumped response revealed the limits of color-blind discourse in the face of policy making with a specific racialized group in mind.

Though Keigher may have been confused by the racial assumptions underlying his own arguments, Pearl Burris-Floyd, a Republican and Gaston's only African American commissioner, understood them clearly. "We are still battling issues in our county and in our country with racial profiling," Burris-Floyd protested. She insisted that maximum-occupancy housing restrictions and police mandates to check immigration status "impact not only illegals, but also impact legal citizens. And if you haven't experienced it in terms of being stopped for a minor traffic infraction and almost have to call in your lord and savior to get you off the hook, then it's very difficult for you to understand how this type of statement coming from the commissioners could impact innocent people. We must be sensitive to the fact that every person who lives in our community who happens to speak another language doesn't necessarily equal an illegal resident."[141] Burris-Floyd immediately recognized a measure whose title referred only to "illegal residents" as a thin shell for racial sentiment and policy making. A Republican, her experiences as a black woman in Gaston County, rather than party politics, motivated her opposition to the ordinance. She also likely presumed that her constituents in Dallas township—one-fifth black and with a considerably poorer white population than that in Torbett's district—were mostly indifferent to the supposed threat of the county's "illegal residents." By contrast, Torbett's constituents represented the exact type of exurban voters that anti-immigrant ordinances were likely to please: middle class, white, and worried not about job competition but rather about changes in schools, neighborhoods, and the clientele of public services. The resolution passed, with only Burris-Floyd opposing.[142]

Like Burris-Floyd, Mecklenburg County's African American commissioners, in this case Democrats with an eye toward long-term coalition-building, declined to jump into the anti-immigrant movement. Anti-immigrant sentiment within Charlotte and Mecklenburg County also emerged from middle-class white far suburbs, but the County Commission's Democratic majority blocked their anti-immigrant proposals and moderated their rhetoric. Only one county commissioner in Mecklenburg spoke out regularly against Latino immigrants: Commissioner Bill James, a onetime anti-busing activist who represented suburban eastern Mecklenburg County, adjacent to Union County.[143] The following exchange in 2008 between James and Commissioners Norman Mitchell and Valerie Woodard, both African American Democrats, shows how the representatives of diverse urban dwellers—even those, like poor African Americans, who faced some job competition from immigrants—held at bay the anti-immigrant sentiments of far suburban white middle-class home owners. Woodard defended the commissioners' earlier decision not to impose additional immigration-related standards on county contractors. "That's alright, just suck up to illegals," responded James, frustrated with his inability to push a class-conscious suburban anti-immigrant agenda onto a Democratic coalition of African Americans and wealthier white pro-business liberals. Later, when Mitchell described his immigration-reform lobbying efforts with the National Association of Counties, he continued, "The Bush administration was not serious about a comprehensive immigration plan. Just the other day in the *Observer*, there was an article written that illegal immigrants also pay taxes." James interrupted him, "And prostitutes and drug dealers. Al Capone paid taxes." Voting "no" on a motion to affirm the commission's earlier decision, James grumbled, "Actually, maybe I should have said 'nada.'"[144] It was a grumble of certain defeat; the Democratic-controlled commission maintained its original position and refrained from implementing new measures to discourage immigration to the county.

The pattern of suburban and exurban anti-immigrant movements and urban moderation repeated itself throughout the state and region, turning state legislatures into immigration battlegrounds. In North Carolina, liberal policy on undocumented immigrant driver's licenses attracted increasing scrutiny. Though opposition to the policy had first begun in response to long waits at DMV offices in metropolitan areas, post-9/11 security concerns quickly became the favored arguments against them. The federal REAL ID Act tied the hands of states, and in 2006 a bipartisan majority required North Carolina driver's license applicants to present a Social Security number. A follow-up bill in 2007 required proof that applicants were legally present in the United States. The policy that had once signaled the state's comparative openness to undocumented immigrants thus came to an end.[145] Discontent born of perceived overuse of government services in the 1990s culminated a decade later in statewide legislation that starkly changed the lives of all the state's undocumented residents.

From there, the exurb-led battles over immigration continued. In 2007, Gaston County's Representative Neumann joined two Republicans from the exurbs of Winston-Salem and one from a military-dominated district to create the "NC Illegal Immigration Prevention Act," HB1485. Notably, none of the act's primary sponsors represented the rural areas that actually had the state's highest concentration of Latinos. The act proposed a host of measures designed to encourage undocumented immigrants to leave the state. These included encouraging local police to enforce immigration law and, perhaps most relevant to middle-class parents like Neumann, banning undocumented immigrants outright from state colleges and universities. In the Democratic-controlled state house, the bill died in committee.

Geographies of Protest

The loss of driver's licenses in North Carolina and the increasingly hostile state and national climate affected all the state's immigrants, whether they hailed from rural areas touting pro-immigrant conservatism, diverse central cities and inner suburbs, or hostile exurban spaces. For one, it meant that encounters with local law enforcement felt more threatening than before. In the past, explained Angelica C., police who caught immigrants driving without a license "would give us a ticket and let us go," but no longer.[146] Another Mexican woman said that in the twenty years since she arrived in Union County in the early 1990s, "I've felt a change. You used to be able to trust the police, but not anymore."[147] This new way of relating to local authorities significantly altered Mexican women's perceptions of whether their communities sought to include or exclude them.[148] Though they were seldom able to pinpoint specific incidents, Union County Mexican immigrant interviewees described a vague yet palpable sense of unwelcome locally as anti-immigrant politics flared nationally and police officers became pursuers rather than protectors.

Even in business-minded Charlotte, Republican mayor Pat McCrory went from courting Latinos to speaking out against them as he sought to broaden his Republican appeal for a gubernatorial campaign. The city's Spanish-language newspaper opined, "We the Latinos have changed in the eyes of McCrory. In the 1990s we were a hard working community, with family values, needed to build downtown Charlotte. Now that it has all been built, he is using us for a different purpose"—courting white suburban votes by stoking anti-immigrant sentiment.[149] Through the previous several decades, different conservative constituencies held diverse views on Mexican and, later, Latino immigration; if anything, southern conservatives had embraced this new workforce more than their counterparts elsewhere had. McCrory's shift in 2008 was just one indication that political space in the immigration debate had narrowed greatly for Republicans in the first decade of the twenty-first century.[150]

In 2005 and 2006, immigrants and their allies protested the hostile turn in Charlotte as throughout the country. Unlike the exurbs, the city had visible public spaces where protestors could gather and public bus routes to help immigrants arrive even if they did not have a driver's license. Thousands convened time and again at Marshall Park inside Charlotte's downtown loop, garnering widespread media coverage as they demanded human rights. And when national Latino leaders called for a boycott of schools and businesses in 2006, more than 800 students skipped school in the Charlotte-Mecklenburg district. The strongest participation was among Latino students at majority-black high schools in the city's diverse middle-ring suburbs.[151] Their political activism signaled that they, like Eréndira Molina, whose school picture began this chapter, felt themselves politically empowered in their diverse urban environments.

The Latin American Coalition, established around 1990 by Latin American professionals, provided the bulk of resources for the area's nascent immigrants' rights movement. From its original purpose as a cultural organization, the agency morphed into a social services agency once poorer Latinos began arriving and finally in the 2000s became a hub of activism, particularly for undocumented youths and their supporters. These students lobbied state legislators for access to higher education, joined in national efforts to pass immigration reform and stop deportations, and registered their U.S. citizen peers to vote.[152]

While some black politicians supported the movement from its inception, others responded skeptically at first. In 2006, the then director of the Latin American Coalition, Angeles Ortega-Moore, received a cool welcome at the Tuesday Morning Breakfast Forum, a weekly meeting of the city's African American power brokers. Rather than beginning a dialogue about black–Latino alliances as Ortega-Moore had hoped, the meeting turned into a venting session in which the black leaders attacked her for the ills that had befallen African Americans as a result of Latino immigration. A blogger for the *Charlotte Post*, the city's black newspaper, reported: "The way folks were gettin' after girlfriend, you would've thought she was bringing in a bunch o' illegals by herself. You can imagine how the ranting took on a life of its own: Forum types get worked up over immigrants taking jobs, don't pay taxes and soak up human services and health care like sponges. Then it turns into an us vs. them Hispanics tirade and the piling on starts."[153] Ortega-Moore characterized the participants' attitude as "Where have you been? You come and ask now for help—where have you been?"[154] In a city, state, and region where an entire generation of African American civic leaders had emerged from the trenches of the civil rights movement and school desegregation battles, the charge carried particular resonance.

The incident, however, proved to be isolated. As Charlotte's immigrants' rights movement gained momentum, African American and Latino leaders cast their lot with coalition politics despite on-the-ground tensions that persisted in some mixed neighborhoods. Black civil rights figures and politicians repeatedly took the speaker's platform at Marshall Park immigrants' rights rallies and defended Latinos in county commission meetings.[155] Even beyond the political elite, African Americans declined time and again to embrace anti-immigrant politics in a public way. When Colorado congressman and national anti-immigrant champion Tom Tancredo tried to stage a rally in a majority-black neighborhood in western Charlotte in 2006, African Americans instead joined Latinos in a counterprotest outside. "For me," said black community organizer Robert Dawkins, "just the fact of calling someone illegal is racially offensive."[156] While Charlotte's schools and neighborhoods were home to both tensions and goodwill between blacks and Latinos, in the public sphere African Americans easily detected the racial underpinnings of the anti-immigrant backlash and defended Latinos against it.

Black–brown coalitions also emerged in other southern cities during the first decade of the twenty-first century.[157] In 2012, black leaders including the Reverend Al Sharpton joined with Latino activists to reenact the civil rights movement's iconic march from Selma to Montgomery; this time, their demands included a repeal of Alabama's punitive anti-immigrant law.[158] In Mississippi, black leaders publicly supported the use of the "Freedom Rides" metaphor that immigrants' rights activists adopted in 2003. "They have the same problems we had in the 1960s as to finding jobs, living wages, and places to live," a state NAACP officer told a reporter. African American leaders also helped organize Mississippi's pro-immigrant marches in 2006.[159] Just as the range of acceptable views on Latino immigration narrowed among southern Republicans in the early 2000s, so too did it narrow—in an opposite way— among diverse constituencies within the Democratic base.

While white churches had offered a prominent pro-immigrant conservative discourse that shaped public discussions and policies in rural agricultural areas like southern Georgia, they did not have a similar effect in greater Charlotte. Prominent Evangelical churches did thrive there, but they attracted a smaller share of the white public than they had in rural areas.[160] And while some Evangelical churches conducted extensive Latino outreach efforts, others, like First Baptist Church of Indian Trail, did so fitfully or not at all.[161] Urban Charlotte's Catholic churches and their more liberal parishioners embraced Latinos, but in far suburbs and fringe counties, where long-standing blue-collar white residents worshipped together with white exurban newcomers, reception of Latinos was inconsistent. Some immediately sprouted volunteers like Georgia's Howdy and Mary Ann Thurman, who wanted to incorporate Latinos, but others made Latinos feel decidedly unwelcome.[162] Meanwhile, the theologically liberal "mainline" denominations, such as Methodists, Lutherans, and Anglicans, which had greater prominence in metropolitan than rural areas, generally kept greater distance from Latino immigrants.[163] In one Methodist church filled with mostly white, middle-class, college-educated, "not particularly conservative" Democrats and Republicans at the southwestern edge of Mecklenburg County, a pastor described immigration as "one of the hardest issues to preach on." A significant subset of congregants, he explained, felt strongly that Latino immigrants threatened their own claims to the benefits of U.S. citizenship. Drawing on a metaphor apt for his suburban setting, the pastor mused, "It's like how people feel about their yards. 'Your tree is climbing over into my yard.'"[164] White middle-class congregants' emphasis on individual rights over Christian universalism prevented churches in greater Charlotte from uniting behind a pro-immigrant discourse, whether liberal or conservative, as they had in southern Georgia.

Among once-potent earlier allies in the U.S. South, not only white churches but also the Mexican state no longer offered decisive political support to metropolitan Mexican immigrants in the 1990s–2000s. Midcentury Mexican migrants to the South could use nationally defined appeals to make their Mexican citizenship a political weapon in new work sites—not so for those in greater Charlotte fifty years later. Once, the bracero-era Mexican Foreign Service had opened a consulate in Memphis within two years of Mexican workers' arrival in the Arkansas Delta and fought successful battles for those workers' rights; now, the Mexican-born population of the Carolinas passed 200,000 before an official Mexican consulate opened to serve the states, in 2000.[165] North Carolina's largely undocumented Mexican immigrant population needed a place to process the Mexican identity documents that, before 2006, could help them get driver's licenses. Furthermore, Mexico's transition out of one-party rule in 2000 brought a redoubling of federal, state, and local policy making designed to give emigrants a voice in the affairs of their hometowns and their nation; this included extending voting rights to Mexicans living abroad and matching their organizations' charitable contributions to public works in their communities of origin.[166] The Raleigh consulate processed more than 15,000 "migrant assistance and protection" cases between 2001 and 2012. The vast majority of these involved basic consular functions: visiting the imprisoned, repatriating the sick and the dead, locating the missing, receiving the deported, securing alimony for the divorced, and producing national identity documents. But just 1 percent of cases, an average of fewer than twenty per year, involved labor, civil, or human rights—contesting abuse by U.S. authorities or demanding unpaid wages and worker's compensation—though both forms of exploitation occurred regularly in migrant communities across the region.[167] The Raleigh consul had more to offer Mexican emigrants than its Atlanta counterpart in the 1980s but still did not provide Mexicans with political leverage in a place where they did not hold citizenship.

As Charlotte's undocumented Mexican adults overcame their fears to go to Marshall Park, link arms with African American ministers and Salvadoran construction workers, and demand immigration reform, exurban Mexican immigrants stayed largely out of sight. "Here?" asked Edith H. in response to a question about immigrants' rights activism in Union County. "No. Maybe in Charlotte."[168] Angelica C. concurred: "Sometimes they do [marches] in Charlotte, but I've never gone."[169] Ana Hernández was a bilingual recent high school graduate and a legal permanent resident when the marches took place; though she was interested in participating, she did not attend either. "Charlotte is like a whole different place," she explained. Mexicans in Union County, she mused, adopted an attitude of "If I don't see it in front of me, then it's not happening."[170] While a rare church bus would transport exurban immigrants to Marshall Park, Charlotte's overwhelmed and underresourced advocates remained almost entirely disconnected from exurban migrant communities.[171]

Nor did parallel organizing develop out in the exurbs. The privatized and car-dependent suburban landscape of Indian Trail and places like it left little public space for immigrants to visibly claim.[172] From the start, Edith H. felt that the lack of sidewalks and public transportation starkly distinguished Union County from Mexico, shaping her experience of her new home.[173] Driving grew riskier each day as licenses issued before 2007 lapsed with no possibility of renewal for the undocumented. Car trips were for necessary excursions to work, school, or local retail centers; the twenty miles of highway between exurban immigrants and the Charlotte immigrants' rights movement was riddled with potential problems. "I can't go to the marches because I have kids," explained Norma C. "What if something happens to me?"[174] Accustomed to living in fear of authority, Angelica C. avoided Charlotte's marches in part because of rumors that immigration authorities would raid them.[175] While Union County's middle-class white residents traveled freely to and from Charlotte on busy highways, the area's Mexican immigrants increasingly made their world apart from the city, immobilized by their lost driver's licenses. Fear erected psychological barriers to undocumented immigrants' political participation everywhere during the mid-2000s, but in the exurbs, geography compounded these with substantial physical barriers.[176] With Mexican transborder state power substantially weakened and liberal Democratic allies seemingly a world away in Charlotte, even the fringe county public spaces that did exist, such as the old downtowns of Monroe and Gastonia, saw no vigils for immigrants' rights.[177]

Yet just as anti-immigrant activists moved in national circles thanks to media and the Internet, so too did Mexicanos, particularly youths. Though they were unlikely to meet political organizers in person, exurban immigrants and their children were keenly aware of the national immigrants' rights movement as a result of both traditional and social media. On the day of a national Latino consumption boycott in 2006, many Union County stores reported that sales were down, signaling that at least some immigrants there were willing to join in the national movement through a low-risk action.[178] Hundreds took a greater risk, telling their bosses that they would not be coming to work at poultry or manufacturing plants in observance of the boycott.[179] Their actions gained little visibility outside their workplaces.

Youths were key catalysts of immigrants' rights marches everywhere during 2005–6, but in Charlotte's exurbs they were the only local catalysts, acting within the confines of their high schools. At majority-white North Mecklenburg High School, in fast-growing Huntersville at the edge of the county, more than fifty students walked out of class to protest a teacher's classroom proclamation that "Latinos were like the rats of New York, and that we were hiding out in corners to evade immigration authorities," reported a student.[180] At Indian Trail's Sun Valley High School, also majority white, a math teacher told students in 2008 that he could not wait until the day when Latino kids would be reassigned to another school; when the principal took no action in response to student complaints, ninth-grader Gaby Aguilar organized two successful student protests.[181] The events recalled 1968 in East Los Angeles, when Chicano high school students walked out of class to protest educational discrimination. But while these earlier "Blowouts" occurred in a rich political ferment of Chicano school board candidates, college activists, and the Brown Berets, among others, students in greater Charlotte forty years later had no such political network in the communities that physically surrounded them.[182] More likely, they found inspiration from news of the national immigrants' rights movement and planned their actions using leadership skills they had developed in student clubs and groups.[183]

Even as some immigrant youths took risks to raise their political voices in the public sphere, their parents focused on accomplishing the goal that had brought them to greater Charlotte in the first place: achieving a middle-class lifestyle. Rather than political rights, they claimed consumer privileges unavailable to them in Mexico. "I will stay here until they kick me out," said Angelica C. flatly in 2011. Despite the economic downturn and increasingly hostile climate, one fact remained: "Here, the kids can go out to eat sometimes, go out to the store, see something that they like, buy it. In Mexico that doesn't happen. You work just to eat."[184] For Norma C., it was impossible to imagine leaving the special education services that a daughter with disabilities could receive for free in Union County. Experiences with social exclusion and hostility at Poplin Elementary School did not change Mercedes R.'s feeling that Union County provided her children with far greater opportunity than Mexico.[185] But even Edith H., a single woman with no children, quipped, "If they would deport me to Paris, great! But they'd send me to Mexico."[186] Raised in a firmly neoliberal Mexico, these women valued their families' economic progress more than the privileges of liberal citizenship.

Rather than march, Union County's Mexican immigrant women carved out spaces for community in an otherwise-harsh environment. They gathered with Latino neighbors on trailer porches or at youth soccer games to watch

FIGURE 33 Family outing to a shopping mall in exurban North Carolina, ca. 2009. Courtesy of Edith V.

children play and attended Spanish story hour at the library. They turned consumption into camaraderie, chatting with friends in the aisles of Compare Foods, attending Zumba classes together, and gathering to sell each other Herbalife, Tupperware, and Mary Kay cosmetics.[187] On weekends, they took their families to church and to the children's play areas within shopping malls. Unlike the family photo albums of Georgia's migrant workers three decades before, which highlighted families' participation in agricultural labor, Charlotte's twenty-first-century exurban migrants collected photographs, now digital, that hewed more to white middle-class norms by capturing their families in moments of leisure, consumption, and education. They showed families relaxing at shopping malls or the zoo and children at their schools (figs. 33, 34, and 35). These women's absence from the immigrants' rights activism of the early twenty-first century did not signal their satisfaction with the political status quo, nor did it result from a form of poverty so extreme as to preclude thinking beyond daily needs. Rather, they affirmed their humanity and that of their families by nurturing social ties the exurban way: via parenting and purchasing. Future research on places like Los Angeles's Antelope Valley, New York's Rockland County, and Virginia's Loudoun County can reveal to what extent exurban space itself has shaped immigrants' choices in consistent ways.

(left) FIGURE 34 Mercedes R.'s daughter Jacqueline talking on a cell phone in front of her school. Courtesy of Mercedes R.

(right) FIGURE 35 Mercedes R. poses playfully at the North Carolina Zoo, ca. 2009. The mural behind her is of the cartoon characters Dora and Diego. Courtesy of Mercedes R.

In Union County, Mexican adults' public silence left the exurbs' anti-immigrant voices unchallenged and unopposed. The exurbs had no Charlotte Way, no liberal allies, no activist consuls, no labor unions, and, ultimately, no immigrants' rights organizing that would push hard-line politicians to soften their tone or moderate their proposals. Some exurban counties' NAACP chapters tried to form a common agenda with Latinos, making significant efforts to register them to vote and invite them to meetings. But those chapters were small to begin with, and they found that frustratingly few Latinos responded to their overtures.[188] The exurbs' anti-immigrant sentiments flourished unchecked.

By the year 2012, it would be easy to mistake the rash of anti-immigrant ordinances and state-level legislation in the South as the inevitable result of the region's notorious racism. Yet this book has told a different story. The rhetoric

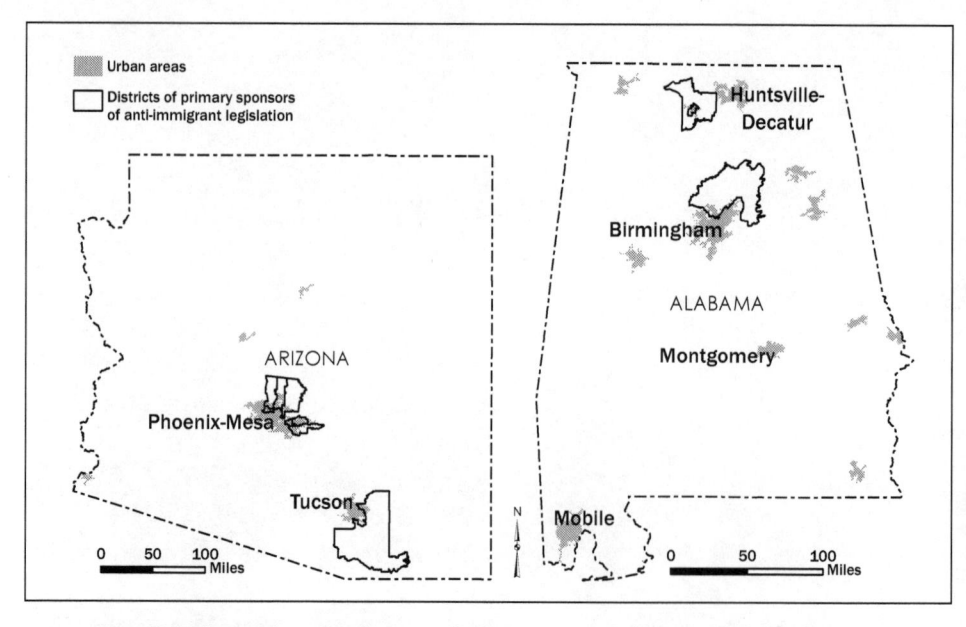

MAP 8 Suburban and exurban districts of primary sponsors of state anti-immigrant legislation in the West and South. Urban areas data (Census 2000) and legislative data (2006) from U.S. Census Cartographic Boundary Files, https://www.census.gov/geo/maps-data/data/tiger-cart-boundary.html; legislative cosponsors data from Arizona State Legislature, www.azleg.com (for SB1070 in 2010), and Alabama Legislative Information System Online, http://www.legislature.state.al.us/aliswww/AlisWWW.aspx (for SB256 in 2011). Map by the author.

of the white taxpayer decrying Latino immigrants' undeserving consumption of public services, rather than the U.S. citizen worker protesting immigrants' effects on jobs and wages, emerged from Southern California's suburbanizing areas in the 1990s; it led to overwhelming voter approval of an anti-immigrant ballot initiative in 1994 and eventually to diminished services for legal immigrants in the federal welfare reform of 1996.[189] As noted in Chapter 4, Atlanta exurbanites expressed similar sentiments in the 1990s. By the twenty-first century, the "taxpayer"-based anti-immigrant discourse ricocheted through the United States, motivating similar initiatives in states as far afield as Arizona and Alabama. What these initiatives and their proponents had in common was their situation in fast-growing exurbs (see map 8). While each of the first four chapters of this book told a story that was significantly distinct from contemporaneous trends in Mexican American history elsewhere, the story of greater Charlotte since 1990 is not only the story of a city or a region but also the story of countless suburbanizing areas throughout the United States.

Conclusion

"For the first time," wrote a journalist in 1999, "significant numbers of people are moving into the South who don't care if the Confederate flag flies over the South Carolina capitol or if Robert E. Lee's picture adorns the flood wall in Richmond."[1] Images of the South's immigrants waving Mexican and American flags in their attempts to gain greater rights (fig. 36) reinforced the claims of journalists, politicians, employers, and social scientists that Latinos' arrival en masse to the region marked a new moment of cultural hybridity and globalization in a region that had once been synonymous with isolation, provinciality, and a binary racial system.

This book has challenged that understanding, revealing new dimensions of U.S., southern, and transnational Mexican history since 1910. Most important, it has recovered and analyzed the beliefs and investments at the heart of Mexicanos' journeys to the U.S. South and the choices they made there within transborder landscapes of pressure, constraint, opportunity, and power. The stories of the South's Mexicanos in New Orleans and the Mississippi and Arkansas Deltas have helped prove that Jim Crow, really a national phenomenon, was always malleable under economic and political pressure. The South's underdevelopment and harsh segregation through the 1960s did not imply isolation and racial oppression in uniform ways for Robert Canedo, Rafael Landrove, Arkansas's braceros, and their fellow Mexicanos during the era of legal segregation. Indeed, stories of Georgia's agricultural areas and Charlotte's sprawling exurbs since 1965 have shown that the South's integration with national economic trends and political ideologies over the second half of the twentieth century opened new avenues for discrimination even as it foreclosed others. At the turn of the twenty-first century, local white officials in the region's metropolitan areas could not try to ban Mexicanos from white schools or restaurants as in the Mississippi and Arkansas Deltas of the interwar years. But legislators could now borrow model legislation from national organizations to exclude Mexicanos from civic and economic life in entire states. Viewed through the lens of the South's working-class immigrant newcomers from 1910 through the early twenty-first century, it also becomes clear that economic, social, and political aspects of globalization have unfolded in profoundly uneven ways across the U.S.-Mexico border. While capital, culture, and information flowed more freely than ever before in

FIGURE 36 Immigrants' rights vigil in Marshall Park, Charlotte, May 1, 2006. Photo by Rosario Machicao, courtesy of *La Noticia*, Charlotte.

the early twenty-first century, the U.S. South's Mexicanos found that political power within their grasp was bounded by national borders more than at any time in the previous century.

Like other studies of "in-between" racial groups, these stories of the South's Mexicanos in New Orleans, Mississippi, and Arkansas during the Jim Crow period have better illuminated segregation's underlying investments, helping U.S. Americans understand exactly how today's still-entrenched racial identities and inequalities came to be. If white elites fomented racial antagonism in the late nineteenth century to ensure that poor white and black laborers did not make common cause, by the interwar period anti-black violence and discrimination most prominently underwrote blacks' labor exploitation. African Americans' alienation from the "American" part of that identity—their inability to use courts and ballots to enforce their rights—curtailed already-limited mobility and opportunity, thwarting efforts to escape or improve jobs in agriculture. But the South's Mexican citizens often had greater access to political rights despite their poverty, and both they and Tejanos had social and familial networks spread across the borderlands. Violent tactics that worked well enough to keep a large black labor force on hand did not suffice with Mexicanos, who appealed to faraway family members and Mexican consuls for support. The Jim Crow system that white elites had constructed now hindered their access to the laborers they desired. So in interwar Mississippi and midcentury Arkansas, these elites pushed their communities to modify the terms of segregation by admitting Mexicans to white schools and businesses. In urban 1910s–30s New Orleans, Mexican immigrants' embodiment of their country's growing economic power gave them a favored racial status from the start, no matter how many "drops" of black or Indian blood they may have had. Thus, the twenty-first-century Nashville elementary school teacher whose Latino student asked, "Which water fountain would I be able to drink from?" could answer: usually the black one at first but eventually the white one.[2] And all can learn from these stories of the South's Mexicanos that even in its most rigid hours, Jim Crow was partially optional for white elites, who could use their power to bend it to their own economic needs.

For this reason, southern distinctiveness, the much-debated notion that the South was somehow "different" from the rest of the nation, looks different from the perspectives of Mexicanos. The recruitment of Mexicanos in the 1910s–20s, the deportations of the 1930s, and the bracero contract worker program of the 1940s–60s may have been national policies, but their implementation, meaning, and implications for the formation of racial boundaries were importantly local. Anglos adapted segregation practices to oppress Mexicanos in Texas and the Southwest. But in the southern locations considered here, where Mexicanos were newcomers, racial ideas about them were less entrenched. In those places, Mexicanos ultimately moved in more expansive racial space than they could have in the Southwest or even the Midwest. For a bracero in Arkansas, this might mean the right to eat in a whites-only restaurant he could not afford anyway, all the while being leered at by white patrons. But for a poor Mexican American child in New Orleans or the Mississippi Delta, it meant far superior education in white schools, vastly improved life chances, and the ability to rise into a middle class whose privilege was bolstered by its exclusion of African Americans. For these Mexicanos and their families, the South's exceptionalism in the first half of the twentieth century was the comparative racial mobility they found there.

This trend looks even clearer in hindsight, from the perspectives of Mexicanos who lived in the South later in the twentieth century and into the twenty-first. In the years when formal segregation became dismantled just as neoliberal economic models gained power in the United States and Mexico, Georgia's white church volunteers and agricultural employers worked to smooth social relations for the Mexicanos who had come to sustain the local agricultural economy. Their efforts built on long-standing intracommunity relationships among white farmers, church leaders, and local politicians and depended little on Atlanta, let alone Washington, D.C. Yet by the 1990s, these local voices competed with national conversations, begun in the West, which insisted on the unfitness of Mexicanos for American citizenship.

Only in the twenty-first century did the supposedly globalizing forces of technology and mobility allow national identity, national citizenship, and national law to create entrenched fault lines excluding Mexicans in the U.S. South. For years, the terms of Mexicanos' inclusion or exclusion had been negotiated locally in southern communities. Now, they were determined on the terrain of the U.S. nation and state: in national debates, blogs, news coverage, talk radio, and marches. Once, small groups of white growers had convinced their neighbors to embrace Mexicans in the name of white post–civil rights conservatism; now, a national Republican Party staked its claim on an enforcement-only approach to immigration, and local Georgia Republicans begrudgingly followed suit. Once, Mexican immigrants had drawn on the power of foreign bureaucrats and racial ideologies to wedge their way into the white side of the color line; now, they bought homes alongside white middle-class exurbanites but were classified as "illegals" by the relentless voices on those neighbors' television sets. Once, Arkansas farmers had created local ordinances banning anti-Mexican discrimination in white public spaces, to ensure their continued access to Mexican labor; now, southern suburban and exurban officials borrowed language from municipalities around the country to craft local ordinances that sought to drive Mexicanos out of town. Even undocumented Mexicanos' most sympathetic spokespeople, college-bound students raised in the United States, lost debates framed by white taxpayer entitlement and became excluded from many of the South's public colleges and universities.[3] The long view of Mexicanos' experiences in the South shows that for them, the South's integration into the nation resulted in greater, not lesser, exclusion and subjugation.

This marginalization resulted not only from the importation of anti-Mexican ideas from the West but also from the globalization of Mexico. Observers of the recent past have pointed to the Mexican government's seemingly redoubled efforts to serve their emigrant populations in the United States.[4] But when viewed over a century from the perspectives of the U.S. South's Mexicans, who relied disproportionately on trans-state power since they lacked access to an ethnic middle class or labor organizing, recent efforts have been less powerful than their midcentury predecessors. The less-globalized Mexico more effectively rallied to its emigrants' cause. From 1910 through the 1950s, the strength of the nation-state system and the widespread belief in its modernist promises of sovereignty, authority, and legitimacy fomented a more balanced two-way exchange of racial ideas and politics between Mexico and the U.S. South. Mexicans' beliefs in these modernist promises, and in the Mexican state's ability to make good on them, gave form to the demands they placed on local southern communities.[5] These promises created expectations of economic and physical mobility, self-determination, and political rights that went unfilled first in Mexico and then in the U.S. South.

Mexicans called on their home state to made good on its promises and support their efforts to claim rights. Sometimes the request of a Mexican official to a local southern one, as in the case of the white schools of Gunnison, Mississippi, could elicit change. More significantly, when the Mexican government controlled the flow of Mexican labor to specific parts of the United States during the late 1940s and early 1950s, it had real power in its dealings with Arkansas's agricultural bosses and local authorities. Most scholars have dismissed the Mexican government's midcentury claim to hold meaningful power over the fates of its workers in the United States.[6] But the heretofore unexplored case of Arkansas proves that for a brief but important period, braceros placed their faith in the Mexican government and used its ideologies and political power to shift their racial—and sometimes economic—position within a southern subregion. This power waned by the late 1950s as undocumented migration from Mexico to the United States increased, unchecked by the control of a weakened Mexican state.

Ruptures in Mexican economic and political life from the 1960s onward increased social inequality and reduced the government's ability to fulfill its populist nationalist promises, undermining individuals' belief in the meaning and value of Mexican citizenship.[7] Emigrants more uniformly mistrusted government officials, and years of austerity meant that those officials had declining resources to invest in emigrant protection. Even as they opened new consulates, processed identity documents, and called emigrants "heroes," Mexican government officials were no longer active or effective political advocates for their compatriots' improved status as a whole.

The simple fact of Mexicans' and other Latinos' presence in the U.S. South may have seemed to herald a new global era since 1990, but from the perspectives of the South's Mexicanos, it has not. While technology enabled their social, cultural, and economic lives to take place in increasingly transnational spaces over the course of the twentieth century, globalization went hand in hand with neoliberalism and the declining usefulness of their Mexican citizenship. In the U.S. South, urban and suburban Mexicanos of all ages, and Mexicano youth in rural and exurban areas, have organized and marched since 2005 to claim their rights. Together with their counterparts throughout the United States, they have won modest yet encouraging changes, as in 2012 when they pushed President Barack Obama to take executive action that spared many undocumented immigrant youths from deportation if they arrived in the country as children. Their movements have engaged primarily with the U.S. federal and state policies that sought to exclude them, such as Georgia's ban on undocumented students at the state's selective public universities. Yet when an activist student asked Mexico's Atlanta consul to sign a petition protesting the ban, he was told that representatives of the Mexican government "could not intervene in U.S. politics"—a far cry from the actions of Mexican consulates in New Orleans and Memphis decades before.[8] Facing profound exclusion in the United States, Mexicans could no longer look for political support to the country where they did hold citizenship. Borders constricted their struggles for rights in the U.S. South more tightly in the early twenty-first century than at any point during the twentieth.

New Orleans's Margarita Rodríguez, Mississippi's Manuel Solís, Arkansas's José Aldama, Georgia's Anselma Gómez, greater Charlotte's Edith H., and millions of other Mexicanos moved through the U.S. South since 1910 with hope or despair but always an eye on the possible. They looked westward to Texas and California, northward to the Midwest, and southward to Mexico as they created and adapted their life strategies. Throughout this vista, they saw points of power, weakness, oppression, and opportunity in communities, churches, schools, work sites, and governments. World War II GI Robert Canedo's single mother found economic stability in 1920s New Orleans while Rafael and Martha Landrove laid roots in Mississippi, hoping they could find greater social mobility than in Texas. Both achieved the cultural and material progress they sought though partial or complete integration with white communities. Bracero José Luís Landa did not actively choose Arkansas as his work site in 1948, but once there, he was determined to be paid as promised and housed like a modern man, not in a shack "once inhabited by blacks." He correctly perceived that withholding his labor and appealing to the Mexican consulate could help him prevail. Departing Mexico in the 1980s, landless Teodora Marín took her family on the migrant circuit to arrest their downward economic spiral; when she eventually settled in southern Georgia, she tolerated difficult labor conditions and whites' standoffishness because it was better than being bullied in Texas or hungry in Guerrero. Angelica C. urged her husband to cross the border with her in 2000 because she dreamed of a consumer lifestyle that her family could not afford with their earnings in Mexico, and she insisted on keeping her family together even through its pursuit of dollars. Once in exurban Union County, North Carolina, she contented herself with her family's increased spending power and did not venture to immigrants' rights marches in nearby Charlotte. Material well-being, which meant different things at different times, in some way motivated all of these migrants. Their cultural and political aspirations fluctuated through time, as ideas about what it meant to live a good life shifted repeatedly in Mexico, the United States, and the world.

Adapting their lives to the U.S. South, Mexicanos often made choices about race: to work in the fields alongside African Americans, fight for admission to the white school, socialize in the black barbershop, live in the white exurb, or attend a rally with the black preacher. In each case, Mexicanos made these choices in a larger context and in pursuit of broader aspirations: higher wages, social mobility, community, power. In no case did Mexico's official racial ideologies, anti-black though they were, inspire Mexicanos to adopt the U.S. version of white supremacy as their own. Mexicanos wanted progress however defined, and over time they used different racial strategies to get it. In every case they declined to make proclamations about their own racial inheritance, and in many cases they worked, lived, and socialized among African Americans even while pursuing public recognition as white. The long view of their experiences suggests that, had African American cotton workers been in a position to offer a potentially victorious strategy for cross-racial organizing in the 1930s–60s, Mexicanos might well have joined up. Mexicanos in the South were connected through family and community networks to the Southwest and the Midwest, and their racial choices suggest that historians of Mexican America must never presume that a public embrace of Caucasian status necessarily implied a private embrace of a white or anti-black racial identity.[9] Reading twenty-first-century survey research on anti-black attitudes among the South's Latino immigrants alongside its recent political history of black–brown political coalitions also suggests the converse is true: animosities in shared neighborhoods or labor markets have not precluded blacks and Latinos from forging powerful alliances in the public sphere.

What are today's southern Mexicanos and their allies to learn from this journey through the *Corazón de Dixie*, the Mexican transnational U.S. South? As southerners of all backgrounds choose how they will engage with the region's future struggles over race and rights, they face a global landscape different from that of their predecessors yet a set of choices that resonates with the past. Latin American home-country governments, once a key source of power for the region's immigrants, are unlikely to assert meaningful political influence on the fates of their co-nationals abroad. As the Charlotte example shows, in the immediate future Mexicanos' most promising political path involves some combination of alliance with other Latinos, with white liberal elites, and with African Americans. Indeed, it was just such a coalition that defeated an English-only ordinance in a Nashville special election in early 2009. Central Nashville residents and particularly African Americans turned out in high numbers to defeat the measure; by contrast, a journalist noted, "the farther voters lived from downtown, the more likely they were to support English-only."[10] This national strategy for coalition politics has the potential to combat an anti-immigrant movement national in scope and ambition, one that, as I write in 2015, has the power to pass state-level anti-immigrant legislation on the strength of white suburban and exurban conservative votes and against the protests of urban liberals or rural pro-immigrant conservatives who may advocate a more accommodating path.

Yet today's liberal coalition politics are surely not permanent. Time and again, changes across the hemisphere have required the South's Mexicanos to craft new strategies and alliances for achieving their aims. None of these were permanent, and the twenty-first century will be no different. This neoliberal era will necessitate new strategies that work between and beyond the U.S. and Mexican states, with labor movements, employers, or international organizations. Today's Mexican and U.S. American youths, including those living undocumented in the U.S. South, have already begun to imagine a new relationship between identity and citizenship that may open new space for Mexicanos' claims on both sides of the border.

However new their presence may feel and however excluded they may be from legal citizenship or social equality, the South's Mexicanos have a traceable history in this region where people, culture, and politics have long crossed international borders. Mexicanos' future choices and strategies will join a longer legacy as they shape these histories of the post–Civil War United States, postrevolutionary Mexico, and the cross-border struggle over the meaning of race and the claiming of rights.

Acknowledgments

"Dear Martie," wrote my grandmother Beverly in 1945. She was visiting Tijuana with a friend and sent this photo (fig. 37) as a postcard to my grandfather Martin, then her boyfriend, who was stationed on an army base in Las Vegas. "Well here we are in dear old Mexico, what a crazy time we are having. So sorry you can't be with us. It's so different down here."

Grandma, of course, was right: both then and now, a lot was "so different" across borders of space, race, and power in the Mexico-U.S. borderlands. In 1945, Grandma Bev was just a year out of Roosevelt High School, where she had attended class in Los Angeles's heavily Mexican Boyle Heights neighborhood. But within a decade, she would be living in a white working-class suburb in the San Fernando Valley, where my dad's elementary school class pictures show that for the first several years, nearly all of his classmates were white. Immigrants and Americans of European descent and those of Mexican descent were well on the road to "difference" in my hometown of Los Angeles and across the Southwest, in matters of housing, education, and indeed the two groups' locations in the cultural and spatial geographies of race.

My desire to understand why and how this came to be has motivated my learning and scholarship in U.S. and Latin American history, ultimately piquing my interest in a region, the U.S. South, whose racial regimes have sometimes functioned differently. Grandma Bev's postcard thus highlights the most important blessings that have graced my career and this book: the love and rootedness of family and friends; the unimaginably good education I have received thanks to the social mobility that my families enjoyed on the white side of "difference"; and the generosity of colleagues, mentors, and students, most from the other side of the borderlands' color line, who have trusted my interest in immigrants' rights and Mexican American history, supported me and my work, and generously educated me with their perspectives and life experiences. I offer this book to my family, teachers, mentors, colleagues, and students as just one piece of my effort to make good on the investments and trust they have placed in me.

When I left Los Angeles for my freshman year of college, I had a mediocre grasp of the Spanish language, the beginnings of an elite education, and little knowledge of Latin America or the Latino communities that had thrived all around me throughout my youth. Mentors in immigrants' rights, social services, and academia helped me grow beyond that younger self. Thank you for trusting and investing in me, Sandra Serrano Sewell, Juan Hernández, Omar de la Torre, and Yvonne Mariajimenez. As an undergraduate student, I was fortunate to join Yale's Ethnicity, Race, and Migration program and to benefit from the stimulation and support of Alicia Schmidt Camacho

FIGURE 37 Photo postcard of the author's grandmother, Beverly Millman (later Weise) (*left*), in Tijuana with friend, 1945. Inscription on the back reads, "Dear Martie, Well here we are in dear old Mexico, what a crazy time we are having. So sorry you can't be with us. It's so different down here." Courtesy of Daniel Weise.

and Patricia Pessar. Patricia's death in 2012 saddened me not just because of our personal connection but because I and the world still had so much more to learn from her. Graduate mentors Seth Fein, Glenda Gilmore, and especially Gil Joseph and Steve Pitti taught me how to be a historian, shaped this project from its inception, and supported me emotionally as I navigated academia. A personally meaningful career has been one of my life's greatest gifts, and for that, my debt to all of you can never be repaid.

A special alchemy of love and shared intellectual experience binds me to those with whom I progressed through graduate school and the professoriate; they have read and discussed this project with me so many times. Thank you, Mike Amezcua, Kaysha Corinealdi, Sarah Cornell, Benjamin Cowan, Lori Flores, Fredy González, Jerry González, Alison Greene, Perla Guerrero, Tammy Ingram, Gerardo Licón, Gustavo Licón, Mireya Loza, Veronica Martínez-Matsuda, Story Matkin-Rawn, April Merleaux, Ana Minian, Isabela Seong Leong Quintana, Abigail Rosas, Ana Elizabeth Rosas, Mario Sifuentez, Angela Stuesse, Louise Walker, Jason Ward, and especially Gerry Cadava and Lisa Pinley Covert. I look forward to many more years of strengthening our work and our bonds. I have also enjoyed learning from a new generation of up-and-coming scholars: Andy Eisen, Adam Goodman, Valeria Jiménez, Cecilia Márquez, Tore Olsson, Yuridia Ramírez, and Richard Velázquez.

The pages of this book are what they are because busy people took the time to read them and tell me what was missing, weak, or wrong. In addition to the graduate school friends named above, thank you for your feedback, José Alamillo, Luís Alvarez, Stephen Aron, Gabriela Arredondo, Carlos Blanton, Al Camarillo, Ernesto

Chávez, Marisela Chávez, Cindy I-Feng Chen, N. D. B. Connolly, Bill Deverell, John Mack Faragher, Lynn Fujiwara, Matt García, David Gutiérrez, Cindy Hahamovitch, Tom Hanchett, Nancy Hewitt, Michael Innis-Jiménez, Matthew Lassiter, Eileen Luhr, Bethany Moreton, Suzanne Oboler, Lorena Oropeza, Mark Overmyer-Velázquez, Yuridia Ramírez, Marc Rodriguez, Vicki Ruíz, Leo Spitzer, Jessica Vasquez, Pamela Voekel, Louis Warren, and Richard White. Three brilliant thinkers who are themselves actors in this story, Richard Enriquez, Javier González, and Wayne Hurder, kindly subjected my chapters to the "ring-true test" and let me know where they did not pass. I am also grateful for helpful support and advice from and conversations with Benny Andres, Carl Brasseaux, Gabriela González, Jesse Hoffnung-Garskof, Natalia Molina, Jocelyn Olcott, George Sánchez, Heather Smith, Jamie Winders, Elliot Young, and the audiences at presentations I had the opportunity to deliver at the University of Alabama, the University of Arkansas at Little Rock, Brown University, Cornell University, Freedom University Georgia, the University of California at Los Angeles and Santa Cruz, the University of Georgia, and the University of Paris—Diderot. In addition to my graduate mentors, a few brave souls provided feedback on the entire draft manuscript. For your utter generosity, thank you Sarah Deutsch, Jerry González, Laurie Green, Chuck Grench, Gerardo Licón, Gustavo Licón, Mary Odem, Paul Ortiz, Isabela Seong Leong Quintana, Matthew Rosenbaum, Karen Weise, Nan Woodruff, and an anonymous peer reviewer. I hope that you all see your intellectual imprints on these pages, because they are certainly there.

A particular joy of border-crossing work is that I have gotten to know scholars in many different academic subfields within U.S. and Latin American history, global migration studies, and the social sciences. I particularly value the opportunity that the Chicano/Latino studies community has given me to grow, write, teach, and act within its fold. Forty years ago when young scholars first proposed to study the histories of Mexicans in the United States, they were forced to matriculate into Latin American history programs because the field of U.S. history did not see a place for them. No sooner did Chicano Studies find a small bit of solid ground in a white-dominated academy than it created a place for me, a white woman, in its ranks. Because I am often asked, it is worth stating publicly that despite the competitiveness of academia, I have never once felt identity politics used against me. I have tried my best to reciprocate by respecting this field's role as not only an intellectual project but also one of the few spaces in the academy where people of color can seek mentorship and camaraderie. I have sometimes fallen short in my attempts to navigate these waters, yet my colleagues in Chicano/Latino Studies have been generous and forgiving. I thank them all for their passionate and expansive approach to this work, for creating this academic field, and for opening a space for me within it.

My colleagues and students at California State University, Long Beach (CSULB), and the University of Oregon (UO) fostered this project and my intellectual development in myriad ways. My chair in CSULB's International Studies program, Richard Marcus, took way too much work on himself in an attempt to allow me more time for research and writing; he continues to inspire me with his indefatigable dedication to creating a meaningful educational experience for students. Collaborating on campus initiatives with Luís Arroyo, Bipasha Baruah, Ali Igmen, Elena Macías, Elizabeth Philipose, Victor Rodríguez, Deborah Thien, and Armando Vasquez-Ramos brought further purpose to those years. Dozens of my students engaged so deeply in the study of migration that I learned at least as much from them as they did from me. Any attempt to list them all will fall short, but I can name a few: Noelan Arbis, J. B. Brown, Casey Burkard, Megan Cutler, Caitlin Dickerson, Araceli González, Deanna Lam, Liliana Montalvo, and Joel Urista. Together, you all made CSULB an incredibly stimulating place to think about migration and globalization. At the University of Oregon, thank you John McCole, Ellen Herman, and the College of Arts and Sciences for ensuring that I had ample writing time on arrival. Lindsay Braun, April Haynes, and Jeff Ostler helpfully checked in on this book's progress, while Reuben Zahler reminded me to just finish it already. Robert Davis, Lynn Fujiwara, Dan Hosang, Claudia Holguín, Lynn Stephen, Melissa Stuckey, and Jessica Vasquez have made UO a warm place to research and teach in Latino and U.S. Ethnic Studies. Sarah Proctor, Luís Sandoval, and Eli Tome at UO's Social Science Instructional Labs patiently supported my novice-level mapmaking.

My year as a Weatherhead Fellow at the School for Advanced Research in Santa Fe, New Mexico, slowed me down in the most wonderful way, enabling me to read widely, rethink my arguments, and rewrite chapters with a depth difficult to muster amid the bustle of my usual academic and personal life. I could not have asked for a more pleasant and supportive scholarly community than the one I enjoyed there, including Rebecca Allahyari, James Brooks, Margaret Bruchac, Kitty King Corbett, Craig Janes, John Martin, Jennifer McCarty, Teresa McCarty, Nancy Marie Mithlo, Malena Mörling, Franklin Peters, Kelsey Potdevin, Nicole Taylor, Wossen Argaw Tegegn, and Aimee Villarreal.

Traveling to archives in multiple states and two countries required substantial financial and logistical support. This research would not have been possible without generous financial support from the Yale Graduate School of Arts and Sciences; California State University, Long Beach; the University of Oregon and its College of Arts and Sciences; the National Endowment for the Humanities; the School for Advanced Research; the Smithsonian's National Museum of American History; the Andrew W. Mellon Fellowship in Humanistic Studies; and several funds within Yale University: the John F. Enders Summer Fellowship, the Howard Lamar Center for the Study of Frontiers and Borders Fellowship, the Mellon Latin American history fund, the Yale Center for International and Area Studies fund, the Yale Agrarian Studies fund, the Yale Council on Latin American and Iberian Studies, and the Fox Fellowship. The Oregon Humanities Center provided a subvention to support the creation of this book's index. The UO Libraries and their Digital Scholarship Center put their wonderful staff on the task of creating the book's website, http://corazondedixie.org. Any views, findings, conclusions, or recommendations expressed in this book do not necessarily represent those of these funders and supporters.

Even when generous, humanities funding is always too limited, and I am grateful to the many people who contributed their couches, guest rooms, desks, and dinner tables to the development of this book. You helped my bottom line, kept me company, and made research fun. In the South, thank you, Benny Andres, Chris Beorkrem and Kelly Moore, Lyn and Steve Boyd, Crata Castleberry, John Diemer, Michelle Johansen and Chris Powell, Diane and Paul Mendelson, Joanna and Lee Mendelson, Tamar and Noam Raucher, Ellen Steeby, Lin and Jackie Stradley, Lindsay Stradley, Shirlee Tevet and Harlan Cohen, and Rayna and Isaac Weiner, for providing shelter and company. In Mexico City, thank you, Yendi Guzmán, Greta Jacobs, Anita and Meir Levin, Lucía Quezada, Sloane Starke and Francisco Caloca, Omar de la Torre, and Simón Zuman. When space to write was at a premium in Los Angeles, the Redner-Shapiro family and Paul Lerner opened their doors and desks to me. Roger Weise also provided a welcome writing retreat, complete with espresso service, in the hills above Eugene.

Though most of the research herein is my own, the contributions of others merit recognition. In cases where others have sent primary documents my way, I have noted that in the notes. I am particularly indebted to those who conducted research in archives I could not visit: research assistants Carla Mendiola at the National Archives at Fort Worth and Christina Davidson at Loyola University of Chicago and friend Diana Greenwold at the Tamiment Library in New York. Cybelle Fox and Adam Goodman generously shared primary documents they had found in their own research at the National Archives in Washington, D.C. Research assistant Christine Hill diligently did all of the data entry from the sample of Mexican-origin households in New Orleans from the 1920 and 1930 manuscript censuses, which is further explained in the Appendix. UO librarian David Woken helped me track down obscure historical data. Diego Barahona cheerily let me turn the offices of Charlotte's *La Noticia* into an archival workstation.

Even more obviously, the credit for oral history research does not accrue to a solitary historian. Gustavo Arévalo, Geraldine Davidson, and Richard Enriquez helped me make key contacts for my interviews. And dozens of people, white, black, Mexicano, and Latino, were willing to share their lives with me on tape and let me scan their photos and personal papers. Many of the most important stories in this book would have been impossible to recount if not for their generosity. Some of their memories, like living as a black man under segregation or risking one's life to cross the border, were extremely painful to revisit. I will be sharing this book with them and only hope they conclude that their time with me was well spent.

The decade of research compiled in *Corazón de Dixie* enters the world through the diligence of Chuck Grench and the amazing staff at the University of North Carolina Press, whose good reputation among authors turns out to be well deserved. Chuck insisted I prioritize quality over speed and then waited patiently each time I took his advice. He and the rest of the staff, particularly Mary Caviness, Heidi Perov, and Iza Wojciechowska, have walked this first-time author through the publication process with great care and attention.

My friends outside of my field know far more than they ever wanted about Mexicans in the South. They showed constant interest in my work while providing a world apart from it during the decade I spent writing this book. In New Haven, Rachel Bergstein, Ona Bloom, Aliza Dzik, David Feder, Justin Florence, Kristi Garroway, Talia Inlender, Adinah Miller, Lisa Stern, and Saul Zipkin brought balance and fun to my life. In Los Angeles, Joanna Arch, Jonathan Bergman, Julia Boorstin, Pamela Collingwood, Victor de la Cruz, Talia Inlender (again), Lindsay Koss, Kathleen Tundermann Niles, Lisa Stern (again), Diana Varat, and the wonderful Shtibl community cheered and supported me. In Eugene, Elsa Johnson, Heidi Kaufman, Stephanie Majewski, Kristi Potter, and Ilana Umansky have offered up friendship in short order. Jillian Catalanotti, Hilary Kaplan, Amanda Levinson, Kathleen McCarthy Baldwin, and Adam Rosenblatt have offered consistent moral support from afar.

My family has never wavered in its support of my academic career and this book project. My mother, Bev, is my biggest cheerleader, showing genuine pride and interest in even the smallest details of my work and helpfully reminding me to keep things in balance. My father, Steven; stepmother, Lori; and step-siblings, Will and Brenna, have supported my comings and goings from Los Angeles (and their house) with cheer and love. A feminist in the 1970s sense of the word, my dad contains a bottomless well of belief that his daughters can and must follow their professional goals to the end. He is the truest believer I know in the transformative power of a liberal arts education, and on that count both he and my mom spent the first sixteen years of my education putting their money where their mouth was. This book would not exist without their investment.

My sister Karen lived with this book for three years, and she and her husband, Noah, have happily and constantly discussed it with me ever since. Karen is also my "perfect" (and, perhaps unfortunately for her, permanent) editor not only because of her journalistic prowess but because she comprehends the intellectual, political, and personal elements at stake in each piece of writing. Even more important, her encouragement, sense of humor, and close friendship have sustained me through the years of writing this book.

And so, in more ways than one, the story of this book's creation comes back to Grandma, indeed, to all four of my grandparents, Bev and Marty Weise and Lil and Joe Liebross, for the historical opportunities of which they took advantage but also for those they defied. Ignoring the individualism of American society, my extended families—now including the Bugattis, Copanses, Gorneys, Liebrosses, Maddises, Mendelsons, Tillipmans, and Weises—have remained close. I was wise enough to pick in-laws with a similar ethos: the Coopers, Gersons, Klines, and Rosenbaums. These large families have supported my academic lifestyle in a flurry of airport pickups; Fedexed cookies; eat-and-run lunches ("Joe! She has to go back to reading her books!"); visits to Mexico City, New Haven, Santa Fe, and Eugene; and amusing e-mail strings that helped me feel connected no matter where I happened to be.

The family that I chose, my spouse, Matthew, has nourished me, my academic career, and this book with his food, presence, and love. The fruits of his labors as a social worker will not have a page on Amazon.com or be reviewed in an academic journal but will continue to live quietly in the immigrants, refugees, criminal defendants, and homeless veterans who have changed their own lives with his support. I and this book have also changed with Matthew's support, as he has helped me become a much fuller human being and therefore a much better historian and teacher. This book's dedication recognizes my life's dual blessings of love and purpose, of which the volume itself is but a small manifestation.

Appendix

Historical Sampling Methodology

Myron Gutmann, Jan Reiff, and Albert Camarillo provided guidance regarding historical sampling methodology and analysis of manuscript census data. Research assistant Christine Hill did most of the New Orleans data entry from the manuscript census pages.

New Orleans, 1920

This analysis results from a sample of one-half of the dwellings in Orleans Parish, Louisiana, that contained at least one resident who was Mexican born. These were identified through searches on Ancestry.com Library Edition. Since there was no race category for "Mexican" in 1920, there was no good way to capture Tejanos, but given how few were in New Orleans even by 1930, it is likely that their number in 1920 was negligible. Mexican-born people, whatever their race listed, were included in the pool, though individuals born to two non-Mexican parents in Mexico, who were not listed as speaking Spanish, were excluded. I randomly selected 226 dwellings from the overall pool of dwellings, utilizing an online random number generator. The sample's 226 dwellings together included 591 of the 1,242 Mexicans listed on the census that year. Analysis of neighborhood composition took into account the census page of the dwelling, in addition to the previous and subsequent pages. Occupational categorizations followed those suggested by Albert Camarillo in his study of Santa Barbara's barrio, with the addition of "domestic" and "maritime" categories to capture women's migrations and New Orleans's unique conditions as a port city, as well as "artist/musician" in response to George Sánchez's note that these professions fit poorly into Camarillo's categorization of "low white-collar" for those professions.[1]

New Orleans, 1930

This analysis results from a sample of 59 percent of the dwellings in Orleans Parish, Louisiana, that contained at least one resident who was Mexican or Mexican American. These were identified through searches on Ancestry.com Library Edition. Mexicans and Mexican Americans were defined as those listed with the race "Mexican" and born in either Mexico or Texas (a few Central Americans listed as race "Mexican" were excluded) or listed with any other race and born in Mexico (individuals born to two non-Mexican parents in Mexico, who were not listed as speaking Spanish, were excluded). I randomly selected 216 dwellings for inclusion in the sample, utilizing an online random number generator to select dwellings from the overall pool of households. The sample's 216 dwellings together included 572 of the 1,184 Mexican-race or Mexican-born white individuals enumerated in the 1930 census in Orleans Parish. Regarding occupational categories, the same were used as in the 1920 analysis described above. On revising this data after completing my dissertation, I discovered a sampling error: either through Ancestry.com or human error, Mexican wives who did not have Mexican husbands were excluded from the original sample. I therefore compiled a list of such women, removed false or repeated hits, used a random number generator to select out 59 percent (the percentage of the original pool that I had sampled), and added them to my data set.

Bolivar County, Mississippi, 1930

I chose to sample Bolivar County because it had the largest population of "Mexican"-race individuals of any Mississippi Delta county in 1930, according to the U.S. census. I utilized Ancestry.com Library Edition to search the 1930 U.S. manuscript census. I generated a list of households in Bolivar County that had at least one member whose race was listed as "Mexican" or who were listed as any race but born in Mexico. After removing false hits, I was left with 121 "Mexican"-race family heads and one Mexican-born "Negro." I then analyzed data from every third family unit on the list, for a total sample of forty-one families consisting of 147 individuals out of the 447 counted by the U.S. census that April.

Notes

Abbreviations Used in the Notes

ACANO	Archives of the Catholic Archdiocese of New Orleans, Louisiana
ACDJ	Archives of the Catholic Diocese of Jackson, Mississippi
ACDS	Archives of the Catholic Diocese of Savannah, Georgia
ADT	"The Arkansas Delta in Transition: Agriculture and Community, 1920–1980," Oral History Collection, Arkansas State University, Jonesboro
AEMEUA	Archivo de la Embajada de México en los Estados Unidos de América, Mexico City
AGENL	Archivo General del Estado de Nuevo León, Monterrey, Mexico
AGEV	Archivo General del Estado de Veracruz, Xalapa, Mexico
AGN	Archivo General de la Nación, Mexico City
AHSRE	Archivo Históricó de la Secretaría de Relaciones Exteriores, Mexico City
AMLN	Archivo Municipal de Lampazos de Naranjo, Nuevo León, Mexico
AP	Associated Press
ASU	Arkansas State University, Jonesboro
BHA	Smithsonian Bracero History Archive Oral Histories
CCES	Catholic Church Extension Society Records, Loyola University, Chicago
CIC	Church of the Immaculate Conception, Blytheville, Arkansas
D&PL	Delta and Pine Land Papers, Mississippi State University Archives, Starkville
DCFS	Department of Children and Family Services series (24-1-31), Georgia Archives, Morrow
DSU	Delta State University Archives and Museum, Cleveland, Mississippi
ECG	E. C. "Took" Gathings Collection, Archives and Special Collections, Arkansas State University, Jonesboro
GA	Georgia Archives, Morrow
GBC	Georgia Baptist Convention Archives, Duluth
HA	Homer M. Adkins Papers, Arkansas History Commission, Little Rock

ICE-FOIA	Freedom of Information Act request to Immigration and Customs Enforcement
JM	Sen. John McClellan Papers, Ouachita Baptist University, Arkadelphia, Arkansas
MDAH	Mississippi Department of Archives and History, Jackson
NAFW RG 33	National Archives at Fort Worth, Record Group 33, Records of the Agricultural Extension Service
NARA RG 85	National Archives and Records Administration, Washington, D.C., Record Group 85, Records of the Immigration and Naturalization Service
NCCC	North Carolina Council of Churches Papers, Duke University Rare Book, Manuscript, and Special Collections Library, Durham
NOPL	New Orleans Public Library, Louisiana Division and City Archives
OLV	Our Lady of Victories Catholic Church, Cleveland, Mississippi
SANC	State Archives of North Carolina, Raleigh
SHCC	Sacred Heart Catholic Church, Vidalia, Georgia
TB	Theodore G. Bilbo Papers, University of Southern Mississippi, McCain Library and Archives, Hattiesburg
UGA	University of Georgia Libraries, Athens
VSU	Valdosta State University Archives, Georgia

Introduction

1. Cónsul Rubén Gaxiola to Secretariat of Foreign Relations, November 19, 1949, folder TM-26-2, AHSRE.

2. Fink, *Maya of Morganton*; Mohl, "Globalization, Latinization, and the Nuevo New South"; Smith and Furuseth, "'Nuevo South'"; Odem, "Latin American Immigration."

3. Tim Whitmire, "Will Fajitas Replace Moon Pie?," *Enquirer Journal*, November 27 2005.

4. The Dustin Inman Society, "No to Georgifornia!," http://www.thedustininman society.org/info/no_to_georgiafornia.html.

5. For reports of tense relations, see McClain, Carter, et al., "Racial Distancing in a Southern City"; Marrow, "Hispanic Immigration, Black Population Size, and Intergroup Relations," 221–23; Gray, *We Just Keep Running the Line*. For reports of actual or potential cooperation, see Stuesse, "Race, Migration, and Labor Control"; Barbara Ellen Smith, "Market Rivals or Class Allies?"; Jones, "Blacks May Be Second Class." For a critique of these discourses, see Jackson, "Shifting Nature of Racism."

6. Winders, *Nashville in the New Millennium*, 127.

7. For arguments about this migration's novelty, see Odem and Lacy, "Introduction"; Peacock, *Grounded Globalism*, 31–32; Mohl, "Globalization, Latinization, and the Nuevo New South"; Torres et al., "Transnational Communities in Eastern North Carolina"; Cravey, "Transnationality, Social Spaces, and Parallel Worlds"; Furuseth and Smith, "From Winn-Dixie to Tiendas," 2. For those who saw old patterns at play,

see Winders and Smith, "New Pasts"; Diaz McConnell, "Racialized Histories; Lovato, "Juan Crow in Georgia"; Watson, "Southern History, Southern Future"; Luna and Ansley, "Global Migrants and Access to Local Housing," 157; Stuesse, "Race, Migration, and Labor Control"; Smith and Furuseth, "Making Real the Mythical Latino Community in Charlotte, North Carolina," 192; Sánchez, "Latinos, the American South, and the Future of U.S. Race Relations"; Stuesse and Helton, "Low-Wage Legacies, Race, and the Golden Chicken in Mississippi."

8. On smaller migrations in the nineteenth century, see Cornell, "Americans in the U.S. South and Mexico"; Jiménez, "Cultural Diplomacy on an International Stage."

9. Here and elsewhere I use "borderland" to denote a space largely beyond the reach of nation-state power. Hämäläinen and Truett, "On Borderlands."

10. Hale, *Making Whiteness*.

11. Grossman, *Land of Hope*; Cobb, *Most Southern Place on Earth*; Woodruff, *American Congo*.

12. Fredrickson, *Racism*; Holt, "Marking"; Omi and Winant, *Racial Formation in the United States*; Spitzer, *Lives in Between*; Balibar, "Racism and Nationalism"; Stern, *Eugenic Nation*.

13. Watson, "Southern History, Southern Future," 280–82.

14. Berthoff, "Southern Attitudes toward Immigration"; Brandfon, "End of Immigration to the Cotton Fields"; Jung, *Coolies and Cane*.

15. Cornell, "Americans in the U.S. South and Mexico," 264.

16. Ibid.; Jung, *Coolies and Cane*; Walter Johnson, *River of Dark Dreams*.

17. Camarillo, *Chicanos in a Changing Society*; Montejano, *Anglos and Mexicans*.

18. Alanís Enciso, *El Primer Programa Bracero y el Gobierno de México, 1917–1918*.

19. Durand, Massey, and Zenteno, "Mexican Immigration to the United States."

20. On cultural racism, see Balibar, "Racism and Nationalism"; Fredrickson, *Racism*; Spitzer, *Lives in Between*.

21. Montejano, *Anglos and Mexicans*.

22. Benton-Cohen, *Borderline Americans*, 162–67; Gordon, *Great Arizona Orphan Abduction*, 194; Alvarez, "Lemon Grove Incident"; Sánchez, *Becoming Mexican American*.

23. Carrigan and Webb, "Lynching of Persons of Mexican Origin or Descent"; Benjamin Heber Johnson, *Revolution in Texas*.

24. Gamboa, *Mexican Labor and World War II*; Valdés, *Al Norte*; Valdés, *Barrios Norteños*; Vargas, *Proletarians of the North*.

25. For more on Texas as both a southern and southwestern state, see Neil Foley, *White Scourge*. On Florida, see Hewitt, *Southern Discomfort*; Connolly, "Timely Innovations."

26. Arredondo, *Mexican Chicago*; Barton, "Borderland Discontents"; Dreby, *Divided by Borders*; Neil Foley, *White Scourge*; Matt García, *A World of Its Own*; Pitti, *Devil in Silicon Valley*; Sifuentez, "By Forests or by Fields"; Vargas, *Proletarians of the North*; Vargas, *Labor Rights Are Civil Rights*; Erika Lee, *At America's Gates*; Matthew Frye Jacobson, *Whiteness of a Different Color*; Hoffnung-Garskof, *Tale of Two Cities*; Deborah Cohen, *Braceros*; Deutsch, *No Separate Refuge*; Goldring, "Mexican State and Transmigrant

Organizations"; Gutiérrez, *Walls and Mirrors*; Perales, *Smeltertown*; Rouse, "Mexican Migration and the Social Space of Postmodernism"; Ruíz, *Cannery Women*; Sánchez, *Becoming Mexican American*; Robert C. Smith, *Mexican New York*; Hsu, *Dreaming of Gold*; Rosas, *Abrazando el Espíritu*; Fink, *Maya of Morganton*; Rodriguez, *Repositioning North American Migration History*; Marc S. Rodriguez, *Tejano Diaspora*.

27. Schmidt Camacho, *Migrant Imaginaries*; Rosas, *Abrazando el Espíritu*.

28. This is true, in part, because I was denied access to the archives of the Catholic Diocese at Little Rock, making it impossible to make conclusive arguments about the role of the Catholic Church in the pivotal middle chapter of this book.

29. See, for example, the dissertation proposal of Yuridia Ramírez, Duke University Ph.D. candidate.

30. Lassiter and Crespino, *Myth of Southern Exceptionalism*.

31. Behnken, *Struggle in Black and Brown*; Stuesse, "Race, Migration, and Labor Control"; Tarasawa, "New Patterns of Segregation"; McClain, Lyle, et al., "Black Americans and Latino Immigrants in a Southern City"; Behnken, *Fighting Their Own Battles*; Krochmal, "Labor, Civil Rights, and the Struggle for Democracy in Texas"; Mantler, *Power to the Poor*; Gray, *We Just Keep Running the Line*.

32. Bow, *Partly Colored*; Jung, *Coolies and Cane*; Lovett, "'African and Cherokee by Choice.'"

33. Hirsch and Lodgson, *Creole New Orleans*.

34. Benjamin Heber Johnson, *Revolution in Texas*; Montejano, *Anglos and Mexicans*.

35. Matt Garcia, *A World of Its Own*; Vargas, *Proletarians of the North*; Valdés, *Barrios Norteños*.

36. Cobb, *Most Southern Place on Earth*.

37. Calavita, *Inside the State*; Deborah Cohen, *Braceros*.

38. Nearly 500,000 migrant workers passed through southern states not including Florida in 1990 alone. Migrant Health Program, "An Atlas of State Profiles." Of these, the majority were of Mexican origin. "Findings from the National Agricultural Workers Survey (NAWS) 1989." The U.S. census found 188,752 Mexican-origin Hispanics living in southern states not including Florida in 1990 and 917,049 in 2000. Social Explorer Tables (SE), Census 1990 and Census 2000, U.S. Census Bureau and Social Explorer, www.socialexplorer.com.

39. On the need not to reify the difference between the two, see Holt, *Problem of Race in the Twenty-First Century*, 14.

40. Smith and Graves, *Charlotte, N.C.: The Global Evolution of a New South City*; O'Toole, "A New Nationalism for a New Era."

41. On connections between neoliberal economic growth patterns in the U.S. Sunbelt and Mexico, see Cadava, *Standing on Common Ground*, 17–18.

42. On globalization's effect on the social and racial landscapes of cities, see Sassen, *Global City*.

43. Walker, *Waking from the Dream*.

44. Lassiter, *Silent Majority*.

45. *Central Alabama Fair Housing Center v. Julie Magee and Jimmy Stubbs*, Civil Action No. 2:11cv982-MHT-CSC (2011).

46. For a critique of this narrative, see Lassiter and Crespino, *Myth of Southern Exceptionalism*.

47. Alabama House Republican Caucus, "Representative Micky Hammon and Illegal Immigration."

Chapter 1

1. See, for example, cover and middle pages of Sánchez, *Becoming Mexican American*.
2. Ibid.
3. Ibid.; Mario García, *Mexican Americans*; Gutiérrez, *Walls and Mirrors*; Monroy, *Rebirth*; Behnken, *Fighting Their Own Battles*.
4. Benjamin Heber Johnson, *Revolution in Texas*; Montejano, *Anglos and Mexicans*; Sánchez, *Becoming Mexican American*.
5. Hazel Canedo, interview by the author.
6. Ibid.
7. The U.S. Census counted 1,242 Mexican-born whites in New Orleans in 1920, and based on my analysis of the 1920 manuscript census (see Appendix), it is likely that an additional 10 percent lived there as well, classified by census workers as Negro or mulatto. For 1930, U.S. Census publications report 467 foreign-born white Mexicans as well as 527 foreign-born individuals with the race "Mexican," for a total of 994. An additional 190 U.S.-born Mexican-race individuals, presumably the children of immigrants, lived there as well. Since my detailed analysis suggests substantial turnover in the Mexicano population between 1920 and 1930, I estimate that around 2,000 Mexicanos lived in the city at some point during the 1910s–30s (see Appendix). Hunt, *Fourteenth Census of the United States*, 3:247, 391; U.S. Census Bureau, *Fifteenth Census of the United States*, 70, 326.
8. For more on the racialized construction of Creole identities, see Dominguez, *White by Definition*. For examples of minority groups deliberately positioning themselves vis-à-vis the color line elsewhere in the U.S. South during the height of Jim Crow, see Bow, *Partly Colored*; Loewen, *Mississippi Chinese*; Lowery, *Lumbee Indians in the Jim Crow South*.
9. This definition is somewhat broader than Omi and Winant's, including realms outside the social, economic, and political and also emphasizing the process through which individuals acquire "race." Omi and Winant, *Racial Formation in the United States*.
10. Fredrickson, *Racism*; Stern, *Eugenic Nation*.
11. Kazal, "Revisiting Assimilation."
12. Leo Spitzer provides an intellectual history of race in Europe, Africa, and Latin America from the nineteenth century into the twentieth, emphasizing the tension between long-standing traditions of cultural assimilation and the rise of eugenics. Spitzer, *Lives in Between*.

13. Gordon, *Great Arizona Orphan Abduction*; Montejano, *Anglos and Mexicans*; Sánchez, *Becoming Mexican American*.

14. Painter, "Assimilation of Latin Americans in New Orleans, Louisiana," 65.

15. For more on the South's global past under European colonialism, see Peacock, *Grounded Globalism*, 31–32.

16. Hudson, "Crossing Stories"; Lima, "Louisiana," 350.

17. Jiménez, "Cultural Diplomacy on an International Stage."

18. Gruesz, "Delta *Desterrados*," 55.

19. Gamio, *Mexican Immigration to the United States*; Sánchez, *Becoming Mexican American*, 22–25, 110.

20. Hunt, *Fourteenth Census of the United States*, 3:402; Truesdell, *Fifteenth Census of the United States*, 992–93.

21. Joseph, *Revolution from Without*, 200–204.

22. Commissioner, U.S. Department of Labor, Immigration Service, to Commissioner-General of Immigration, Washington, D.C., in Vecoli, *Records of the Immigration and Naturalization Service*, reel 5, frame 0083.

23. "Many May Face Trial for Aiding Mexican Rebels," *Times-Picayune*, December 22, 1923; "Mexican Revolt Plotters Start Hurried Exodus," *Times-Picayune*, December 24, 1923.

24. Analysis of 1930 "Protección" logs of the Mexican Consulate at New Orleans, AHSRE.

25. Joseph, *Revolution from Without*, 73–91; Tutino, *From Insurrection to Revolution*, 288–97.

26. Joseph, *Revolution from Without*; Falcón and García, *La Semilla en el Surco*.

27. Joseph, *Revolution from Without*, 73–79.

28. Fowler-Salamini, "Women Coffee Sorters"; Koth, *Waking the Dictator*.

29. Fowler-Salamini, "Women Coffee Sorters," 40.

30. Joseph, *Revolution from Without*.

31. Falcón, "Veracruz"; Joseph, *Revolution from Without*; Koth, *Waking the Dictator*, 255–57.

32. Alanís Enciso, *El Primer Programa Bracero y el Gobierno de México, 1917–1918*. Train fare is calculated from Zacatecas to Eagle Pass via Torreón in 1924, the only year for which I could find figures. Ferrocarriles Nacionales de México y Anexos, "Tarifa de Pasajes por Distancias Kilométricas para Uso de los Conductores de Trenes," Secretaría de Comunicaciones y Obras Publicas. I use an exchange rate of two pesos to one dollar from U.S. Department of Commerce, *Commercial Traveler's Guide to Latin America, Revised Edition, 1926*.

33. Secretaría de Gobernación to C. Delfino Victoria, Gob. Interino del Estado de Veracruz, Circular #30, 1918, Box 86, Folder 53, "Consultas contratación de braceros," AGEV.

34. Acuse, Municipio de Xoxocotla, Canton de Zongolica, November 15, 1918, Box 86, Folder 53, "Consultas contratacion de braceros," AGEV.

35. J. de la Torre to Alberto J. Pani, July 1, 1918, Box 137, Folder 10, AGN; Alanís Enciso, *El Primer Programa Bracero y el Gobierno de México, 1917–1918*, 87.

36. For more on the henequen plant and its importance to Yucatán's economic, social, and political history, see Joseph, *Revolution from Without*, 13.

37. Michael Nelken (grandson of Francisco Enseñat), interview by the author.

38. "Nuestra Colonia Hace Veinte Años-Según los Archivos de los Periódicos Lozano," *La Prensa*, January 17, 1934.

39. Kenneth Nieto (Peter's grandson), interview by the author; Peter Nieto household, *Fifteenth Census of the United States: 1930*, New Orleans, La., Enumeration District 36-102, Sheet 24A, accessed via Ancestry.com.

40. Painter, "Assimilation of Latin Americans in New Orleans, Louisiana," 13; Fowler-Salamini, "Women Coffee Sorters Confront the Mill Owners."

41. Painter, "Assimilation of Latin Americans in New Orleans, Louisiana," 13.

42. 1930 manuscript census analysis; see Appendix for more information.

43. Jesus Reséndez household, *Fifteenth Census of the United States: 1930*, New Orleans, La., Enumeration District 36-82, Sheet 18A, accessed via Ancestry.com.

44. Carrigan and Webb, "Lynching of Persons of Mexican Origin or Descent"; Benjamin Heber Johnson, *Revolution in Texas*; Montejano, *Anglos and Mexicans*.

45. Frank Cervantes (grandson of Francisco Cervantes), telephone interview by the author.

46. Francis D. Cervantes, *Fifteenth Census of the United States: 1930*, New Orleans, La., Enumeration District 36-188, Sheet 4-B, accessed via Ancestry.com.

47. U.S. Department of Commerce, *Commercial Traveler's Guide to Latin America, Revised Edition, 1931*, 55–56.

48. "Thirty-Second Report of the Board of Commissioners of the Port of New Orleans"; "Thirty-Third Report of the Board of Commissioners of the Port of New Orleans"; U.S. Department of Commerce, *Commercial Traveler's Guide to Latin America, Revised Edition, 1931*.

49. "Trade Gain Seen in Recognition of Obregon Rule," *Times-Picayune*, September 1, 1923.

50. "Mexico's Trade Belongs to City," *Times-Picayune*, August 5, 1923.

51. Connolly, "Timely Innovations," 254.

52. "Un Mexicano es Enviado Especial de Louisiana," *La Prensa*, December 24, 1929.

53. "El Problema de Irigación en México," *La Prensa*, September 24, 1930. On anti-Mexican sentiment in other newspapers, see Fox, *Three Worlds of Relief*, 124–49.

54. Sánchez, *Becoming Mexican American*, 59; Stern, "Buildings, Boundaries, and Blood"; Hernandez, *Migra!*

55. Stern, "Buildings, Boundaries, and Blood," 45–46.

56. Fairchild, *Science at the Borders*, 141.

57. Ibid., 140–44.

58. Lehrbas, "Immigration Station Here Place of Hope and Frustration," *Times-Picayune*, February 21, 1932.

59. This description is based on observations from the early 1930s in ibid.; Federal Writers' Project, *WPA Guide to New Orleans*, 60–61, 150–51, 261.

60. Based on descriptions and photographs in Sánchez, *Becoming Mexican American*, 71–73; Stern, "Buildings, Boundaries, and Blood," 32; Romo, *Ringside Seat to a Revolution*, 228.

61. Of Mexican-born people whose arrival dates were cataloged by enumerators on the 1920 census, 60 percent arrived in 1917 or later. See 1920 census analysis, explained in Appendix.

62. Hunt, *Fourteenth Census of the United States*, 3:247, 391. In 1920, "white" was the technical racial categorization of Mexican-origin people on the census.

63. This extrapolates from my analysis of the 1920 manuscript census. See Appendix for methodological information.

64. "Se organiza una Cia naviera mexicana en este país," *La Prensa*, July 31, 1917.

65. Camarillo, *Chicanos in a Changing Society*, 173; Sánchez, *Becoming Mexican American*, 192. Camarillo's figures are precisely for 1920 while Sánchez's are based on naturalization petitions filed before 1940 and thus represent the 1910s–30s as a whole.

66. Bennett, *Religion and the Rise of Jim Crow in New Orleans*, 197, 209–10.

67. Huber, *Our Lady of Guadalupe Church*.

68. Heck and Wheeler, *Religious Architecture in Louisiana*.

69. "Re-dedication and Blessing, Our Lady of Guadalupe Church, February 3, 1952," 15, ACANO.

70. Anne M. Martínez, *Catholic Borderlands*.

71. Massey, Alarcón, Durand, and González, *Return to Aztlan*.

72. Prayedeo Lozano household, *Fifteenth Census of the United States: 1930*, New Orleans, La., Enumeration District 36-100, Sheet 9A, accessed via Ancestry.com.

73. Vincente Gonzales, *Fifteenth Census of the United States: 1930*, New Orleans, La., Enumeration District 36-78, Sheet 8A, accessed via Ancestry.com.

74. Nationally, 43 percent of Mexican immigrants counted in the 1920 census were women. U.S. Census Bureau, *Abstract of the Fourteenth Census of the United States—1920*, 2:299. In 1930, 47 percent of Mexicans counted nationally were women. U.S. Census Bureau, *Fifteenth Census of the United States*, 101.

75. This figure counts Mexican and Mexican American women over the age of sixteen listed as single, divorced, or widowed. See Appendix for more information.

76. This figure is based on arrival dates of immigrant women in the 1930 census. This date was meant to indicate arrival to the country, if not necessarily the current city of residence. As a port city, however, New Orleans was the first destination for the vast majority of Mexican immigrants, as evidenced by the fact that 90 percent of the immigrants' U.S.-born children were born in Louisiana. See Appendix.

77. Analeta Cruz, *Fifteenth Census of the United States: 1930*, New Orleans, La., Enumeration District 36-80, Sheet 17B, accessed via Ancestry.com.

78. Ethel Sastre, *Fifteenth Census of the United States: 1930*, New Orleans, La., Enumeration District 36-199, Sheet 8B, accessed via Ancestry.com.

79. Gardner, *Qualities of a Citizen*.

80. Sánchez, *Becoming Mexican American*, 194–95.

81. For more on Ramos, see Jiménez, "Cultural Diplomacy on an International Stage."

82. Migel Henriquez, *Fourteenth Census of the United States: 1920*, New Orleans, La., Enumeration District 87, Sheet 10B, accessed via Ancestry.com; Miguel Henriquez, *Fifteenth Census of the United States: 1930*, New Orleans, La., Enumeration District 36-80, Sheet 6A, accessed via Ancestry.com.

83. Leon and Marguerite Rodriguez, *Fourteenth Census of the United States: 1920*, New Orleans, La., Enumeration District 9, Sheet 3A, accessed via Ancestry.com; Arron and Margarite Rodriguez, *Fifteenth Census of the United States: 1930*, New Orleans, La., Enumeration District 36-225, Sheet 25A, accessed via Ancestry.com.

84. Due to New Orleans census workers' quixotic spellings of Mexicans' last names as well as my sampling methodology, it was not possible to conduct a systematic longitudinal analysis. However, of four matches I was able to make between the 1920 and 1930 samples, two remained stable and two experienced upward mobility. Naturalization petitions would have identified a limited slice of the immigrant population (those who remained in New Orleans and naturalized there) but would have allowed for a robust longitudinal analysis of that slice, as in Sánchez, *Becoming Mexican American*.

85. Painter, "Assimilation of Latin Americans in New Orleans, Louisiana," 16.

86. Based on analysis of extant AHSRE records. There were sixty-three cases that definitively originated in New Orleans from 1930 to 1935.

87. Carlos Zervigón, interview by the author; Kenneth Nieto, interview by the author; Frank Cervantes, telephone interview by the author; Hazel Canedo, interview by the author; Michael Nelken, interview by the author; David Resendez, telephone interview by the author.

88. Carlos Zervigón, interview by the author; David Resendez, telephone interview by the author.

89. Arredondo, "Navigating Ethno-Racial Currents," 44; Sánchez, *Becoming Mexican American*; Camarillo, *Chicanos in a Changing Society*, 146.

90. Just 26 percent of Mexicans in 1920 had at least one Latin American neighbor; in 1930, 31 percent did. See Appendix.

91. Woodward, *Strange Career of Jim Crow*, 31–44.

92. Arnold Hirsch, "Simply a Matter of Black and White," 268.

93. 1920 and 1930 census analyses (see Appendix).

94. Federal Writers' Project, *WPA Guide to New Orleans*, 44.

95. Based on analysis of 1920 manuscript census. See Appendix for methodology. Matthew Frye Jacobson, *Whiteness of a Different Color*.

96. August Pradillo, *Fifteenth Census of the United States: 1930*, New Orleans, La., Enumeration District 36-87, Sheet 8-B, accessed via Ancestry.com; Ralph Gutierrez, *Fifteenth Census of the United States: 1930*, New Orleans, La., Enumeration District 36-227, Sheet 11, accessed via Ancestry.com.

97. Hunt, *Fourteenth Census of the United States*, 3:402; Sánchez, *Becoming Mexican American*; Arredondo, *Mexican Chicago*. For methodology in determining neighborhood composition, see explanation of census research in Appendix.

98. Montejano, *Anglos and Mexicans*, 37.

99. Sánchez, *Becoming Mexican American*, 138–39.

100. Gerino Morantes household, *Fifteenth Census of the United States: 1930*, New Orleans, La., Enumeration District 36-172, Sheet 4A, accessed via Ancestry.com.

101. Dray, *At the Hands of Persons Unknown*; Hale, *Making Whiteness*.

102. Joaquin Sanchez household, *Fifteenth Census of the United States: 1930*, New Orleans, La., Enumeration District 36-126, Sheet 29B, accessed via Ancestry.com.

103. U.S. Census Bureau, *Fifteenth Census of the United States*, 2.

104. Ibid., 1399.

105. Ibid., 69, 323.

106. The 1930 U.S. census publications report 467 foreign-born white Mexicans as well as 527 foreign-born individuals listed with the race "Mexican" lived in New Orleans that year; this means that 47 percent of Mexican-born individuals were returned as white. An additional 190 U.S.-born Mexican-race individuals lived there as well, presumably the children of immigrants. Ibid., 70, 326. Examination of the manuscript census reveals that in some cases, Central Americans were racially categorized as Mexican, causing official statistics to be inexact. In the households I sampled for this study, 41 percent of Mexican-born individuals were returned as white on the 1930 census, 56 percent were returned as Mexican, and 3 percent were returned as Negro. See Appendix for details.

107. A random sample of enumerators was identified as white through searches on Ancestry.com; I identified approximately 60 percent as female on the basis of first names and use of the titles "Mrs." or "Miss."

108. Painter, "Assimilation of Latin Americans in New Orleans, Louisiana."

109. See, for example, C.N.S., "Mexicans Warring against 'Jim Crow,'" *Louisiana Weekly*, October 24 1931.

110. "Economics," *The Crisis* 5, no. 4 (1913).

111. Blair Legendre, *Fifteenth Census of the United States: 1930*, New Orleans, La., Enumeration District 36-106, Sheet 31B, accessed via Ancestry.com; Joseph Ducoing, *Fifteenth Census of the United States: 1930*, New Orleans, La., Enumeration District 36-217, Sheet 47B, accessed via Ancestry.com.

112. For more on hierarchies within whiteness during this period, see Matthew Frye Jacobson, *Whiteness of a Different Color*; Guglielmo, *White on Arrival*.

113. This is in contrast to another Gulf Coast city, Tampa, where Cubans were classed as "Latins" alongside Spanish and Italian immigrants. Hewitt, *Southern Discomfort*.

114. Cleary, "Education of Mexican-Americans in Kansas City, Kansas"; Valdés, *Al Norte*; Valdés, *Barrios Norteños*, 80.

115. Arredondo, *Mexican Chicago*; Valdés, *Barrios Norteños*, 44, 109; Vargas, *Labor Rights Are Civil Rights*, 88; Innis-Jiménez, *Steel Barrio*.

116. "'The Hooked' Labor System," *Louisiana Planter and Sugar Manufacturer*, October 28, 1911.

117. "Our Need of Immigration," *Louisiana Planter and Sugar Manufacturer*, June 3, 1911.

118. Cornell, "Americans in the U.S. South and Mexico," 266–67.

119. "Louisiana Sugar News," *Louisiana Planter and Sugar Manufacturer*, June 1, 1918.

120. Wooton, "Mexican Labor May Aid Sugar Planters Here—Serious Situation Can Be Met by Importation of Cane Laborers," *Times-Picayune*, June 21, 1918.

121. "Louisiana Sugar News," *Louisiana Planter and Sugar Manufacturer*, July 6, 1918.

122. Truesdell, *Fifteenth Census of the United States*, vol. 3, part 1, 992.

123. "Mexican Involved in Fight at Negro Dance Hall," *Times-Picayune*, September 19, 1922.

124. "Trabajadores Mexicanos," *La Prensa*, June 24, 1918; "Dos Mil Braceros Seran Llamados de México: Los necesitan para la zafra en el Estado de Louisiana," *La Prensa*, September 22, 1918.

125. "Trabajadores Mexicanos," *La Prensa*, June 24, 1918.

126. "Consul Probes Mexican Appeal at Paper Mill," *Times-Picayune*, August 26, 1923.

127. The question would be foremost in the minds of Cuban elites in Tampa as well. Hewitt, *Southern Discomfort*, 219.

128. Ibid.

129. For Shreveport, see Consul Fernando Alatorre to Sra. Petra S. Viuda de Hernandez, August 30, 1933, Folder IV-642-25, AHSRE. For Cleveland, Mississippi, see Chapter 2. For the West and Midwest, see Vargas, *Labor Rights Are Civil Rights*, 135. For the Southwest, see Sánchez, *Becoming Mexican American*, 117.

130. "Visitation Report for the Parish of St. Louis Cathedral," 1934, Parish files, Our Lady of Guadalupe, ACANO.

131. Interviews with descendants of New Orleans's Mexican immigrants (Michael Nelken, Kenneth Nieto, and Carlos Zervigón) revealed no memories of communal organizations. Painter had a similar finding for Latin Americans in general. Painter, "Assimilation of Latin Americans in New Orleans, Louisiana."

132. For more on the Mexican consulate in Los Angeles, see Sánchez, *Becoming Mexican American*, 108–25.

133. Agustin Valles household, *Fourteenth Census of the United States: 1920*, New Orleans, La., Enumeration District 217, Sheet 16B, accessed via Ancestry.com.

134. Arnesen, *Waterfront Workers of New Orleans*; Claire Nee Nelson, "Redeeming Whiteness in New Orleans."

135. Dominguez, *White by Definition*, 141–48.

136. Lodgson and Cossé Bell, "Americanization of Black New Orleans," 253–57.

137. "Diplomat Protests Ban on Mexicans," September 19, 1923, newspaper clipping from unknown source, in Folder 1451/1, AEMEUA.

138. Prescott, "Journeying through Jim Crow," 10–11.

139. Basave Benítez, *México Mestizo*, 130.

140. Ibid.; María Elena Martínez, *Genealogical Fictions*.

141. Knight, "Racism, Revolution, and *Indigenismo*."

142. Ibid.

143. Ibid.

144. Basave Benítez, *México Mestizo*, 92; Rénique, "Race, Region, and Nation." For the subversive potential of mestizaje, see Benjamin Heber Johnson, "Cosmic Race in Texas."

145. Basave Benítez, *México Mestizo*, 141.

146. For more on the prerevolution history of this relationship, see Cornell, "Americans in the U.S. South and Mexico."

147. Horne, *Black and Brown*, 182–83; Gellman, *Good Neighbor Diplomacy*, 30.

148. Embassy of Mexico to Secretary of Foreign Relations, November 15, 1929, Folder IV-122-4, AHSRE.

149. Horne, *Black and Brown*, 182–83; Cornell, "Americans in the U.S. South and Mexico."

150. Mauricio Tenorio-Trillo argues that European-influenced Porfirian ideas of nation and modernity shaped the contours of "post"-revolutionary Mexican culture and intellectual life, including in matters of race. See Tenorio-Trillo, *Mexico at the World's Fairs*.

151. "Expediente personal de Armando Cuitlahuac Amador Sandoval," Folder 14-29-4, AHSRE.

152. Ibid.

153. "El Renacimiento del Arte Mexicano," lecture by Armando Amador, February 16, 1929, Tulane University, New Orleans, Folder IV-263-58, AHSRE.

154. Text of radio talk over Station WSMB, by Armando Amador, January 19, 1930, Folder IV-490-22, AHSRE.

155. López, "The Noche Mexicana," 40.

156. Benjamin Heber Johnson, *Revolution in Texas*.

157. "Present Disorganization of Mexico," *Louisiana Planter and Sugar Manufacturer*, July 11, 1914.

158. "Sugar in Mexico—A Summary," *Louisiana Planter and Sugar Manufacturer*, July 8, 1916.

159. "Says Mexico Had but One Real Revolution," *Morning Advocate*, May 7, 1930, clipping in Folder IV-263-62, AHSRE; Brunk, "Remembering Emiliano Zapata," 464.

160. On the Jung Hotel, see Federal Writers' Project, *WPA Guide to New Orleans*, xxxiii.

161. Cónsul Octavio Barreda to C. Secretario de Relaciones Exteriores, September 22, 1930, and Program of Independence Day Celebration, September 16, 1930, Folder IV-265-33, AHSRE.

162. Anita González, *Jarocho's Soul*.

163. On Amador in Chicago, see Arredondo, *Mexican Chicago*, 80.

164. This information is based on analysis of extant documentation of New Orleans

consular protection cases originating in New Orleans in 1930–32: Folders IV-188-16, IV-358-14, IV-358-43, and IV-69-44, AHSRE.

165. The regionally specific historiography of racial ideas in twentieth-century Mexico is sparse and has not yet explored Veracruz. On the colonial period, see Carroll, *Blacks in Colonial Veracruz*.

166. Painter, "Assimilation of Latin Americans in New Orleans, Louisiana," 118, fn. 16.

167. Fox, *Three Worlds of Relief*.

168. Sánchez, *Becoming Mexican American*, 214.

169. Fox, *Three Worlds of Relief*, 125–86.

170. Hoffman, *Unwanted Mexican Americans in the Great Depression*, 3; Balderrama and Rodriguez, *Decade of Betrayal*.

171. Fox, *Three Worlds of Relief*, 127–30.

172. "New Act Facilitates Naturalization Steps," *New York Times*, June 12, 1929; "Unregistered Mexicans Safe," *Los Angeles Times*, July 5, 1929; "Mexicanos Alarmados por las Medidas de Migración," *La Prensa*, June 11, 1929.

173. "Mexicanos Alarmados por las Medidas de Migración," *La Prensa*, June 11, 1929.

174. "Mexicanos en Desesperada Situación," *La Prensa*, May 5, 1930.

175. U.S. Department of Labor, Immigration Service, Manifest #33594, Bernardo Velasco Mendoza, admission at Laredo, Tex., April 29, 1929, accessed via Ancestry.com.

176. List of Consular Protection Activities, Mexican Consulate in New Orleans, 1930, Folder IV-69-44, AHSRE.

177. "Será Deportado por Quinta Vez un mexicano de 14 años," *La Prensa*, January 9, 1929.

178. This is based on all extant records from the New Orleans consulate from 1929 to 1935 and key-word searches of the *Times-Picayune* and Newsbank's Hispanic American Periodicals database, which includes several papers that reported on New Orleans at the time, as well as *La Prensa*, which had a correspondent there. Furthermore, Cybelle Fox has conducted an exhaustive review of federal records pertaining to the deportation and repatriation of Mexicans in the early 1930s. She found no evidence of large-scale repatriation or deportation campaigns targeted at Mexicans in New Orleans. Cybelle Fox, e-mail to the author, July 27, 2014; and Fox, *Three Worlds of Relief*.

179. U.S. Department of Labor, *Annual Report*, 94–96.

180. Fox, *Three Worlds of Relief*.

181. District Director, New Orleans District, U.S. Department of Labor Immigration Service, to Commissioner of Immigration and Naturalization, Department of Labor, Washington, D.C., August 16, 1934, Entry 9, 55598/568A, Box 412, NARA RG 85. I am grateful to Cybelle Fox for finding and sending me this primary source.

182. Commissioner of Immigration, New Orleans District, U.S. Department of Labor, Immigration Service, to Commissioner General of Immigration, U.S. Department of Labor, Washington, D.C., July 28, 1931, Entry 9, 55753–917, NARA RG 85. I am grateful to Adam Goodman for finding and sending me this primary source; Lehrbas, "Immigration Station Here Place of Hope and Frustration," *Times-Picayune*, February 21, 1932.

183. In lieu of a criminal charge, the records of New Orleans Police Department arrests sometimes read, "Held for U.S. immigration authorities." See, for example, the arrest cards of laborers Antonio López (July 30, 1928) and Federico López (April 10, 1929), NOPL.

184. Assistant Commissioner of Immigration, New Orleans, La., to Commissioner, May 27, 1924, and Assistant Commissioner of Immigration, New Orleans, La., to Commissioner, February 14, 1928, Entry 9, 55396/17, NARA RG 85; Commissioner, U.S. Department of Labor, New Orleans, La., to Commissioner-General of Immigration, Washington, D.C., July 28, 1930, Entry 9, 55727/917, NARA RG 85.

185. In addition to several cases in consulate files that clearly originated outside New Orleans, federal documents suggest that of Mexican immigrants permanently departing the United States for any reason from July 1, 1929, through June 30, 1930, just twenty-three listed Louisiana as their last state of residence, though this is almost certainly an undercount. U.S. Department of Labor, *Annual Report*, 96.

186. List of Consular Protection Activities, Mexican Consulate in New Orleans, 1930, Folder IV-69-44, AHSRE.

187. List of Consular Protection Activities, Mexican Consulate in New Orleans, 1931, Folder IV-188-16, AHSRE.

188. The total number of ship records was determined from a search for Antonio Benavides on Ancestry.com and by confirming Benavides's identity via his age and nationality and/or race. See, for example, "List or Manifest of Aliens Employed on the Vessel as Members of Crew," Vessel Crawford Ellis, arriving at New Orleans, La., October 4, 1932, from the port of Veracruz, accessed via Ancestry.com.

189. "List or Manifest of Aliens Employed on the Vessel as Members of Crew," Vessel Santa Marta, arriving at New Orleans, La., June 1, 1936, from the port of Havana, Cuba. Accessed via Ancestry.com.

190. Fox, *Three Worlds of Relief*, 160–86.

191. List of Consular Protection Activities, Mexican Consulate in New Orleans, 1931, Folder IV-188-16, AHSRE.

192. List of Consular Protection Activities, Mexican Consulate in New Orleans, 1930, Folder IV-69-44, AHSRE; for Los Angeles, see Fox, *Three Worlds of Relief*, 173.

193. List of Consular Protection Activities, Mexican Consulate in New Orleans, 1930, Folder IV-69-44, AHSRE.

194. Ibid.

195. My overall analysis is based on repatriations reported in ibid. and List of Consular Protection Activities, Mexican Consulate in New Orleans, 1931, Folder IV-188-16, AHSRE.

196. It is unclear whether this indicates Laguna, Texas, or Laguna, California, though Manuel Gamio's text indicates the latter. William Deverell posits that this lyric refers to the backbreaking labor at Simons Brick Company in "Simons, Laguna" east of Los Angeles. Deverell, *Whitewashed Adobe*, 169.

197. Gamio, *Mexican Immigration to the United States*, 84–104.

198. Report of Protection Activities, 1930. Reference to a letter from Consul of New Orleans to Consul General in San Antonio, October 27, 1930, Folder IV-69-44, AHSRE.

199. Report of Protection Activities, 1930, Folder IV-69-44, AHSRE.

200. "Visitation Report for the Parish of St. Louis Cathedral," 1934, Parish files, Our Lady of Guadalupe, ACANO.

201. Archdiocese of New Orleans, *Catholic Directory*, 1920–39, ACANO.

202. Arredondo, *Mexican Chicago*; Balderrama and Rodriguez, *Decade of Betrayal*; Camarillo, *Chicanos in a Changing Society*; Deutsch, *No Separate Refuge*; Matt García, *A World of Its Own*; Montejano, *Anglos and Mexicans*; Pitti, *Devil in Silicon Valley*; Sánchez, *Becoming Mexican American*; Valdés, *Al Norte*; Vargas, *Proletarians of the North*.

Chapter 2

1. Natanson, *Black Image in the New Deal*, 3, 78.

2. The full collection of Wolcott's photographs is available from the Library of Congress at http://www.loc.gov/pictures/collection/fsa/. I am grateful to April Merleaux for calling these photographs to my attention.

3. For Bauxite, Arkansas, see Keltner, "Tar Paper Shacks in Arcadia." For Floyd County, Kentucky, see U.S. manuscript census, 1930. For rural Louisiana, see Chapter 1 of this book.

4. Quoted in Jung, *Coolies and Cane*, 78.

5. Loewen, *Mississippi Chinese*.

6. Cobb, *Most Southern Place on Earth*, 110–11; Milani, "Peonage at Sunnyside"; Brandfon, "End of Immigration to the Cotton Fields."

7. Berthoff, "Southern Attitudes toward Immigration"; Brandfon, "End of Immigration to the Cotton Fields"; Jung, *Coolies and Cane*.

8. For 1904–5, see Cornell, "Americans in the U.S. South and Mexico," 264. For 1908, see Bishop Gunnis to Rev. Father Jeanard, September 23, 1908, Bishop Gunnis correspondence, File 9, ACDJ. Another mention of Mexicans in Mississippi in 1908 is in McWilliams, *Ill Fares the Land*, 249.

9. Cornell, "Americans in the U.S. South and Mexico," 262–68.

10. U.S. Census Bureau, *Thirteenth Census of the United States Taken in the Year 1910*, 1044–59.

11. De P. Araujo, "¡Alto Ahi Bandidos!," *Regeneración*, August 17, 1912.

12. Benjamin Heber Johnson, *Revolution in Texas*.

13. Daniel, *Breaking the Land*, 9.

14. Woodruff, *American Congo*, 41–49; Grossman, *Land of Hope*, 38–59.

15. Woodruff, *American Congo*, 61–62.

16. "Plan to Bring in Mexican Laborers," *Arkansas Gazette*, August 11, 1918. I am grateful to Story Matkin-Rawn for sending me this primary source.

17. Woodruff, *American Congo*, 23–28.

18. Ibid., 76–146; Daniel, *Shadow of Slavery*.

19. Cobb, *Most Southern Place on Earth*, 104–6.

20. Alanís Enciso, *El Primer Programa Bracero y el Gobierno de México, 1917–1918*, 35–38; Valdés, *Al Norte*, 9–11.

21. Benjamin Heber Johnson, *Revolution in Texas*.

22. Montejano, *Anglos and Mexicans*, 168–78; San Miguel, *Let All of Them Take Heed*, 51.

23. Carrigan and Webb, "Lynching of Persons of Mexican Origin or Descent," 423.

24. Hernández, *Migra!*, 47–65.

25. Benjamin Heber Johnson, *Revolution in Texas*; Montejano, *Anglos and Mexicans*; Sánchez, *Becoming Mexican American*.

26. Hernandez, *Migra!*, 54–55; Montejano, *Anglos and Mexicans*, 219.

27. Pitti, *Devil in Silicon Valley*, 107; Vargas, *Proletarians of the North*, 88; Rivera, *Y no se le tragó la tierra*, 23; Rivas-Rodriguez, "Ignacio E. Lozano," 81. For the Mexican American exodus from Texas in the 1920s, see also Montejano, *Anglos and Mexicans*, 200–219; Sánchez, *Becoming Mexican American*, 65–6; Valdés, *Al Norte*; Valdés, *Barrios Norteños*.

28. For settlement in the 1910s, see, for example, Celso Palacios, Draft Registration Card, Serial number 3295, Order number 1988, Skene, Mississippi, 1918, MDAH.

29. D. A. Davidson to Delta & Pine Land Co. of Mississippi, March 29, 1927, Oscar Johnston General Correspondence, Series 6, D&PL.

30. Description based on "Malaria among Mexican Cotton Pickers in Mississippi," *Monthly Labor Review* 25:50–51; Federal Writers' Project, *Mississippi: The WPA Guide to the Magnolia State*.

31. Downing to Gerow, November 19, 1927, File 11, Folder "Downing," File "Downing, Rev. Nelius 1927," ACDJ.

32. Whatever the crop, the vast majority of Mexican agricultural laborers in South Texas were wage workers, not sharecroppers, by 1930. Montejano, *Anglos and Mexicans*, 173.

33. Excerpt of Report of Department of Justice, Concerning Alleged Persecution of Mexican Citizens at Mayersville, Mississippi, Folder 1451/8, AEMEUA.

34. Juan Marshall, Acting Consul General, to Hon. Agent in Charge, Bureau of Investigation, Department of Justice, August 21, 1924, Folder 1451/6, AEMEUA.

35. Excerpt of Report of Department of Justice, Concerning Alleged Persecution of Mexican Citizens at Mayersville, Mississippi, Folder 1451/8, AEMEUA.

36. "El Algunos Campos Agricolas se Trata con Suma Dureza a los Trabajadores Mexicanos," *La Prensa*, June 5, 1924; "Centenares de Mexicanos se Encuentran Sufriendo en los Campos de Trabajo," *La Prensa*, August 28, 1924.

37. "Las Penalidades de los Braceros Mexicanos en el Mississipi," *La Prensa*, November 24, 1925. Anthropologist Manuel Gamio reported in the late 1920s that Mexicans earned about $1.75 daily for picking cotton in Texas: Gamio, *Mexican Immigration to the United States*, 39.

38. "Los mexicanos que sean maltratados en los campos de trabajo deben quejarse,"

La Prensa, September 24, 1925; "Una Compatriota se Queja de los Enganchadores," *La Prensa*, March 31, 1926.

39. "Continua la Demanda de Pizcadores," *La Prensa*, September 30, 1925.

40. "Correspondencia de Nueva Orleans," *El Heraldo de México*, September 26, 1925.

41. Nelius Downing to Rev. R. O. Gerow, October 15, 1925, File 11, Folder "Downing," File "Downing, Rev. Nelius 1927," ACDJ.

42. Report of St. Elizabeth's Parish, Clarksdale, 1925, "Reports—Parishes," ACDJ. My analysis shows that approximately one-fifth of ethnic Mexicans in the Delta in 1930 were Texas born. See Appendix.

43. Report of St. Elizabeth's Parish, Clarksdale, 1925, "Reports—Parishes," ACDJ.

44. Downing to Gerow, October 29, 1925, File 11, Folder "Downing," File "Downing, Rev. Nelius 1927," ACDJ.

45. "Las Penalidades de los Braceros Mexicanos en el Mississipi," *La Prensa*, November 24, 1925.

46. Ibid.

47. "Una Compatriota se Queja de los Enganchadores," *La Prensa*, March 31, 1926.

48. "Varios Mexicanos son Aprehendidos en Clarksdale, Mississippi," *La Prensa*, November 4, 1925.

49. "Una Compatriota se Queja de los Enganchadores," *La Prensa*, March 31, 1926.

50. "Las Penalidades de los Braceros Mexicanos en el Mississipi," *La Prensa*, November 24, 1925.

51. Ibid.

52. Woodruff, *American Congo*, 116; Grossman, *Land of Hope*; Benjamin Heber Johnson, *Revolution in Texas*; Sánchez, *Becoming Mexican American*; Vargas, *Labor Rights Are Civil Rights*.

53. Simmons, "The Week," *Chicago Defender*, August 19, 1922; "C.W.A.," *The Crisis* 41, no. 2 (1934).

54. Namorato, *Catholic Church in Mississippi*, 64.

55. Prendergast to Gerow, May 17, 1928, File 11, Folder "Prendergast"—"Prendergast, Rt. Rev. Msgr. J. M., V.G.—1928," ACDJ.

56. Lawrence J. Nelson, "Welfare Capitalism on a Mississippi Plantation," 235–36.

57. Downing to Gerow, October 17, 1925, File 11, Folder "Downing," File "Downing, Rev. Nelius 1927," ACDJ.

58. "To the Mexican Workers/Para los Trabajadores Mexicanos" from Rev. Father Nelius Downing, Catholic Priest, September 25, 1925, File 11, Folder "Downing," File "Downing, Rev. Nelius 1927," ACDJ.

59. Downing to Gerow, October 17, 1925, File 11, Folder "Downing," File "Downing, Rev. Nelius 1927," ACDJ.

60. "Las Penalidades de los Braceros Mexicanos en el Mississipi," *La Prensa*, November 24, 1925.

61. Translation of letter from Embassy of Mexico, Washington, D.C., to the Honorable Frank Kellogg, Secretary of State, December 4, 1925, in Daniel, *The Peonage Files of*

the U.S. Department of Justice, Reel 19, Casefile 50-636, frames 0368–82; "Los Mexicanos No Deben Ir a las Haciendas de Mississipi," *La Prensa*, November 28, 1925.

62. "Los Mexicanos No Deben Ir a las Haciendas de Mississipi," *La Prensa*, November 28, 1925.

63. "Los braceros mexicanos en Mississippi, piden que se les auxilie," *La Prensa*, December 28, 1925; "Mexicanos Abandonados a Su Propia Suerte," *El Cronista del Valle*, January 30, 1926.

64. Quoted in Woodruff, *American Congo*, 149.

65. This is in contrast to east-central Texas. Neil Foley, *White Scourge*.

66. U.S. Census Bureau, *Fifteenth Census of the United States*, 66. Thirty-one of the thirty-seven Mexican and Mexican American household heads in the sample who were enumerated in the 1930 census listed their occupation as "farmer," rather than "laborer" or "day laborer." See Appendix on sampling methodology.

67. Throughout this section, my most careful analysis has focused on Bolivar County, the Mississippi county that enumerated more Mexicans and Mexican Americans than any other in the 1930 census.

68. See Appendix.

69. See Appendix.

70. Sacrament Records, OLV.

71. This description is based on African American cotton farmer Ned Cobb's, as told in his autobiography, as well as James Cobb's details of the cotton cycle. Cobb, *Most Southern Place on Earth*, 156–60; Nate Shaw, *All God's Dangers*, 177–87.

72. Joe Enriquez, telephone interview by the author, 2005.

73. Report of Protection Activities, 1930, Folder IV-69-44, AHSRE.

74. Cobb, *Most Southern Place on Earth*, 106.

75. This is based on the families' residence at the time of their children's baptism. Sacrament Records, OLV.

76. "Llegaron a 5,000 los Mexicanos que Sufrieron Considerablemente a Causa de las Inundaciones del Mississippi," *El Heraldo de México*, September 8, 1927; Daniel, *Deep'n as It Come*, 84.

77. Cobb, *Most Southern Place on Earth*, 185; Daniel, *Breaking the Land*, 69–70; Woodruff, *American Congo*, 153.

78. Entry for May 22, 1927, *Diary of Bishop Gerow: Vol. VI, 1924–34*, ACDJ.

79. Rotondo to Gerow, April 29, 1929, File 11, Folder "Rotondo—1927," ACDJ.

80. "Excitativa a Nuestra Colonia," *El Heraldo de México*, May 15, 1927; "La Confederación de Sociedades Mexicanas Pide Ayuda para los Damnificados Mexicanos del Mississippi," *El Heraldo de México*, June 11, 1927; "Actividades de la Cruz Azul Mexicana, Primera Division," *La Epoca*, May 29, 1927; "Los mexicanos de Oklahoma socorren a los damnificados del Misisipi," *La Prensa*, June 12, 1927; "Los mexicanos residentes en Nueva Orleans ayudan a los damnificados," *La Prensa*, May 23, 1927.

81. "Excitativa a Nuestra Colonia," *El Heraldo de México*, May 15, 1927.

82. Ibid.

83. D. A. Davidson to Delta & Pine Land Co. of Mississippi, March 29, 1927, D&PL.

84. It appears that they arrived in 1926 or 1927, as Delta & Pine Land's 1925 plantation census listed no Spanish surnames. Ledger #26, Series L1-L9, D&PL.

85. Downing to Gerow, October 6, 1927; Gerow to Downing, October 8, 1927, File 11, Folder "Downing," File "Downing, Rev. Nelius 1927," ACDJ. For more on Delta & Pine Land's management practices, see Lawrence J. Nelson, "Welfare Capitalism on a Mississippi Plantation"; Woodruff, *American Congo*, 23–28.

86. Downing to Gerow, November 23, 1927, File 11, Folder "Downing," File "Downing, Rev. Nelius 1927," ACDJ.

87. "Elecciones de Funcionarios en la Comisión Honorifica de Gunnison, Mississippi," *El Heraldo Mexicano*, August 8, 1928; "Celebraron el 5 de Mayo en Gunnison, Mississippi," *El Heraldo Mexicano*, May 6, 1928.

88. Sánchez, *Becoming Mexican American*, 114–15.

89. "Elecciones de Funcionarios en la Comisión Honorifica de Gunnison, Mississippi," *El Heraldo Mexicano*, August 8, 1928; "Celebraron el 5 de Mayo en Gunnison, Mississippi," *El Heraldo Mexicano*, May 6, 1928.

90. "Celebraron el 5 de Mayo en Gunnison, Mississippi," *El Heraldo Mexicano*, May 6, 1928.

91. Cobb, *Most Southern Place on Earth*, 177–83.

92. For the historical debate on this question, see Blanton, "George I. Sánchez, Ideology, and Whiteness"; Neil Foley, "Partly Colored or Other White"; Guglielmo, "Fighting for Caucasian Rights"; Benjamin Heber Johnson, "Cosmic Race in Texas."

93. This is based on my analysis of the 1930 manuscript census; see Appendix.

94. Kit Mason household, *Fifteenth Census of the United States: 1930*, Bolivar County, Mississippi, Enumeration District 6-5, Sheet 32OB, accessed via Ancestry.com; Antonio Martinez household, *Fifteenth Census of the United States: 1930*, Bolivar County, Mississippi, Enumeration District 6-17, Sheet 9A, accessed via Ancestry.com.

95. Ocie Jones household, *Fifteenth Census of the United States: 1930*, Carroll County, Enumeration District 8-4, Sheet 16B, accessed via Ancestry.com. Carroll is also a Delta county.

96. Frank Torres household, *Fifteenth Census of the United States: 1930*, Bolivar County, Mississippi, Enumeration District 6-16, Sheet 2B, accessed via Ancestry.com.

97. Cobb, *Most Southern Place on Earth*, 159.

98. Loewen, *Mississippi Chinese*; Higham, *Strangers in the Land*, 169.

99. For more on Blumenbach's contribution to modern eugenic thought, see Fredrickson, *Racism*, 62.

100. *Rice v. Gong Lum*, 139 Miss. 760, 104 So. 105 (1925).

101. Loewen, *Mississippi Chinese*; San Miguel, *Let All of Them Take Heed*; Montejano, *Anglos and Mexicans*.

102. Orenstein, "Void for Vagueness."

103. Castro to Bilbo, March 22, 1930, Folder 5, Box 73, TB.

104. Eckles to Bilbo, February 22, 1930, Folder 20, Box 71, TB.

105. "Elecciones de Funcionarios en la Comisión Honorifica de Gunnison, Mississippi," *El Heraldo Mexicano*, August 8, 1928. On Landrove's movements, see Rafael

Jaime Landrove, Petition for Naturalization No. 422, U.S. District Court of Mississippi at Clarksdale, Mississippi, accessed via Ancestry.com..

106. Gunnison Consolidated School Records, 1928–29, 2nd grade, Race: white, Teacher: Mrs. E. M. Pease; 1929–30, 2nd grade, Teacher: Mrs. Edwina M., DSU. The latter book does not have a racial designation in its title, but I know it to be the white school because several of its pupils were the children of plantation managers.

107. Eckles to Bilbo, February 22, 1930, Folder 20, Box 71, TB.

108. Cobb, *Most Southern Place on Earth*, 116; Gunnison Consolidated School Records, "Negro" schools, 1929–30, 1934–35, DSU.

109. Alvarez, "Lemon Grove Incident"; San Miguel, *Let All of Them Take Heed*, 77–81.

110. Sacrament Records, OLV.

111. Diocese of Natchez Annual Reports, 1925–35, ACDJ.

112. Downing to Gerow, February 18, 1929, File 12, Folder "Mexicans," ACDJ.

113. Downing to Gerow, January 18, 1927, File 11, Folder "Downing," File "Downing, Rev. Nelius 1927," ACDJ.

114. Downing to Gerow, November 17, 1927, File 11, Folder "Downing," File "Downing, Rev. Nelius 1927," ACDJ.

115. Rafael Landrove and Petra Jayme, marriage record, 1879, San Juan Bautista parish, Lampazos de Naranjo, Nuevo León, Mexico, International Genealogical Index, Church of Jesus Christ of Latter-day Saints, www.familysearch.org; Tomás González Landrove (great-nephew of Mississippi's Rafael J. Landrove), interview by the author.

116. Knight, *Porfirians, Liberals and Peasants*, 11, 43–44.

117. Constancio Landrove household, *Fifteenth Census of the United States: 1930*, San Antonio, Bexar County, Texas, Enumeration District 15-55, Sheet 55A, accessed via Ancestry.com.

118. Actas #113, 114, 115, *Nacimientos 1922*, Civil Registry of Lampazos de Naranjo. "Lista de patentes, 1916," lists Constancio Landrove owing twenty pesos for a liquor license, 1911 Caja 301 (misfiled), AMLN.

119. Tomás González Landrove, interview by the author.

120. Acta #99, *Nacimientos 1921*, Civil Registry of Lampazos de Naranjo; Acta # 171, and Acta #306, *Nacimientos 1908, Lampazos de Naranjo*, AGENL; Acta # 8 and Acta #71, *Nacimientos 1911, Lampazos de Naranjo*, AGENL; Manuel Saenz household, *Thirteenth Census of the United States: 1910*, Laredo, Webb County, Texas, Enumeration District 148, Sheet 10A, accessed via Ancestry.com.

121. Tomás González Landrove, interview by the author.

122. Tutino, *From Insurrection to Revolution*, 297–305.

123. Vaughan, *Cultural Politics in Revolution*, 26–27.

124. Rafael Jaime Landrove, Petition for Naturalization.

125. Census and school records identify her brother as Perry, while baptismal records identify her as Pérez. On Mexican cotton workers in East-Central Texas, see Neil Foley, *White Scourge*.

126. Rafael Jaime Landrove, Petition for Naturalization.

127. Omi and Winant, *Racial Formation in the United States*, 60–61; Stern, "Buildings, Boundaries, and Blood," 78.

128. Rafael Landrove household, *Fifteenth Census of the United States: 1930*, Bolivar County, Mississippi, Enumeration District 6-5, Sheet 27A, accessed via Ancestry.com.

129. Acta #113, *Nacimientos 1922*, Civil Registry of Lampazos de Naranjo. Great-nephew Tomás González Landrove also was not aware of any familial connection to Cuba. Tomás González Landrove, interview by the author.

130. Nicolas and Mary Enriquez identified this photograph's subjects as Rafael and Martha Landrove to their grandson, Richard Enriquez. I was able to confirm Landrove's identity because his naturalization documents indicate that he had a shortened first (pointer) finger on his right hand, which is visible in the photograph. I date the photo to early 1928 because the first child Rafael and Martha had together, Martina, was born in May 1927. Rafael Jaime Landrove, Petition for Naturalization.

131. Rose emphasizes the importance of interpreting such contexts, rather than treating photographs as stand-alone texts. Rose, *Doing Family Photography*.

132. Holland, "Introduction"; Rose, *Doing Family Photography*, 11.

133. Shawn Michelle Smith, *American Archives*.

134. Levine, *Images of History*, 62.

135. Rosas, *Abrazando el Espíritu*, loc. 1130.

136. This is based on my 1930 Bolivar County census analysis; see Appendix.

137. Neil Foley, "Partly Colored or Other White"; Neil Foley, "Becoming Hispanic."

138. Alvarez, "Lemon Grove Incident."

139. For example, see Folders IV-69-44 and IV-188-16, AHSRE.

140. Report of Protection Activities, 1930, Folder IV-69-44, AHSRE.

141. San Miguel, *Let All of Them Take Heed*, 77–81.

142. Alvarez, "Lemon Grove Incident," 8.

143. Ibid.; Behnken, *Fighting Their Own Battles*, 28.

144. For Mexican schools in Texas, see Montejano, *Anglos and Mexicans*, 192; San Miguel, *Let All of Them Take Heed*. For educational segregation of Mexicans in Southern California, see Sánchez, *Becoming Mexican American*, 258–59.

145. Neil Foley, "Partly Colored or Other White"; Neil Foley, "Becoming Hispanic"; Guglielmo, "Fighting for Caucasian Rights." More convincingly, historian Carlos Blanton argues that the "Caucasian strategy" was merely a legal argument chosen because it could win in court—but that its Mexican American proponents in the 1950s and 1960s made common cause with African American civil rights leaders even as they argued for their own legal whiteness. Blanton, "George I. Sánchez, Ideology, and Whiteness."

146. Castro to Bilbo, February 12, 1931, Folder 11, Box 71, TB.

147. Vázquez and Meyer, *México frente a Estados Unidos*, 157–62.

148. Gunnison Consolidated School Record, DSU. These records show that the Landrove and Robledo children did not attend school regularly until December that year.

149. Fligstein, *Going North*, 94–95.

150. For more on these collaborations, see Fox, *Three Worlds of Relief*.

151. Daniel, *Breaking the Land*, 66–70.

152. List of Consular Protection Activities, Mexican Consulate in New Orleans, 1930, Folder IV-69-44, AHSRE.

153. Sacrament Records, OLV.

154. Folder IV-188-16, AHSRE.

155. Cónsul Fernando Alatorre to Rafael J. Landrove, October 13, 1932, Folder IV-358-76, AHSRE.

156. Rafael Jaime Landrove, Petition for Naturalization.

157. Social Security Death Index, R. Landrove, SSN 428-36-4156, and Martha Landrove, SSN 428-36-4011, accessed via Ancestry.com; R. J. Landrove obituary, *Sacramento Bee*, December 28, 1976.

158. Cobb, *Most Southern Place on Earth*, 188–89; Daniel, *Breaking the Land*, 94–105.

159. Joe Enriquez, interview by the author, 2006.

160. Weise, "Mississippi."

161. SRE to Consulate of Mexico in New Orleans, January 31, 1931, Folder IV-186-1, AHSRE.

162. J. G. Chastain Sr., "Work Among the Mexicans in the Delta," *Baptist Record*, December 7, 1933. I am grateful to Alison Greene for sending me this primary source.

163. McKenna to Gerow, August 14, 1946, File 11, Folder "McKenna 1946–7," ACDJ.

164. Phillip Laro, interview by the author; Weise, "Mississippi."

165. Joe Enriquez, interview by the author; Mary Palacios Ybarra, interview by the author.

166. This is based on personal observation as well as Márquez, "Chicanos in SNCC."

Chapter 3

1. Cónsul Rubén Gaxiola to Secretariat of Foreign Relations, November 19, 1949, Folder TM-26-2, AHSRE.

2. Ibid.

3. On the desegregation flashpoint in Hoxie, Arkansas, see Lewis, *Massive Resistance*, 35–39.

4. Klein, *For All These Rights*, 4–7; Sullivan, *Days of Hope*.

5. Calavita, *Inside the State*; Deborah Cohen, *Braceros*; Rosas, *Abrazando el Espíritu*; Galarza, *Merchants of Labor*; Gamboa, *Mexican Labor and World War II*.

6. This extrapolates from Holley's calculation that 251,298 braceros worked in Arkansas between 1953 and 1965 and uses his figures for braceros as a part of the overall cotton labor force during those years. Holley, *Second Great Emancipation*, 152.

7. Rosas, *Abrazando el Espíritu*.

8. Deborah Cohen, "Caught in the Middle"; Calavita, *Inside the State*, 27–28; García y Griego, *Importation of Mexican Contract Laborers to the United States*.

9. Fligstein, *Going North*, 159–63; Woodruff, *American Congo*, 191–227.

10. Woodruff, *American Congo*, 191–227.

11. Agricultural Extension Service Annual Reports, Crittenden County, Arkansas, Narrative Report of Negro County Agent, December 1, 1944, and January 5, 1945, NAFW RG 33. Research assistant Carla Mendiola, Southern Methodist University, conducted the research at NAFW RG 33.

12. Lemann, *Promised Land*.

13. Agricultural Extension Service Annual Reports, N. Mississippi County, Arkansas, Narrative Report of County Agent, November 30, 1943, NAFW RG 33; Holley, *Second Great Emancipation*, 178.

14. U.S. Manuscript Census, 1930, accessed via Ancestry.com; Sacrament Records, CIC. For more on the earlier Mexican American history of Arkansas, see Striffler and Weise, "Arkansas."

15. Woodruff, *American Congo*, 154.

16. "Fiestas Patrias en Nuestra Colonia," *La Prensa*, September 7, 1940.

17. Whayne, *A New Plantation South*, 222; Agricultural Extension Service Annual Reports, Crittenden County, Arkansas, Narrative Report of County Agent, November 30, 1943, NAFW RG 33.

18. Woodruff, *American Congo*, 208.

19. Montejano, *Anglos and Mexicans*, 212, 19; George B. Franklin and Son to W. H. Farmer, Manager, Louisiana Delta Council, excerpted in Statement of W. H. Farmer, Manager, Louisiana Delta Council, Delhi., La., to the House Committee on Agriculture, Subcommittee on Farm Labor, *Farm Labor Investigations: Hearings in Greenville, Miss., Memphis, Tenn., and Midland, Tex*, 81st Congress, 2nd Session, 1950, 57.

20. "Necesitanse 500 Pizcadores," *La Prensa*, October 2, 1944; "Necesito 400 Pizcadores de Algodón para el Estado de Arkansas," *La Prensa*, August 20, 1946; "Necesitamos Pizcadores de Algodón para los Estados de Arkansas y Mississippi," *La Prensa*, September 20, 1946; "Atención Trabajadores," *La Prensa*, August 17, 1947.

21. W. P. Boyer, County Agent, to farmers ("Dear Sir,"), Agricultural Extension Service Annual Reports, Jefferson County, Arkansas, August 9, 1946, NAFW RG 33.

22. Agricultural Extension Service Annual Reports, S. Mississippi County, Arkansas, Narrative Report of County Agent, November 30, 1947, NAFW RG 33.

23. Statement of Joe Cromer, Osceola, Arkansas, to the House Committee on Agriculture, in *Farm Labor Investigations*.

24. "Multados por Traer Braceros al País," *La Prensa*, September 12, 1947.

25. Agricultural Extension Service Annual Reports, Crittenden County, Arkansas, Narrative Report of County Agent, November 30, 1948, NAFW RG 33.

26. List of braceros contracted 1952–53 in Eagle Pass, Folder 30-16-45, AHSRE; Arkansas Certifications Adjusted, September 11, 1950, HA.

27. Agricultural Extension Service Annual Reports, S. Mississippi County, Arkansas, Narrative Report of County Agent, November 30, 1948, NAFW RG 33.

28. Thom E. Beasley, interview, BHA.

29. Deborah Cohen, *Braceros*; Rosas, *Abrazando el Espíritu*.

30. Deborah Cohen, *Braceros*; Rosas, *Abrazando el Espíritu*.

31. Gabino Solís Aguilera, interview, BHA.

32. Declaration of I. G. García and J. P. Yepes, October 14, 1948, Folder 1453/3, AEMEUA.

33. Declaration of Antonio Vega Aguiniga, October 16, 1948, Folder 1453/3, AEMEUA.

34. Declaration of Pedro Villarreal Jr., October 14, 1948, Folder 1453/3, AEMEUA.

35. Declarations of Nemesio Puente H. and José Cifuentes Martínez, October 17, 1948, Folder 1453/3, AEMEUA.

36. Miguel Jáquez López, interview, BHA.

37. Declaration of F. Moreno, J. Chávez, D. Jiménez, October 16, 1948, Folder 1453/3, AEMEUA.

38. A. Cano del Castillo to Ed McDonald, October 11, 1952, Folder TM-10-30, AHSRE.

39. A. Cano del Castillo to Ed McDonald, approximately 1952, Folder TM-24-18, AHSRE.

40. A. Cano del Castillo to Ed McDonald, October 11, 1952, Folder TM-10-30, AHSRE.

41. Declaration of F. Moreno, J. Chávez, D. Jímenez, October 16, 1948, Folder 1453/3, AEMEUA.

42. Jack McNeil, interview, ADT; Declaration of F. Moreno, J. Chávez, D. Jiménez, October 16, 1948, Folder 1453/3, AEMEUA.

43. J. W. Speck to E. C. Gathings, June 18, 1951, ECG.

44. For more on the ways California's growers employed discourse to denigrate local workers, see Deborah Cohen, *Braceros*, 47–65.

45. Statement of W. M Garrard Jr., Chairman, Delta Council Agricultural Committee, Indianola, Miss., and Statement of A. W. Oliver, President, the Agricultural Council of Arkansas, to the House Committee on Agriculture, Subcommittee on Farm Labor, in *Farm Labor Investigations*.

46. Statement of Sanford Joiner, Tennessee Department of Employment Security, Nashville, Tenn.; Statement of George Twine, Truck Driver, Memphis, Tenn.; Statement of Cora Townes, Truck Driver, Memphis, Tenn., House Committee on Agriculture, in *Farm Labor Investigations*.

47. Gabino Solís Aguilera, telephone interview by the author.

48. Report of Joint Investigation of Mexican National Agricultural Workers, Crittenden Farm Association, October 2, 1952, Folder TM-6-3; A. Cano del Castillo to Ed McDonald, September 29, 1952, Folder TM-10-22; A. Cano del Castillo to Claude A. Caldwell, October 1, 1952, Folder TM-6-3; A. Cano del Castillo to Sr. José Aldama, October 1, 1952; A. Cano del Castillo to Ed McDonald, October 8, 1952, Folder TM-6-3; A. Cano to Claude Caldwell, October 8, 1952, Folder TM-6-3; A. Cano del Castillo to Claude Caldwell, October 11, 1952, Folder TM-10-30, AHSRE.

49. Report of Joint Investigation of Mexican National Agricultural Workers, Crittenden Farm Association, October 2, 1952, Folder TM-6-3, AHSRE.

50. John Collier, interview, BHA; Thom Beasley, interview, BHA.

51. Calvin King, interview, BHA.

52. For interpretations of braceros' relationship to the money they earned in the United States, see Deborah Cohen, *Braceros*; Rosas, *Abrazando el Espíritu*.

53. Jesús Ortíz Torres, interview, BHA.

54. John Gray, interview, BHA.

55. "Fiestas Patrias en Nuestra Colonia," *La Prensa*, September 7, 1940.

56. Kirby, *Rural Worlds Lost*, 271; Woodruff, *American Congo*, 194–214; Whayne, *A New Plantation South*, 220.

57. Whayne, *A New Plantation South*, 226–27.

58. Delores Atkins, interview, BHA.

59. "Looking and Listening," *The Crisis* 59, no. 1 (1952).

60. Calvin King, interview, BHA.

61. Green, *Battling the Plantation Mentality*, 205–6.

62. For more on this myth, see Neil Foley, *White Scourge*.

63. James O. Scarlett to E. C. Gathings, February 2, 1952, Folder 4153, Box 272—Farm Labor—Mexican, ECG.

64. Daniel, *Shadow of Slavery*.

65. Bobby Wood, interview, ADT. John Grisham also recalled practicing Spanish with braceros in his semiautobiographical *A Painted House* (New York: Doubleday, 2001), 5.

66. Delores Atkins, interview, BHA.

67. Memorandum from Gustavo Garcia, transmitted by telephone from Pine Bluff, Arkansas, October 21, 1949, Folder 1453/3, AEMEUA.

68. Preliminary report given by Canciller Rafael Linares Navarro about the official commission conferred on Pine Bluff, Arkansas, November 15, 1948, Folder 1453/3, AEMEUA.

69. Royce Stubblefield to E. C. Gathings, February 4, 1952, Folder 4153, Box 272—Farm Labor—Mexican, ECG.

70. Bernard Lipsey, interview, BHA.

71. On braceros as dehumanized economic "input factors," see Galarza, *Merchants of Labor*, 16.

72. On the importance of program experiences for bracero reputations in their families and home towns, see Deborah Cohen, *Braceros*; Rosas, *Abrazando el Espíritu*.

73. Gabino Solís Aguilera, telephone interview with the author.

74. Vice Consul Daniel Mancha Macias to Consul General Miguel G. Calderón, November 5, 1948, Folder 1453/3, AEMEUA.

75. Statement of A. W. Oliver, President, Agricultural Council of Arkansas, before the House Committee on Agriculture, in *Farm Labor Investigations*, 1950.

76. Deborah Cohen, *Braceros*; Rosas, *Abrazando el Espíritu*.

77. Joe García, interview, ADT.

78. Royce Stubblefield to E. C. Gathings, February 4, 1953, Folder 4153, Box 272—Farm Labor—Mexican, ECG.

79. Declaration of Pablo Soto Amaya and Cristóbal Vázquez Martínez, October 17, 1948, Folder 1453/3, AEMEUA.

80. Gabino Solís Aguilera, interview, BHA.

81. Vaughan, *Cultural Politics in Revolution*.

82. For more on the modern promises of the bracero program, see Deborah Cohen, *Braceros*.

83. Formal Joint Investigation Report, Employer Coy Scott, England, Arkansas, October 15, 1952, TM-10-30; A. Cano de Castillo, Consul in Dallas, to Ed McDonald, Regional Director, U.S. Department of Labor, Dallas, February 3, 1953, Folder TM-11-24, AHSRE.

84. Declaration of José Luís Landa and Manuel Gallegos, October 16, 1948, Folder 1453/3, AEMEUA.

85. In addition to Chapter 2 of this book, see Sánchez, *Becoming Mexican American*, 144–45.

86. Berry, "Use of Mexicans as Farm Laborers in the Delta." Berry supervised bracero contracting for farmers in Phillips, Lee, and St. Francis counties starting in June 1948.

87. Report of Investigation of Mexican National Agricultural Workers, October 21, 1952, Folder TM-11-27, AHSRE.

88. Gomez, "*Braceros* in the Arkansas Delta," 14.

89. C. A. Dawson to E. C. Gathings, July 29, 1950, Folder 4150, Box 272—Farm Labor—Mexican, ECG.

90. Dan Felton to E. C. Gathings, July 29, 1950, Folder 4150, Box 272—Farm Labor—Mexican, ECG.

91. Juan Antonio Mérigo to Consul General, San Antonio, December 12, 1953, Folder 1455/1, AEMEUA.

92. Joint Report of Investigation of Mexican National Agricultural Workers: A. H. Barnhill, April 11, 1953, Folder TM-21-30, AHSRE; Don W. Walker, Arkansas State Police, To Whom It May Concern, August 10, 1953, Folder 4463, Box 298—Foreign Agricultural Labor, ECG.

93. Joint Report of Investigation of Mexican National Agricultural Workers: A. H. Barnhill, April 11, 1953, TM-21-30, AHSRE.

94. For an example of federal immigration officers working to keep braceros from leaving their farms, see Frank O. Wilson to E. C. Gathings, July 27, 1950, Folder 4150, Box 272—Farm Labor—Mexican, ECG.

95. Woodruff, *American Congo*.

96. A. Cano de Castillo to W. B. McFarland, March 13, 1952, Folder TM-6-3, AHSRE.

97. "Memorandum," October 24, 1951, 56321/448 (A), NARA RG 85. I am grateful to Andy Eisen for finding and sending me this primary source.

98. On the limits of "free" labor in the absence of citizenship rights, see Woodruff, *American Congo*, 3–4.

99. Report about the Protection Case of the Mexican Workers of the Area of Pine Bluff, Arkansas, November 22, 1948, Folder 1453/3, AEMEUA.

100. Rafael Jiménez Castro, Consul in New Orleans, to Consul General of Mexico, San Antonio, October 29, 1949, Folder 1453/3, AEMEUA.

101. See, for example, Tenorio Trillo, "Cosmopolitan Mexican Summer"; Delpar, *Enormous Vogue of Things Mexican*; Olsson, "Agrarian Crossings."

102. On STFU joining the Congress of Industrial Organizations (CIO), see Woodruff, *American Congo*, 185–86. For CIO attempts to stop the importation of Mexican workers to Arkansas, see Philip M. Weightman, CIO-PAC Field Director, to Mrs. Ethel B. Dawson, Field Representative, National Council of Churches, Pine Bluff, Arkansas, June 3, 1955, Box 1, Folders 4–6, Philip M. Weightman Papers, Tamiment Library, New York University. I am grateful to Michael C. Pierce for alerting me to this collection and Diana Greenwold for consulting the archive on my behalf in New York.

103. Whitlow, *Annual of the Arkansas Baptist State Convention*, 111; Bishop of Little Rock to Most Reverend William D. O'Brian, June 28, 1948, Series I, Box 64, Folder 4, CCES. I am grateful to research assistant Christina Davidson for conducting CCES research in Chicago.

104. Whitlow, *Annual of the Arkansas Baptist State Convention*, 1957. Regarding Catholics, there is no evidence of their advocacy in other records or those of the Catholic Church Extension Society (Boxes 64, 65, and 112, CCES). However, Little Rock's Catholic diocese was the only one to deny me access to their archive, so a key source is missing from this analysis.

105. Loza, "Braceros on the Boundaries," 31–69; Pitti, *Devil in Silicon Valley*, 136–47.

106. Loza, "Braceros on the Boundaries," 25–27, 33.

107. "42 Braceros Abandonados Pasan 35 Horas sin Probar Alimento," *La Prensa*, October 16, 1948; "Noticias Sintéticas Mundiales," *La Prensa*, February 2, 1950.

108. "Brillante Carrera Diplomática del Nuevo Cónsul Mex. en Laredo," *La Prensa*, November 3, 1955; García y Griego, *Importation of Mexican Contract Laborers to the United States*.

109. See, for example, Cano de Castillo to Casildo Caldera Hurtado c/o Crain Company, Wilson Arkansas, September 19, 1952, Folder TM-10-25, AHSRE; Report of Consul Angel Cano de Castillo about the official commission that was conferred in Pine Bluff, Ark., November 15, 1948, Folder 1453/3, AEMEUA.

110. AP, "Triste Odisea de Cien Pizcadores Mexicanos," *La Prensa*, November 24, 1951.

111. My description of the weather conditions is informed by local weather data for November 23, 1951, from the National Climatic Data Center, http://www.ncdc.noaa.gov.

112. Hahamovitch, *Fruits of Their Labor*, 151.

113. Kester, *Revolt among the Sharecroppers*, 72.

114. This analysis extrapolates from a careful analysis of thirty-nine out of the ninety-six folders in Mexico's Foreign Relations archive relating to Arkansas employers, dated 1948–53.

115. A. Cano to Ed McDonald, September 22, 1953, Folder TM-10-22, AHSRE.

116. A. Cano to Ed McDonald, October 20, 1953, Folder TM-23-15, AHSRE.

117. Esteban Saldaña, interview, BHA.

118. Conversation between Mr. P. M. Kenefick, Mr. Holly, and Mr. Gathings, July 28, 1953, Folder 4155, Box 272—Farm Labor—Mexican, ECG.

119. Testimony of J. C. Baird, President of the Delta Council, October 2, before the House Committee on Agriculture, in *Farm Labor Investigations*.

120. Robert C. Goodwin, Director, U.S. Department of Labor Bureau of Employment Security, to Hon E. C. Gathings, April 21, 1952, Folder 4153, Box 272—Farm Labor—Mexican, ECG.

121. Rocco Siciliano, Assistant Secretary of Labor, to E. C. Gathings, March 31, 1955, Folder 4464, Box 298—Foreign Agricultural Labor, ECG.

122. Earl C. Beck Jr. to E. C. Gathings, April 4, 1952, Folder 4153, Box 272—Farm Labor—Mexican, ECG.

123. E. D. McKnight, Parkin Farmers' Association, to Don Larin, March 14, 1952, Folder 4153, Box 272—Farm Labor—Mexican, ECG.

124. A. Cano del Castillo to Ed McDonald, August 25, 1953, Folder 1455/1, AEMEUA.

125. See, for example, the entire folder TM-9-19, AHSRE.

126. A. Cano de Castillo to W. B. McFarland, March 13, 1952, Folder TM-6-3, AHSRE.

127. A. Cano de Castillo to Ed McDonald, March 14, 1952, Folder TM-24-31, AHSRE.

128. A. Cano de Castillo to Ed McDonald, December 18, 1952, Folder TM-11-29, AHSRE.

129. Woodruff, *American Congo*.

130. Gamboa, *Mexican Labor and World War II*, 113; Galarza, *Merchants of Labor*, 77.

131. Deborah Cohen, "Caught in the Middle."

132. Ngai, *Impossible Subjects*, 146.

133. Gamboa observes a similar phenomenon in the case of the Pacific Northwest. Gamboa, *Mexican Labor and World War II*.

134. M. G. Calderón, Consul General in San Antonio, to SRE, October 26, 1948, Folder 1453/3, AEMEUA.

135. Notice to Mexican Nationals, October 23, 1948, Folder 1453/3, AEMEUA.

136. M. G. Calderón, Consul General in San Antonio, to SRE, November 6, 1948, Folder 1453/3, AEMEUA.

137. For more on how these dynamics played out at the U.S.-Mexico border, see Deborah Cohen, "Caught in the Middle."

138. A. Cano de Castillo to Ed McDonald, November 6, 1952, Folder TM-6-3; A. Cano to M. W. McFarland, U.S. Department of Labor, Dallas, June 16, 1952, Folder TM-24-31, AHSRE.

139. Telegram from J. W. Fulbright to Gov. Homer Adkins, September 20, 1950, HA.

140. Arturo Garza Cantú, Vice Consul in Memphis, to Embassy of Mexico, Washington, May 9, 1956, Folder TM-67-20, AHSRE.

141. E. C. Gathings to Luis Padilla Nervo, Minister of Foreign Relations, Mexico, April 30, 1957, Folder 4463, Box 298—Foreign Agricultural Labor, ECG.

142. Paul Kenefick to Rafael Aveleyra, Consul General of Mexico, Washington, D.C., August 15, 1952, Folder TM-23-16, AHSRE.

143. A. Cano to Ed McDonald, September 8, 1953, Folder Leo Powell, AHSRE.

144. A. H. Barnhill to Ed McDonald, May 13, 1953, Folder 4463, Box 298—Foreign Agricultural Labor, ECG.

145. For an example of D.C. bureaucrats' efforts, see Paul M. Kenefick, Special Assistant to the Secretary of Labor, to Señor Hector Blanco-Melo, Mexican Embassy, September 18, 1952, Folder TM-11-26, AHSRE. On long-standing patterns of local federal employees beholden to local power structures thwarting D.C.-initiated liberal initiatives in the South, see Daniel, *Shadow of Slavery*, 149–66; Woodruff, *American Congo*; Scott Beck, interview by the author.

146. Vice Consul Daniel Mancha Macías to Consul General Miguel G. Calderón, November 5, 1948, Folder 1453/3, AEMEUA.

147. Ibid.

148. For more on the histories of these counties' establishment for "whites only," see Woodruff, *American Congo*, 31.

149. Rubén Gaxiola, Memphis Consul, to Consul General, San Antonio, November 5, 1949, Folder TM-26-32, AHSRE.

150. D. O. Rushing, Agricultural Employment Specialist, to Angel Cano, May 3, 1951, Folder TM-26-2, AHSRE.

151. Rubén Gaxiola to SRE, November 19, 1949, Folder TM-26–32, AHSRE.

152. Memorandum to McDonald from Rushing, November 23, 1949, ibid.

153. J. G. Waskom, Mayor of Marked Tree, to D. O. Rushing, Employment Service, Little Rock, November 21, 1949; Telegram from E. Ritter and Co. to D. O. Rushing, Employment Service, Little Rock, November 22, 1949, Folder TM-26-32; Manuel Aguilar, Director General of the Consular Service, to Consul of Mexico, Memphis, Tennessee, December 20, 1949, Folder TM-26-2, AHSRE.

154. Consul A. Cano de Castillo to Secretariat of Foreign Relations, January 12, 1951; Joint Investigation of Consul Cano and United States Employment Service, January 15, 1951, Folder TM-26-2, AHSRE.

155. Sherriff of Poinsett County, Mayor of Marked Tree, and Chief of Police, Marked Tree, to Cano de Castillo, August 31, 1951, Folder TM-26-2, AHSRE.

156. Declaration to A. Cano de Castillo, August 29, 1951, Folder TM-26-2, AHSRE.

157. Consular report from V. Harwood Blocker, October 28, 1951, Folder TM-26-32, AHSRE.

158. Joint Investigation Report Alleged Discrimination in Marked Tree, Arkansas, October 8, 1951, Folder TM-26-32, AHSRE.

159. José Antonio Mérigo to SRE, November 27, 1951, Folder TM-26-32, AHSRE.

160. Joint Investigation by A. Cano del Castillo, Consul of Mexico, and Ted T. Critenson and Ray O. Bronander, USES Representative, in Trumann, Arkansas, October 18, 1951, Folder TM-26-32, AHSRE.

161. Supplement to Joint Investigation Report Alleged Discrimination, Trumann, Arkansas, November 16, 1951, Folder TM-26-32, AHSRE.

162. A. Cano de Castillo to Consul General of Mexico, San Antonio, November 24, 1951, and November 28, 1951; Consul General Cosme Hinojosa, San Antonio, to Ambassador of Mexico, Washington, D.C., January 9, 1952, Folder TM-26-32, AHSRE.

For more on Ritter's outsize holdings and influence in Poinsett County, see Whayne, *A New Plantation South*, 142.

163. Ordinance 29—An Ordinance Prohibiting Discrimination against Mexican Nationals Because of Their Ancestry or Nationality, October 9, 1952, Folder 4153, Box 272—Farm Labor—Mexican, ECG.

164. Jess Wike, Mayor of Marked Tree, to Consul A. Cano de Castillo, October 2, 1952, Folder TM-26-2, AHSRE.

165. Marked Tree Chamber of Commerce to A. Cano de Castillo, October 8, 1952, Folder TM-26-2, AHSRE.

166. Miguel Calderón to Consul of Mexico, Memphis, August 29, 1952, Folder TM-26-32, AHSRE.

167. Consul Cano, Memphis, to Mexican Bracero Reception Center, Harlingen, Texas, September 23, 1952, Folder TM-26-32, AHSRE.

168. Miguel Calderón, Director of Office of Migratory Workers, to Consul of Mexico, Memphis, October 22, 1952, Folder TM-26-32, AHSRE.

169. J. D. Harlan to A. Cano de Castillo, May 8, 1953, Folder 1455/1, AEMEUA.

170. Leslie Bow argues that southern African American memoirs decry immigrants' superior racial mobility as a way to call out "the irrationality of segregation." Bow, *Partly Colored*, 37–38.

171. Claude Kennedy, telephone interview by the author.

172. Bernard Lipsey, interview, BHA.

173. John Collier, interview, BHA; Gomez, "*Braceros* in the Arkansas Delta," 13.

174. José Gutiérrez, interview by the author and Joel Urista. I am grateful to Urista, then an undergraduate at California State University, Long Beach, for arranging our interview of Gutiérrez.

175. Ibid.

176. Harrison Locke, interview, BHA.

177. Claude Kennedy, interview by the author.

178. For additional accounts of blacks' and Mexicanos' memories of warm encounters in Arkansas, see Lucas and Buss, *Forged under the Sun*, 78; Gomez, "*Braceros* in the Arkansas Delta."

179. Telegram to E. C. Gathings, September 8, 1953, Folder 4441, Box 297—Foreign Agricultural Labor and Agricultural Labor, General, ECG.

180. Joint Report of Investigation, January 12, 1953, Folder TM-10-22, AHSRE.

181. For braceros as a share of cotton pickers in 1950s Arkansas, see Grove, "Economics of Cotton Harvest Mechanization in the United States," 42; Holley, *Second Great Emancipation*, 152.

182. Grove, "Economics of Cotton Harvest Mechanization in the United States," 19.

183. Willey Planting Company to Ed McDonald, April 21, 1953, Folder 1455/1, AEMEUA. James R. Orton, one of the tenants listed, is identified as African American through the 1930 U.S. manuscript census. James R. Orton, *Fifteenth Census of the United States: 1930*, Jefferson County, Ark., Enumeration District 35-10, Sheet 10, accessed via Ancestry.com.

184. J. L. Bland to Benton M. Kitchens, Manager, Employment Security Division, Paragould, Arkansas, November 17, 1958, Folder 4164, Box 273—Farm Labor—Mexican, ECG. I assume Hensen was white because a black person would have had no reason to believe that Governor Faubus, a dedicated proponent of segregation, would respond to his concerns.

185. Conversation between Albert D. Misler (Labor Department), P. N. Kenefick (special assistant to secretary of labor), Lloyd Godley, Osceola, and Mr. Gathings, April 24, 1953, Folder 4463, Box 298—Foreign Agricultural Labor, ECG.

186. Letter, October 5, 1956, Folder TM-25-40, AHSRE.

187. Grove, "Economics of Cotton Harvest Mechanization in the United States," 40.

188. Holley, *Second Great Emancipation*.

189. Green, *Battling the Plantation Mentality*.

190. "Probe Bias In Cotton Labor Wages," *Tri-State Defender*, July 17, 1954. Thanks to Story Matkin-Rawn for leading me to this article.

191. For more on this work, see Green, *Battling the Plantation Mentality*.

192. "Cotton Workers Express Gratitude for Petition during Picnic Here," *Memphis World*, July 30, 1954.

193. Green, *Battling the Plantation Mentality*, 205–6.

194. Story Matkin-Rawn has conducted a thorough review of these organizations' files for Little Rock and did not find any reference to Mexican labor. I reviewed files from the Arkansas Delta and Memphis and also found no references. NAACP papers, Urban League papers, Library of Congress, Washington, D.C.

195. Lee Beegle to Mr. Gathings, handwritten letter, July 5, 1955, Folder 4136, Box 271—Farm Labor and Foreign Agricultural Labor, ECG.

196. W. J. Stoddard, Brookland, Arkansas, to E. C. Gathings, April 10, 1961, Folder 4136, Box 271—Farm Labor and Foreign Agricultural Labor, ECG.

197. On Fulbright, see Gomez, "*Braceros* in the Arkansas Delta," 15–16. On McClellan, see Arthur J. Goldberg, Secretary of Labor, to Honorable John L. McClellan, United States Senate, April 23, 1963, JM.

198. Holley, *Second Great Emancipation*, 158.

199. On the relationship between agricultural and racial systems in the Delta, see Woodruff, "Mississippi Delta Planters."

200. Monette Growers Association to Gathings, February 3, 1958, Folder 4162, Box 273—Farm Labor—Mexican, ECG.

201. Oliver Clark, McAllen, Texas, to Gathings, July 20, 1962, Folder 4112, Box 270—Farm Labor and Foreign Agricultural Labor, ECG.

202. Joint Investigation, October 13, 1956, Folder TM-69-2, AHSRE.

203. José Ines Cano, Consul of Mexico in Memphis, to Mexican Ambassador, Washington, D.C., October 28, 1959; Roy Haynes to Jim [Bland, Arkansas Employment Security Division], November 20, 1959, TM-110-5, AHSRE.

204. Berry, "Use of Mexicans as Farm Laborers in the Delta."

205. Roy Haynes to Jim [Bland, Arkansas Employment Security Division], November 20, 1959, TM-110-5, AHSRE.

206. Hundreds of Spanish-surnamed children were baptized at Blytheville's Church of the Immaculate Conception alone during the bracero years. Since braceros traveled as single men, these children's parents were most likely Tejanos and undocumented immigrants. CIC.

207. Dray, *At the Hands of Persons Unknown*.

208. Berry, "Use of Mexicans as Farm Laborers in the Delta," 5.

209. José Ines Cano to SRE, April 14, 1960, Folder TM-110-5, AHSRE; Letter about F. C. Centro Mexicano printed in *Congressional Record*, Folder 4454, Box 298—Foreign Agricultural Labor, ECG.

210. M. G. Calderón, General Office of Migrant Worker Affairs, to Consul of Mexico, Memphis, April 30, 1960, Folder TM-110-5, AHSRE.

211. Galarza, *Merchants of Labor*, 238; Deborah Cohen, *Braceros*.

212. John M Stevens Jr. to Gathings, April 14, 1964, Folder 4099, Box 270—Farm Labor and Foreign Agricultural Labor, ECG.

213. Mrs. B. C. Burnette to Gathings, July 16, 1965, Folder 4483, Box 298—Foreign Agricultural Labor, ECG.

214. Grove, "Economics of Cotton Harvest Mechanization in the United States," 40.

215. Holley, *Second Great Emancipation*, 152.

216. Ibid., 159.

217. Ibid., 154–55.

218. Extensive attempts to find ex-braceros through local contacts in the Arkansas Delta between 2006 and 2008 revealed only rumors of two who had stayed but no solid evidence of their or others' presence.

219. On how these men came to see themselves as full citizens of Mexico, see Deborah Cohen, *Braceros*.

220. Declaration of I. G. Garcia and J. P. Yepes, Folder 1453-3, AEMEUA; Declaration of Manuel Avila Rosales, Folder 1453-3, AEMEUA; Jose Antonio Contreras to Consul General of Mexico in San Antonio, Folder 1453-3, AEMEUA; Joint Report of Investigation of Mexican National Agricultural Workers—AH Barnhill, Folder TM-21-30, AHSRE.

221. Juan Loza, telephone interview by the author. I am grateful to Mireya Loza for helping me make contact with her uncle.

222. Grove, "Economics of Cotton Harvest Mechanization in the United States," 40.

223. Woodruff, *American Congo*.

224. Requests for Foreign Labor Processed by USES, January 1 to December 31, 1949, Folder 4440, Box 297, ECG; Adolfo G. Domínguez, Consul of Mexico in New Orleans, to Ernest L. Marbury, Regional Director, USES Atlanta, February 24, 1953, Folder TM-10-22, AHSRE.

Chapter 4

1. Friendly, *Harvest of Shame*, November 24, 1960, CBS. The complete documentary is available at https://www.youtube.com/watch?v=yJTVF_dya7E.

2. On the distinction between "transnational" and "trans-state," see Waldinger and Fitzgerald, "Transnationalism in Question."

3. Moreton, *To Serve God and Wal-Mart*, 268–69.

4. For more on this "silent bargain" in rural North Carolina, see Torres, Popke, and Hapke, "South's Silent Bargain." Marrow, *New Destination Dreaming*. This chapter explains the historical process through which a similar (though not identical) "bargain" was struck in rural Georgia.

5. "Summary Report of Georgia, State Departments of Public Health, Education and Welfare, for Conference on Migrants, Washington, DC, May 17–19, 1954," Series 26-4-21, Box 5, Accession No. 2851-13, Folder "Migrant Labor," GA.

6. Riley, *Florida's Farmworkers in the Twenty-First Century*, 5–7.

7. Marc S. Rodriguez, *Tejano Diaspora*.

8. Griffith, "Hay Trabajo," 131.

9. Andrea and Bernardo Avalos, interview by the author. Migrant camp surveys confirm that Slim Avalos had whites, blacks, and Mexicans in his crews. 1981 survey, "Migrant and Seasonal Farmworkers Association" folder, Box 132; and 1982 survey, "Migrant and Seasonal Farmworkers Association 1983" file, Box 146, DCFS.

10. The earliest mention I have found of "Spanish-speaking" migrants in North Carolina is in the papers of the North Carolina Council of Churches' Migrant Ministry, which cover the 1960s and 1970s. See, for example, North Carolina Public School Bulletin, Raleigh, N.C., Vol. 32, No. 2, October 1967, "Our Migrant Story," 4–5, by Y. A. Taylor, State Supervisor Program Development, Title I, ESEA, Folder "Migrant Ministry (2 of 3)," Box 53, NCCC. The first mention that these "Spanish-speaking" migrant agricultural workers are Mexican and Mexican American is in 1973: Migrant Family Health Service report, June 18–November 2, 1973, Henderson County, North Carolina, Folder "Migrant (2 of 2)," Box 53, NCCC. For South Carolina, see AP, "Aliens," *Valdosta (Ga.) Daily Times*, June 18, 1976. For Virginia, see Heppel, "Harvesting the Crops of Others." Additionally, Mexican consulate records report that Mexican nationals performed farm labor in Alabama as early as 1986. Ramon Moreno Llamas, Third Level Consul, to Minister Luisa Virginia Junco, Consul of Mexico in Atlanta, July 17, 1986, Folder IV-343-2 2a parte, AHSRE.

11. Hahamovitch, *Fruits of Their Labor*.

12. Ibid., 89–92.

13. U.S. Census Bureau, *1987 Census of Agriculture*.

14. "Migrant and Seasonal Farmworkers in Georgia," in Frank Brewer's report, Box 16, Series 1-9-95, "Governor-Special Affairs Office" collection, GA.

15. Smigielski, "Farmers Need Migrants," *Valdosta (Ga.) Daily Times*, April 15, 1990; Deborah Cohen, *Braceros*.

16. Nixon, White, and Miller, "Hired Labor Management Practices among Georgia Farmers," Department of Agricultural Economics.

17. "Interview Excerpts on South Georgia Seasonal Agricultural Workers collected by Laurie Kay Sommers, 1997–2002," South Georgia Folklife Project, UA 22-12, Box 14, Folder 13, "Last Harvest Project Echols County Field Notes Clippings," VSU.

18. Tirso Moreno, interview by Laurie Sommers, Apopka, Fla., March 6, 1998, Last Harvest Documentation Project, UA 22-12, Box 14, VSU.

19. Israel Cortez, interview by Laurie Sommers, Valdosta, Ga., December 7, 2004, South Georgia Folklife Project, UA 22-12, Box 19, DAT 1010.37, VSU.

20. M. L. Brockette, Commissioner of Education, Texas Education Agency, to Hon. Jack P. Nix, Georgia Superintendent of Schools, May 7, 1976, Georgia Department of Education papers, 12-9-89, Box 9, Folder "Migrant 1975–76," GA.

21. "Migrant and Seasonal Farmworkers in Georgia," in Frank Brewer's report, Box 16, Series 1-9-95, "Governor—Special Affairs Office" collection, GA.

22. AP, "Aliens," *Valdosta (Ga.) Daily Times*, June 18, 1976.

23. Cortez interview.

24. For discussion of the role of unemployment benefits in shaping migrant routes, see Olga Martinez, interview by Laurie Sommers, El Pozo camp, Apopka, Fla., March 6, 1998, Last Harvest Documentation Project, UA 22-12, Box 14, Folder 8, VSU.

25. Cortez interview.

26. Ibid. Crop types were deduced from Migrant Housing Surveys analysis. See note 32.

27. José and Anselma Gómez, interview by the author.

28. Sacrament Records, SHCC.

29. U.S. Census Bureau, *1987 Census of Agriculture*.

30. Olsson, "Peeling Back the Layers."

31. Art Harris, "Letter from Dixie: Growers in Vidalia Savor the Sweet Success of Their Onions," *Washington Post*, July 3, 1983.

32. This is based on my analysis of migrant camp surveys conducted in 1980, 1981, and 1982. "Directions to Migrant Camps," 1980, compiled by Dawn Blum and Patricia Mendoza, Governor's Interns for WIC, August 13, 1980, Box 38, Series 1-9-95, "Governor—Special Affairs Office" collection, GA; 1981 survey, "Migrant and Seasonal Farmworkers Association" folder, Box 132, and 1982 survey, "Migrant and Seasonal Farmworkers Association 1983" file, Box 146, DCFS. For 1980 survey, Spanish surnamed crew leaders' camps were included in the analysis. For 1981 and 1982, camps were included if "Hispanic" was among the groups listed in the "race/origin" category.

33. See note 32.

34. Sister Patricia Brown, Report, October 1982, "Migrant Ministry" files, ACDS.

35. María Villegas, interview by the author.

36. Massey, Alarcón, Durand, and González, *Return to Aztlan*.

37. Teresa and Abel Aguilar, Rosa and Albert Aguilar, Carlos Alcantar, Mary Ann and Howdy Thurman, joint interview by the author; Studstill and Nieto-Studstill, "Hospitality and Hostility," 73.

38. Teresa and Abel Aguilar, Rosa and Albert Aguilar, Carlos Alcantar, and Mary Ann and Howdy Thurman, joint interview by the author.

39. See note 32.

40. Memorandum from Keith Yarbrough, District Director, to Ms. Barbara Ferrell, Refugee Coordinator, Georgia Department of Children and Family Services, Au-

gust 21, 1981, Folder "Migrant and Seasonal Farmworkers Association," Box 121, DCFS. For a discussion of race and Caribbean farm labor in the U.S. South, see Hahamovitch, *No Man's Land*.

41. Cortez interview; Cynthia Anderson, "New Law Changes Life for Migrants," *Tifton (Ga.) Gazette*, July 6, 1989.

42. "Findings from the National Agricultural Workers Survey (NAWS) 1989."

43. Cortez interview; Anderson, "New Law Changes Life for Migrants."

44. Cornelius, "Los Migrantes de la Crisis," 178–79.

45. The 1977 survey sampled workers in Kentucky, North Carolina, Tennessee, South Carolina, Georgia, Alabama, Mississippi, and Florida. Rowe, "Hired Farm Working Force of 1977"; "Findings from the National Agricultural Workers Survey (NAWS) 1989."

46. For the demographics of Georgia farm labor in the 1970s, see "Migrant and Seasonal Farmworkers in Georgia," in Frank Brewer's report, Box 16, Series 1-9-95, "Governor—Special Affairs Office" collection, GA. On the rise of poultry processing in the South, see Striffler, *Chicken*.

47. Cornell, "Americans in the U.S. South and Mexico," 264; Jung, *Coolies and Cane*; and Chapters 1–3 of this book.

48. Sister Patricia Brown, Report, October 1982, "Migrant Ministry" files, ACDS.

49. Javier González, telephone interview by the author.

50. "Report of Georgia Migrant Education Program-Title I, ESEA 1976–77," Georgia Department of Education Papers, GA, Series 12-4-182, Box 13, Folder "Georgia Migrant Education Program Report."

51. Sister Patricia Brown, Report, October 1982, "Migrant Ministry" files, ACDS; "Holy Family Catholic Church, Metter, Georgia, Parish Profile," May 2006, ACDS.

52. "On the Road with the Georgia Migrant Education Program," newsletter, Vol. 2, No. 4, 1982, p. 4, Georgia Department of Education Papers, GA, Series 12-9-137, Box 9, Folder "Migrant Education."

53. Javier González, telephone interview by the author.

54. Ibid.

55. Beck, "'We Were the First Ones,'" 141.

56. Robert Marín and Teodora Marín, interview by the author.

57. Cortez interview.

58. Diana (Avalos) Mendieta, interview by the author.

59. Javier González, telephone interview by the author.

60. For more on the racial work that discourses of difference and exoticism can do, see Bow, *Partly Colored*, 30–31; Holt, *Problem of Race in the Twenty-First Century*, 111.

61. Diana (Avalos) Mendieta, interview by the author.

62. José and Anselma Gómez, interview by the author.

63. Diana (Avalos) Mendieta, interview by the author.

64. Robert Marín and Teodora Marín, interview by the author.

65. Andrea Hinojosa, interview by the author.

66. Jerome Woody, interview by the author.

67. John Raymond Turner, interview by the author.

68. On African Americans perceiving Latinos as political competitors in the rural South, see Marrow, *New Destination Dreaming*.

69. Heppel, "Harvesting the Crops of Others."

70. Migrant Housing Surveys analysis. See note 32.

71. Migrant Ministry Project, November 1982 report, "Migrant Ministry" files, ACDS.

72. Jim Auchmutey, "FBI Asked to Probe Threats in Cedartown," *Atlanta Journal-Constitution*, June 19, 1983.

73. "Opinion" of Minister Luisa Virginia Junco, Consul of Mexico in Atlanta, August 15, 1986, Folder IV-343-2, 2a parte, AHSRE; Hernández-León and Zúñiga, "Appalachia Meets Aztlán."

74. Griffith, "Hay Trabajo."

75. Wade, *Fiery Cross*, 276–79; MacLean, *Behind the Mask of Chivalry*.

76. Jeff Nesmith and Clifford Krauss, "An Alien's Tragic Odyssey: Distrust, Death at Cedartown," *Atlanta Journal-Constitution*, November 29, 1981, clipping in "Georgia—Aliens and Immigrants" vertical file, UGA.

77. Ibid. For other examples, see "Opinion" of Minister Luisa Virginia Junco, Consul of Mexico in Atlanta, August 15, 1986, regarding the workplace death of Pablo Jacobo Moscones, which mentions his widow, "norteamericana" Sandra Lavonne Dawson of Cedartown, Folder IV-343-2, 2a parte, AHSRE.

78. Wells, "Cedartown Story."

79. Nesmith and Krauss, "An Alien's Tragic Odyssey"; Wells, "Cedartown Story."

80. "Mexican's Death Tied to Ethnic Prejudice," *Atlanta Journal-Constitution*, April 16, 1983.

81. Wells, "Cedartown Story," 75.

82. Statement of Dwayne Welton Pruitt, 9:20 a.m., interview conducted by Special Agent J. R. Longino, *The State vs. Dwayne Welton Pruitt*, May 1983, Criminal case CR 165–83, Polk County Superior Court, Georgia.

83. Jim Auchmutey, "Mexican's Shooting Explained in Taped Statement," *Atlanta Journal-Constitution*, October 5, 1983.

84. Auchmutey, "FBI Asked to Probe Threats in Cedartown."

85. Auchmutey, "Mexican's Shooting Explained in Taped Statement."

86. Auchmutey, "FBI Asked to Probe Threats in Cedartown."

87. John Harmon, "As More Hispanics Find Jobs in Poultry Industry, Tensions Rise in Gainesville," *Atlanta Journal-Constitution*, June 8, 1987, clipping in Folder IV-432-3, 6a parte, AHSRE.

88. Zúñiga and Hernández-León, "A New Destination for an Old Migration."

89. "1981 Survey of Migrant Housing in Georgia: Location Information," Folder "Migrant and Seasonal Farmworkers Association," Box 132, DCFS.

90. "1982 Survey of Migrant Housing in Georgia: Location Information," Folder "Migrant and Seasonal Farmworkers Association 1983," Box 146, DCFS.

91. "Summary Observations and Comments on 1981 Migrant Housing Survey," Folder "Migrant and Seasonal Farmworkers Association," Box 132, DCFS.

92. "Final Report, Governor's Internship for WIC, Migrant Outreach," by Dawn Blum, August 19, 1980, Box 37, Series 1-9-95, "Governor—Special Affairs Office" collection, GA.

93. Sister Patricia Brown, "Report on Migrant Housing Site in Metter, Georgia," December 9, 1982, "Hispanic Ministry" file, ACDS.

94. See note 32.

95. "Migrant Workers Paddle against a Tide That Hasn't Turned since Steinbeck's Era," *Macon (Ga.) Telegraph-News*, September 6, 1987, clipping in "Migrants" vertical file, UGA.

96. "They Tramp Dusty Fields, Dingy Camps to Make Migrant Workers' Lives Better," *Macon (Ga.) Telegraph and News*, September 7, 1987.

97. Sister Patricia Brown, "Report on Migrant Housing Site in Metter, Georgia."

98. Robert Marín and Teodora Marín, interview by the author; Anderson, "New Law Changes Life for Migrants"; Beck, "'We Were the First Ones.'"

99. Beck, "'We Were the First Ones,'" 1–3.

100. U.S. Bureau of Labor Statistics, "Fatal Occupational Injuries to Workers in the Agriculture, Forestry, and Fishing Industries, All Ownerships, Georgia, 1992–2002," and "Fatal Work Injuries in the Farming, Forestry and Fishing Industries involving Hispanic Workers, Georgia, 2003–2013," both requested via e-mail and in author's possession.

101. Sabia, "Challenges of Solidarity," 99–102.

102. Numbers of fatal injuries are from U.S. Bureau of Labor Statistics, "Fatal Occupational Injuries to Workers in the Agriculture, Forestry, and Fishing Industries, All Ownerships, Georgia, 1992–2002" and "Fatal Work Injuries in the Farming, Forestry and Fishing Industries involving Hispanic Workers, Georgia, 2003–2013." Estimates of the total Latino farmworker population in those states were difficult to locate, as neither the U.S. Census Bureau nor the Bureau of Labor Statistics releases statistics for farmworkers on the state level. So I have used statistics from Migrant Health Program, *An Atlas of State Profiles Which Estimate Number of Migrant and Seasonal Farmworkers and Members of Their Families*.

103. Asbed, "'Coalition of Immokalee Workers'"; Estabrook, *Tomatoland*, 87.

104. Gloria Shaw Jackson, interview by the author.

105. "Final Report, Governor's Internship for WIC, Migrant Outreach," by Dawn Blum, August 19, 1980, Box 37, Series 1-9-95, "Governor—Special Affairs Office" collection, GA.

106. Sister Patricia Brown, Report, October 1982, "Migrant Ministry" files, ACDS.

107. Daniel, *Breaking the Land*, 66–87.

108. Heppel, "Harvesting the Crops of Others."

109. Cortez interview.

110. Moreno interview.

111. Ramón Moreno Llamas, Third Level Consul, to Minister Luisa Virginia Junco, Consul of Mexico in Atlanta, July 25, 1986, Folder IV-343-2, 2a parte, AHSRE.

112. Anderson, "New Law Changes Life for Migrants."

113. Ramón Moreno Llamas, Third level Consul, to Minister Luisa Virginia Junco, Consul of Mexico in Atlanta, July 25, 1986, Folder IV-343-2, 2a parte, AHSRE.

114. See, for example, Joe D. King and Randy King to Congressman Richardson Pryor, August 11, 1977, Governor Hunt papers, Box 31, Folder "Migrant Workers," SANC.

115. Marc S. Rodriguez, *Tejano Diaspora*, 96–97; Sifuentez, "By Forests or by Fields," 104–234; Lucas and Buss, *Forged under the Sun*.

116. Sellers, "'Del pueblo, para el pueblo,'" 59–60; Randy Shaw, *Beyond the Fields*, 147; Alfonso Pulido Sisniega, Consul General of Mexico in Miami, to SRE, January 20, 1977, Folder PAC-F-87-17, Mexicanos en Miami, AHSRE

117. Mary Otto, "Born-Again Union Leader Helps Migrant Laborers Get Their Due," *Houston Chronicle*, September 4, 1998.

118. Fink, *Maya of Morganton*; Sellers, "'Del pueblo, para el pueblo,'" 61–66; Melody Gonzalez, "Awakening the Consciousness of the Labor Movement"; Giagnoni, *Fields of Resistance*; Coalition of Immokalee Workers, "Consciousness + Commitment = Change."

119. For the long history of Mexican and Mexican American labor organizing, including in agricultural industries, see Vargas, *Labor Rights Are Civil Rights*.

120. See Chapters 2 and 3 of this book.

121. Heppel, "Harvesting the Crops of Others," 217.

122. Michael W. Foley, "Agenda for Mobilization."

123. Coin, "Pickles and Pickets after NAFTA."

124. See Chapter 3.

125. Deborah Cohen, *Braceros*.

126. Michael W. Foley, "Agenda for Mobilization."

127. Zolov, *Refried Elvis*; Aguayo, *1968: Los Archivos de la Violencia*.

128. Michael W. Foley, "Privatizing the Countryside."

129. O'Toole, "A New Nationalism for a New Era."

130. Robert Marín and Teodora Marín, interview by the author.

131. Héctor Mena, former consul of Mexico in Atlanta, telephone interview by the author, January 29, 2008.

132. Visits to Work Sites, 1986, Folder IV-43203, 1a parte, AHSRE; "Opinion" of Consul Luisa Virginia Junco, September 8, 1987, Folder IV-432-3, 8a parte, AHSRE; "Opinion" of Minister Luisa Virginia Junco, Consul of Mexico in Atlanta, August 25, 1986, Folder IV-343-2, 2a parte, AHSRE.

133. "Opinion" of Minister Luisa Virginia Junco, Consul of Mexico in Atlanta, July 31, 1986, Folder IV-343-2, 2a parte, AHSRE; O'Toole, "A New Nationalism for a New Era."

134. O'Toole, "A New Nationalism for a New Era."

135. Teodoro Alonso to Luisa Virginia Junco, February 21, 1985, Folder IV-343-1, 1a parte, AHSRE.

136. "Opinion"—attachment to letter 874, June 1, 1987, Folder IV-432-3, 6a parte, AHSRE.

137. Cornelius, "Los Migrantes de la Crisis," 161–2; Cadava, *Standing on Common Ground*.

138. I am grateful to Aimee Villareal Garza for this insight.

139. José and Anselma Gómez, interview by the author.

140. Heppel, "Harvesting the Crops of Others," 182–83.

141. While scholars believe that the details of daily life and routines can be accurately recalled decades later, emotional memory is notoriously fickle. Abrams, *Oral History Theory*, 87. For more on nostalgia even for times and places of great suffering, see Marianne Hirsch and Spitzer, *Ghosts of Home*.

142. Otero, "Refusing to Be 'Undocumented'"; Rosas, *Abrazando el Espíritu*, loc. 1130.

143. Augustus Wolfman, "Wolfman Report on the Photographic & Imaging Industry in the United States," *Modern Photography Magazine*, 1979–80 through 1991–92 editions. On photography in twentieth-century Mexico, see Mraz, "Technologies of Seeing."

144. Marianne Hirsch, *Family Frames*; Richard Chalfen, *Turning Leaves*, 12.

145. Richard Chalfen, *Turning Leaves*, 7–9. Indeed, while ideologies of family have varied across time and space, family albums where present have served as a tool to prop up those ideologies in the lives of family members. Some scholars construct this idea narrowly, claiming that family photographs specifically advance the ideology of white middle-class families. See, for example, Spence and Holland, *Family Snaps*; Rose, *Doing Family Photography*; Langford, "Speaking the Album"; Holland, "Introduction," 7. More useful are those who apply the framework to the experiences of immigrants, minorities, and other subcultures, including Marianne Hirsch, *Family Frames*; Marianne Hirsch, *Familial Gaze*; Kunimoto, "Intimate Archives"; Spitzer, "Album and the Crossing"; Campt, *Image Matters*; Otero, "Refusing to Be 'Undocumented'"; Rosas, *Abrazando el Espíritu*.

146. Stanley, "'Well, Who'd Want an Old Picture of Me at Work?'"; Richard Chalfen, *Turning Leaves*, 92.

147. Rosas, *Abrazando el Espíritu*, loc. 2769.

148. Richard Chalfen found a similar pattern among Japanese Americans, some of whom carefully preserved photos of farm labor in their albums. Richard Chalfen, *Turning Leaves*, 86–92. For more on how male-led agricultural labor migration created a labor–leisure divide where none had previously existed in the Mexican countryside, see Deborah Cohen, *Braceros*.

149. Robert Marín and Teodora Marín, interview by the author.

150. For the theorist Roland Barthes, the best photography reaches beyond its cultural context to prick the heart of the viewer. Barthes, *Camera Lucida*.

151. José and Anselma Gómez, interview by the author.

152. Ibid.

153. While lower-income Americans did own cameras at rates comparable to those in other income levels, they were far less likely than higher-income earners to own a Polaroid. Wolfman, "Wolfman Report on the Photographic & Imaging Industry in the United States," 1987–88, 45.

154. José and Anselma Gómez, interview by the author.

155. Richard Chalfen, *Turning Leaves*, 71.

156. José and Anselma Gómez, interview by the author.

157. Perales, *Smeltertown*; Bodnar, "Power and Memory in Oral History."

158. Perales, *Smeltertown*.

159. Lucas and Buss, *Forged under the Sun*; Marc S. Rodriguez, *Tejano Diaspora*; Sifuentez, "By Forests or by Fields"; Asbed, "Coalition of Immokalee Workers."

160. For another example of contemporary discourses shaping workers' narratives as they formed, see Bodnar, "Power and Memory in Oral History."

161. Tuck, *Beyond Atlanta*, 21–22, 35, 78–79.

162. For more on the difficult struggle for civil rights in southern Georgia, particularly the challenge of desegregating Albany, Georgia, see Carson, "SNCC and the Albany Movement"; Michael M. Chalfen, "Rev. Samuel B. Wells and Black Protest in Albany, 1945–1965"; Tuck, *Beyond Atlanta*, 34.

163. Montejano, *Chicano Politics and Society in the Late 20th Century*, 282–86; Ernesto Chávez, *"Mi Raza Primero!"*; Marc S. Rodriguez, *Tejano Diaspora*. Rodriguez argues that even the Mexican American activism of Texas has substantial roots in the progressive traditions of Wisconsin, a place where many activists had once lived.

164. Randy Shaw, *Beyond the Fields*, 147.

165. This was unlike in the Mississippi Delta. Dittmer, *Local People*; Payne, *I've Got the Light of Freedom*. For the Albany movement in southern Georgia, see Carson, "SNCC and the Albany Movement"; Michael M. Chalfen, "Rev. Samuel B. Wells and Black Protest in Albany, 1945–1965."

166. For the demographics of Georgia farm labor, see "Migrant and Seasonal Farmworkers in Georgia," in Frank Brewer's report, Box 16, Series 1-9-95, "Governor—Special Affairs Office" collection, GA.

167. For the relationship between black attitudes toward farm labor and organizing, see Heppel, "Harvesting the Crops of Others," 222.

168. José and Anselma Gómez, interview by the author.

169. Heppel found a similar phenomenon among black and Mexican workers on the Virginia shore. There, blacks and Mexicans created their identities in part through contrast with the other. Heppel, "Harvesting the Crops of Others," 221.

170. Reagan, "Radio Address to the Nation on Welfare Reform."

171. Migrant Workers Service Providers, Georgia, "Hispanic Ministry" file, ACDS.

172. Beck, "'We Were the First Ones,'" 5.

173. Lynn Brazen, "The Kiddie Kastle Opens," Migrant and Seasonal Farmworkers Association newsletter, April 16, 1982, Folder "Migrant and Seasonal Farmworkers Association," Box 132, DCFS; "WIC Migrant Outreach and Internship Activities, Presented by Dawn Blum and Patricia Mendoza, Georgia Governor's Interns for Department of Human Resources," October 1980; Patricia Mendoza's intern report, Box 38, Series 1-9-95, "Governor—Special Affairs Office" collection, GA.

174. Ramón Moreno Llamas, Third Level Consul, to Minister Luisa Virginia Junco, Consul of Mexico in Atlanta, July 14, 1986, in Folder IV-343-2, 2a parte, AHSRE.

175. Jane Ruffin, "Agencies Spar over Migrant Aid," *Raleigh News and Observer*, August 24, 1987.

176. Marc S. Rodriguez, *Tejano Diaspora*, 98–118.

177. Germany, "Poverty Wars in the Louisiana Delta."

178. Gloria Shaw Jackson interview. Helen Marrow observes that teachers and social service workers in rural North Carolina were highly receptive to their new Hispanic clients but does not comment on the implications for black–Mexican relations. Marrow, *New Destination Dreaming*. This point bears further exploration as many social service workers in the black-belt South are African American veterans of the region's civil rights struggles. This case and Marrow's contrast with scholarly observations of white and black social service workers limiting Latinas' access to health and social services in North Carolina's Research Triangle metropolitan area. Deeb-Sossa and Mendez, "Enforcing Borders in the Nuevo South."

179. Jerome Woody, interview by the author, Claxton, Ga., April 2, 2008. Helen Marrow has shown that in rural North Carolina counties where blacks do not comprise a majority (as they don't in most of southeastern Georgia), black activists have seen Hispanics as potentially advantageous political allies over the long term. Marrow, *New Destination Dreaming*, 136. Furthermore, Angela Stuesse documents that even in Mississippi, with its many majority-black counties, African American civil rights leaders have adopted the immigrants' rights cause as their own. Stuesse, "Race, Migration, and Labor Control."

180. See, for example, Montejano, *Chicano Politics and Society in the Late 20th Century*; Marc S. Rodriguez, *Tejano Diaspora*.

181. Andrea Hinojosa, interview by the author.

182. Ibid.

183. Crespino, *In Search of Another Country*.

184. Moreton, *To Serve God and Wal-Mart*. Southern Georgia's agricultural counties in 2000 ranged from one-third to two-thirds practicing Evangelical Protestant. "Maps and Reports Religious Groups Evangelical Denominations—Rates of Adherence per 1000 Population (2000)," Association of Religious Data Archives, http://www.thearda.com/mapsReports/maps/map.asp?alpha=0&variable=6&state=10&variable2=1&GRP=1&Var2=15.

185. In 1987, 89 percent of farms in Georgia were individual- or family-owned. U.S. Census Bureau, *1987 Census of Agriculture*.

186. Ibid.

187. Mary Ann and Howdy Thurman, interview by the author.

188. AP, "Farmers Resent Federal Field Sanitation Effort," *Valdosta (Ga.) Daily Times*, March 21, 1987; AP, "Georgia Farmers Resent the New Immigration Law," *Valdosta (Ga.) Daily Times*, June 8, 1987.

189. AP, "Farmers Fight Migrant Protection Bills," *Valdosta (Ga.) Daily Times*, May 10, 1993; AP, "Vidalia Onion Growers Hot about Labor Regulations," *Valdosta (Ga.) Daily Times*, June 3, 1994.

190. For more on similar discourses during the bracero program, see Deborah Cohen, *Braceros*, 51.

191. Mary Ann Thurman believed that growers have successfully influenced police in

Fort Valley to be more sympathetic to immigrants. Mary Ann and Howdy Thurman, interview by the author. Andrea Hinojosa reported that by the mid-2000s, however, police harassment of undocumented immigrants was the norm in Vidalia. Sabia, "Anti-Immigrant Fervor in Georgia."

192. Moreton, *To Serve God and Wal-Mart*, 237–40.

193. Sally Scherer, "Harvest of Help: Tragedy Allows Community to Discover How Much Migrant Workers Mean to Them," *Macon (Ga.) Telegraph-News*, April 21, 1994.

194. "Level of Development Assessment, Sacred Heart Church, Vidalia, Georgia, May 29–40, 1985," Glenmary Research Center, Washington, D.C., ACDS.

195. Lichterman, *Elusive Togetherness*, 135; Emerson and Smith, *Divided by Faith*, 52–63.

196. Keane, *Christian Moderns*, 49–52; Emerson and Smith, *Divided by Faith*, 75–79; Crespino, *In Search of Another Country*, 269–70; Elisha, *Moral Ambition*, 199.

197. Bartkowski and Regis, *Charitable Choices*, 103–18.

198. Elisha, *Moral Ambition*, 198.

199. For discussion of "moral ambition" in white churches, see ibid. Studying conservative Christian charity in the Midwest, Paul Lichterman found that for white church volunteers, African American and Guatemalan charity clients were "interchangeable 'others' on the group's social map." Lichterman, *Elusive Togetherness*, 158.

200. AP, "Retired Foreign Missionary Helps Rural Georgia Workers," *Valdosta (Ga.) Daily Times*, November 27, 1988.

201. Handwritten draft of personal history of Mary Ann Thurman, Thurman personal papers.

202. Ruth and Sonny Bridges, interview by the author.

203. Though Protestant evangelization efforts in Mexico were well under way in the 1970s and 1980s, they were most successful by far in Mexico's southeastern and northeastern states, while most Mexican migrants to southern Georgia in this time were from the central and north-central part of the country. For example, Israel Cortez's home state of Mexico was 97 percent Catholic in 1970, 95 percent in 1980, and 91 percent in 2000. Teodora Marín's home state of Guerrero was 97 percent Catholic in 1970, 93 percent in 1980, and 89 percent in 2000. In contrast, the southeastern Mexican state of Tabasco was 87 percent Catholic in 1970, 79 percent in 1980, and 70 percent in 2000. Instituto Nacional de Estadística, Geografía e Informática, *La diversidad religiosa en México*; Instituto Nacional de Estadística, Geografía e Informática, "Censo General de Población y Vivienda."

204. Sally Scherer, "'They're Walking Saints': Fort Valley Couple Gives Spiritual, Material Comfort to Migrant Farm Workers in Peach County," *Macon (Ga.) Telegraph-News*, August 28, 1994.

205. Ibid.

206. Jerry K. Baker, "Ethnics in Georgia Baptist Life, 1985–1995," GBC; John D. Pierce, "Growing Hispanic Ministry Result of Vision, Commitment," *Christian Index*, July 27, 1995; Waits, "'They've Come for the True Gospel.'"

207. Carolyn Flowers, interview by the author.

208. Sister Patricia Brown, Report, October 1982, "Migrant Ministry" files, ACDS.

209. Cynthia Anderson, "Church Fights to Make Area Bilingual," *Tifton (Ga.) Gazette*, date unknown (circa 1989), clipping in "Migrants/Hispanics—Press" folder, ACDS.

210. Ruth and Sonny Bridges, interview by the author. For another example, see Pierce, "Growing Hispanic Ministry Result of Vision."

211. Sister Patricia Brown, Report, October 1982, "Migrant Ministry" files , ACDS.

212. Ruth and Sonny Bridges, interview by the author.

213. Mary Ann Thurman to Duke Lane, President, Lane Packing Co., October 10, 1988, Thurman personal papers.

214. "Migrant Ministry" newsletter, April 23, 1991, Thurman personal papers.

215. Jarrett K. Reagan, "Westfield Students Host Easter Egg Hunt," *Leader-Tribune (Peach County)*, April 12, 1990, clipping in Thurman personal papers.

216. Crespino, *In Search of Another Country*, 240. Dozens of photographs on the school's website even in 2008 showed only white students. See www.westfieldschool.org.

217. See, for example, Ayers, *Southern Crossing*; Grossman, *Land of Hope*.

218. See, for example, Gilmore, *Gender and Jim Crow*, 266; Hewitt, *Southern Discomfort*, 27.

219. AP, "Vidalia Onion Growers Hot about Labor Regulations." For more on farmers' turn away from paternalistic labor relationships, see Hahamovitch, *No Man's Land*, 91.

220. Emerson and Smith, *Divided by Faith*, 117–18.

221. For further discussion of the pitfalls of liberalism in the arena of race and rights, see HoSang, *Racial Propositions*.

222. Hahamovitch, "Creating Perfect Immigrants."

223. Janis Roberson, interview by the author.

224. For more on the role of deportability in exacerbating the power gulf between guest workers and employers, see Hahamovitch, "Creating Perfect Immigrants"; Hahamovitch, *No Man's Land*.

225. Janis Roberson, interview by the author.

226. Anderson, "Church Fights to Make Area Bilingual."

227. AP, "Georgia Farmers Resent the New Immigration Law," *Valdosta (Ga.) Daily Times*, June 8, 1987.

228. Marianne Hirsch, *Family Frames*, 43–48.

229. Richard Chalfen notes that photos typically provide "visual maps of kinship networks." Chalfen, *Snapshot Versions of Life*, 95.

230. Janis Roberson, interview by the author. For a nineteenth-century example of an employer using individual portraits to promote a paternalistic view of their relations with an immigrant workforce, see Anthony W. Lee, *A Shoemaker's Story*, 60–65.

231. Janis Roberson, interview by the author.

232. For more on coercive settings in photography, see Richard Chalfen, *Snapshot Versions of Life*, 74–75. Also see Anthony W. Lee, *A Shoemaker's Story*, 219.

233. Handwritten draft of personal history of Mary Ann Thurman, Thurman personal papers.

234. Elisha, *Moral Ambition*.

235. Ruth and Sonny Bridges, interview by the author.

236. For more on how "intensive benevolence" at churches can help the poor gain greater social capital, see Bartkowski and Regis, *Charitable Choices*, 70. On Latino immigrants gaining social capital through white churches in the South, see López-Sanders, "Bible Belt Immigrants."

237. For a similar case, see López-Sanders, "Bible Belt Immigrants."

238. José and Anselma Gómez, interview by the author.

239. Mary Ann and Howdy Thurman, interview by the author.

240. On the importance of community building in blacks' response to white supremacy, see Connolly, "Colored, Caribbean, and Condemned."

241. Mary Ann and Howdy Thurman, interview by the author.

242. Barton, "Borderland Discontents," 141.

243. For other examples of Latino community building in southern churches, see Marquardt, "From Shame to Confidence"; Odem, "Our Lady of Guadalupe in the New South"; Waits, "'They've Come for the True Gospel.'"

244. Margarita to Mary Anne Thurman, December 21, 1988, Thurman personal papers.

245. Postcard from Jesús and María to "Mr. Howdy y Mary Anne," August 23, year obscured, Thurman personal papers.

246. Eujenio Moreno to "Mariana," February 27, 1990, postmarked McAlpin, Fl., Thurman personal papers.

247. Bernice Gallegos, Nixon, Tex., to Mary Ann Thurman, July 15, 1990, Thurman personal papers.

248. José and Anselma Gómez, interview by the author.

249. Andrea and Bernardo Avalos, interview by the author.

250. Cortez interview.

251. Javier González, interview by the author.

252. Petra Soto interview, interview by the author.

253. Cortez interview.

254. The Coalition of Immokalee Workers, for example, was founded in a meeting room at a supportive Catholic church. Coalition of Immokalee Workers, "Consciousness + Commitment = Change."

255. Marc S. Rodriguez, *Tejano Diaspora*, 160.

256. Though mostly associated with the Republican Party, the anti-immigrant movement in California also enjoyed wide support from Democrats. HoSang, *Racial Propositions*, 173–74.

257. Dean Poling, "Roundup Targets Illegal Workers," *Valdosta (Ga.) Daily Times*, April 6, 1995.

258. Southern Poverty Law Center, "Close to Slavery." On the origins of H2 visas, see Hahamovitch, *No Man's Land*, loc. 2725.

259. Diana (Avalos) Mendieta, interview by the author.

260. Thomas P. Fischer, telephone interview by the author, March 18, 2012; Thomas P. Fischer, District Director, INS, Atlanta District Office, to the Honorable Zell Miller, February 24, 1997, Governor—Intergovernmental Relations—Subject Files—1993-7—Gov. Zell Miller 001-24-133, Box 20 (RCB 35852), GA; Joyner, "H2A Agricultural Guestworker Program."

261. Ben Butler, "Chambliss Wants Migrant Restrictions Eased," *Valdosta (Ga.) Daily Times*, October 12, 1997.

262. John Lewis to the Hon. Zell Miller, May 12, 1997, Governor—Intergovernmental Relations—Subject Files—1993-7—Gov. Zell Miller 001-24-133, Box 20 (RCB 35852), GA; Butler, "Chambliss Wants Migrant Restrictions Eased."

263. John R. Beverly III and John R. Fraser to Hon. Sanford D. Bishop Jr., January 8, 1998, and Bishop to the Hon. Zell Miller, January 12, 1998, Governors' papers, GA.

264. Joyner, "H2A Agricultural Guestworker Program."

265. Teodoro Maus, telephone interview by the author.

266. Observations of South Georgia Areas, April 4, 1998, ICE-FOIA #12-14822.

267. Teodoro Maus, telephone interview by the author; Joyner, "H2A Agricultural Guestworker Program."

268. "Southeast: Vidalia Onions," *Rural Migration News* 4 (July 1998); Joyner, "H2A Agricultural Guestworker Program"; Steven Greenhouse, "Going after Migrants, but Not Employers," *New York Times*, April 16, 2006.

269. Agreement between Vidalia Onion Growers Association and the Immigration and Naturalization Service, ICE-FOIA #12-14822; "Southeast: Vidalia Onions"; Joyner, "H2A Agricultural Guestworker Program."

270. Peter James Stelling, Smyrna, Ga., to Gov. Zell Miller, April 3, 1995, Governor—Intergovernmental Relations—Subject Files—1993-7—Gov. Zell Miller 001-24-133, Box 20 (RCB 35852), GA.

271. "Mark in East Cobb" to Smyrna Mayor Max Bacon, June 1, 1995, Governor—Intergovernmental Relations—Subject Files—1993-7—Gov. Zell Miller 001-24-133, Box 20 (RCB 35852), GA.

272. Robin Dale Jacobson, *New Nativism*; HoSang, *Racial Propositions*, 161–98.

273. Andrea Hinojosa recalled once seeing Klan members in hoods distributing anti-immigrant pamphlets in Vidalia during the late 1980s or early 1990s. This was the extent of anti-immigrant Klan activity that she or other southern Georgia interviewees could recall. Andrea Hinojosa, interview by the author.

274. AP, "South Georgia Hispanic Festival Finds New Home, Plans Census 2000 Drive," *Athens Banner-Herald*, October 1, 1999, clipping in Luz Marti personal papers.

275. Luz Marti, interview by the author.

276. See, for example, *Ojeda-Sanchez et al. v. Bland Farms*, Case No. CV608-096, Decision, 2009 U.S. Dist. LEXIS 66238, U.S. District Court, S.D. Georgia, Statesboro Division, July 31, 2009, accessed via Lexis-Nexis.

277. *Jaime Guijosa-Silva et al. v. Wendell Roberson Farms, Inc.*, Complaint, 2010 WL 1788998 (M.D. Ga.), United States District Court, M.D. Georgia, Valdosta Division,

March 12, 2010, accessed via Westlaw; *Jaime Guijosa-Silva et al. v. Wendell Roberson Farms, Inc.*, Decision, 2010 U.S. Dist. LEXIS 33358, U.S. District Court, M.D. Georgia, Valdosta Division, March 13, 2012, accessed via Lexis-Nexis.

278. Janis Roberson, interview by the author.

279. Andrea Hinojosa, interview by the author.

280. Dan Chapman, "Equal but Separate in Lyons," *Atlanta Journal-Constitution*, April 11, 2004, clipping in Andrea Hinojosa personal papers.

281. Andrea Hinojosa, interview by the author; "Ga. High School Holds Segregated Proms," May 17, 2004, http://www.foxnews.com/story/2004/05/17/ga-high-school-holds-segregated-proms/.

282. On the need to examine politics at scales below the nation and state, see Lassiter, "Political History beyond the Red-Blue Divide."

283. For examples of the former analysis, see Shailagh Murray, "Conservatives Split in Debate on Curbing Illegal Immigration," *Washington Post*, March 25, 2005; Richard W. Stevenson, "Bush Renews Push to Overhaul Immigration," *New York Times*, November 29, 2005.

284. Blathnaid Healy, "Graham, Other Senators Hope to Break Impasse," *Spartanburg Herald Journal*, April 17, 2006.

285. Tom Crawford, "Rogers Introduces Latest Bill on Immigration," *CapitolImpact.net*, February 9, 2006.

286. JD Sumner, "Thousands March in Support of Equality for Immigrants," *Tifton (Ga.) Gazette*, April 11, 2006, clipping in Luz Marti personal papers.

287. Lori Glenn, "Immigrant Protest Patchy in Colquitt County," *Moultrie Observer*, May 1, 2006. On this generational divide elsewhere, see Abrego, "Legal Consciousness of Undocumented Latinos."

288. Glenn, "Immigrant Protest Patchy in Colquitt County."

289. Nor did it in majority-white Yell County in Arkansas, another small haven of pro-immigrant conservatism. Hallett, "'Better than White Trash.'"

290. Bill Torpy, "Crimes Highlight a Culture," *Atlanta Journal-Constitution*, October 15, 2005, clipping in Marti personal papers. On the barber, see Jana Cone, "Hollis Flanders: Tifton's 'Political Barometer'" *Tifton (Ga.) Gazette*, April 25, 2007.

291. Mary Lou Pickel, "Raid of Illegals Hits Home in Georgia Town," *Atlanta Journal-Constitution*, September 25, 2006. Shoe saleswoman Vanecia Glover, quoted in the article, identifies herself as black on her MySpace page, http://www.myspace.com/189165515.

292. Ruth and Sonny Bridges, interview by the author.

293. Carolyn Flowers, interview by the author.

294. "Solving the Farm Crisis," *Valdosta (Ga.) Daily Times*, June 16, 2011.

295. American Civil Liberties Union, "Republican Mayor Opposes Georgia's Anti-immigrant Law."

296. Paul Bridges, "Why I'm Suing Georgia over Immigration Law," CNNOpinion, June 20, 2012, http://www.cnn.com/2011/OPINION/06/19/bridges.georgia.immigration/index.html.

297. Catherine E. Shoichet, "Republican Mayor in the South Becomes Unlikely Advocate for Immigrants," CNN, June 28, 2012, http://www.cnn.com/2011/US/06/28/immigration.georgia.mayor/index.html?_s=PM:US; Trymaine Lee, "Republican Mayor Paul Bridges, an Unlikely Ally in the Fight against Anti-Immigration Laws," *Huffington Post*, March 1, 2012, http://www.huffingtonpost.com/2012/03/01/republican-mayor-paul-bri_n_1313862.html.

298. Kathy Bradford, "Uvalda, GA Mayor Paul Bridges Convenes an Immigration Reform Roundtable," *Vidalia (Ga.) Advance*, June 1, 2011.

299. AP, "Georgia Legislators Likely to Focus Less on Immigration," *Chattanooga Times Free Press*, December 12, 2011.

300. "NationsBank donó $1 million al Consejo Nacional de La Raza," *La Noticia*, March 13, 1998; Mark Bixler and Sheila M. Poole, "Updates: Latino Rights Group Opens Office Here," *Atlanta Journal-Constitution*, January 8, 2003.

Chapter 5

1. Lassiter, *Silent Majority*; Gaillard, *Dream Long Deferred*.

2. Laura Mendoza and Eréndira Molina, interview by the author. Berryhill was located in a census tract that had attracted Latino immigrants since the early 1990s. Smith and Furuseth, "Housing, Hispanics."

3. Since 1955, scholars have used a combination of factors to define "exurbia" as opposed to suburbia or urban areas. Depending on the scholar, these factors have included distance from urban areas, rate of population growth since 1970 (sometimes as compared with prior population growth), commuting patterns, population density, and education levels of residents. Berube, Singer, Wilson, and Frey, "Finding Exurbia." Because he is interested primarily in the relationship between exurbia and politics, Ruy Texeira provides the most useful working definition of exurbia: a combination of "emerging suburbs" (places that are already suburbanizing) and "true exurbs" (rural areas that include increasing numbers of commuters but where large-scale suburban development has not yet taken root). Texeira, "Next Frontier." Texeira relies on Lang and Sanchez's typology of metropolitan counties: cores, inner suburbs, mature suburbs, emerging suburbs, and exurbs, noting that while "true exurbs" are overwhelmingly white and conservative, "emerging suburbs" are increasingly diverse. In the case of Charlotte's Metropolitan Statistical Area, it is indeed these "emerging suburbs" that host substantial Latino populations. Given its focus on Latino populations and city- and county-level politics, the present book uses the word "suburbs" to refer to suburban areas within the city of Charlotte. It uses the word "exurbs" to refer to more recently developed cities in outer Mecklenburg County (such as Mint Hill) and to surrounding Lincoln, Gaston, Union, Cabarrus, and York (South Carolina) counties. The last three are categorized as "emerging suburbs" by Lang and Sanchez and thus would be considered exurbs under Texeira's definition, while Gaston is considered a "mature suburb" and Lincoln is not categorized. Lang and Sanchez, "New Metro Politics: Interpreting Recent Presidential Elections Using a County-Based Regional

Typology," http://www.mi.vt.edu/uploads/NationalElectionReport.pdf. Thus, my use of the term "exurb" is intended to be not precise from the perspective of demography but rather, following Texeira, useful from the perspective of political history.

4. For example, 39 percent of domestic newcomers to Union County between 1995 and 2000 came from urban/suburban Mecklenburg, and an additional 46 percent arrived from out of state, while smaller numbers arrived from more rural counties nearby, such as Anson and Stanly. LINC (Log Into North Carolina), "Migration Report for Union County."

5. For more on suburban diversity, see Singer, Hardwick, and Brettell, *Twenty-First Century Gateways*.

6. Mercedes R., interview by the author. For more on Latino parents' alienation even in public schools that conscientiously serve their children, see Winders, *Nashville in the New Millennium*, 124–25.

7. Lippard and Gallagher, "Introduction," 17–20; Luna and Ansley, "Global Migrants and Access to Local Housing"; Mohl, "Globalization and Latin American Immigration in Alabama"; Odem, "Unsettled in the Suburbs."

8. A fast-developing literature on suburban immigrant settlement has largely ignored the exurban frontier of "emerging suburbs" and "true exurbs." Caroline Brettell's study of Plano, Texas, is a notable exception within the seminal collection. See Singer, Hardwick, and Brettell, *Twenty-First Century Gateways*.

9. For evidence of "Spanish-speaking" migrants in North Carolina since the 1960s, see note 10 of Chapter 4.

10. For more on the relationship between the global financial industry and low-wage, nonwhite labor forces, see Sassen, *Global City*. On immigration to Sunbelt service economies, see Cadava, *Standing on Common Ground*.

11. Associated Press, "Illegal Aliens Abandoning Crop Fields in Carolinas for Construction Sites," *Charlotte Observer*, August 24, 1986.

12. Scholars commonly assume that IRCA legal status allowed immigrants to settle in new destinations since now they would not fear deportation. Though often asserted, this maxim has yet to be proven in the case of the South, a region that had comparatively little immigration enforcement in the late twentieth century. See, for example, Cravey, "Transnationality, Social Spaces, and Parallel Worlds," 6; Zúñiga and Hernández-León, "A New Destination for an Old Migration"; Massey and Durand, *Crossing the Border*. The argument about the IRCA's effects on the labor market is more convincing in the context of the South. Cornelius, "Los Migrantes de la Crisis."

13. Census 2000 Summary, File 4, "Sex by Place of Birth by Year of Entry for the Foreign-Born Population [89]," accessed via Census.gov; "Table A4.11: Leading Non-Farm Private-Sector Industries for Hispanic Employment in Mecklenburg County, 2000," in Kochar, Suro, and Tafoya, "New Latino South." Because it is based on census data, this estimate of 27.6 percent of Mecklenburg County's Hispanic workforce would not include crews brought in from other states such as Texas. Smith and Furuseth, "Housing, Hispanics."

14. "Table A4.11: Leading Non-Farm Private-Sector Industries for Hispanic Em-

ployment in Mecklenburg County, 2000," in Kochar, Suro, and Tafoya, "New Latino South," 70.

15. Alicia E., interview by the author. For other accounts of Latino immigrants reporting comparatively favorable economic possibilities in the U.S. South during the 1990s, see Passel and Zimmerman, "Are Immigrants Leaving California? Settlement Patterns of Immigrants in the Late 1990s"; Light, *Deflecting Immigration*; Weeks, Weeks, and Weeks, "Latino Immigration in the U.S. South," 53; Mohl, "Globalization, Latinization, and the Nuevo New South," 35, 43; Zúñiga and Hernández-León, "Dalton Story," 36–38.

16. Smith and Furuseth have called this the "Welcome amigos" phase. Smith and Furuseth, "Localized Immigration Policy."

17. Wayne Cooper, interview by the author.

18. Angeles Ortega-Moore, interview by the author.

19. "Staffmark equipada y experimentada en la contratación de personal Latino," *La Noticia*, January 30, 1998.

20. Clinton, "Convention Acceptance."

21. Brown, "New Racial Politics of Welfare."

22. Robin Dale Jacobson, *New Nativism*; HoSang, *Racial Propositions*.

23. Robin Dale Jacobson, *New Nativism*, 140.

24. Brown, "New Racial Politics of Welfare."

25. "Participantes y asistentes al Festival," *La Noticia*, October 24, 1997; "Don Reid busca la reelección y el apoyo de la población Latina," *La Noticia*, October 10, 1997.

26. Wayne Cooper, interview by the author; "Crónica del VII Festival Latinoamericano," *La Noticia*, October 24, 1997.

27. In 1996, Piedmont residents surveyed in the Carolina poll were twice as likely to tell telephone pollsters that the influx of Hispanics was "bad" (45 percent) as opposed to "good" (23 percent). Since Charlotte is the Piedmont's largest city, this must reflect at least somewhat the sentiments there. "Carolina Poll," Spring 1996.

28. "La Feria de la Salud cumplió expectativas," *La Noticia*, December 5, 1997; "International House: Inscríbase en las clases de ciudadanía," *La Noticia*, October 24, 1997; Manuel Rey-Salinas, "UNCC apoya a la población Latina en Charlotte," *La Noticia*, November 21, 1997; "Día de México celebra Charlotte Country Day School," *La Noticia*, April 9, 1999; Ted Mellnik, "Soaring Population Gets Advocate," *Charlotte Observer*, November 9, 1991.

29. Deeb-Sossa and Mendez, "Enforcing Borders in the Nuevo South"; Dreby and Schmalzbauer, "Relational Contexts of Migration."

30. On Latino settlement in racially mixed Charlotte neighborhoods that include significant African American populations, see Smith and Furuseth, "Housing, Hispanics," 223.

31. The 1996 Carolina poll found that 28 percent of blacks thought the Hispanic influx was "good," compared with 22 percent of whites, and that 38 percent thought it was "bad," as opposed to 44 percent of whites. "Carolina Poll," Spring 1996. For negative attitudes, see McClain, Carter, et al., "Racial Distancing in a Southern City";

Marrow, "Hispanic Immigration, Black Population Size, and Intergroup Relations in the Rural and Small-Town South."

32. "Crónica del VII Festival Latinoamericano," *La Noticia*, October 24, 1997; Watlington, "Enfocando su compañía hacia el éxito trabajando en las cosas grandes," *La Noticia*, April 30 1999; Danica Coto, "More Historically Black Colleges Recruiting Latinos," *Charlotte Observer*, February 18, 2007.

33. Mercedes R., interview by the author.

34. For example, see Alicia E., interview by the author; Rosa Elba Gutiérrez, interview by the author.

35. Dianne Whitacre, "Relief on the Way for DMV Lines," *Charlotte Observer*, August 26, 2001.

36. Hurder, "Almost Definitive History of Licensing Undocumented Aliens in North Carolina."

37. Ibid.

38. Park, *Entitled to Nothing*; Robin Dale Jacobson, *New Nativism*. For more on shifts in U.S. culture toward consumption-based ideas of race, rights, and citizenship, see Holt, *Problem of Race in the Twenty-First Century*, 73–75; Lizabeth Cohen, *A Consumers' Republic*.

39. Chang, *Disposable Domestics*; Hondagneu-Sotelo, *Doméstica*; Flores-González, Guevarra, and Toro-Morn, *Immigrant Women Workers in the Neoliberal Age*; Singer, Hardwick, and Brettell, *Twenty-First Century Gateways*.

40. Smith and Furuseth, "'Nuevo South'"; Singer, Hardwick, and Brettell, *Twenty-First Century Gateways*.

41. Hondagneu-Sotelo, *Gendered Transitions*.

42. The 2004 American Community Survey showed that like these interviewees, more than 90 percent of North Carolina's "Hispanics" were forty-four years old or younger. Kasarda and Johnson, "Economic Impact of the Hispanic Population on the State of North Carolina," http://www.kenan-flagler.unc.edu/assets/documents/2006 _KenanInstitute_HispanicStudy.pdf.

43. Interviewees from newer out-migration areas included Guerrero (four), Mexico City (two), and the State of Mexico (one). Those from more traditional emigration states included Michoacán (four), Durango (one), and Tamaulipas (one). While there are no reliable survey data on states of origin among Mexicans in North Carolina, data about identity cards (*matrículas consulares*) processed by the Mexican consulate can approximate this information. These data may underestimate the number of immigrants from traditional origin states who first lived in California or Texas and acquired their matricula consular prior to moving to North Carolina. "Consulmex Raleigh, Matrículas Consulares Expedidas por Estado de Procedencia, 2003," in author's possession; Kasarda and Johnson, "Economic Impact of the Hispanic Population on the State of North Carolina," 3.

44. Hernández-León, *Metropolitan Migrants*; Marcelli and Cornelius, "Changing Profile of Mexican Migrants to the United States," 121; Cornelius, "Los Migrantes de la Crisis," 162.

45. Dreby and Schmalzbauer, "Relational Contexts of Migration"; Mahler and Pessar, "Gendered Geographies of Power"; Hondagneu-Sotelo, *Gendered Transitions*.

46. Jennifer S. Hirsch, *A Courtship after Marriage*; Dreby and Schmalzbauer, "Relational Contexts of Migration."

47. These interviewees signed a release form based on the American Association of University Presses' model form, which I adapted to allow them to explicitly choose whether I would use their names and biographical data. As a practical matter, however, I did not anticipate that their names would be public beyond this book's readership, as e-books now necessitate. After consulting with sociologists, anthropologists, and journalist experts in this area (some advocated using full names and others advocated using only pseudonyms), I struck this compromise position, using real first names and last initials, to honor the women's decisions to make their names known while acting cautiously in a changed publishing climate and still-uncertain policy future for undocumented immigrants. The few immigrants whose full names are used are not undocumented and not part of the sample described in note 43.

48. Angelica C., interview by the author.

49. Ibid.

50. Deborah Cohen, *Braceros*, 174–75; Ben Hyneman, interview, ADT.

51. Bauer, *Goods, Power, History*; García Canclini, *Consumers and Citizens*.

52. Deborah Cohen, *Braceros*; Rosas, *Abrazando el Espíritu*.

53. De la Calle and Rubio, *Mexico*, 60; García Canclini, *Consumers and Citizens*; Walker, *Waking from the Dream*; Bauer, *Goods, Power, History*.

54. Castañeda, *Mexican Shock*; Oppenheimer, *Bordering on Chaos*.

55. González Chávez and Macías, "Vulnerabilidad alimentaria y política agroalimentaria en México."

56. De la Calle and Rubio, *Mexico*, 32.

57. María and Alejandra N., interview by the author.

58. Edith H., interview by the author.

59. De la Calle and Rubio, *Mexico*.

60. Hondagneu-Sotelo, *Gendered Transitions*.

61. Rosas, *Abrazando el Espíritu*.

62. Dreby, *Divided by Borders*.

63. Cornelius, "Los Migrantes de la Crisis," 170–71.

64. Mercedes R., interview by the author.

65. Greene, "Cablevision(nation) in Rural Yucatán"; Jennifer S. Hirsch, *A Courtship after Marriage*.

66. On women's attitudes toward family separation during the bracero program, see Rosas, *Abrazando el Espíritu*.

67. Massey, Durand, and Malone, *Beyond Smoke and Mirrors*.

68. Dreby, *Divided by Borders*; Jennifer S. Hirsch, *A Courtship after Marriage*; Hondagneu-Sotelo, *Gendered Transitions*.

69. María F., interview by the author.

70. Rosas, "Breaking the Silence."

71. De la Calle and Rubio, *Mexico*, 22.

72. U.S. Census Bureau, Population Division, "Census 2000 County-to-County Worker Flow Files"; U.S. Census Bureau, Population Division, "1990 County-to-County Worker Flow Files."

73. Kirsten Valle Pittman, "People Still Flocking to Charlotte—Area's Population Surges Even as Economy Has Taken a Slide over Last Decade," *Charlotte Observer*, March 3, 2011.

74. Property taxes in Gaston County were comparable to Mecklenburg's, but for all the other counties in question, they were lower.

75. Kent Bernhard Jr., "Fastest-Growing N.C. County? Ours," *Charlotte Observer*, May 5, 2002.

76. LINC, "Census 2000, Summary File 3, Indian Trail, N.C."

77. Ibid. On Cobb County, Georgia, see Lassiter, "Big Government and Family Values."

78. LINC, "Migration Report for Union County."

79. LINC, "Census 2000, Summary File 1, Indian Trail, N.C."; LINC, "Census 2000, Summary File 3, Indian Trail, N.C"; LINC, "Census 1990, Summary File 1, Indian Trail, N.C."

80. LINC, "Census 2000, Summary File 3, Indian Trail, N.C." For national educational attainment by race, see Bauman and Graf, *Educational Attainment*, 5.

81. LINC, "Census 2000, Summary File 3, Indian Trail, N.C.," 41.

82. Data from Summary Files 1 and 3, Census 2000, accessed via http://socialexplorer.com.

83. Data from Summary File 1, Census 1990, accessed via http://socialexplorer.com.

84. Data from Summary File 1, Census 2000, accessed via http://socialexplorer.com.

85. LINC, "Census 2000, Summary File 3, Indian Trail, N.C."

86. Joie Lapolla, "Growth Leads All Election Issues," *Charlotte Observer*, April 28, 1996.

87. Lizabeth Cohen, *A Consumers' Republic*, 397.

88. Smith and Furuseth, "Housing, Hispanics"; Smith and Furuseth, "'Nuevo South.'"

89. Singer, Hardwick, and Brettell, *Twenty-First Century Gateways*.

90. See, for example, ads in *La Noticia*, Charlotte, October 10, 1997, 42, and March 27, 1998, 44, 48.

91. Smith and Furuseth, "Housing, Hispanics," 218; Gill, *Latino Migration Experience in North Carolina*, 21–23.

92. Kochar, Suro, and Tafoya, "New Latino South," 47.

93. Gene Stowe, "Growing Hispanic Community Gives Union County a Spanish Accent," *Charlotte Observer*, September 8, 1991.

94. LINC, "Census 2000, Summary File 3, Indian Trail, N.C."; LINC, "Census 2000, Summary File 3, Mecklenburg County, N.C."; Kochar, Suro, and Tafoya, "New Latino South." Other census data are from Summary File 1, available on http://socialexplorer.com. This refers to the official seven-county Metropolitan Statistical Area.

95. In 2000, 32 percent of nonfarm Hispanic employment was in construction, 20 percent was in manufacturing (durable and nondurable combined), 12 percent was in service industries, and 10 percent was in retail. Kochar, Suro, and Tafoya, "New Latino South," 72.

96. María and Alejandra N., interview by the author; Ana Hernández, interview by the author; Rosa Elba Gutiérrez, interview by the author.

97. Edith H., interview by the author; María F., interview by the author.

98. On Latino avoidance of black neighborhoods, see Price and Singer, "Edge Gateways."

99. Alicia E., interview by the author.

100. Walker, *Waking from the Dream*, 7; de la Calle and Rubio, *Mexico*, 38.

101. Advertisement for Regent Homes, *La Noticia*, November 7, 2007, 41V.

102. Advertisement for Fleetwood Homes, *La Noticia*, July 13, 2005, 7V.

103. Advertisement for Adams Homes, *La Noticia*, July 19, 2006, 11V.

104. Doris Cevallos, interview by the author.

105. Celia Estrada, interview by the author.

106. Bocian, Li, Reid, and Quercia, "Lost Ground, 2011."

107. Doris Cevallos, interview by the author.

108. Barton, "Borderland Discontents," 141.

109. Data is from Zillow.com.

110. This echoes earlier battles over black home ownership in white neighborhoods, which also equated consumption with citizenship and identity. Holt, *Problem of Race in the Twenty-First Century*, 73–75. It also draws on Perla Guerrero's concept of "acts of spatial illegality," which she defines as "any instance where Latinas/os do not break laws, customs, or social norms of the community yet their activity is constructed as objectionable and illicit, where their mere presence is a violation of community." Guerrero, "Impacting Arkansas," 258.

111. Kruse, *White Flight*; Lassiter, *Silent Majority*; HoSang, *Racial Propositions*.

112. Robin Dale Jacobson, *New Nativism*; HoSang, *Racial Propositions*; Lippard and Gallagher, "Introduction," 17.

113. On the historical construction of the illegal immigrant, see Ngai, *Impossible Subjects*.

114. Wil Neumann, interview by the author.

115. O'Neil, "Challenging Change," 102.

116. Laura Sullivan, "Prison Economics Help Drive Ariz. Immigration Law," *Morning Edition*, National Public Radio, October 28, 2010.

117. Michael Powell and Michelle García, "Pa. City Puts Illegal Immigrants on Notice," *Washington Post*, August 22, 2006; Sandoval and Tambini, *Farmingville*; "Hispanics March in Milwaukee against Immigration Bills," CNN, March 23, 2006, http://www.cnn.com/2006/US/03/23/latino.march/.

118. For an account that pins anti-immigrant sentiment on southern particularities, see Sabia, "Anti-Immigrant Fervor in Georgia," 73. For arguments against southern exceptionalism in the civil rights era, see Kruse, *White Flight*; Lassiter, *Silent Majority*.

119. On Cobb County, see Lassiter, "Big Government and Family Values"; Odem, "Unsettled in the Suburbs."

120. Deeb-Sossa and Mendez, "Enforcing Borders in the Nuevo South."

121. William Gheen, telephone interview by the author.

122. NCListen, "Contact."

123. Deeb-Sossa and Mendez, "Enforcing Borders in the Nuevo South," 620.

124. William Gheen, telephone interview by the author.

125. Dustin Inman Society, "No to Georgifornia!"

126. On the white racial subtext of "taxpayer" identities, see HoSang, *Racial Propositions*, 167.

127. Anti-Defamation League, "Immigrants Targeted." For more on these discourses, see Leo R. Chavez, *Latino Threat*, and Deeb-Sossa and Mendez, "Enforcing Borders in the Nuevo South."

128. Letter to the Latin American Coalition, postmarked November 2005. Courtesy of Angeles Ortega-Moore.

129. This is in contrast to older, inner southern suburbs, where neighborhood identities structured discourse on Latino newcomers. Winders, *Nashville in the New Millennium*, 56–58, 169, 233–34.

130. Dotti Jenkins, e-mail to Wil Neumann and Pearl Burris-Floyd, September 29, 2009. Courtesy of Wil Neumann.

131. John Love e-mail to Wil Neumann, September 30, 2009. Courtesy of Wil Neumann.

132. Terry Lewis e-mail to Wil Neumann, March 6, 2009. Courtesy of Wil Neumann.

133. Tish Huss e-mail to Wil Neumann, April 14, 2009. Courtesy of Wil Neumann.

134. "Tish Huss, Mooresville, NC signature," Stand with Joe, http://www.standwithjoe.com/totals.php?pageNum_WallNew=6&totalRows_WallNew=51150 (accessed November 26, 2013).

135. Monte Monteleone e-mail to Bill Current, September 22, 2009. Courtesy of Wil Neumann.

136. Gleaned from Fair Immigration Reform Movement, "Overview of Recent Local Ordinances on Immigration—Draft," in author's possession; Puerto Rican Legal Defense and Education Fund, "Database of Local Anti-Immigration Ordinances."

137. Census 2000 data is from http://socialexplorer.com.

138. "2006-414: Commissioner Torbett–BOC–To Adopt Policies and Apply Staff Direction Related to Illegal Residents in Gaston County," Gaston County, North Carolina Commissioner's Court minutes, November 9, 2006, http://egov2.co.gaston.nc.us/WebLink8/Browse.aspx?startid=1269239&dbid=0.

139. "Gaston County Board of Commissioners Meeting."

140. Luna and Ansley, "Global Migrants and Access to Local Housing," 161–63.

141. "Gaston County Board of Commissioners Meeting."

142. Ibid.

143. Mecklenburg County, North Carolina Board of County Commissioners, "Meet

the Board"; Debbie Cenziper and Celeste Smith, "Beyond Busing: The Choice is Ours," *Charlotte Observer*, April 6, 1997.

144. "Mecklenburg County Commissioners Meeting."

145. Hurder, "Almost Definitive History of Licensing Undocumented Aliens in North Carolina."

146. Angelica C., interview by the author.

147. Focus group with Mexican immigrant women, Monroe, N.C., August 12, 2011.

148. Deeb-Sossa and Mendez, "Enforcing Borders in the Nuevo South."

149. "Comunidad reacciona ante datos falsos dados por el alcalde McCrory," *La Noticia*, January 30, 2008.

150. Little scholarship has probed the relationship between conservatism and anti-immigrant sentiment in the United States. Phillips-Fein, "Conservatism," 735–36.

151. Rosario Machicao, "Más de 10,000 piden reforma migratoria integral," *La Noticia*, May 3, 2006.

152. Jess George, interview by the author; Angeles Ortega-Moore, interview by the author.

153. The Fly, "Illegal Latino's 'Don't Pay Taxes,' 'Soak up Human Services ... like Sponges' and Are Taking Black Jobs," *Charlotte Post*, exact date unknown, 2006. Reprinted in "BillJames.org: Conservative Republican News for Charlotte and Mecklenburg County," http://billjames.org/listbuilder/2006/2006-7-8-Democrats%20to %20discuss%20Black%20-%20Latino%20Rift.htm (accessed November 28, 2008).

154. Angeles Ortega-Moore, interview by the author.

155. Rosario Machicao, "En manifestación en Charlotte, más de 6,000 piden reforma migratoria," *La Noticia*, March 29, 2006; Machicao, "Más de 10,000 piden reforma migratoria integral," *La Noticia*, May 3, 2006.

156. Aníbal Calderón, "Comunidad se una contra mensaje antiinmigrante," *La Noticia*, February 1, 2006.

157. Rosario Machicao, "Más de 2300 Latinos alzan su voz para hacer oír sus derechos," *La Noticia*, June 1, 2005; Rosario Machicao, "En manifestación en Charlotte, más de 6,000 piden reforma migratoria," *La Noticia*, March 29, 2006. For more on black–Latino political coalitions and social ties in other southern cities, see Jones, "Blacks May Be Second Class"; Nestor Rodríguez, "New Southern Neighbors."

158. Charles J. Dean, "Selma March to Alabama Capital Relaunched with New Spirit, Purpose," Alabama Media Group, http://blog.al.com/spotnews/2012/03/selma_march_to_alabama_capital.html.

159. Riva Brown, "Immigrants in U.S. Pay Hefty Price," *Clarion Ledger*, September 2003; Weise, "Mississippi."

160. Religious Congregations & Membership Study 2000, accessed via www.social explorer.com.

161. On Evangelical outreach efforts, see Pastor José Torres, interview by the author; Clark, "A Mission of Hope: Hispanics Helped through Baptist Church," *Charlotte Observer*, June 26, 1988; Stowe, "Churches Reach out to Hispanics," *Charlotte Observer*,

September 8, 1991; "Se Expanden Servicios de Iglesias en Español," *La Noticia*, January 11, 2006. A Spanish-language service at First Baptist Church of Indian Trail was listed in a 2009 directory (http://www.ihclt.org/resources.php?cat=50) but by 2014 no longer existed according to the church's website (http://www.fbcit.org/our-history) and a phone call to its office placed by the author on November 19, 2014.

162. On Charlotte Catholics' Hispanic ministries, see Sister Andrea Inkrott, interview by the author; and "Colabore con la Campaña de Recolección de Fondos para Construir el Centro Católico Hispano," *La Noticia*, October 10, 1997. On inconsistent Catholic responses in exurban counties, see Father Frank Cancro, interview by the author; Father José Antonio Juya, interview by the author; Angelica C., interview by the author.

163. "Se Expanden Servicios de Iglesias en Español," *La Noticia*, January 11, 2006.

164. Tom Stinson-Wesley, interview by the author. Alex and Anne Smythers recounted a similar reluctance toward Latino outreach in their Methodist church in Mint Hill, at Mecklenburg County's eastern edge. Alex and Anne Smythers, interview by the author.

165. Census 2000 collapsed Summary Files 1 and 3, accessed via http://socialexplorer.com.

166. Robert C. Smith, *Mexican New York*, 284–85; FitzGerald, *A Nation of Emigrants*.

167. Consular Assistance and Protection Cases handled in the Mexican consulate in Raleigh, N.C., 2001–9 and 2010–12, acquired via "Infomex" Mexican government public records request, in author's possession. I am grateful to Louise Walker for facilitating the completion of this request in Mexico City.

168. Edith H., interview by the author.

169. Angelica C., interview by the author.

170. Ana Hernández, interview by the author.

171. Jess George, interview by the author.

172. For more on the ways space constrains political activism among southern Latinos, see Odem, "Latino Immigrants and the Politics of Space in Atlanta."

173. Edith H., interview by the author.

174. Norma C., interview by the author.

175. Angelica C., interview by the author.

176. For more on the role of fear in limiting the political claims of adult undocumented immigrants, see Abrego, "Legal Consciousness of Undocumented Latinos."

177. *La Noticia* mentioned a march in Gastonia on April 1, 2007, but I was unable to corroborate this from other newspaper sources. Gastonia's Catholic priest, an immigrant advocate, asked around for information in response to a request. He wrote in an e-mail that "there was a protest but no one remembers who sponsored it—local ministers were involved and possibly the council of churches. No one from [the Catholic church] was present nor do they think the protest itself was well attended." Father Frank Cancro, e-mail to the author, October 22, 2013.

178. "Pilgrim's Pride to Close for Protest," *Enquirer-Journal*, April 29, 2006, Union County Public Library, "Hispanic" vertical file.

179. Ibid.; Ordoñez, "Latino Shopping Boycott May Grow: Work Absences, Student Walkouts Expected Locally in 1-Day Protest," *Charlotte Observer*, April 9, 2006.

180. Aníbal Calderón, "Estudiantes latinos salen de las aulas a manifestarse," *La Noticia*, April 19, 2006.

181. Rosario Machicao, "Estudiantes rechazan actitud del profesor," *La Noticia*, May 21, 2008.

182. Ernesto Chávez, *"Mi Raza Primero!,"* 47–48; García and Castro, *Blowout!*.

183. Gonzales, "Left Out but Not Shut Down," 232.

184. Angelica C., interview by the author.

185. Mercedes R., interview by the author.

186. Edith H., interview by the author.

187. Cahn, *Direct Sales and Direct Faith in Latin America*; Cahn, "Using and Sharing."

188. Nathel Hailey, President of Union County NAACP, interview by the author; Annie Young, President of Gaston County NAACP, interview by the author.

189. Robin Dale Jacobson, *New Nativism*, 86–88; HoSang, *Racial Propositions*, 198.

Conclusion

1. Gil Klein Media General News Service, "Chorus of Different Accents Growing Louder in the South: Growing Number of Hispanics Settling in," *Times-Picayune*, October 3, 1999.

2. Winders, *Nashville in the New Millennium*, 127.

3. Sara Hebel, "Georgia Regents Ban Illegal Immigrants From Selective Public Colleges," *Chronicle of Higher Education*, October 13, 2010; Russell, "State Policies Regarding Undocumented College Students."

4. Robert C. Smith, *Mexican New York*; Smith and Guarnizo, *Transnationalism from Below*; FitzGerald, *A Nation of Emigrants*.

5. For more on these modernist promises, see Deborah Cohen, *Braceros*.

6. Galarza, *Merchants of Labor*; Gilbert G. González, *Mexican Consuls and Labor Organizing*, 212; García y Griego, *Importation of Mexican Contract Laborers to the United States*.

7. Joseph, Rubenstein, and Zolov, "Assembling the Fragments," 13.

8. Erik Morin, personal communication, Atlanta, November 16, 2014.

9. Blanton, "George I. Sánchez, Ideology, and Whiteness."

10. Chris Echegaray, "Nashville's Core Tilted English-Only Vote," *Tennessean*, January 25, 2009.

Appendix

1. Camarillo, *Chicanos in a Changing Society*, 247–49; Sánchez, *Becoming Mexican American*, 312, n. 14.

Bibliography

Archives in Mexico

Mexico City
   Archivo de la Embajada de México en los Estados Unidos de América
   Archivo General de la Nación
   Archivo Histórico de la Secretaría de Relaciones Exteriores
Nuevo León
   Archivo General del Estado de Nuevo León (Monterrey)
   Archivo Municipal de Lampazos de Naranjo, Nuevo León
Veracruz
   Archivo General del Estado de Veracruz (Xalapa)

Archives in the United States

Arkansas
   Archives and Special Collections, Arkansas State University (Jonesboro)
   Arkansas History Commission (Little Rock)
     Homer M. Adkins Papers
   Church of the Immaculate Conception (Blytheville)
     Sacrament Records
   Ouachita Baptist University (Arkadelphia)
     Sen. John McClellan Papers
Georgia
   Archives of the Catholic Diocese of Savannah
   Georgia Archives (Morrow)
   Georgia Baptist Convention Archives (Duluth)
   Sacred Heart Catholic Church (Vidalia)
     Sacrament Records
   University of Georgia Libraries (Athens)
   Valdosta State University Archives (Georgia)
Illinois
   Loyola University (Chicago)
     Catholic Church Extension Society Records
Louisiana
   Archives of the Catholic Archdiocese of New Orleans

Louisiana Division and City Archives, New Orleans Public Library
Mississippi
   Archives of the Catholic Diocese of Jackson
   Delta State University Archives and Museum (Cleveland)
   Mississippi Department of Archives and History (Jackson)
   Mississippi State University Archives (Starkville)
      Delta & Pine Land Papers
   Our Lady of Victories Catholic Church (Cleveland)
      Sacrament Records
   University of Southern Mississippi, McCain Library and Archives (Hattiesburg)
      Theodore G. Bilbo Papers
North Carolina
   Duke University Rare Book, Manuscript, and Special Collections Library (Durham)
      North Carolina Council of Churches Papers
   State Archives of North Carolina (Raleigh)
Texas
   National Archives at Fort Worth
      Record Group 33, Records of the Agricultural Extension Service
Washington, D.C.
   National Archives and Records Administration
      Record Group 85, Records of the Immigration and Naturalization Service

Newspapers

(Online access noted where applicable.)
Arkansas Gazette
Atlanta Journal-Constitution (microfilm, paper, and via Lexis-Nexis)
Baptist Record (Jackson, Miss.)
Boston Globe (via Lexis-Nexis)
Charlotte Observer (paper and via Newsbank, Lexis-Nexis, and www.charlotteobserver.com)
Charlotte Post
Christian Index (Georgia Baptist Convention)
City Paper (Nashville, Tenn.) (www.nashvillecitypaper.com)
Clarion Ledger (Jackson, Miss.)
Crisis (via GoogleBooks)
Daily World (Atlanta, Ga.) (via Proquest)
El Cronista del Valle (Brownsville, Tex.) (via Newsbank)
El Heraldo de México (Los Angeles, Calif.) (via Newsbank)
Enquirer-Journal (Union County, N.C.)
Florida Catholic
Gainesville (Ga.) Times

Houston Chronicle
Knight Ridder (via Lexis-Nexis)
La Epoca (San Antonio, Tex.) (via Newsbank)
La Noticia (Charlotte, N.C.)
La Prensa (San Antonio, Tex.) (via Newsbank)
Leader-Tribune (Peach County, Ga.)
Los Angeles Times (via Lexis-Nexis)
Loudon (Va.) Times Mirror
Louisiana Planter and Sugar Manufacturer (New Orleans, La.)
Macon (Ga.) Telegraph-News
Memphis World
Mi Gente (Charlotte, N.C.)
Morning Advocate (Baton Rouge, La.)
Morning Tribune (New Orleans, La.)
New York Times (via ProQuest and Lexis-Nexis)
News & Observer (Raleigh, N.C.)
Regeneración (Los Angeles, Calif.) (via Newsbank)
Tennessean (www.tennessean.com)
Tifton (Ga.) Gazette (via Lexis-Nexis)
Times-Picayune (New Orleans, La.)
Tri-State Defender (Memphis, Tenn.)
Valdosta (Ga.) Daily Times
Vidalia (Ga.) Advance
Washington Post (via Lexis-Nexis)
Winston-Salem (N.C.) Journal and Sentinel

Interviews Conducted by the Author

All interview recordings and notes are in the author's possession.
Teresa and Abel Aguilar, Rosa and Albert Aguilar, Carlos Alcantar, and Mary Ann and Howdy Thurman, Fort Valley, Ga., April 4, 2008
Gustavo Arévalo, Monroe, N.C., July 20, 2014
Beth Arnow, Atlanta, Ga., April 8, 2008
Andrea and Bernardo "Slim" Avalos, Omega, Ga., July 11, 2010
David Balderas, telephone interview, May 8, 2007
Ana Barba, Charlotte, N.C., August 10, 2011
Gov. Roy Barnes, Marietta, Ga., April 8, 2008
Scott Beck, Statesboro, Ga., March 31, 2008
Curtis Blackwood, Waxhaw, N.C., August 2, 2011
Ruth and Sonny Bridges, Moultrie, Ga., July 13, 2010
Sister Patricia Brown, Savannah, Ga., March 28, 2008
Angelica C. (pseudonym), Wingate, N.C., August 16, 2011
Norma C., Monroe, N.C., August 19, 2011

Rosario Campos Sandoval, Monroe, N.C., September 16, 2008
Father Frank Cancro, Gastonia, N.C., August 25, 2011
Hazel Canedo, New Orleans, La., May 3, 2007
Frank Cervantes, telephone interview, August 20, 2007
Doris Cevallos, Charlotte, N.C., August 1, 2011
Wayne Cooper, Charlotte, N.C., September 8, 2008
Alicia E. (pseudonym), Indian Trail, N.C., August 4, 2011
María E., Indian Trail, N.C., August 4, 2014
Joe Enriquez, Cleveland, Miss., January 12, 2006; telephone interview, June 6, 2005
Celia Estrada, Charlotte, N.C., August 17, 2011
María F., Indian Trail, N.C., July 25, 2011
Carolyn Flowers, Doeren, Ga., July 12, 2010
Vincent Frisina, Charlotte, N.C., September 17, 2008
Jess George, Charlotte, N.C., August 17, 2011
William Gheen, telephone interview, September 4, 2008
Doris Goedeke, Concord, N.C., September 11, 2008
José and Anselma Gómez, Nicholls, Ga., April 2, 2008
Javier González, telephone interview, February 13, 2008
Tomás González Landrove, Monterrey, Mexico, July 9, 2006
José Gutiérrez, interview by the author and Joel Urista, Long Beach, Calif., June 1, 2011
Rosa Elba Gutiérrez, Monroe, N.C., September 16, 2008
Edith H. (pseudonym), August 8, 2011
Elvia H. (pseudonym), August 8, 2011
Nathel Hailey, Monroe, N.C., August 16, 2011
Clara Harden, Claxton, Ga., April 2, 2008
Ana Hernández, Monroe, N.C., August 24, 2011
Andrea Hinojosa, Lyons, Ga., March 31, 2008
Gloria Shaw Jackson, Lyons, Ga., April 1, 2008
Father José Antonio Juya, Gastonia, N.C., September 11, 2008
Claude Kennedy, telephone interview, October 7, 2008
Sister Andrea Inkrott, Charlotte, N.C., September 11, 2008
Fathers Brian Laburt, Mike Smith, and Ed Frank, Statesboro, Ga., March 31, 2008
Phillip Laro, Cleveland, Miss., October 22, 2006
María Laury, Monroe, N.C., July 25, 2014
Denisa Leach, Charlotte, N.C., September 17, 2008
Flora López, Monroe, N.C., September 10, 2008
Juan Loza, telephone interview, April 11, 2007
Maria Macon, telephone interview, September 5, 2008
Robert Marín and Teodora Marín, Cedar Crossing, Ga., April 2, 2008
Luz Marti, Tifton, Ga., July 12, 2010

Pastor Wiley Martin, Charlotte, N.C., September 16, 2008
Teodoro Maus, telephone interview, May 11, 2004
Héctor Mena, telephone interview, January 29, 2008
Diana (Avalos) Mendieta, Omega, Ga., July 11, 2010
Laura Mendoza and Eréndira Molina, Charlotte, N.C., September 18, 2008
María and Alejandra N., Monroe, N.C., August 19, 2011
Michael Nelken, New Haven, Conn., August 5, 2007
Wil Neumann, Gastonia, N.C., August 5, 2011
Kenneth Nieto, Covington, La., May 2, 2007
Lizbeth Olivares, Monroe, N.C., September 10, 2008
Angeles Ortega-Moore, Charlotte, N.C., September 10, 2008, and August 3, 2011
Mercedes R., Monroe, N.C., August 19, 2011
David Resendez, telephone interview, May 9, 2007
Janis Roberson, Tifton, Ga., July 10, 2010
Alex and Anne Smythers, Mint Hill, N.C., September 18, 2008, and August 2, 2011
Gabino Solís Aguilera, telephone interview, April 15, 2007
Petra Soto, Omega, Ga., July 12, 2010
Frank Stilp, Lyons, Ga., April 1, 2008
Tom Stinson-Wesley, Pineville, N.C., August 22, 2011
Pastor José Torres, Matthews, N.C., August 22, 2011
John Raymond Turner, Vidalia, Ga., April 1, 2008
Edith V. (pseudonym), Wingate, N.C., August 4, 2011
Héctor Vaca, Charlotte, N.C., August 4, 2011
María Villegas, Lyons, Ga., April 1, 2008
Susan Webster, Monroe, N.C., September 10, 2008
Rev. Frank Wilson, Charlotte, N.C., September 17, 2008
Jerome Woody and Tina Hagan, Claxton, Ga., April 2, 2008
Mary Palacios Ybarra, Merigold, Miss., June 7, 2005
Annie Young, Belmont, N.C., August 18, 2011
Carlos Zervigón, New Orleans, La., May 3, 2007

Publicly Available Oral History Interviews

"The Arkansas Delta in Transition: Agriculture and Community, 1920–1980,"
    Oral History Collection, Arkansas State University, Jonesboro
  Joe García, interview by John "Pat" Snodgrass, Parkin, Ark., March 29, 2000
  Ben Hyneman, interview by John "Pat" Snodgrass, Trumann, Ark., April 26, 1999
  Jack McNeil, interview by Brady Banta, Jonesboro, Ark., February 8, 2000
  Bobby Wood, interview by Brady Banta and Larry Ball, Lake City, Ark., May 2, 1999
Smithsonian Bracero History Archive Oral Histories, available at http://bracero
    archive.org
  Delores Atkins, interview by Julie Weise, September 25, 2008, http://bracero
    archive.org/items/show/3076

Thom E. Beasley, interview by Melany Bowman, September 24, 2008, http://braceroarchive.org/items/show/3077

John Collier, interview by Mireya Loza, September 25, 2008, http://braceroarchive.org/items/show/3089

John Gray, interview by Mike Bowman, September 24, 2008, http://braceroarchive.org/items/show/3080

Calvin King, interview by Julie Weise and Nicole Smith-Neal, September 24, 2008, http://braceroarchive.org/items/show/3085

Bernard Lipsey, interview by Julie Weise, September 22, 2008, http://braceroarchive.org/items/show/3090

Harrison Locke, interview by Julie Weise and Nicole Smith-Neal, September 24, 2008, http://braceroarchive.org/items/show/3087

Miguel Jáquez López, interview by Laureano Martínez, May 27, 2003, http://braceroarchive.org/items/show/214

Juán Loza, interview by Mireya Loza, August 31, 2005, http://braceroarchive.org/items/show/175

Esteban Saldaña, interview by Myrna Parra-Mantilla, February 14, 2003, http://braceroarchive.org/items/show/49

Gabino Solís Aguilera, interview by Steve Velásquez, July 28, 2005, http://braceroarchive.org/items/show/155

Interviews conducted by students of Professor Michelle Shaul, Queens University, Charlotte, N.C. (transcripts in the author's possession)

Francisco Ramos, interview by Anna Helms, Charlotte, N.C., ca. 2004

Consuela Ramos, interview by Melissa Mary Grove, Charlotte, N.C., ca. 2004

Personal Papers and Photographs

All personal papers and photographs are in the author's possession.
Andrea and Bernardo "Slim" Avalos, Omega, Ga.
Ruth and Sonny Bridges, Moultrie, Ga.
Sister Patricia Brown, Savannah, Ga.
Hazel Canedo and family, New Orleans, La.
Richard Enriquez, Nick Enriquez, and families, Collierville, Tenn.
José and Anselma Gómez, Nicholls, Ga.
Andrea Hinojosa, Lyons, Ga.
Maria Macon, minutes, agendas, and clippings of "Ad-Hoc Immigration Committee," Charlotte, N.C.
Luz Marti, Tifton, Ga.
Eréndira Molina and Laura Mendoza, Charlotte, N.C.
Janis Roberson, Tifton, Ga.
Mary Ann and Howdy Thurman, Fort Valley, Ga.
Carlos Zervigón and family, New Orleans, La.

Government Sources

Alabama House Republican Caucus. "Representative Micky Hammon and Illegal Immigration." 2011. http://www.youtube.com/watch?v=nCZoxSBjeEw.

Bauman, Kurt J., and Nikki L. Graf. *Educational Attainment: 2000*. Washington, D.C.: U.S. Census Bureau, 2003.

Central Alabama Fair Housing Center v. Julie Magee and Jimmy Stubbs. Civil Action No. 2:11cv982-MHT-CSC (2011).

Clinton, Bill. "Convention Acceptance." *Congressional Digest* (October 1992): 230–32.

Daniel, Pete, comp. *The Peonage Files of the U.S. Department of Justice, 1901–1945*. Bethesda, Md.: University Microfilms of America.

"Findings from the National Agricultural Workers Survey (NAWS) 1989." Washington, D.C.: U.S. Department of Labor, 1991.

"Gaston County Board of Commissioners Meeting, November 9, 2006." Video provided by Gaston County government. In the author's possession.

Instituto Nacional de Estadística Geografía e Informática. "Censo General de Población y Vivienda." http://www.inegi.org.mx/sistemas/TabuladosBasicos/default.aspx?c=16762&s=est.

Instituto Nacional de Estadística Geografía e Informática. *La diversidad religiosa en México*. Aguascalientes, Mexico, 2005. http://www.inegi.org.mx/prod_serv/contenidos/espanol/bvinegi/productos/integracion/sociodemografico/religion/div_rel.pdf

Joyner, Carlotta C. "H2A Agricultural Guestworker Program: Experiences of Individual Vidalia Onion Growers." Washington, D.C.: U.S. General Accounting Office, Health, Education and Human Services Division, 1998.

LINC (Log Into North Carolina). "Census 1990, Summary File 1, Indian Trail, N.C." State of North Carolina, http://data.osbm.state.nc.us/pls/census/dyn_census_profiles_1.show.

———. "Census 2000, Summary File 1, Indian Trail, N.C." State of North Carolina, http://data.osbm.state.nc.us/pls/census/dyn_census_profiles_1.show.

———. "Census 2000, Summary File 3, Indian Trail, N.C." State of North Carolina, http://data.osbm.state.nc.us/profiles/2000/sf3_00_179_6.pdf.

———. "Census 2000, Summary File 3, Mecklenburg County, N.C." State of North Carolina, http://data.osbm.state.nc.us/profiles/2000/sf3_00_119_6.pdf.

———. "Migration Report for Union County." http://data.osbm.state.nc.us/migrate/migrate_00_179.pdf.

"Mecklenburg County Commissioners Meeting, April 15, 2008." http://charmeck.org/mecklenburg/county/CountyManagersOffice/BOCC/Meetings/Pages/Watch-Meetings.aspx.

Mecklenburg County, North Carolina Board of County Commissioners. "Meet the Board." http://charmeck.org/mecklenburg/county/CountyManagersOffice/BOCC/District6/Pages/James.aspx.

Migrant Health Program. *An Atlas of State Profiles which Estimate Number of Migrant and Seasonal Farmworkers and Members of Their Families.* Rockville, Md.: U.S. Department of Health and Human Services, 1990.

U.S. Census Bureau. *Abstract of the Fourteenth Census of the United States–1920.* Vol. 2. Washington, D.C.: Government Printing Office, 1923.

———. *Fifteenth Census of the United States–1930–Population–General Report, Statistics by Subject.* Vol. 2. Washington, D.C.: Government Printing Office, 1933.

———. *1987 Census of Agriculture.* Vol. 1: Geographic Area Series, Part 10: Georgia, State and County Data. Washington, D.C.: U.S. Department of Commerce, 1989.

———. *Thirteenth Census of the United States Taken in the Year 1910.* Vol. 2: Population. Washington, D.C.: Government Printing Office, 1913.

U.S. Census Bureau, Population Division. "Census 2000 County-to-County Worker Flow Files." http://www.census.gov/population/www/cen2000/commuting/index.html.

———. "1990 County-to-County Worker Flow Files." http://www.census.gov/population/www/socdemo/jtw_workerflow.html.

U.S. Department of Labor. *Annual Report of the Commissioner General of Immigration—1930.* Washington, D.C.: Government Printing Office, 1930.

Vecoli, Rudolph, comp. *Records of the Immigration and Naturalization Service.* Bethesda, Md.: University Publications of America.

Published Primary Sources

Anti-Defamation League. "Immigrants Targeted: Extremist Rhetoric Moves into the Mainstream." Anti-Defamation League, http://archive.adl.org/civil_rights/anti_immigrant/alipac.html#.VJtf7F4APk.

Bocian, Debbie Gruenstein, Wei Li, Carolina Reid, and Roberto G. Quercia. "Lost Ground, 2011: Disparities in Mortgage Lending and Foreclosures." Center for Responsible Lending, http://www.responsiblelending.org/mortgage-lending/research-analysis/Lost-Ground-2011.pdf.

"Carolina Poll, Spring 1996." School of Journalism and Mass Communication, University of North Carolina at Chapel Hill. http://arc.irss.unc.edu/dvn/dv/odvn/faces/study/StudyPage.xhtml?globalId=hdl:1902.29/D-30962&studyListingIndex=2_d8c853a21f0fa71929139b482ddo.

Dustin Inman Society. "No to Georgifornia!" http://www.thedustininmansociety.org/info/no_to_georgiafornia.html.

Fair Immigration Reform Movement. "Overview of Recent Local Ordinances on Immigration—Draft." 2007. In the author's possession.

Ferrocarriles Nacionales de México y Anexos. "Tarifa de Pasajes por Distancias Kilométricas para Uso de los Conductores de Trenes." Mexico City: Secretaría de Comunicaciones y Obras Públicas, 1924.

Kasarda, John D., and James H. Johnson Jr. "The Economic Impact of the Hispanic

Population on the State of North Carolina." Chapel Hill: Kenan-Flagler Business School, University of North Carolina, 2006.

Kochar, Rakesh, Roberto Suro, and Sonya Tafoya. "The New Latino South: The Context and Consequences of Rapid Population Growth." Washington, D.C.: Pew Hispanic Center, 2005.

Lang, Robert E., and Thomas W. Sanchez. "The New Metro Politics: Interpreting Recent Presidential Elections Using a County-Based Regional Typology." Blacksburg, Va.: Metropolitan Institute at Virginia Tech, 2006.

"Malaria among Mexican Cotton Pickers in Mississippi." *Monthly Labor Review* 25 (1927): 50–51.

NCListen. "Contact," http://Nclisten.com/contact. Accessed January 14, 2009.

Nixon, John W., Fred C. White, and Bill R. Miller. "Hired Labor Management Practices among Georgia Farmers." Athens, Ga.: Department of Agricultural Economics, 1976.

Passel, Jeffrey, and Wendy Zimmerman. "Are Immigrants Leaving California? Settlement Patterns of Immigrants in the Late 1990s." Washington, D.C.: Urban Institute, 2001.

Puerto Rican Legal Defense and Education Fund. "Database of Local Anti-Immigration Ordinances." www.ailadownloads.org/advo/PRLDEF-ListOfLocal Ordinances.xls.

Rowe, Gene. "The Hired Farm Working Force of 1977." Washington, D.C.: United States Department of Agriculture, Economics, Statistics, and Cooperatives Service, 1979.

Southern Poverty Law Center. "Close to Slavery: Guestworker Programs in the United States." http://www.splcenter.org/pdf/static/SPLCguestworker.pdf.

"Thirty-Second Report of the Board of Commissioners of the Port of New Orleans." New Orleans: Board of Commissioners of the Port of New Orleans, 1928.

"Thirty-Third Report of the Board of Commissioners of the Port of New Orleans." New Orleans: Board of Commissioners of the Port of New Orleans, 1929.

Secondary Sources

Abrams, Lynn. *Oral History Theory*. London: Routledge, 2010.

Abrego, Leisy J. "Legal Consciousness of Undocumented Latinos: Fear and Stigma as Barriers to Claims Making for First- and 1.5-Generation Immigrants." *Law & Society Review* 45, no. 2 (2011): 337–69.

Aguayo, Sergio. *1968: Los Archivos de la Violencia*. Mexico City: Editorial Grijalbo, 1998.

Alanís Enciso, Fernando Saúl. *El Primer Programa Bracero y el Gobierno de México 1917–1918*. San Luis Potosí, Mexico: El Colegio de San Luis, 1999.

Alvarez, Robert R., Jr. "The Lemon Grove Incident: The Nation's First Successful Desegregation Court Case." *Journal of San Diego History* 32, no. 2 (Spring 1986). http://www.sandiegohistory.org/journal/86spring/lemongrove.htm.

American Civil Liberties Union. "Republican Mayor Opposes Georgia's Anti-Immigrant Law." 2012. http://www.aclu.org/immigrants-rights/republican-mayor-opposes-georgias-anti-immigrant-law.

Arnesen, Eric. *Waterfront Workers of New Orleans: Race, Class, and Politics, 1863–1923*. New York: Oxford University Press, 1991.

Arredondo, Gabriela. *Mexican Chicago: Race, Identity, and Nation, 1916–39*. Urbana: University of Illinois Press, 2008.

———. "Navigating Ethno-Racial Currents: Mexicans in Chicago, 1919–1939." *Journal of Urban History* 30, no. 3 (March 2004): 399–427.

Asbed, Greg. "Coalition of Immokalee Workers: 'Golpear a Uno es Golpear a Todos!' To Beat One of Us Is to Beat Us All!" In *Bringing Human Rights Home*, edited by Cynthia Soohoo, Catherine Albisa, and Martha Davis, 1–23. Santa Barbara, Calif.: Greenwood, 2008.

Ayers, Edward L. *Southern Crossing: A History of the American South, 1877–1906*. Oxford: Oxford University Press, 1995.

Balderrama, Francisco E., and Raymond Rodriguez. *Decade of Betrayal: Mexican Repatriation in the 1930s*. Albuquerque: University of New Mexico Press, 1995.

Balibar, Etienne. "Racism and Nationalism." In *Race, Nation, Class: Ambiguous Identities*, edited by Etienne Balibar and Immanuel Wallerstein, 37–67. London: Verso, 1991.

Barthes, Roland. *Camera Lucida: Reflections on Photography*. Translated by Richard Howard. 1980. Reprint, New York: Hill and Wang, 1981.

Bartkowski, John P., and Helen A. Regis. *Charitable Choices: Religion, Race, and Poverty in the Post-Welfare Era*. New York: New York University Press, 2004.

Barton, Josef. "Borderland Discontents: Mexican Migration in Regional Contexts, 1880–1930." In *Repositioning North American Migration History: New Directions in Modern Continental Migration, Citizenship, and Community*, edited by Marc S. Rodriguez, 141–205. Rochester, N.Y.: University of Rochester Press, 2005.

Basave Benítez, Agustín. *México Mestizo: Análisis del nacionalismo mexicano en torno a la mestizophilia de Andrés Molina Enríquez*. Mexico City: Fondo de Cultura Económica, 1992.

Bauer, Arnold J. *Goods, Power, History: Latin America's Material Culture*. Cambridge: Cambridge University Press, 2001.

Beck, Scott A. L. "'We Were the First Ones': Oral Histories of Mexican Heritage Women Pioneers in the Schools of Rural Southeast Georgia, 1978–2002." Ph.D. diss., University of Georgia, 2003.

Behnken, Brian D. *Fighting Their Own Battles: Mexican Americans, African Americans, and the Struggle for Civil Rights in Texas*. Chapel Hill: University of North Carolina Press, 2011.

———, ed. *The Struggle in Black and Brown: African American and Mexican American Relations during the Civil Rights Era*. Lincoln: University of Nebraska Press, 2011.

Bennett, James B. *Religion and the Rise of Jim Crow in New Orleans*. Princeton, N.J.: Princeton University Press, 2005.

Benton-Cohen, Katherine. *Borderline Americans: Racial Division and Labor War in the Arizona Borderlands*. Cambridge, Mass.: Harvard University Press, 2009.

Berry, Harold. "The Use of Mexicans as Farm Laborers in the Delta." *Phillips County Historical Review* 31, no. 1–2 (Spring 1993): 2–10.

Berthoff, Rowland T. "Southern Attitudes toward Immigration, 1865–1914." *Journal of Southern History* 17, no. 3 (August 1951): 328–60.

Berube, Alan, Audrey Singer, Jill H. Wilson, and William H. Frey. "Finding Exurbia: America's Fast-Growing Communities at the Metropolitan Fringe." Living Cities Census Series. Brookings Institution, 2006, http://www.brookings.edu/~/media/Files/rc/reports/2006/10metropolitanpolicy_berube/20061017_exurbia.pdf.

Blanton, Carlos K. "George I. Sánchez, Ideology, and Whiteness in the Making of the Mexican American Civil Rights Movement, 1930–1960." *Journal of Southern History* 72, no. 3 (August 2006): 569–604.

Bodnar, John. "Power and Memory in Oral History: Workers and Managers at Studebaker." *Journal of American History* 75, no. 4 (March 1989): 1201–21.

Bow, Leslie. *Partly Colored: Asian Americans and Racial Anomaly in the Segregated South*. New York: New York University Press, 2010.

Brandfon, Robert L. "The End of Immigration to the Cotton Fields." *Mississippi Valley Historical Review* 50, no. 4 (March 1964): 591–611.

Brown, Hana. "The New Racial Politics of Welfare: Ethno-Racial Diversity, Immigration, and Welfare Discourse Variation." *Social Service Review* 87, no. 3 (2013): 586–612.

Brunk, Samuel. "Remembering Emiliano Zapata: Three Moments in the Posthumous Career of the Martyr of Chinameca." *Hispanic American Historical Review* 78, no. 3 (August 1998): 457–90.

Cadava, Geraldo L. *Standing on Common Ground: The Making of a Sunbelt Borderland*. Cambridge, Mass.: Harvard University Press, 2013.

Cahn, Peter. *Direct Sales and Direct Faith in Latin America*. New York: Palgrave Macmillan, 2011.

———. "Using and Sharing: Direct Selling in the Borderlands." In *Land of Necessity: Consumer Culture in the United States–Mexico Borderlands*, edited by Alexis McCrossen, 274–98. Durham, N.C.: Duke University Press, 2009.

Calavita, Kitty. *Inside the State: The Bracero Program, Immigration, and the INS*. New York: Routledge, 1992.

Camarillo, Albert. *Chicanos in a Changing Society: From Mexican Pueblos to American Barrios in Santa Barbara and Southern California, 1848–1930*. Cambridge, Mass.: Harvard University Press, 1979.

Campt, Tina. *Image Matters: Archive, Photography, and the African Diaspora in Europe*. Durham, N.C.: Duke University Press, 2012.

Carrigan, William D., and Clive Webb. "The Lynching of Persons of Mexican Origin or Descent in the United States, 1848 to 1928." *Journal of Social History* 37, no. 2 (Winter 2003): 411–38.

Carroll, Patrick James. *Blacks in Colonial Veracruz: Race, Ethnicity, and Regional Development*. 2nd ed. Austin: University of Texas Press, 2001.

Carson, Clayborne. "SNCC and the Albany Movement." *Journal of Southwest Georgia History* 2 (Fall 1984): 15–25.

Castañeda, Jorge. *The Mexican Shock: Its Meaning for the United States*. New York: New Press, 1995.

Chalfen, Michael M. "Rev. Samuel B. Wells and Black Protest in Albany, 1945–1965." *Journal of Southwest Georgia History* 9 (Fall 1994): 37–64.

Chalfen, Richard. *Snapshot Versions of Life*. Bowling Green, Ohio: Bowling Green State University Popular Press, 1987.

———. *Turning Leaves: The Photograph Collections of Two Japanese American Families*. Albuquerque: University of New Mexico Press, 1991.

Chang, Grace. *Disposable Domestics: Immigrant Women Workers in the Global Economy*. Cambridge, Mass.: South End Press, 2000.

Chávez, Ernesto. *"Mi Raza Primero!" (My People First!): Nationalism, Identity, and Insurgency in the Chicano Movement in Los Angeles, 1966–1978*. Berkeley: University of California Press, 2002.

Chavez, Leo R. *The Latino Threat: Constructing Immigrants, Citizens, and the Nation*. Stanford, Calif.: Stanford University Press, 2008.

Cleary, Robert Martin. "The Education of Mexican-Americans in Kansas City, Kansas, 1916–1951." M.A. thesis, University of Missouri–Kansas City, 2002.

Coalition of Immokalee Workers. "Consciousness + Commitment = Change." In *Globalize Liberation: How to Uproot the System and Build a Better World*, edited by David Solnit, 347–60. San Francisco: City Lights Books, 2004.

Cobb, James C. *The Most Southern Place on Earth: The Mississippi Delta and the Roots of Regional Identity*. New York: Oxford University Press, 1992.

Cohen, Deborah. *Braceros: Migrant Citizens and Transnational Subjects in the Postwar United States and Mexico*. Chapel Hill: University of North Carolina Press, 2011.

———. "Caught in the Middle: The Mexican State's Relationship with the United States and Its Own Citizen-Workers, 1942–1954." *Journal of American Ethnic History* 20, no. 3 (2001): 110–32.

Cohen, Lizabeth. *A Consumers' Republic: The Politics of Mass Consumption in Postwar America*. New York: Knopf, 2003.

Coin, Francesca. "Pickles and Pickets after NAFTA: Globalization, Agribusiness, the U.S.-Mexico Food Chain, and Farm-Worker Struggles in North Carolina." Ph.D. diss., Georgia State University, 2007.

Connolly, Nathan. "Colored, Caribbean, and Condemned: Miami's Overtown District and the Cultural Expense of Progress, 1940–1970." *Caribbean Studies* 34, no. 1 (January–June 2006): 3–60.

———. "Timely Innovations: Planes, Trains, and the 'Whites Only' Economy of a Pan American City." *Urban History* 36, no. 2 (August 2009): 243–61.

Cornelius, Wayne. "Los Migrantes de la Crisis: The Changing Profile of Mexican Migration to the United States." In *Social Responses to Mexico's Economic Crisis of the 1980s*, edited by Mercedes González de la Rocha and Agustín Escobar Latapí, 155–93. San Diego: Center for U.S.-Mexican Studies, University of California, San Diego, 1991.

Cornell, Sarah E. "Americans in the U.S. South and Mexico: A Transnational History of Race, Slavery, and Freedom, 1810–1910." Ph.D. diss., New York University, 2008.

Cravey, Altha. "Transnationality, Social Spaces, and Parallel Worlds." In *Latinos in the New South: Transformations of Place*, edited by Heather A. Smith and Owen J. Furuseth, 217–34. Burlington, Vt.: Ashgate, 2006.

Crespino, Joseph. *In Search of Another Country: Mississippi and the Conservative Counterrevolution*. Princeton, N.J.: Princeton University Press, 2007.

Daniel, Pete. *Breaking the Land: The Transformation of Cotton, Tobacco, and Rice Cultures since 1880*. Urbana: University of Illinois Press, 1985.

———. *Deep'n as It Come: The 1927 Mississippi River Flood*. New York: Oxford University Press, 1977.

———. *The Shadow of Slavery: Peonage in the South, 1901–1969*. Urbana: University of Illinois Press, 1972.

Deeb-Sossa, Natalia, and Jennifer Bickham Mendez. "Enforcing Borders in the Nuevo South: Gender and Migration in Williamsburg, Virginia, and the Research Triangle, North Carolina." *Gender and Society* 22, no. 5 (2008): 613–38.

de la Calle, Luís, and Luís Rubio. *Mexico: A Middle Class Society*. Translated by Cara Goodman. 2010. Reprint, Washington, D.C.: Woodrow Wilson Center for Scholars, 2012.

Delpar, Helen. *The Enormous Vogue of Things Mexican: Cultural Relations between the United States and Mexico, 1920–1935*. Tuscaloosa: University of Alabama Press, 1992.

Deutsch, Sarah. *No Separate Refuge: Culture, Class, and Gender on an Anglo-Hispanic Frontier in the American Southwest, 1880–1940*. New York: Oxford University Press, 1987.

Deverell, William Francis. *Whitewashed Adobe: The Rise of Los Angeles and the Remaking of Its Mexican Past*. Berkeley: University of California Press, 2004.

Diaz McConnell, Eileen. "Racialized Histories and Contemporary Population Dynamics in the New South." In *Being Brown in Dixie: Race, Ethnicity, and Latino Immigration in the New South*, edited by Cameron D. Lippard and Charles A. Gallagher, 77–98. Boulder, Colo.: FirstForumPress, 2011.

Dittmer, John. *Local People: The Struggle for Civil Rights in Mississippi*. Urbana: University of Illinois Press, 1994.

Dominguez, Virginia R. *White by Definition: Social Classification in Creole Louisiana*. New Brunswick, N.J.: Rutgers University Press, 1986.

Dray, Philip. *At the Hands of Persons Unknown: The Lynching of Black America.* New York: Random House, 2002.

Dreby, Joanna. *Divided by Borders: Mexican Migrants and Their Children.* Berkeley: University of California Press, 2010.

Dreby, Joanna, and Leah Schmalzbauer. "The Relational Contexts of Migration: Mexican Women in New Destination Sites." *Sociological Forum* 28, no. 1 (March 2013): 1–26.

Durand, Jorge, Douglas Massey, and Rene M. Zenteno. "Mexican Immigration to the United States: Continuities and Changes." *Latin American Research Review* 36, no. 1 (2001): 107–27.

Elisha, Omri. *Moral Ambition: Mobilization and Social Outreach in Evangelical Megachurches.* Berkeley: University of California Press, 2011.

Emerson, Michael O., and Christian Smith. *Divided by Faith: Evangelical Religion and the Problem of Race in America.* Oxford: Oxford University Press, 2000.

Estabrook, Barry. *Tomatoland: How Modern Industrial Agriculture Destroyed Our Most Alluring Fruit.* Kansas City: Andrews McMeel Publishing, 2011.

Fairchild, Amy L. *Science at the Borders: Immigrant Medical Inspection and the Shaping of the Modern Industrial Labor Force.* Baltimore: Johns Hopkins University Press, 2003.

Falcón, Romana. "Veracruz: Los Límites del Radicalismo en el Campo." *Revista Mexicana de Sociología* 41, no. 3 (July–September 1979): 671–98.

Falcón, Romana, and Soledad García. *La Semilla en el Surco: Adelberto Tejeda y el Radicalismo en Veracruz, 1883–1860.* Mexico City: El Colegio de México, 1986.

Federal Writers' Project. *Mississippi: The WPA Guide to the Magnolia State.* 1938. Reprint, Jackson: University of Mississippi Press, 1988.

——— . *The WPA Guide to New Orleans: The Federal Writers' Project Guide to 1930s New Orleans.* 1938. Reprint, New York: Pantheon Books, 1983.

Fink, Leon. *The Maya of Morganton: Work and Community in the Nuevo New South.* Chapel Hill: University of North Carolina Press, 2003.

——— . *Workers across the Americas: The Transnational Turn in Labor History.* New York: Oxford University Press, 2011.

FitzGerald, David. *A Nation of Emigrants: How Mexico Manages Its Migration.* Berkeley: University of California Press, 2009.

Fligstein, Neil. *Going North: Migration of Blacks and Whites from the South, 1900–1950.* New York: Academic Press, 1981.

Flores-González, Nilda, Anna Romina Guevarra, and Maura Toro-Morn, eds. *Immigrant Women Workers in the Neoliberal Age.* Urbana: University of Illinois Press, 2013.

Foley, Michael W. "Agenda for Mobilization: The Agrarian Question and Popular Mobilization in Contemporary Mexico." *Latin American Research Review* 26, no. 2 (1991): 39–74.

——— . "Privatizing the Countryside: The Mexican Peasant Movement and Neoliberal Reform." *Latin American Perspectives* 22, no. 1 (1995): 59–76.

Foley, Neil. "Becoming Hispanic: Mexican Americans and the Faustian Pact with Whiteness." In *Reflexiones 1997: New Directions in Mexican American Studies*, edited by Neil Foley, 53 –70. Austin, Tex.: CMAS Books, 1998.

———. "Partly Colored or Other White: Mexican Americans and Their Problem with the Color Line." In *Beyond Black and White: Race, Ethnicity, and Gender in the U.S. South and Southwest*, edited by Stephanie Cole and Allison Parker, 123–44. College Station: Texas A&M University Press, 2004.

———. *The White Scourge: Mexicans, Blacks, and Poor Whites in Texas Cotton Culture*. Berkeley: University of California Press, 1997.

Fowler-Salamini, Heather. "Women Coffee Sorters Confront the Mill Owners and the Veracruz Revolutionary State, 1915–1918." *Journal of Women's History* 14, no. 1 (Spring 2002): 34–63.

Fox, Cybelle. *Three Worlds of Relief: Race, Immigration, and the American Welfare State from the Progressive Era to the New Deal*. Princeton, N.J.: Princeton University Press, 2012.

Fredrickson, George M. *Racism: A Short History*. Princeton, N.J.: Princeton University Press, 2002.

Friendly, Fred W., director. *Harvest of Shame*. CBS Reports. November 24, 1960.

Furuseth, Owen J., and Heather A. Smith. "From Winn-Dixie to Tiendas: The Remaking of the New South." In *Latinos in the New South: Transformations of Place*, edited by Heather A. Smith and Owen J. Furuseth, 1–18. Burlington, Vt.: Ashgate, 2006.

Gaillard, Frye. *The Dream Long Deferred*. Chapel Hill: University of North Carolina Press, 1988.

Galarza, Ernesto. *Merchants of Labor: The Mexican Bracero Story*. Charlotte: McNally & Loftin, 1964.

Gamboa, Erasmo. *Mexican Labor and World War II: Braceros in the Pacific Northwest, 1942–1947*. Austin: University of Texas Press, 1990.

Gamio, Manuel. *Mexican Immigration to the United States: A Study of Human Migration and Adjustment*. 1930. Reprint, New York: Dover Publications, 1971.

García, Mario T. *Mexican Americans: Leadership, Ideology, and Identity, 1930–1960*. New Haven, Conn.: Yale University Press, 1989.

García, Mario T., and Sal Castro. *Blowout! Sal Castro and the Chicano Struggle for Educational Justice*. Chapel Hill: University of North Carolina Press, 2011.

García, Matt. *A World of Its Own: Race, Labor, and Citrus in the Making of Greater Los Angeles, 1900–1970*. Chapel Hill: University of North Carolina Press, 2001.

García Canclini, Néstor. *Consumers and Citizens: Globalization and Multicultural Conflicts*. Minneapolis: University of Minnesota Press, 2001.

García y Griego, Manuel T. *The Importation of Mexican Contract Laborers to the United States, 1942–1964: Antecedents, Operation, and Legacy*. La Jolla, Calif.: Program in U.S.-Mexican Studies, University of California, San Diego, 1981.

Gardner, Martha Mabie. *The Qualities of a Citizen: Women, Immigration, and Citizenship, 1870–1965*. Princeton, N.J.: Princeton University Press, 2005.

Gellman, Irwin. *Good Neighbor Diplomacy: U.S. Policies in Latin America, 1933–1945.* Baltimore: Johns Hopkins University Press, 1979.

Germany, Kent B. "Poverty Wars in the Louisiana Delta: White Resistance, Black Power, and the Poorest Place in America." In *The War on Poverty: A New Grassroots History, 1964–1980*, edited by Annelise Orleck and Lisa Gayle Hazirjian, 231–55. Athens: University of Georgia Press, 2011.

Giagnoni, Silvia. *Fields of Resistance: The Struggle of Florida's Farmworkers for Justice.* Chicago: Haymarket Books, 2011.

Gill, Hannah E. *The Latino Migration Experience in North Carolina: New Roots in the Old North State.* Chapel Hill: University of North Carolina Press, 2010.

Gilmore, Glenda Elizabeth. *Gender and Jim Crow: Women and the Politics of White Supremacy in North Carolina, 1896–1920.* Chapel Hill: University of North Carolina Press, 1996.

Goldring, Luin. "The Mexican State and Transmigrant Organizations: Negotiating the Boundaries of Membership and Participation in the Mexican Nation." *Latin American Research Review* 37, no. 3 (2002): 55–99.

Gomez, Rocio. "*Braceros* in the Arkansas Delta, 1943–1964." *Ozark Historical Review* 39 (Spring 2010): 1–18.

Gonzales, Roberto G. "Left Out but Not Shut Down: Political Activism and the Undocumented Student Movement." *Northwestern Journal of Law and Social Policy* 3 (Spring 2008): 219–39.

González, Anita. *Jarocho's Soul: Cultural Identity and Afro-Mexican Dance.* Lanham, Md.: University Press of America, 2004.

González, Gilbert G. *Mexican Consuls and Labor Organizing: Imperial Politics in the American Southwest.* Austin: University of Texas Press, 1999.

Gonzalez, Melody. "Awakening the Consciousness of the Labor Movement: The Case of the Coalition of Immokalee Workers." Undergraduate thesis, University of Notre Dame, 2005.

González Chávez, Humberto, and Alejandro Macías. "Vulnerabilidad alimentaria y política agroalimentaria en México." *Desacatos*, no. 25 (September–December 2007): 47–78.

Gordon, Linda. *The Great Arizona Orphan Abduction.* Cambridge, Mass.: Harvard University Press, 1999.

Gray, LaGuana. *We Just Keep Running the Line: Black Southern Women and the Poultry Processing Industry.* Baton Rouge: Louisiana State University Press, 2014.

Green, Laurie B. *Battling the Plantation Mentality: Memphis and the Black Freedom Struggle.* Chapel Hill: University of North Carolina Press, 2007.

Greene, Allison. "Cablevision(nation) in Rural Yucatán: Performing Modernity and Mexicanidad in the Early 1990s." In *Fragments of a Golden Age: The Politics of Culture in Mexico since 1940*, edited by Gilbert M. Joseph, Anne Rubenstein, and Eric Zolov, 415–51. Durham, N.C.: Duke University Press, 2001.

Griffith, David. "Hay Trabajo: Poultry Processing, Rural Industrialization, and the Latinization of Low-Wage Labor." In *Any Way You Cut It: Meat Processing and*

Small-Town America, edited by Donald D. Stull, Michael J. Broadway, and David Griffith, 129–52. Lawrence: University Press of Kansas, 1995.

Grossman, James R. *Land of Hope: Chicago, Black Southerners, and the Great Migration*. Chicago: University of Chicago Press, 1989.

Grove, Wayne Allison. "The Economics of Cotton Harvest Mechanization in the United States, 1920–1970." Ph.D. diss., University of Illinois, 2000.

Gruesz, Kirsten Silva. "Delta *Desterrados*: Antebellum New Orleans and New World Print Culture." In *Look Away! The U.S. South in New World Studies*, edited by Jon Smith and Deborah N. Cohn, 52–79. Durham, N.C.: Duke University Press, 2004.

Guerrero, Perla M. "Impacting Arkansas: Vietnamese and Cuban Refugees and Latina/o Immigrants, 1975–2005." Ph.D. diss., University of Southern California, 2010.

Guglielmo, Thomas A. "Fighting for Caucasian Rights: Mexicans, Mexican Americans, and the Transnational Struggle for Civil Rights in World War II Texas." *Journal of American History* 94, no. 4 (March 2006): 1212–37.

———. *White on Arrival: Italians, Race, Color, and Power in Chicago, 1890–1945*. New York: Oxford University Press, 2003.

Gutiérrez, David. *Walls and Mirrors: Mexican Americans, Mexican Immigrants, and the Politics of Ethnicity*. Berkeley: University of California Press, 1995.

Hahamovitch, Cindy. "Creating Perfect Immigrants: Guestworkers of the World in Historical Perspective." *Labor History* 44, no. 1 (2003): 69–94.

———. *The Fruits of Their Labor: Atlantic Coast Farmworkers and the Making of Migrant Poverty, 1870–1945*. Chapel Hill: University of North Carolina Press, 1997.

———. *No Man's Land: Jamaican Guestworkers in America and the Global History of Deportable Labor*. Kindle ed. Princeton, N.J.: Princeton University Press, 2011.

Hale, Grace Elizabeth. *Making Whiteness: The Culture of Segregation in the South, 1890–1940*. New York: Pantheon Books, 1998.

Hallett, Miranda Cady. "'Better than White Trash': Work Ethic, *Latinidad* and Whiteness in Rural Arkansas." *Latino Studies* 10, no. 1–2 (Spring/Summer 2012): 81–106.

Hämäläinen, Pekka, and Samuel Truett. "On Borderlands." *Journal of American History* 98, no. 2 (2011): 338–61.

Heck, Robert W., and Otis B. Wheeler. *Religious Architecture in Louisiana*. Baton Rouge: Louisiana State University Press, 1995.

Heppel, Monica L. "Harvesting the Crops of Others: Migrant Farm Labor on the Eastern Shore of Virginia." Ph.D. diss., American University, 1982.

Hernández, Kelly Lytle. *Migra! A History of the U.S. Border Patrol*. Berkeley: University of California Press, 2010.

Hernández-León, Rubén. *Metropolitan Migrants: The Migration of Urban Mexicans to the United States*. Berkeley: University of California Press, 2008.

Hernández-León, Rubén, and Víctor Zúñiga. "Appalachia Meets Aztlán: Mexican Immigration and Intergroup Relations in Dalton, Georgia." In *New Destinations:*

Mexican Immigration in the United States, edited by Víctor Zúñiga and Rubén Hernández-León, 244–74. New York: Russell Sage Foundation, 2005.

Hewitt, Nancy A. *Southern Discomfort: Women's Activism in Tampa, Florida, 1880s–1920s*. Urbana: University of Illinois Press, 2001.

Higham, John. *Strangers in the Land: Patterns of American Nativism, 1860–1925*. New York: Atheneum, 1963.

Hirsch, Arnold R. "Simply a Matter of Black and White: The Transformation of Race and Politics in Twentieth-Century New Orleans." In *Creole New Orleans: Race and Americanization*, edited by Arnold R. Hirsch and Joseph Lodgson, 262–319. Baton Rouge: Louisiana State University Press, 1992.

Hirsch, Arnold R., and Joseph Lodgson, eds. *Creole New Orleans: Race and Americanization*. Baton Rouge: Louisiana State University Press, 1992.

Hirsch, Jennifer S. *A Courtship after Marriage: Sexuality and Love in Mexican Transnational Families*. Berkeley: University of California Press, 2003.

Hirsch, Marianne. *Family Frames: Photography, Narrative, and Postmemory*. Cambridge, Mass.: Harvard University Press, 1997.

———, ed. *The Familial Gaze*. Hanover, N.H.: University Press of New England, 1999.

Hirsch, Marianne, and Leo Spitzer. *Ghosts of Home: The Afterlife of Czernowitz in Jewish Memory*. Berkeley: University of California Press, 2010.

Hoffman, Abraham. *Unwanted Mexican Americans in the Great Depression: Repatriation Pressures, 1929–1939*. Tucson: University of Arizona Press, 1974.

Hoffnung-Garskof, Jesse. *A Tale of Two Cities: Santo Domingo and New York after 1950*. Princeton, N.J.: Princeton University Press, 2008.

Holland, Patricia. "Introduction: History, Memory, and the Family Album." In *Family Snaps: The Meanings of Domestic Photography*, edited by Jo Spence and Patricia Holland, 1–14. London: Virago, 1991.

Holley, Donald. *The Second Great Emancipation: The Mechanical Cotton Picker, Black Migration, and How They Shaped the Modern South*. Fayetteville: University of Arkansas Press, 2000.

Holt, Thomas C. "Marking: Race, Race-Making, and the Writing of History." *American Historical Review* 100, no. 1 (February 1995): 1–20.

———. *The Problem of Race in the Twenty-First Century*. Cambridge, Mass.: Harvard University Press, 2000.

Hondagneu-Sotelo, Pierrette. *Doméstica: Immigrant Workers Cleaning and Caring in the Shadows of Affluence*. Berkeley: University of California Press, 2001.

———. *Gendered Transitions: Mexican Experiences of Immigration*. Berkeley: University of California Press, 1994.

Horne, Gerald. *Black and Brown: African Americans and the Mexican Revolution, 1910–1920*. New York: New York University Press, 2005.

HoSang, Daniel. *Racial Propositions: Ballot Initiatives and the Making of Postwar California*. Berkeley: University of California Press, 2010.

Hsu, Madeline Yuan-yin. *Dreaming of Gold, Dreaming of Home: Transnationalism and Migration between the United States and South China, 1882–1943*. Stanford, Calif.: Stanford University Press, 2000.

Huber, Leonard V. *Our Lady of Guadalupe Church, New Orleans, Louisiana*. Hackensack, N.J.: Custombook, 1976.

Hudson, Sara. "Crossing Stories: Circulating Citizenships in an Americas du Golfe." Ph.D. diss., Yale University, 2011.

Hunt, William C. *Fourteenth Census of the United States Taken in the Year 1920*. Vol. 3. Washington, D.C.: Government Printing Office, 1922.

Hurder, Wayne. "The Almost Definitive History of Licensing Undocumented Aliens in North Carolina." 2013. Unpublished manuscript in author's possession.

Innis-Jiménez, Michael. *Steel Barrio: The Great Mexican Migration to South Chicago, 1915–1940*. New York: New York University Press, 2013.

Jackson, Regine O. "The Shifting Nature of Racism." In *Being Brown in Dixie: Race, Ethnicity, and Latino Immigration in the New South*, edited by Cameron D. Lippard and Charles A. Gallagher, 25–51. Boulder, Colo.: FirstForumPress, 2011.

Jacobson, Matthew Frye. *Whiteness of a Different Color: European Immigrants and the Alchemy of Race*. Cambridge, Mass.: Harvard University Press, 1999.

Jacobson, Robin Dale. *The New Nativism: Proposition 187 and the Debate over Immigration*. Minneapolis: University of Minnesota Press, 2008.

Jiménez, Valeria P. "Cultural Diplomacy on an International Stage: The Eighth Cavalry Mexican Band at the 1884 World's Fair and the Life of Florencio Ramos." Paper presented at the annual meeting of the Southern Historical Association, Atlanta, 2014.

Johnson, Benjamin Heber. "The Cosmic Race in Texas: Racial Fusion, White Supremacy, and Civil Rights Politics." *Journal of American History* 98, no. 2 (2011): 404–19.

———. *Revolution in Texas: How a Forgotten Rebellion and Its Bloody Suppression Turned Mexicans into Americans*. New Haven, Conn.: Yale University Press, 2003.

Johnson, Walter. *River of Dark Dreams: Slavery and Empire in the Cotton Kingdom*. Cambridge, Mass.: Harvard University Press, 2013.

Jones, Jennifer A. "Blacks May Be Second Class, but They Can't Make Them Leave: Mexican Racial Formation and Immigrant Status in Winston-Salem." *Latino Studies* 10, no. 1–2 (2012): 60–80.

Joseph, Gilbert M. *Revolution from Without: Yucatan, Mexico, and the United States, 1880–1924*. Cambridge: Cambridge University Press, 1982.

Joseph, Gilbert M., Anne Rubenstein, and Eric Zolov. "Assembling the Fragments: Writing a Cultural History of Mexico since 1940." In *Fragments of a Golden Age: The Politics of Culture in Mexico since 1940*, edited by Gilbert M. Joseph, Anne Rubenstein, and Eric Zolov, 3–22. Durham, N.C.: Duke University Press, 2001.

Jung, Moon-Ho. *Coolies and Cane: Race, Labor, and Sugar in the Age of Emancipation*. Baltimore: Johns Hopkins University Press, 2006.

Kazal, Russell A. "Revisiting Assimilation: The Rise, Fall, and Reappraisal of a Concept in American Ethnic History." *American Historical Review* 100, no. 2 (April 1995): 437–71.

Keane, Webb. *Christian Moderns: Freedom and Fetish in the Mission Encounter.* Berkeley: University of California Press, 2007.

Keltner, Robert W. "Tar Paper Shacks in Arcadia: Housing for Ethnic Minority Groups in the Company Town of Bauxite, Arkansas." *Arkansas Historical Quarterly* 60, no. 4 (2001): 341–59.

Kester, Howard. *Revolt among the Sharecroppers.* New York: Covici Friede, 1936.

Kirby, Jack Temple. *Rural Worlds Lost: The American South, 1920–1960.* Baton Rouge: Louisiana State University Press, 1987.

Klein, Jennifer. *For All These Rights: Business, Labor, and the Shaping of America's Public-Private Welfare State.* Princeton, N.J.: Princeton University Press, 2003.

Knight, Alan. *Porfirians, Liberals and Peasants.* Vol. 1 of *The Mexican Revolution.* Cambridge: Cambridge University Press, 1986.

———. "Racism, Revolution, and *Indigenismo*: Mexico, 1910–1940." In *The Idea of Race in Latin America, 1870–1940*, edited by Richard Graham, 71–113. Austin: University of Texas Press, 1990.

Koth, Karl B. *Waking the Dictator: Veracruz, the Struggle for Federalism and the Mexican Revolution, 1870–1927.* Calgary, Alberta, Canada: University of Calgary Press, 2002.

Krochmal, Max. "Labor, Civil Rights, and the Struggle for Democracy in Texas, 1935–1965." Ph.D. diss., Duke University, 2011.

Kruse, Kevin M. *White Flight: Atlanta and the Making of Modern Conservatism.* Princeton, N.J.: Princeton University Press, 2005.

Kunimoto, Namiko. "Intimate Archives: Japanese-Canadian Family Photography, 1939–1949." *Art History* 27, no. 1 (February 2004): 129–55.

Langford, Martha. "Speaking the Album: An Application of the Oral-Photography Framework." In *Locating Memory: Photographic Acts*, edited by Annette Kuhn and Kirsten Emiko McAllister, 223–46. New York: Berghan Books, 2006.

Lassiter, Matthew D. "Big Government and Family Values: Political Culture in the Metropolitan Sunbelt." In *Sunbelt Rising: The Politics of Place, Space, and Region*, edited by Michelle M. Nickerson and Darren Dochuk, 82–109. Philadelphia: University of Pennsylvania Press, 2011.

———. "Political History beyond the Red-Blue Divide." *Journal of American History* 98, no. 3 (December 2011): 760–64.

———. *The Silent Majority: Suburban Politics in the Sunbelt South.* Princeton, N.J.: Princeton University Press, 2006.

Lassiter, Matthew D., and Joseph Crespino, eds. *The Myth of Southern Exceptionalism.* Oxford: Oxford University Press, 2010.

Lee, Anthony W. *A Shoemaker's Story: Being Chiefly about French Canadian Immigrants, Enterprising Photographers, Rascal Yankees, and Chinese Cobblers in a Nineteenth Century Town.* Princeton, N.J.: Princeton University Press, 2008.

Lee, Erika. *At America's Gates: Chinese Immigration during the Exclusion Era, 1882–1943*. Chapel Hill: University of North Carolina Press, 2003.

Lemann, Nicholas. *The Promised Land: The Great Black Migration and How It Changed America*. New York: Vintage Books, 1992.

Levine, Robert M. *Images of History: Nineteenth and Early Twentieth Century Latin American Photographs as Documents*. Durham, N.C.: Duke University Press, 1989.

Lewis, George. *Massive Resistance: The White Response to the Civil Rights Movement*. London: Hodder Arnold, 2006.

Lichterman, Paul. *Elusive Togetherness: Church Groups Trying to Bridge America's Divisions*. Princeton, N.J.: Princeton University Press, 2005.

Light, Ivan. *Deflecting Immigration: Networks, Markets, and Regulation in Los Angeles*. New York: Russell Sage Foundation, 2006.

Lima, Lázaro. "Louisiana." In *Latino America: A State-by-State Encyclopedia*, edited by Mark Overmyer-Velázquez, 347–61. Westport, Conn.: Greenwood Press, 2008.

Lippard, Cameron D., and Charles A. Gallagher. "Introduction: Immigration, the New South, and the Color of Backlash." In *Being Brown in Dixie: Race, Ethnicity, and Latino Immigration in the New South*, edited by Cameron D. Lippard and Charles A. Gallagher, 1–24. Boulder, Colo.: FirstForumPress, 2011.

Lodgson, Joseph, and Caryn Cossé Bell. "The Americanization of Black New Orleans, 1850–1900." In *Creole New Orleans: Race and Americanization*, edited by Arnold R. Hirsch and Joseph Lodgson, 201–61. Baton Rouge: Louisiana State University Press, 1992.

Loewen, James W. *The Mississippi Chinese: Between Black and White*. Cambridge, Mass.: Harvard University Press, 1971.

López, Rick. "The Noche Mexicana and the Exhibition of Popular Arts: Two Ways of Exalting Indianness." In *The Eagle and the Virgin: Nation and Cultural Revolution in Mexico, 1920–1940*, edited by Mary K. Vaughan and Stephen E. Lewis, 23–42. Durham, N.C.: Duke University Press, 2006.

López-Sanders, Laura. "Bible Belt Immigrants: Latino Religious Incorporation in New Immigrant Destinations." *Latino Studies* 10, no. 1–2 (2012): 128–54.

Lovett, Laura. "'African and Cherokee by Choice': Race and Resistance under Legalized Segregation." In *Confounding the Color Line: The Indian-Black Experience in North America*, edited by James Brooks, 192–222. Lincoln: University of Nebraska Press, 2002.

Lowery, Malinda Maynor. *Lumbee Indians in the Jim Crow South: Race, Identity, and the Making of a Nation*. Chapel Hill: University of North Carolina Press, 2010.

Loza, Mireya. "Braceros on the Boundaries: Activism, Race, Masculinity, and the Legacies of the Bracero Program." Ph.D. diss., Brown University, 2011.

Lucas, María Elena, and Fran Leeper Buss. *Forged under the Sun: The Life of María Elena Lucas*. Ann Arbor: University of Michigan Press, 1993.

Luna, Guadalupe T., and Fran Ansley. "Global Migrants and Access to Local Housing: Anti-Immigrant Backlash Hits Home." In *Global Connections & Local Receptions: New Latino Immigration to the Southeastern United States*, edited by

Fran Ansley and Jon Shefner, 155–93. Knoxville: University of Tennessee Press, 2009.

MacLean, Nancy. *Behind the Mask of Chivalry: The Making of the Second Ku Klux Klan*. New York: Oxford University Press, 1994.

Mahler, Sarah, and Patricia Pessar. "Gendered Geographies of Power: Analyzing Gender across Transnational Spaces." *Identities: Global Studies in Culture and Power* 7, no. 4 (January 2001): 441–59.

Mantler, Gordon Keith. *Power to the Poor: Black-Brown Coalition and the Fight for Economic Justice, 1960–1974*. Chapel Hill: University of North Carolina Press, 2013.

Marcelli, Enrico A., and Wayne A. Cornelius. "The Changing Profile of Mexican Migrants to the United States: New Evidence from California and Mexico." *Latin American Research Review* 36, no. 3 (2001): 105–31.

Marquardt, Marie Friedmann. "From Shame to Confidence: Gender, Religious Conversion, and Civic Engagement of Mexicans in the U.S. South." *Latin American Perspectives* 32, no. 1 (2005): 27–56.

Márquez, Cecilia. "Chicanos in SNCC: Black and Latino Alliances during the Civil Rights Movement." Paper presented at the annual meeting of the Southern Historical Association, Mobile, Ala., 2012.

Marrow, Helen. "Hispanic Immigration, Black Population Size, and Intergroup Relations in the Rural and Small-Town South." In *New Faces in New Places: The Changing Geography of American Immigration*, edited by Douglas Massey, 211–48. New York: Russell Sage Foundation, 2008.

———. *New Destination Dreaming: Immigration, Race, and Legal Status in the Rural American South*. Stanford, Calif.: Stanford University Press, 2011.

Martínez, Anne M. *Catholic Borderlands: Mapping Catholicism onto American Empire, 1905–1935*. Lincoln: University of Nebraska Press, 2014.

Martínez, María Elena. *Genealogical Fictions: Limpieza de Sangre, Religion, and Gender in Colonial Mexico*. Stanford, Calif.: Stanford University Press, 2008.

Massey, Douglas, and Jorge Durand, eds. *Crossing the Border: Research from the Mexican Migration Project*. New York: Russell Sage Foundation, 2004.

Massey, Douglas, Jorge Durand, and Nolan J. Malone. *Beyond Smoke and Mirrors: Mexican Immigration in an Era of Economic Integration*. New York: Russell Sage Foundation, 2002.

Massey, Douglas S., Rafael Alarcón, Jorge Durand, and Humberto González. *Return to Aztlan: The Social Process of International Migration from Western Mexico*. Berkeley: University of California Press, 1990.

McClain, Paula D., Niambi M. Carter, Victoria M. DeFrancesco Soto, Monique L. Lyle, Jeffrey D. Grynaviski, Shayla C. Nunnally, Thomas C. Scotto, J. Alan Kendrick, Gerald F. Lackey, and Kendra Davenport Cotton. "Racial Distancing in a Southern City: Latino Immigrants' Views of Black Americans." *Journal of Politics* 68, no. 3 (2006): 571–84.

McClain, Paula D., Monique L. Lyle, Niambi M. Carter, Victoria M. DeFrancesco Soto, Gerald F. Lackey, Kendra Davenport Cotton, Shayla C. Nunnally,

Thomas J. Scotto, Jeffrey D. Grynaviski, and J. Alan Kendrick. "Black Americans and Latino Immigrants in a Southern City: Friendly Neighbors or Economic Competitors?" *DuBois Review* 4, no. 1 (2007): 97–117.

McWilliams, Carey. *Ill Fares the Land: Migrants and Migratory Labor in the United States*. Boston: Little, Brown, 1942.

Milani, Ernesto R. "Peonage at Sunnyside and the Reaction of the Italian Government." *Arkansas Historical Quarterly* 50, no. 1 (Spring 1991): 30–39.

Mohl, Raymond A. "Globalization and Latin American Immigration in Alabama." In *Latino Immigrants and the Transformation of the U.S. South*, edited by Mary E. Odem and Elaine Lacy, 51–69. Athens: University of Georgia Press, 2009.

———. "Globalization, Latinization, and the Nuevo New South." *Journal of American Ethnic History* 22, no. 4 (Summer 2003): 31–66.

Monroy, Douglas. *Rebirth: Mexican Los Angeles from the Great Migration to the Great Depression*. Berkeley: University of California Press, 1999.

Montejano, David. *Anglos and Mexicans in the Making of Texas, 1836–1986*. Austin: University of Texas Press, 1987.

———, ed. *Chicano Politics and Society in the Late 20th Century*. Austin: University of Texas Press, 1999.

Moreton, Bethany. *To Serve God and Wal-Mart: The Making of Christian Free Enterprise*. Cambridge, Mass.: Harvard University Press, 2009.

Mraz, John. "Technologies of Seeing: Photography and Culture." In *Technology and Culture in Twentieth-Century Mexico*, edited by Araceli Tinajero and J. Brian Freeman, 73–89. Tuscaloosa: University of Alabama Press, 2013.

Namorato, Michael V. *The Catholic Church in Mississippi, 1911–1984: A History*. Westport, Conn.: Greenwood Press, 1998.

Natanson, Nicholas. *The Black Image in the New Deal: The Politics of FSA Photography*. Knoxville: University of Tennessee Press, 1992.

Nelson, Claire Nee. "Redeeming Whiteness in New Orleans: Politics and Race in the 1891 Lynchings." Paper presented at the Southern Historical Association conference, Atlanta, 2005.

Nelson, Lawrence J. "Welfare Capitalism on a Mississippi Plantation in the Great Depression." *Journal of Southern History* 50, no. 2 (May 1984): 225–50.

Ngai, Mae M. *Impossible Subjects: Illegal Aliens and the Making of Modern America*. Princeton, N.J.: Princeton University Press, 2004.

Odem, Mary E. "Latin American Immigration and the New Multiethnic South." In *The Myth of Southern Exceptionalism*, edited by Matthew D. Lassiter and Joseph Crespino, 234–62. Oxford: Oxford University Press, 2010.

———. "Latino Immigrants and the Politics of Space in Atlanta." In *Latino Immigrants and the Transformation of the U.S. South*, edited by Mary E. Odem and Elaine Lacy, 112–25. Athens: University of Georgia Press, 2009.

———. "Our Lady of Guadalupe in the New South: Latino Immigrants and the Politics of Integration in the Catholic Church." *Journal of American Ethnic History* 24, no. 1 (2004): 26–57.

———. "Unsettled in the Suburbs: Latino Immigration and Ethnic Diversity in Metro Atlanta." In *Twenty-First Century Gateways: Immigrant Incorporation in Suburban America*, edited by Audrey Singer, Susan W. Hardwick, and Carolina B. Brettell, 105–36. Washington, D.C.: Brookings Institution Press, 2008.

Odem, Mary E., and Elaine Lacy. "Introduction." In *Latino Immigrants and the Transformation of the U.S. South*, edited by Mary E. Odem and Elaine Lacy, ix–xvii. Athens: University of Georgia Press, 2009.

Olsson, Tore C. "Agrarian Crossings: The American South, Mexico, and the Twentieth-Century Remaking of the Rural World." Ph.D. diss., University of Georgia, 2013.

———. "Peeling Back the Layers: Vidalia Onions and the Making of a Global Agribusiness." *Enterprise and Society* 13, no. 4 (2012): 832–61.

Omi, Michael, and Howard Winant. *Racial Formation in the United States: From the 1960s to the 1990s*. 2nd ed. New York: Routledge, 1994.

O'Neil, Kevin Singleton. "Challenging Change: Local Policies and the New Geography of American Immigration." Ph.D. diss., Princeton University, 2011.

Oppenheimer, Andres. *Bordering on Chaos: Mexico's Roller-Coaster Journey toward Prosperity*. 1996. Reprint, Boston: Back Bay, 1998.

Orenstein, Dara. "Void for Vagueness: Mexicans and the Collapse of Miscegenation Law in California." *Pacific Historical Review* 74, no. 3 (August 2005): 367–407.

Otero, Lydia R. "Refusing to Be 'Undocumented': Chicana/os in Tucson during the Depression Years." In *Picturing Arizona: The Photographic Record of the 1930s*, edited by Katherine G. Morrissey and Kirsten Jensen, 43–59. Tucson: University of Arizona Press, 2005.

O'Toole, Gavin. "A New Nationalism for a New Era: The Political Ideology of Mexican Neoliberalism." *Bulletin of Latin American Research* 22, no. 3 (July 2003): 269–90.

Painter, Norman Wellington. "The Assimilation of Latin Americans in New Orleans, Louisiana." M.A. thesis, Tulane University, 1949.

Park, Lisa Sun-Hee. *Entitled to Nothing: The Struggle for Immigrant Health Care in the Age of Welfare Reform*. New York: New York University Press, 2011.

Payne, Charles M. *I've Got the Light of Freedom: The Organizing Tradition and the Mississippi Freedom Struggle*. Berkeley: University of California Press, 1995.

Peacock, James L. *Grounded Globalism: How the U.S. South Embraces the World*. Athens: University of Georgia Press, 2007.

Perales, Monica. *Smeltertown: Making and Remembering a Southwest Border Community*. Chapel Hill: University of North Carolina Press, 2010.

Phillips-Fein, Kim. "Conservatism: A State of the Field." *Journal of American History* 98, no. 3 (December 2011): 723–43.

Pitti, Stephen J. *The Devil in Silicon Valley: Northern California, Race, and Mexican Americans*. Princeton, N.J.: Princeton University Press, 2003.

Prescott, Laurence E. "Journeying through Jim Crow: Spanish American Travelers in the United States during the Age of Segregation." *Latin American Research Review* 42, no. 1 (February 2007): 3–28.

Price, Marie, and Audrey Singer. "Edge Gateways: Immigrants, Suburbs, and the Politics of Reception in Metropolitan Washington." In *Twenty-First Century Gateways: Immigrant Incorporation in Suburban America*, edited by Audrey Singer, Susan W. Hardwick, and Carolina B. Brettell, 137–70. Washington, D.C.: Brookings Institution Press, 2008.

Reagan, Ronald. "Radio Address to the Nation on Welfare Reform." American Presidency Project, February 15, 1986, http://www.presidency.ucsb.edu/ws/?pid=36875.

Rénique, Gerardo. "Race, Region, and Nation: Sonora's Anti-Chinese Racism and Mexico's Postrevolutionary Nationalism, 1920s–1930s." In *Race and Nation in Modern Latin America*, edited by Nancy P. Appelbaum, Anne S. Macpherson, and Karin Alejandra Rosemblatt, 211–36. Chapel Hill: University of North Carolina Press, 2003.

Riley, Nano. *Florida's Farmworkers in the Twenty-First Century*. Gainesville: University Press of Florida, 2002.

Rivas-Rodriguez, Maggie. "Ignacio E. Lozano: The Mexican Exile Publisher Who Conquered San Antonio and Los Angeles." *American Journalism* 21, no. 1 (Winter 2004): 75–89.

Rivera, Tomás. *Y no se le tragó la tierra*. Houston, Tex.: Arte Público Press, 1987.

Rodriguez, Marc S. *Repositioning North American Migration History: New Directions in Modern Continental Migration, Citizenship, and Community*. Rochester, N.Y.: University of Rochester Press, 2005.

———. *The Tejano Diaspora: Mexican Americanism and Ethnic Politics in Texas and Wisconsin*. Chapel Hill: University of North Carolina Press, 2011.

Rodríguez, Nestor. "New Southern Neighbors: Latino Immigration and Prospects for Intergroup Relations between African-Americans and Latinos in the South." *Latino Studies* 10, no. 1–2 (2012): 18–40.

Romo, David Dorado. *Ringside Seat to a Revolution: An Underground Cultural history of El Paso and Juárez, 1893–1923*. El Paso, Tex.: Cinco Puntos Press, 2005.

Rosas, Ana Elizabeth. *Abrazando el Espíritu: Bracero Families Confront the U.S.–Mexico Border*. Kindle ed. Oakland: University of California Press, 2014.

———. "Breaking the Silence: Mexican Children and Women's Confrontation of Bracero Family Separation, 1942–64." *Gender & History* 23, no. 2 (2011): 382–400.

Rose, Gillian. *Doing Family Photography: The Domestic, the Public and the Politics of Sentiment*. Burlington, Vt.: Ashgate, 2010.

Rouse, Roger. "Mexican Migration and the Social Space of Postmodernism." *Diaspora* 1, no. 1 (Spring 1991): 8–23.

Ruíz, Vicki. *Cannery Women, Cannery Lives: Mexican Women, Unionization, and the California Food Processing Industry, 1930–1950*. Albuquerque: University of New Mexico Press, 1987.

Russell, Alene. "State Policies Regarding Undocumented College Students." American Association of State Colleges and Universities, 2011. http://www.nacacnet.org/research/KnowledgeCenter/Documents/UndocumentedCollegeStudents.pdf.

Sabia, Debra D. "The Anti-Immigrant Fervor in Georgia: Return of the Nativist or Just Politics as Usual?" *Politics & Policy* 38, no. 1 (2010): 53–80.

———. "Challenges of Solidarity and Lessons of Community Empowerment: The Struggle of Migrant Farm Workers in Rural South Georgia." *SECOLAS Annals: Journal of the Southeastern Council on Latin American Studies* 30 (1999): 95–109.

Sánchez, George J. *Becoming Mexican American: Ethnicity, Culture, and Identity in Chicano Los Angeles, 1900–1945.* New York: Oxford University Press, 1993.

———. "Latinos, the American South, and the Future of U.S. Race Relations." *Southern Spaces*, April 26, 2007.

Sandoval, Carlos, and Catherine Tambini, directors. *Farmingville*. Camino Bluff Productions, 2004.

San Miguel, Guadalupe. *Let All of Them Take Heed: Mexican Americans and the Quest for Educational Equality.* Austin: University of Texas Press, 1987.

Sassen, Saskia. *The Global City: New York, London, Tokyo.* Princeton, N.J.: Princeton University Press, 1991.

Schmidt Camacho, Alicia R. *Migrant Imaginaries: Latino Cultural Politics in the U.S.–Mexico Borderlands.* New York: New York University Press, 2008.

Sellers, Sean. "'Del pueblo, para el pueblo': The Coalition of Immokalee Workers and the Fight for Fair Food." M.A. thesis, University of Texas at Austin, 2009.

Shaw, Nate. *All God's Dangers: The Life of Nate Shaw.* 1974. Reprint, New York: Vintage Books, 1989.

Shaw, Randy. *Beyond the Fields: Cesar Chavez, the UFW, and the Struggle for Justice in the 21st Century.* Berkeley: University of California Press, 2008.

Sifuentez, Mario. "By Forests or by Fields: Organizing Immigrant Labor in the Pacific Northwest, 1940–1990." Ph.D. diss., Brown University, 2010.

Singer, Audrey, Susan W. Hardwick, and Carolina B. Brettell, eds. *Twenty-First Century Gateways: Immigrant Incorporation in Suburban America.* Washington, D.C.: Brookings Institution Press, 2008.

Smith, Barbara Ellen. "Market Rivals or Class Allies? Relations between African American and Latino Immigrant Workers in Memphis." In *Global Connections & Local Receptions: New Latino Immigration to the Southeastern United States*, edited by Fran Ansley and Jon Shefner, 299–317. Knoxville: University of Tennessee Press, 2009.

Smith, Heather A., and Owen J. Furuseth. "Housing, Hispanics, and Transitioning Geographies in Charlotte, North Carolina." *Southeastern Geographer* 44, no. 2 (2004): 216–35.

———. "Localized Immigration Policy: The View from a New Immigrant Gateway (Charlotte, North Carolina)." Paper presented at the State and Local Immigration Policy in the U.S. Conference, San Diego, May 8, 2008.

———. "Making Real the Mythical Latino Community in Charlotte, North Carolina." In *Latinos in the New South: Transformations of Place*, edited by Heather A. Smith and Owen J. Furuseth, 191–216. Burlington, Vt.: Ashgate, 2006.

———. "The 'Nuevo South': Latino Place Making and Community Building in the Middle-Ring Suburbs of Charlotte." In *Twenty-First Century Gateways: Immigrant Incorporation in Suburban America*, edited by Audrey Singer, Susan W. Hardwick, and Carolina B. Brettell, 281–307. Washington, D.C.: Brookings Institution Press, 2008.

Smith, Heather A., and William Graves, eds. *Charlotte, N.C.: The Global Evolution of a New South City*. Athens: University of Georgia Press, 2012.

Smith, Michael P., and Luis Guarnizo, eds. *Transnationalism from Below*. New Brunswick, N.J.: Transaction Publishers, 1998.

Smith, Robert C. *Mexican New York: Transnational Lives of New Immigrants*. Berkeley: University of California Press, 2006.

Smith, Shawn Michelle. *American Archives: Gender, Race, and Class in Visual Culture*. Princeton, N.J.: Princeton University Press, 1999.

Spence, Jo, and Patricia Holland, eds. *Family Snaps: The Meanings of Domestic Photography*. London: Virago, 1991.

Spitzer, Leo. "The Album and the Crossing." In *The Familial Gaze*, edited by Marianne Hirsch, 208–20. Hanover, N.H.: University Press of New England, 1999.

———. *Lives in Between: The Experience of Marginality in a Century of Assimilation*. New York: Hill & Wang, 1999.

Stanley, Jo. "'Well, Who'd Want an Old Picture of Me at Work?'" In *Family Snaps: The Meanings of Domestic Photography*, edited by Jo Spence and Patricia Holland, 60–71. London: Virago, 1991.

Stern, Alexandra Minna. "Buildings, Boundaries, and Blood: Medicalization and Nation-Building on the U.S.–Mexico Border, 1910–1930." *Hispanic American Historical Review* 79, no. 1 (1999): 41–81.

———. *Eugenic Nation: Faults and Frontiers of Better Breeding in Modern America*. Berkeley: University of California Press, 2005.

Striffler, Steve. *Chicken: The Dangerous Transformation of America's Favorite Food*. New Haven, Conn.: Yale University Press, 2005.

Striffler, Steve, and Julie M. Weise. "Arkansas." In *Latino America: A State-by-State Encyclopedia*, edited by Mark Overmyer-Velázquez, 63–75. Westport, Conn.: Greenwood Press, 2008.

Studstill, John D., and Laura Nieto-Studstill. "Hospitality and Hostility: Latino Immigrants in Southern Georgia." In *Latino Workers in the Contemporary South*, edited by Arthur D. Murphy, Colleen Blanchard, and Jennifer A. Hill. Athens: University of Georgia Press, 2001.

Stuesse, Angela. "Race, Migration, and Labor Control: Neoliberal Challenges to Organizing Mississippi's Poultry Workers." In *Latino Immigrants and the Transformation of the U.S. South*, edited by Elaine Lacy and Mary E. Odem, 91–111. Athens: University of Georgia Press, 2009.

Stuesse, Angela, and Laura E. Helton. "Low-Wage Legacies, Race, and the Golden Chicken in Mississippi: Where Contemporary Immigration Meets African American Labor History." *Southern Spaces*, December 31, 2013, http://southernspaces.org/2013/low-wage-legacies-race-and-golden-chicken-mississippi.

Sullivan, Patricia. *Days of Hope: Race and Democracy in the New Deal Era*. Chapel Hill: University of North Carolina Press, 1996.

Tarasawa, Beth. "New Patterns of Segregation: Latino and African American Students in Metro Atlanta High Schools." *Southern Spaces*, January 19, 2009.

Tenorio Trillo, Mauricio. "The Cosmopolitan Mexican Summer, 1920–1949." *Latin American Research Review* 32, no. 3 (1997): 224–42.

———. *Mexico at the World's Fairs: Crafting a Modern Nation*. Berkeley: University of California Press, 1996.

Texeira, Ruy. "The Next Frontier: A New Study of Exurbia." Washington, D.C.: New Politics Institute, 2006.

Torres, Rebecca, Jeff Popke, and Holly Hapke. "The South's Silent Bargain: Rural Restructuring, Latino Labor and the Ambiguities of Migrant Experience." In *Latinos in the New South: Transformations of Place*, edited by Heather A. Smith and Owen J. Furuseth, 37–68. Burlington, Vt.: Ashgate, 2006.

Torres, Rebecca, Jeff Popke, Holly Hapke, Matilde Elisa Suarez, Heidi Serrano, Brian Chambers, and Paula Andrea Castaño. "Transnational Communities in Eastern North Carolina: Results from a Survey of Latino Families in Greene County." *North Carolina Geographer* 11 (2003): 88–107.

Truesdell, Leon E. *Fifteenth Census of the United States: 1930*. Vol. 3, Part 1, Washington, D.C.: Government Printing Office, 1932.

Tuck, Stephen G. N. *Beyond Atlanta: The Struggle for Racial Equality in Georgia, 1940–1980*. Athens: University of Georgia Press, 2003.

Tutino, John. *From Insurrection to Revolution in Mexico: Social Bases of Agrarian Violence, 1750–1940*. Princeton, N.J.: Princeton University Press, 1986.

U.S. Department of Commerce. *Commercial Traveler's Guide to Latin America, Revised Edition, 1926*. 2nd revised ed. Washington, D.C.: Government Printing Office, 1926.

———. *Commercial Traveler's Guide to Latin America, Revised Edition, 1931*. 4th ed. Washington, D.C.: Government Printing Office, 1931.

Valdés, Dennis Nodín. *Al Norte: Agricultural Workers in the Great Lakes Region, 1917–1970*. Austin: University of Texas Press, 1991.

———. *Barrios Norteños: St. Paul and Midwestern Mexican Communities in the Twentieth Century*. Austin: University of Texas Press, 2000.

Vargas, Zaragosa. *Labor Rights Are Civil Rights: Mexican American Workers in Twentieth-Century America*. Princeton, N.J.: Princeton University Press, 2005.

———. *Proletarians of the North: A History of Mexican Industrial Workers in Detroit and the Midwest, 1917–1933*. 1993. Reprint, Berkeley: University of California Press, 1999.

Vaughan, Mary K. *Cultural Politics in Revolution: Teachers, Peasants, and Schools in Mexico, 1930–1940*. Tucson: University of Arizona Press, 1997.

Vázquez, Josefina Zoraida, and Lorenzo Meyer. *México frente a Estados Unidos: Un Ensayo Histórico, 1776–1980*. Mexico City: Colegio de México, 1982.

Wade, Wyn Craig. *The Fiery Cross: The Ku Klux Klan in America*. New York: Oxford University Press, 1987.

Waits, Hannah. "'They've Come for the True Gospel': Southern Baptists and Latino Immigrants in the American South." Paper presented at the annual meeting of the American Society of Church History, Chicago, 2012.

Waldinger, Roger, and David Fitzgerald. "Transnationalism in Question." *American Journal of Sociology* 109, no. 5 (2004): 1177–95.

Walker, Louise E. *Waking from the Dream: Mexico's Middle Classes after 1968*. Stanford, Calif.: Stanford University Press, 2013.

Watson, Harry L. "Southern History, Southern Future: Some Reflections and a Cautious Forecast." In *The American South in a Global World*, edited by James L. Peacock, Harry L. Watson, and Carrie R. Matthews, 277–88. Chapel Hill: University of North Carolina Press, 2005.

Weeks, Gregory B., John R. Weeks, and Amy J. Weeks. "Latino Immigration in the U.S. South: 'Carolatinos' and Public Policy in Charlotte, North Carolina." *Latino(a) Research Review* 6, no. 1–2 (2006–7): 50–71.

Weise, Julie M. "Mississippi." In *Latino America: A State-by-State Encyclopedia*, edited by Mark Overmyer-Velázquez, 445–61. Westport, Conn.: Greenwood Press, 2008.

Wells, Lyn. "The Cedartown Story: The Ku Klux Klan and Labor in 'the New South.'" *Labor Research Review* 8 (1986): 69–79.

Whayne, Jeannie M. *A New Plantation South: Land, Labor, and Federal Favor in Twentieth-Century Arkansas*. Charlottesville: University Press of Virginia, 1996.

Whitlow, S. A., ed. *Annual of the Arkansas Baptist State Convention*. Little Rock: The Convention, 1944–65.

Winders, Jamie. *Nashville in the New Millennium: Immigrant Settlement, Urban Transformation, and Social Belonging*. New York: Russell Sage Foundation, 2013.

Winders, Jamie, and Barbara Ellen Smith. "New Pasts: Historicizing Immigration, Race, and Place in the South." *Southern Spaces*, November 4, 2010, http://www.southernspaces.org/print/21564.

Woodruff, Nan Elizabeth. *American Congo: The African American Freedom Struggle in the Delta*. 2003. Reprint, Chapel Hill: University of North Carolina Press, 2012.

———. "Mississippi Delta Planters and Debates over Mechanization, Labor, and Civil Rights in the 1940s." *Journal of Southern History* 60, no. 2 (May 1994): 263–84.

Woodward, C. Vann. *The Strange Career of Jim Crow*. 3rd ed. New York: Oxford University Press, 1974.

Zolov, Eric. *Refried Elvis: The Rise of the Mexican Counterculture*. Berkeley: University of California Press, 1999.

Zuñiga, Víctor, and Rubén Hernández-León. "The Dalton Story: Mexican Immigration and Social Transformation in the Carpet Capital of the World." In *Latino Immigrants and the Transformation of the U.S. South*, edited by Mary E. Odem and Elaine Lacy, 34–50. Athens: University of Georgia Press, 2009.

———. "A New Destination for an Old Migration: Origins, Trajectories, and Labor Market Incorporation of Latinos in Dalton, Georgia." In *Latino Workers in the Contemporary South*, edited by Arthur D. Murphy, Colleen Blanchard, and Jennifer A. Hill, 126–35. Athens: University of Georgia Press, 2001.

Index

African American elites, attitude toward Mexican immigrants, 187–88, 205–6, 209
African American middle class: and Mexican agricultural migrant laborers, 124, 131, 149, 171, 275 (n. 178), 275 (n. 179); and African American agricultural migrant laborers, 147, 172; in exurbs, 196
African American press, 62, 209. *See also specific newspapers*
African Americans: violence experienced by, 1, 4, 57, 92, 218; Mexican immigrants' attitudes toward, 1, 61, 68–69, 109–10, 148, 187, 223; southern out-migration in 1910s–60s, 4, 9, 51, 55, 56, 57, 63, 67, 68, 86, 88, 92, 96, 106, 117; emancipation from slavery, 4, 38, 55, 56, 86, 112, 129; sharecropping of, 4, 57, 65, 92, 111; response to Mexican Americans, 6, 8, 13; lynching of, 6, 31, 114; attitudes toward Mexican immigrants, 7, 34–35, 62, 68–69, 108–10, 131–32, 187, 204, 206, 209–10, 211, 215, 224, 264 (n. 170), 283 (n. 31); identities of, 9; in New Orleans, 25, 30; and civil rights movement, 34, 62, 77, 125, 209; and Italians of New Orleans, 38; Mexican policy on, 40; and history of slavery, 44, 51, 92, 156; intermarriage with Mexican immigrants in Mississippi Delta, 68–69; Great Migration period, 86; white elites' attitudes toward, 86, 129, 185, 186–87; citizenship rights of, 97, 105, 111, 112, 116, 218; in urban areas, 112; racial threat of black masculinity, 114; and neoliberal ideology, 122; and Garveyism, 147; and labor unions, 147; and white Evangelical Protestants, 152; stereotypes of, 186; as welfare recipients, 186; in exurban Charlotte, 195–96; homeownership in white neighborhoods, 287 (n. 110)
African American working class: popular understandings of, 4; white elites' attitudes toward, 4, 6, 55–56, 57, 86, 128, 148; in Mississippi Delta, 51, 55, 57, 61, 62, 63, 66, 80; in Arkansas Delta, 86, 88, 89, 90–91, 92, 93, 96, 97, 101, 104, 110–12, 116, 125; organizational efforts of, 88, 92, 98; violence toward, 92; in Georgia, 125, 128, 129, 131–32, 147–48; as migrant laborers, 125, 131–32, 137, 147–48, 172; and labor unions, 147
Afro-Mexicans, 44
Agricultural Adjustment Administration (AAA), 80, 99
Aguilar, Abel, 128, 170
Aguilar, Albert, 128, 170
Aguilar, Gaby, 213
Alabama, 12–13, 210, 267 (n. 10)
Albany, Georgia, 147
Aldama, José, 90, 222
La Alianza de Braceros, 98
Amador, Armando, 41–44, 76
Amador, Nick C., 105
American Civil Liberties Union (ACLU), 133, 177

American Community Survey, 284 (n. 42)
Americans for Legal Immigration Political Action Committee (ALIPAC), 202, 203
Anti-immigrant movements: in Charlotte, 12, 187, 200, 201, 203–4, 206, 208, 209; in Alabama, 12–13, 210; national network of, 124, 184, 189, 203, 208; in Georgia, 154, 155, 171, 173, 175–76, 202–3, 204, 220, 222, 279 (n. 273); and Republican Party, 171, 173, 174, 175–76, 177, 178, 207, 208, 210, 220, 278 (n. 256); in California, 173–74, 185, 186, 201, 202–3; in exurban Charlotte, 200, 201, 203–5, 206, 207, 215, 220; state legislation on, 201–2, 224; and Internet-based networks, 202, 203–4; and Democratic Party, 204, 206, 278 (n. 256); and coalition politics, 224
Arizona, 6, 13, 58, 87
Arkansas Delta: bracero program in, 1, 3, 82, 83–84, 87–91, 102–3, 116–17, 217, 219, 221, 256 (n. 6), 261 (n. 104); Mexican immigration in, 1, 6, 10, 53, 57, 63, 137, 138, 171, 217; recruitment of Mexican labor in, 60, 86; white assimilation of bracero workers in, 85, 106, 107, 108–9, 115–16, 117, 219, 220; resistance of bracero workers in, 94–97, 98, 100, 101, 138; ex-bracero workers remaining in, 117, 266 (n. 218). *See also specific cities*
Arpaio, Joe, 204
Arroyo, Timotea, 78
Aryan Nation, 203
Asian immigration, 5
Athens, Georgia, 178
Atkins, Delores, 92, 93
Atlanta, Georgia: Mexican migrants in, 11; Mexican consulate in, 139; anti-immigration politics in, 175–76, 177, 178, 204, 216; exurbs of, 195, 216

Atlanta Journal-Constitution, 133
Auverge, Arkansas, 113
Avalos, Andrea, 120, 122, 124–25, 126, 168
Avalos, Bernardo "Slim," 120, 122, 124–25, 126, 131, 172, 267 (n. 9)
Avalos family, 120, 122, 125, 126, 129, 131, 168, 170

Ballew, Theresa Ann, 132
Bank, Charles, 131
Baptist Church, 98, 153, 166, 210, 290 (n. 161)
Barnhill, A. H., 96–97, 101, 103–4
Baumann, M. C., 90–91
Bauxite, Arkansas, 53
Beck, Earl, Jr., 101
Beegle, Lee, 112
Benavides, Antonio, 47, 248 (n. 188)
Berryhill Elementary School, Charlotte, North Carolina, 179–80, 281 (n. 2)
Big Brothers and Big Sisters, 156
Bilbo, Theodore, 77
Bishop, Sanford, Jr., 172
Blumenbach, Johann Friedrich, 69–70
Blytheville, Arkansas, 110, 113, 266 (n. 206)
Bolivar County, Mississippi, 64–65, 68, 70, 252 (n. 67)
borderlands, 3, 5, 58, 237 (n. 9)
Bowling, Benjamin, 32
Bowling, Ernestine, 32
Bracero program of 1942–64: in Arkansas Delta, 1, 3, 82, 83–84, 87–91, 102–3, 116–17, 217, 219, 221, 256 (n. 6), 261 (n. 104); and agricultural labor in Southwest, 5; contracts of, 10, 82, 85, 87, 88–90, 91, 95, 96, 97, 99, 100, 102–3, 104, 105, 106, 107, 108, 110, 111, 113, 116, 118; and agricultural labor in South, 57; in Texas, 80, 87, 96, 100, 102; and white elites, 82, 83–84, 85, 87–88, 89, 90, 90–91, 93, 96, 98, 101, 102, 104, 110, 113, 114–16, 117, 118; and Mexican

consulate's monitoring of discrimination, 82, 88, 99, 102, 104–10, 113, 114, 115–16, 117, 118, 174; remittances to families, 84, 94; African American laborers' attitudes toward, 92; white working-class attitudes toward, 92–93; resistance of bracero workers in Arkansas Delta, 94–97, 98, 100, 101, 104, 138; deportation of bracero workers, 96; petitions of bracero workers for economic security, 99–100; and blacklisting, 101, 102–3, 106, 107, 108, 114; racialization of bracero workers, 116; ending of, 116, 129, 139, 173; agricultural migrant laborers compared to bracero workers, 122; and immigration enforcement, 171; and consumer culture, 191; local impact of, 219
Braya Carlos, Juán, 96
Bretherick, R. S., 102
Bridges, Paul, 177–78
Bridges, Ruth, 153, 154, 155, 162, 165, 166, 170
Bridges, Sonny, 153, 154, 162, 165, 166, 170, 177
Brown, Patricia, 154
Brown Berets, 213
Brown v. Board of Education (1954), 82
Burris-Floyd, Pearl, 205–6
Bush, George, 206

Caballero, Dagoberto, 90
Cabarrus County, North Carolina, 194, 197, 199
California: Mexican immigration in, 6, 10, 22, 28, 58, 59; bracero program in, 87, 96, 98; Mexican American farmworkers in, 120; Mexican agricultural migrant laborers in, 128–29, 137, 147, 170; anti-immigration initiative in, 173–74, 185, 186, 201, 202–3; suburbanizing areas of, 216. *See also specific cities*

Camarillo, Albert, 233
Campeche, Mexico, 19
Canchola García, Ignacio, 117
Canedo, Hazel, 15
Canedo, Robert, 14–16, 17, 38, 217, 222
Cano del Castillo, Angel, 98–99, 100, 101–4, 107
Carillo Puerto, Felipe, 19
Carranza, Venustiano, 20, 43
Carvajal, Francisco, 19
Cary, North Carolina, 202, 203
Castillo, Santiago, 61, 68
Catholic Charities, 47–48
Catholic Church: and segregation in New Orleans, 25–26; on Mexican identity in New Orleans, 25–26, 37, 49, 72; and segregation in Mississippi Delta, 62, 71; and Mexicano migrants in Mississippi Delta, 62–63, 65, 67, 71, 76; perspectives on Mexicano migrants, 72, 76, 238 (n. 28); and bracero program in Arkansas Delta, 98, 118, 261 (n. 104); and Mexican agricultural migrant laborers, 135, 152, 153, 154; and Mexican immigrants in Charlotte, 210; and Coalition of Immokalee Workers, 278 (n. 254)
Catholic Church Extension Society, 261 (n. 104)
Catholic Social Services, 133
Caucasian Strategy for Mexican American desegregation, 76–77, 78, 255 (n. 145)
Cauffield (mayor), 39
Cecil, J. S., 103
Cedartown, Georgia, 132–33, 139, 200
Central America, 170, 174–75
Cervantes, Francisco, 22, 25
Cevallos, Doris, 199
Chambliss, Saxby, 172, 173, 175
Charity: and Mexican agricultural migrant laborers in Georgia, 123–24, 151–52, 155–62, 165, 166–67, 170, 210,

219–20; and white middle class, 153–54, 155, 156, 165–66, 170; photo albums of charity work, 158–62, 165, 166, 170
Charleston, South Carolina, 29–30
Charlotte, North Carolina: Mexican immigration in, 6, 11, 12, 182–83, 184, 185, 186, 187–88, 197, 200, 210, 211, 223–24, 283 (n. 27); anti-immigrant movement in, 12, 187, 200, 201, 203–4, 206, 208, 209; school desegregation in, 179–80; suburban areas within, 180–81, 194, 196, 281 (n. 3); African Americans' political role in, 196; immigrants' rights movement in, 208, 209, 211–12. *See also* Exurban Charlotte
Charlotte Way, 179, 182, 187, 188, 204, 215
Chicago, Illinois: Mexican immigrants in, 24, 46; white attitudes toward Mexican immigrants in, 28; settlement patterns of Mexican immigrants in, 29, 30; Mexican consulate in, 44; bracero workers relocating to, 96, 97, 98, 103; African Americans settling in, 117
Chicago Defender, 34
Chicano Movement, 28, 213
Chinese immigrants, 4, 8, 47, 55–56, 69–70
Churches: and charities for Mexican agricultural migrant laborers, 123, 138, 152–53, 154, 155, 157–62, 171, 178, 210, 219–20; Mexican agricultural migrant laborers' views of, 165–71; and pro-immigrant conservatism, 210. *See also* Catholic Church; Evangelical Protestantism; Protestant Church
Cinco de Mayo, 68
Citizenship: concepts of, 3, 4; Mexicans' experiences of, 5; Mexicano immigrants' beliefs about, 7, 55; regional and national politics of, 8; Mexican Americans' rights of, 8–9; Mexicans' expectations of, 10, 11, 13, 14, 220–21; Tejanos' rights of, 61–62, 79, 97, 218; and Mexican Caucasian strategy on educational desegregation, 76, 77; bracero workers' rights of, 88, 94, 96, 97, 99, 104, 105, 107, 108–9, 112–13, 118; African Americans' rights of, 97, 105, 111, 112, 116, 218; of agricultural migrant laborers, 122; of Mexican agricultural migrant laborers, 126–27, 138, 139, 140, 147; and civil rights movement era, 147; of Mexican immigrants to Charlotte, 182–83, 210–11
Civil Rights Act (1964), 117, 118
Civil rights movement: African Americans' involvement in, 34, 62, 77, 125, 209; and Mexican immigrants, 62; in World War II era, 86; and school integration, 117; and Lyndon Johnson, 118; and Mexican American farmworkers, 120; and opportunities for African American working class, 125; in Georgia, 147, 150; and Mexican agricultural migrant laborers, 148, 149–50, 275 (n. 178), 275 (n. 179); liberal ideologies of, 150
Clark, Clayton, 131
Class: local southern subcultures defined by, 3; changing regimes of, 4; Mexicans' experiences of, 5; Mexicano migrants' beliefs about, 7; regional and national politics of, 8; and consumer consciousness, 11; and Mexican immigrants in New Orleans, 51; cross-class nationalism, 55, 139; and bracero program, 91; and New Deal's class-based coalition, 99, 117. *See also* African American elites; African American middle class; African American working class; Latino working class; Mexican immigrant middle class; Mexican immigrant

upper class; Mexican immigrant working class; Social mobility; White elites; White middle class; White working class
Clinton, Bill, 171, 186
Coalition of Immokalee Workers, 278 (n. 254). *See also* Immokalee, Florida
Cobb, James, 252 (n. 71)
Cobb, Ned, 252 (n. 71)
Cobb County, Georgia, 195, 202
Colar C., Alejandro, 48
Collier, John, 109
Colorado, 202
Color line, 17, 22, 55, 64, 68–72
Columbus, Christopher, 42
Comisiones Honoríficas (Honorary Commissions), 58, 67
Concord, North Carolina, 194, 196
Congress of Industrial Organizations (CIO), 98
Conservatism: changing politics in South, 7, 11; and white populism, 12; of white elites, 83, 85; pro-immigrant conservatism, 124, 156–62, 165, 170, 171, 173–78, 204, 207, 208, 210, 224; in Georgia, 149, 150; of exurban Charlotte, 184, 201; of suburbs, 201; and anti-immigrant movements, 202, 208
Construction industry, 184, 185, 187, 196, 197–98, 200, 282 (n. 13), 287 (n. 95)
Consumer culture: consumer consciousness, 11–12, 13; and exurbs, 182, 192, 194, 198, 213, 214, 222; in Mexico, 191–92
Conteras, Antonio, 66
Conteras, Aurelia, 66
Contreras family, 136
Convict leasing, 57
Corridos: "Los Betabeleros" (The Beet Pickers), 48; "Los Enganchados" (The Contracted Ones), 48; on Louisiana, 48, 248 (n. 196)

Cortez, Israel, 126–27, 128, 130, 136, 138, 168–69, 170, 276 (n. 203)
Cortez family, 126–27, 128, 129, 136, 138, 168–69
Coverdell, Paul, 173
Cramerton, North Carolina, 201
Creoles, 16, 38–39, 43
The Crisis, 34, 92
Cruz, Analeta, 27
Cubans, 74, 128, 184

Dalton, Georgia, 133–34
Dawkins, Robert, 209
Debt peonage, 57
de la Huerta, Adolfo, 19
de la Torre, J., 20
Del Rio, Texas, 71, 76, 77
Delta & Pine Land (D&PL), 67, 253 (n. 84)
Democratic Party: and Dixiecrats, 99, 104, 117, 118; and immigration enforcement, 172; and Latino working class, 186; and anti-immigrant movement, 204, 206, 278 (n. 256); and immigrants' rights movement, 210, 212
Department of Motor Vehicles (DMV), North Carolina, 188, 190, 207
Depression era: anti-immigrant sentiments of, 5; and economic progress of Mexican migrants in Mississippi, 10, 55, 78–79; white attitudes toward Mexican immigrants in, 27, 45, 86, 129; and deportation campaigns, 45, 46, 48, 78; and sharecropping, 78, 80
Díaz, Porfirio, 19, 39, 41, 73, 74–75, 80, 95, 246 (n. 150)
Dixiecrats, 99, 104, 117
Dodson, Hank, 125, 168
Dole, Elizabeth, 187
Douglas, Georgia, 127, 131, 166
Downing, Nelius, 60–63
Ducoing, Joseph, 34
Dustin Inman Society, 202–3

Eastern European immigrants, 30
Economic crash of 2008, 199
Education: segregation in, 4, 6, 15, 58, 69–70, 76, 78, 82–83, 86, 117; of Mexican immigrants in Mississippi Delta, 58, 67–68, 70–71, 76, 77–78, 81, 86, 91, 217, 219, 221, 254 (n. 106); Mexican immigrants attending white schools, 70–71, 76, 81, 254 (n. 106); of African Americans in Mississippi Delta, 71; desegregation of, 76–78, 82–83, 113, 130, 175, 179, 209, 255 (n. 145); Mexican Caucasian strategy on educational desegregation, 76–77, 255 (n. 145); of Mexican immigrants in Arkansas Delta, 91, 109, 217; migrant education programs, 129–30, 148, 149–50; Christian private schools, 155–56
Elizondo, Jesús, 26
El Paso, Texas, 23, 24, 193
Enganchadores (labor recruitment agencies), 57–58, 59, 61, 64, 65
English language, and Mexican agricultural migrant laborers, 136, 137, 146, 148, 162, 165–66, 170
Enriquez, Mary, 255 (n. 130)
Enriquez, Nicolas, 255 (n. 130)
Enriquez, Richard, 255 (n. 130)
Enriquez family, 74, 81, 255 (n. 130)
Enseñat, Francisco, 21
Enseñat family, 21
Esparza, José, 66
Esparza, Sara, 66
Estrada, Celia, 199
Eugenics, 39–40, 80, 239 (n. 12)
European immigration, 5, 47
European Union, 191
Evangelical Protestantism, 150, 151–52, 210, 275 (n. 184)
Evans, Chop, 128, 132
Exclusion: legal and social politics of, 8, 12–13, 106, 178, 224; lack of regional continuity of, 13, 220

Exurban Charlotte: Mexican immigrants moving to, 11, 12, 184, 189, 196, 197–99, 220, 222–23; spatial segregation in, 13; white middle class in, 181–82, 189, 194–96, 198–99, 200, 201, 203–4, 206; Mexican immigrants' lack of participation in immigrants' rights movement, 190, 211–12, 214, 215, 223; Mexican immigrant women in, 190, 211–14, 222–23; property taxes in, 195, 196, 200–201, 286 (n. 74); African Americans in, 195–96; anti-immigrant movements in, 200, 201, 203–5, 206, 207, 215, 220; youth involvement in immigrants' rights movement, 213
Exurbs: defining of, 180, 281–82 (n. 3); and consumer culture, 182, 192, 194, 198, 213, 214, 222; anti-immigrant movement in, 202, 204, 206–7, 216

Fair Labor Standards Act, 174
Farm Placement Service, 106
Farm Security Administration (FSA), 51, 55
Farmworkers Legal Services, 149
Faubus, Orval, 265 (n. 184)
First Baptist Church, Indian Trail, North Carolina, 210, 290 (n. 161)
Flores, Román, 128, 131
Flores family, 21
Flores Magón, Ricardo, 18, 56
Flores Ortiz, Enrique, 136
Florida: multiethnic heritage of, 6; Mexican migration to, 10; bracero program in, 119; Mexican agricultural migrant laborers in, 122, 124–25, 126, 127, 128, 135, 137, 158, 170; Tejanos as laborers in, 124–25; Haitian farmworker activists in, 147; migrant education in, 149; size of farms in, 151; and anti-immigrant movement, 202. *See also specific cities*
Flowers, Carolyn, 153–54, 166, 177

328   Index

Ford, Henry, 146
Forrest City, Arkansas, 97, 115
Fort Valley, Georgia, 152, 153
Freedom University, 178
Fulbright, J. William, 103, 113

Gainesville, Georgia, 132, 133–34, 140, 200
Galarza, Ernesto, 98
Gallegos, Bernice, 167
Gallegos, Manuel, 95, 138
Galván, 131
Gamboa, Erasmo, 262 (n. 133)
Gamio, Manuel, 248 (n. 196), 250 (n. 37)
Ganier, E. J., 96
García, I. G., 88
García, Joe, 94
García, Rosa, 38
Garvey, Marcus, 41, 147
Gaston County, North Carolina, 194, 196, 199, 201, 204–6, 207, 281 (n. 3), 286 (n. 74)
Gastonia, North Carolina, 194, 204, 290 (n. 177)
Gathings, E. C., 100, 103, 112, 113
Gaxiola, Rubén, 1, 82, 105–6
Gender: and Mexicano migrants' worldviews, 7; gender balance of women as Mexican immigrants, 27, 242 (n. 74); gender-specific racial ideas, 31; masculinity, 114; shifts in ideas of gender and family in Mexico, 192–94, 198, 222–23
Georgia: history of Mexican and Mexican American laborers in, 1, 124; Mexican immigration in, 6, 10–11; bracero program in, 119, 124; Mexican American farmworkers of, 120; neoliberal ideology in, 122; Mexican agricultural migrant laborers in, 123–24, 125, 127, 137–38, 139, 150–51, 219, 267 (n. 4); charity for Mexican agricultural migrant laborers in, 123–24, 151–52, 155–62, 165, 166–67, 170, 210, 219–20; pro-immigrant conservatism in, 124, 156–62, 165, 170, 171, 173–78; agricultural industry changes in, 125–26; majority-white factory towns of, 126, 132–34; white attitudes toward Mexican immigrants in, 130–31; anti-immigrant movements in, 154, 155, 171, 173, 175–76, 202–3, 204, 220, 222, 279 (n. 273); federal immigration enforcement in, 171–73, 175. *See also specific cities*
Georgia Association of Latino Elected Officials, 178
Georgia Latino Alliance for Human Rights, 178
Georgia Legal Services Program, 148–49, 174
Georgia Pine Straw, 128
German prisoners, 80, 86
Gheen, William, 202
Gille, Karl, 33–34
Globalization, 11
Goggans, Greg, 176
Gomes, Francisco, 48
Gómez, Anselma: as agricultural migrant laborer, 127; experiences with white attitudes toward Mexicans, 131; on outdoor work, 140; family narrative of, 142, 144–46, 148; political discussions with African American agricultural migrant laborers, 147–48; on churches' interaction, 166; relationship with growers, 167–68; possibilities for, 222
Gómez, José, 127, 147–48
Gómez family, 142, 144–46, 167, 170
Gómez Farías, Valentín, 17
Gong Lum v. Rice (1925), 69
González, A., 65
González, Javier, 129–30, 169, 170
González, Vicente, 26
Gracios Mora, Eduardo, 96

Graham, Lindsey, 175
Gray, John, 91
Great Society programs, 148–50
Great Southern Lumber Company, 37
Gress, Ron, 133
Grisham, John, 259 (n. 65)
Gulf of Mexico: steamship connections through, 17, 22, 23–24, 46; as route of Mexican immigrants to New Orleans, 17–24, 44, 47; and effects of Mexican Revolution, 18–19; laboring classes of Gulf Coast, 19–20
Gutiérrez, José, 109
Gutiérrez, Ralph, 30
Gutiérrez, Rosa Elba, 197

H2A agricultural guest worker program, 157, 162, 171, 172–73, 174, 175
Haitians, 128, 147, 170
Hamilton, Kent, 154
Hammon, Micky, 12–13
Hannity, Sean, 204
Hardin, C. E., 94–95
Hardy, Ralph, 175
Harvest of Shame (documentary), 120, 162
Head Start, 148, 149
Helena, Arkansas, 110, 118
Helms, Jesse, 149
Henriquez, Miguel, 28
Hensen, E. Z., 110–11, 265 (n. 184)
El Heraldo de México, 66
Hernández, 131
Hernández, Ana, 197, 211–12
Hernández, Nacario, 47–48
Hernández family, 21
Hinojosa, Andrea, 131, 149, 175, 276 (n. 191), 279 (n. 273)
Hispanics: and census data, 9, 129, 238 (n. 38); in construction industry, 185; in Mecklenburg County, 197
Honduras, 153

Horcasitas, Andrés, 42
Horcasitas, Hortensia, 14, 16, 17, 38, 42, 76
Hurder, Wayne, 188
Hurricane Katrina, 28
Huss, Tish, 204

Idaho, 102
Illinois, 137. *See also* Chicago, Illinois
Immigrants and immigration: federal restrictions on, 5, 11, 173, 202, 205, 207, 208; twenty-first-century national politics of, 8; and deportation campaigns, 45–46, 219; and segregation in education, 70; pro-immigrant conservatism, 124, 156–62, 165, 170, 171, 173–78, 204, 207, 208, 210, 224; and Ku Klux Klan's anti-immigrant activity, 133; and public services, 188, 189. *See also* Anti-immigrant movements; Mexican agricultural migrant laborers; Mexican immigrants; Mexican immigration
Immigrants' rights movement: youth involvement in, 12, 212–13, 221–22; in urban areas, 183, 184, 190, 208–9, 211, 221–22; exurban Mexican immigrants' lack of participation in, 190, 211–12, 214, 215, 223; geography of, 207–16; in Charlotte, 208, 209, 211–12
Immigration Act (1965), 11
Immigration Reform and Control Act (IRCA, 1986), 128, 136, 171, 185, 282 (n. 12)
Immokalee, Florida, 137–38
Indian Trail, North Carolina: as exurb, 180–81, 184; Latino working class in, 181–82, 197, 198, 199–200; white middle class of, 194, 195, 198; African Americans in, 196; lack of immigrants' rights movement in, 212
Industrial workers, 83, 99, 100, 113, 196–97

Institutional Revolutionary
  Party (Partido Revolucionario
  Institucional, PRI), 138
International House, Charlotte, North
  Carolina, 187
Internet-based networks, and anti-
  immigrant movement, 202, 203–4
Interwar period: prototypical milieu of
  Mexican migration in, 9; and white
  assimilation of Mexican immigrants
  in New Orleans, 9, 14–15, 16, 17, 29;
  and settlement patterns of Mexican
  immigrants, 29; anti-black violence
  during, 218
Israel, 191
Italian immigrants, 4, 16, 30, 38, 56, 69, 71

James, Bill, 206
Jamison, Terry, 99
Japan, 191
Japanese Americans, photo albums of,
  273 (n. 148)
Jáquez López, Miguel, 89
Jenkins, Dotti, 203
Jenkins, M. C., 97
Jim Crow system: as applied to Latino
  population, 3; in South Texas, 5–6, 22,
  55, 58, 59, 61, 68; in New Orleans, 9,
  16, 31, 38, 39, 40, 41, 50; and marriage
  patterns, 31; in Mississippi Delta, 71,
  72, 219; and Mexican consulates, 76;
  understandings of race in, 80; fall of,
  82; in Arkansas Delta, 82, 104, 106,
  108–9, 110, 113, 118, 119, 219; and Mexi-
  can agricultural migrant laborers, 134;
  malleability of, 217, 219
Johnson, Lyndon, 118, 148
Johnson, Paul, 176
Johnston, Oscar, 67
Johnstown, Pennsylvania, 39, 41, 44
Joiner, Arkansas, 113
Juárez, Benito, 17
Jung, Louise, 33

Keigher, Tom, 205
Kennedy, Claude, 108–10
King, Calvin, 91, 92
King, D. A., 201, 202–3
Ku Klux Klan, 132, 133, 134, 184, 279
  (n. 273)

Labor-leisure divide, 141, 142, 144, 145–
  46, 273 (n. 148)
Labor rights: of Mexican immigrants in
  Georgia, 11; of Mexican immigrants
  in Louisiana, 37; of Mexican immigrants in Mississippi Delta, 62–63,
  137; of New Deal legislation, 83, 99,
  104; of braceros in Arkansas Delta,
  99–101; white elites' resistance to,
  113, 117
Labor strikes: and Mexican consulates'
  political support for bracero workers,
  10; of bracero workers in Arkansas
  Delta, 94, 95, 96, 98, 100, 101, 138;
  of Mexican agricultural migrant
  laborers, 137
Labor unions: and sharecropping, 88,
  92, 99; and bracero workers, 98, 99;
  and Mexican agricultural migrant
  laborers, 122, 137, 146, 170; and African
  Americans, 147
Landa, José Luís, 95, 138, 222
Landres, Byron, 100
Landrove, Constancio, 73–74
Landrove, Hortensia, 70–71, 72, 74, 77,
  78, 255 (n. 148)
Landrove, José, 73
Landrove, Margarita, 73, 74
Landrove, María, 73
Landrove, Melchor, 73
Landrove, Petra Jayme, 72, 74
Landrove, Rafael: children enrolled in
  white school, 70–71, 76–77, 78, 86,
  255 (n. 145); and Mexican Honorary
  Commission, 72; family migration
  within Mexico, 72–73; and Mexican

Index 331

Revolution, 73–74, 95; migration to Mississippi Delta, 74, 192, 217, 222; photograph of, 74–76, 255 (n. 130); social mobility of, 78, 79; naturalization petition of, 79; repatriation request of, 79; descendants living in Mississippi Delta, 81

Landrove, Rafael (father), 72

Landrove, Tomás González, 255 (n. 129)

Lane, Duke, 154–55

Latin America: anti-black prejudices in, 1; as transnational, 3; U.S. limitations on immigration from, 11; Louisiana's cultural ties with, 17; immigrants from, 17, 184; and filibusters, 18; and New Orleans trade, 22–23, 32

Latin American Coalition, 203, 208–9

Latino consumption boycott of 2006, 176, 208, 212

Latino working class: anti-immigrant movement targeted at, 12, 184; and public services, 181, 187, 189, 200, 201, 205, 216; in Indian Trail, 181–82, 197, 198, 199–200; in urban areas, 184–85; in service industry, 184–85, 189, 197–98, 287 (n. 95); stereotypes of, 186–87, 203, 205; attitudes toward African Americans, 187; recruitment of, 196

Law enforcement officials: and deportation campaigns in New Orleans, 47, 248 (n. 183); restrictions on bracero workers' mobility, 96, 97, 107, 108, 113; Mexican agricultural migrant laborers harassed by, 133, 151, 275–76 (n. 191); and federal immigration enforcement, 173, 202, 205, 207, 208

League of United Latin American Citizens (LULAC), 62, 76

Lee, George W., 111

Lee, Robert E., 217

Legal Aid, 136, 148–49

Legendre, Blair, 34

Lemon Grove, California, 71, 76–77

Lepanto, Arkansas, 93, 109, 113, 115

Lewis, John, 172

Lewis, Terry, 203

Liberalism: changing politics in South, 7; and expectations of citizenship, 10, 98; on African American laborers, 51; and education policies, 71, 72, 77; and New Deal, 83, 85, 99, 100, 104, 113, 117; cross-border liberalism, 99–100, 104; and investigations of violence against Mexican agricultural migrant laborers, 133; and school desegregation, 179; coalition politics of, 224. *See also* Neoliberalism

Lichterman, Paul, 276 (n. 199)

Lincoln County, North Carolina, 281 (n. 3)

Lincolnton, North Carolina, 194

Lipsey, Bernard, 93, 109

Little Rock Central High School, Arkansas, desegregation of, 82–83, 113

Locke, Harrison, 109

Longview Farms, 103

López, Gregorio, 47

López, Ramiro, 132–33

Los Angeles, California: Mexican revolutionaries in, 18, 19; Mexican immigrants in, 24, 27; Spanish-surnamed men in white-collar professions, 25; settlement patterns in, 30; marriage patterns in, 31; racial identity of Mexican immigrants in, 33; deportation campaign in, 45; repatriation cases in, 48; suburban barrios of, 180; Chicano high school students' activism in, 213

Louisiana: attitudes toward Mexican immigrants in rural areas, 35–37, 46, 56, 57; and *corridos*, 48; Mexican immigrants as laborers in, 53, 60. *See also* New Orleans, Louisiana

Louisiana Planter and Sugar Manufacturer, 36, 43

Louisiana Weekly, 34

Love, John, 203
Loza, Juan, 118
Lucio, Carmen, 66
Lucio, Herminio, 66
Luckie, John B., 103
Lum, Martha, 69
Lynching: African Americans as victims of, 6, 31, 114; Mexicanos as victims of, 6, 58; Italians as victims of, 38, 69
Lyons, Georgia, 130, 149

Mackenzie, Maggie, 69
Madero, Francisco, 43
Marín, Angelina, 168
Marín, Robert, 130, 131, 168
Marín, Teodora, 131, 139, 142, 168, 222, 276 (n. 203)
Marín family, 170
Marked Tree, Arkansas, 1, 3, 82, 105–8
Martínez, Antonio, 69
Martínez, Sarah, 69
Mason, Kit, 68–69
Mason, Lula, 68–69
Maus, Teodoro, 172–73
McClellan, John, 103, 113
McCrory, Pat, 187, 208
McDonald, Ed, 101
McGehee, J. G., 67, 70
McKnight, E. D., 94
McNeil, Jack, 89
Mecklenburg County, North Carolina, 185, 187, 195, 196, 197, 204, 206, 281 (n. 3), 282 (n. 13), 286 (n. 74)
Meeks, Roscoe, 167–68
Memphis, Tennessee, 86, 90, 97–99, 103, 105, 111–12, 117, 211, 222
Mendieta, Diana Avalos, 130, 172
Mendoza, Laura, 180, 184, 185
Mestizaje, ideology of, 39, 41, 42–43, 44, 76, 80, 107, 223
Methodist churches, 210, 290 (n. 164)
Mexican agricultural migrant laborers: violence experienced by, 122, 132–33, 134; crews of, 125, 126, 135–36, 140, 170, 267 (n. 9); in North Carolina, 125, 137, 170, 184, 267 (n. 10), 275 (n. 178); and family labor, 126, 140, 141–42, 146, 170; legal status of, 128–29; living conditions of, 129, 134, 135–36, 154, 156, 157–58, 172, 222; migrant education programs, 129–30; relationship with African American agricultural migrant laborers, 131–32, 148, 274 (n. 169); intermarriage with whites in Georgia, 132, 133, 177; working conditions of, 134, 135–36, 139, 140, 141–42, 151, 154, 156; resistance of, 136; discrimination against, 140; narratives of, 141, 142, 168–70, 171; views of churches, 165–71; remittances to families, 192; surveys of, 267 (n. 9), 268 (n. 32); population of, 271 (n. 102)
Mexican American farmworkers, 120
Mexican American Fruit Corporation, 22
Mexican American generation, 14
Mexican American Legal Defense and Education Fund (MALDEF), 133
Mexican Americans: aspirations of, 6; limited citizenship rights of, 8–9; as U.S. citizens of Mexican descent, 9; attitudes toward in Southwest, 35, 55, 91; as laborers in Mississippi Delta, 60–61; organizations challenging educational segregation, 71; as middle-class citizens in Southwest, 79; youths' attitude toward immigration, 174, 175, 176. *See also* Tejanos
Mexican consuls and consulates: as representative of Mexican immigrants in New Orleans, 9, 28, 38, 40, 41–44, 47, 50, 62, 76, 77, 78, 79–80, 95–96, 97, 104–5, 222, 243 (n. 86), 246–47 (n. 164); discrimination-related protests to, 10, 28, 82, 88, 99, 102, 104–10, 113, 114, 115–16, 117, 118,

174, 218, 243 (n. 86); and political support for bracero workers, 10, 97, 98–104, 117, 118, 174; neutralization of, 13; and deportation campaigns, 46, 47, 48–49; and repatriations, 47–48, 49, 78, 79; as representative of Mexican immigrants in Mississippi Delta, 50, 55, 59–60, 62, 63, 66, 72, 76, 78, 79–80, 81, 95–96, 221; and Comisiones Honoríficas, 67, 72; and educational desegregation, 76–78; as representative of Mexican immigrants in Arkansas Delta, 82, 93, 94, 97, 211, 221; and bracero program, 84, 85, 93, 94, 221; in San Antonio, 97; decline in resources and power of, 122–23, 139, 149, 221, 222; and Mexican agricultural migrant laborers, 135, 149, 172, 222, 267 (n. 10); as representative of Mexican immigrants in North Carolina, 185, 211; and region of origin of Mexican immigrants, 284 (n. 43)

Mexican Foreign Service, 1, 40, 211

Mexican Honorary Commission, Gunnison, Mississippi, 67, 68, 70, 72, 79

Mexicanidad, 17, 41–44, 49, 104–5

Mexican immigrant middle class: white assimilation in New Orleans, 14, 16–17, 24–25, 38, 44, 46, 50; from Veracruz, 21; returning to Mexico, 26; and racial identity, 42, 95; white assimilation in Mississippi Delta, 55, 79, 81; organizations of, 66; and Comisiones Honoríficas, 67; photographs of, 74–76; and educational segregation, 79; Mexican agricultural migrant laborers as, 140, 170

Mexican immigrants: and Mexican archives, 7; migration routes of, 7; places of origin, 7, 8; photo albums of, 7, 16–17, 74–76; white assimilation in New Orleans, 9, 14–15, 16, 17, 24–35, 36, 37, 38, 41, 43, 44, 49–50, 55; white assimilation in Mississippi Delta, 10, 55, 64, 68–72, 76, 77–78, 79, 81, 91, 219; Gulf Coast routes to New Orleans, 17–24; social mobility of, 28, 50, 53, 55, 65–66, 67, 68, 74–76, 78–79, 81, 122, 124, 128, 136, 140, 162, 183, 185, 243 (n. 84). *See also* Mexican agricultural migrant laborers; Undocumented Mexican immigrants; Women as Mexican immigrants

Mexican immigrant upper class: from Veracruz, 21; in New Orleans, 21, 22, 26, 38, 39, 40, 44, 45, 46, 49, 76; and racial identity, 39, 40, 41–42, 45; Texans' attitudes toward, 93

Mexican immigrant working class: white assimilation in New Orleans, 16, 17, 25, 26, 30, 31, 44, 49; and women as Mexican immigrants, 27; marriage patterns of, 31; in rural Louisiana, 35–37; and deportation campaigns, 45; in New Orleans, 46, 48; organizations of, 66; and Comisiones Honoríficas, 67. *See also* Mexican agricultural migrant laborers

Mexican immigration: in Arkansas Delta, 1, 6, 10, 53, 57, 63, 137, 138, 171, 217; increases in, 5; in Southwest, 5–6, 14, 15, 185, 219, 223; in New Orleans, 6, 9, 14, 18–24, 26, 51, 217, 242 (n. 61); in California, 6, 10, 22, 28, 58, 59; in Midwest, 6, 10, 22, 45, 58, 59, 68, 79, 219, 223; in Mississippi Delta, 6, 10, 53, 55, 59, 192, 217; in Charlotte, 6, 11, 12, 182–83, 184, 185, 186, 187–88, 197, 200, 210, 211, 223–24, 283 (n. 27); in Texas, 9, 10, 18, 19, 20, 44, 139, 190; in South, 10–11, 56, 58, 183, 185, 217, 238 (n. 38)

Mexican Independence Day, 79, 95, 138

Mexicanos, as Mexicans and Mexican Americans, 9

Mexican Patriotic Committee, Hughes, Arkansas, 86

Mexican Revolution of 1910–17: and working-class Mexican nationalism, 5; and Mexican migration, 9, 14, 18–24, 26, 36, 56, 64; political and economic instability created by, 18, 21, 58; and New Orleans, 18–19, 21, 26; political legacy of, 42, 43, 44–45, 80, 95; and social mobility, 73–74

Mexicans: white elites' recruitment of, 4, 6, 219; mixed white and Indian genetic background of, 5, 38, 39, 41–42, 44, 74, 113, 114, 131; aspirations of, 6, 8; reasons for migration to South, 7; as Mexican nationals, 9

Mexico: changes of 1910s, 5; and whitening through culture, 5, 39–40, 41, 42, 80, 104, 105; changes in state power, 7; as Europeanized, 9; north-central Mexico as origin of Mexican immigrants, 9, 18, 19, 20–22, 23, 36, 44; World War II and post–World War II economic expansion in, 10; postrevolutionary state, 10, 58, 95; and free trade, 11; crisis era of 1965–2004, 11, 129, 138, 221; middle-class ideal in, 12; cultural ideas of race in, 16; Díaz's capitalist development of, 19; positivist tradition in, 39, 41, 42, 72, 73, 74–75, 79; African American immigration to, 40–41; and folk culture, 42, 43, 44; African influences in heritage, 43, 44; historiography of racial ideas in, 44, 247 (n. 165); church–state conflicts in, 71; paternalistic concept of *protección*, 76; nationalist agenda of, 76, 77, 80, 84, 95, 98, 103, 105, 107, 139, 221; education of Mexican immigrants, 77; economic growth during World War II, 84; and bracero program, 85, 88, 94, 98–101, 102; populist land redistributions in, 95; liberalism in, 99–100; agricultural migrant laborers in, 122; postnationalist era in, 122; and neoliberal ideology, 122–23, 191, 213, 219, 221; peasant organizing in, 137, 170; individual self-sufficiency discourse of, 140; and globalization, 182, 220, 221; regions of origin of outmigration, 189, 284 (n. 43); consumer culture in, 191–92; and North American Free Trade Agreement, 191–92

Mexico City, Mexico, massacre of student protesters in Tlatelolco district, 138

Mexico Society of New Orleans, 43

Mexico-U.S. border: as international boundary line, 10; effect of Mexican Revolution on, 18, 23; and enganchadores, 58; bracero program contracting sites of, 88; and Operation Gatekeeper, 193; and globalization, 217

Michigan, 10, 127

Midwest: Mexican immigration in, 6, 10, 22, 45, 58, 59, 68, 79, 219, 223; attitudes toward Mexican immigrants in, 35; and *corridos*, 48; racial attitudes in, 50; Mexican agricultural migrant laborers in, 124, 126, 127, 128; white migrants to North Carolina from, 195

Migrant Education, 148

Migrant health clinics, 148

Migrant Health Program, 271 (n. 102)

Migrant Labor Agreement, 101

Migration history, studies of, 6–7

Miller Lumber Company, Marianna, Arkansas, 96

Milwaukee, Wisconsin, 149, 175, 202

Mint Hill, North Carolina, 203, 281 (n. 3), 290 (n. 164)

Mississippi: Mexican immigrants as laborers in, 56, 60; Mexican community organizations in, 67, 79; and immigrants' rights movement, 210. *See also* Mississippi Delta

Mississippi Delta: Mexican immigration in, 6, 10, 53, 55, 59, 192, 217; sharecrop-

Index 335

ping of Mexican immigrants in, 10, 53, 55, 59–60, 64–68, 78, 80; white assimilation of Mexican immigrants in, 10, 55, 64, 68–72, 76, 77–78, 79, 81, 91, 219; and repatriation of Mexican immigrants, 48, 78; social mobility of Mexican immigrants in, 50, 53, 55, 65–66, 67, 68, 74–76, 78–79, 81; Texas as origin of Mexican immigration in, 51, 53, 55, 58, 60, 61, 64, 67, 251 (n. 42); Mexicano laborers in, 51, 53, 60–63, 136, 137; African American laborers in, 51, 55, 57, 61, 62, 63; color line in, 55, 64, 68–72, 78; Mexican immigrants recruited as laborers in, 57, 59, 86; education of Mexican immigrants in, 58, 67–68, 70–71, 76, 77–78, 81, 86, 91, 217, 219, 221, 254 (n. 106); Tejanos as laborers in, 61–62, 64, 79, 80–81; demographic profile of Mexicano migrants of, 64–65, 252 (n. 66), 252 (n. 67); and bracero program, 80–81
Mississippi River, flood of 1927, 66–67
Mitchell, Norman, 206
Modernity, of Mexico, 75, 77, 95, 96, 105, 220–21
Molina, Eréndira, 179–80, 184, 185, 208
Monroe, North Carolina, 182, 184, 194, 195, 197
Monteleone, Monte, 204
Morantes, Gerino, 31
Moreno, Eujenio, 167
Morganton, North Carolina, 137, 138
Moultrie, Georgia, 153, 154
Mount Holly, North Carolina, 196
Mount Olive, North Carolina, 137
Murrow, Edward R., 120
Myrick, Sue, 187

Nashville, Tennessee, 11, 219, 224
National Association for the Advancement of Colored People (NAACP), 34, 62, 92, 111, 149, 196, 210, 215

National Association of Counties, 206
National belonging, concepts of, 3
National Council of La Raza (NCLR), 175, 178
National Farm Labor Union, 98
Nation-states, 7
Native Americans, 8
NC Illegal Immigration Prevention Act, 207
NCListen, 202
Neelly, Richard, 59–60
Nelken, Michael, 245 (n. 131)
Neoliberalism: and changing politics in South, 11, 13, 122, 219, 224; in Mexico, 122–23, 191, 213, 219, 221; and white elites, 123–24; in exurbs, 198
Neumann, Wil, 201, 203, 204, 207
New Brothers, 127–28
New Deal, 83, 85, 99, 100, 104, 113, 117
New Mexico, 87, 124
New Orleans, Louisiana: Mexican immigration in, 6, 9, 14, 18–24, 26, 51, 217, 242 (n. 61); white assimilation of Mexican immigrants in, 9, 14–15, 16, 17, 24–35, 36, 37, 38, 41, 43, 44, 49–50, 55, 76, 104–5, 219; segregation in, 9, 24, 29–31, 33–34, 35, 38–44, 45, 50; racial identities in, 9, 24, 33–34, 35, 38–44, 45; Mexicans as European-style white immigrants, 14, 16; Spanish-language culture in, 17; Gulf Coast routes of Mexican immigrants, 17–24; and effects of Mexican Revolution, 18–19, 21, 26; Texas as origin of Mexican immigrants to, 21–22; and trade with Mexico and Latin America, 22, 23, 32, 42, 43, 50; census data on Mexican-born whites in, 24, 32–33, 38, 239 (n. 7), 242 (n. 62), 244 (n. 106), 244 (n. 107); women as Mexican immigrants in, 26–27, 242 (n. 76); settlement patterns of Mexican immigrants in, 29, 30, 34, 35,

46; marriage patterns in, 31–32, 35; lack of collective activity of Mexican immigrants in, 37–38, 44, 49; and deportation campaigns, 45–47, 247 (n. 178), 248 (n. 183), 248 (n. 185); and repatriation of Mexican immigrants, 47–48
Nieto, Kenneth, 245 (n. 131)
Nieto, Laura, 21
Nieto, Peter, 21
9/11 terrorist attacks, national security concerns of, 188, 207
Norfolk, Virginia, 202, 204
North American Free Trade Agreement (NAFTA), 191–92, 196–97
North Carolina: Mexican agricultural migrant laborers in, 125, 137, 170, 184, 267 (n. 10), 275 (n. 178); Farmworkers Legal Services in, 149; Mexican immigrants to, 188, 189; origin of Mexican immigrants to, 189, 284 (n. 43); anti-immigrant movements in, 203–4, 206–7; African American activists in, 275 (n. 179). *See also specific cities*
North Carolina Council of Churches, Migrant Ministry, 267 (n. 10)
North Mecklenburg High School, Huntersville, North Carolina, 213
Northwest: Mexican immigration in, 6, 45, 262 (n. 133); Mexican agricultural migrant laborers in, 126, 170; white migrants to North Carolina from, 195
La Noticia, 186–87, 290 (n. 177)

Obama, Barack, 222
Oblates of Mary Immaculate, 25–26
Obregón, Alvaro, 40
Oglethorpe, Georgia, 154
Ohio, 127, 137, 146
Oklahoma, 124, 126
Omega, Georgia, 125, 130, 174
Operation Gatekeeper, 193
Operation Southern Denial, 172, 175

Oral history interviews: of Mexican agricultural migrant laborers, 7, 135, 140, 141, 142, 168; of bracero workers in Arkansas Delta, 108; and nostalgia, 140, 273 (n. 141); of Mexican immigrants in Union County, 184, 189–90, 191, 192, 193–94
Oregon, 100, 137, 147
Ortega-Moore, Angeles, 185, 209
Ortíz Torres, Jesús, 91

Palacios family, 81
Pan-American Petroleum, 48
Parano Chávez, Feliciano, 97
Parkin Farmers' Association, 89, 101
Paternalism: of slavery, 4–5; of Catholic Church, 72; of Mexican government, 76, 98; of white community leaders in Georgia, 151, 156; of Protestant Church, 156
Perdue, Sonny, 176
Pérez, George, 71, 77
Perry (Pérez), Martha, 70–71, 72, 74–75, 78, 79, 222, 254 (n. 125)
Photographs and photo albums: of Mexican immigrants, 7, 16–17, 74–76; of Mexican immigrants in New Orleans, 14, 15–16; as idealized versions of domestic life, 74–76, 141, 273 (n. 145); of Mexican American farmworkers, 120; of Mexican agricultural migrant laborers, 140–41, 142, 144–47; and Polaroid cameras, 142, 145–46, 273 (n. 153); of charity work with Mexican agricultural migrant laborers, 158–62, 165, 166, 170; of growers, 167–68; of Mexican immigrants in exurban Charlotte, 214; Rose on interpreting contexts of, 255 (n. 131); Barthes on, 273 (n. 150); of Japanese Americans, 273 (n. 148); Chalfen on, 277 (n. 229)
Pine Bluff, Arkansas, 102–3, 104

Index 337

Plano, Texas, 282 (n. 8)
Plessy, Homer, 16, 39, 40, 41, 50
Political coalition building, 1, 99, 117, 224
Poplin Elementary School, Indian Trail, North Carolina, 180–82, 183, 192, 200, 213
Poultry production: in North Carolina, 11, 137, 181, 182, 194, 196, 197, 212; in Georgia, 129, 131, 132, 133, 177
Powell, Leo, 103
Pozos Mora, Blas, 174
Pradillo, August, 30
La Prensa, 23, 45, 60, 62, 63, 247 (n. 178)
Proposition 187, California, 173–74, 186, 201
Protestant Church: and bracero program in Arkansas Delta, 98; alignment with business, 150, 151, 154, 155, 156; and charity for Mexican agricultural migrant laborers, 151–52; evangelization efforts in Mexico, 153, 276 (n. 203); mission work with Mexican agricultural migrant laborers, 153–54; and Mexican agricultural migrant laborers' conversion, 170
Pruitt, Dwayne, 133
Public services: and Latino working class, 181, 187, 189, 200, 201, 205, 216; debates over entitlement to, 188, 189, 201, 203–4, 205, 207; in exurban Charlotte, 196, 200, 201, 206
Puebla, battle of (May 5, 1862), 68
Puerto Ricans, 128

Race: and binary of black and white, 3, 16, 50, 72, 109, 122, 130, 137, 217; southern race relations, 3, 85; changing regimes of, 4; Mexicans' concepts of, 5; Mexicano migrants' beliefs about, 7; regional and national politics of, 8; cultural definitions of, 11, 80, 93; one-drop rule, 16, 74; color line, 17, 22, 55, 64, 68–72; scientific racism, 31; historiography of racial ideas in Mexico, 44, 247 (n. 165); cross-racial labor organizing, 62, 99; definitions of, 69–70, 72, 74, 80; and bracero program, 85, 91–93, 104–10; and anti-immigrant movements, 203, 205, 209
Racial identities: Mexican, compared to American, 5, 74; composition of racial groups, 8–9; in New Orleans, 9, 24, 33–34, 35, 38–44, 45; intra-Mexican racial distinctions, 38; of Creoles in New Orleans, 38–39, 43; of Mexican immigrant middle class, 39, 40, 41–42, 42, 45, 95; of Mexican Americans in Southwest, 79; entrenchment of, 218
Racialization: and biological ideas of race, 16; and cultural ideas of race, 16; definition of, 16, 239 (n. 9); and border crossings, 23; and white perceptions of Mexicans as working class, 25, 37; in Southwest, 25, 106, 116; uneven process of, 81; in Arkansas Delta, 116; of Mexican agricultural migrant laborers, 141
Railroads, 20, 240 (n. 32)
Ramírez López, Angel, 96, 117
Ramos, Florencio, 27–28
Ramos Cervantes, Raquel, 22
Ranes, T. P., 76
Raza cósmica (cosmic race), 40, 44, 76, 80
Reagan, Ronald, 148
REAL ID Act, 207
Red Cross, 66
Reece, Carroll, 111
Reed, Jill, 195, 198
Regeneración (newspaper), 56
Reid, Don, 186–87
Republican Party: and anti-immigrant movement, 171, 173, 174, 175–76, 177, 178, 207, 208, 210, 220, 278 (n. 256); and immigration enforcement,

172–73, 175; and Latino working class, 186–87
Reséndez, Jesus, 21–22
Reséndez, Mary, 21
Resistance: of Mexican immigrant upper class to white supremacy, 39, 40, 41–42; of Mexican laborers in Mississippi Delta, 59–62, 68, 71; of bracero workers in Arkansas Delta, 94–97, 98, 100, 101, 104, 138; of Mexican agricultural migrant laborers in Georgia, 136–37; of Mexican immigrants in North Carolina, 200
Reyna Torres, Margarito, 117
Richardson, David Wayne, 132–33
Río Grande Valley, Texas, 64
Ritter, E., 82, 105–8
Roberson, Janis, 154, 157–62, 165, 171, 174
Roberson, Wendell, 154, 157, 159, 161, 171
Robledo, Freddo, 71, 72
Robledo, Jubertina, 71, 72
Robledo, María, 70–71, 72
Robledo, Telesforo, 67, 70–71, 72, 77
Robledo, Trinidad, 77, 255 (n. 148)
Rodríguez, Benny, 128
Rodríguez, León, 28
Rodríguez, Margarita, 28, 222
Rome, Georgia, 132
Rosales Pozos, Armando, 174
Rural areas: attitudes toward Mexican immigrants in Louisiana, 35–37, 46, 56, 57; as origin of Mexican immigrants, 189–90, 191; and pro-immigrant conservatism, 204, 207, 224

St. Juliana Catholic Church, Fort Valley, Georgia, 153, 162, 166
Salas Ochoa, Heriberto, 90
Saldaña, Esteban, 96, 100
San Antonio, Texas, 18, 22, 73, 74
Sánchez, Alfonso, 49
Sánchez, George J., 233
Sánchez, Joaquín, 32
Sánchez, Leonor, 32
Sánchez, Vicente, 49
San Diego, California, 193
Santa Barbara, California, 25
Santiago, Miguel, 100
Sastre, Ethel, 27
Save the Old Dominion, 202
Scarlett, James O., 92–93
Scientific racism, 31
Scott, C. E., 89
Seasonal agricultural workers (SAW), legalization of, 128, 129, 185, 282 (n. 12)
Segregation: in education, 4, 6, 15, 58, 69–70, 76, 78, 82–83, 86, 117; politics of, 7; in New Orleans, 16, 25–26, 29–31, 33–34, 35, 38–44, 45, 50; and Catholic Church, 25–26, 62, 71; residential segregation in interwar period, 29; in Texas, 58; in Mississippi Delta, 62, 68, 217; separate but equal doctrine, 82, 117; in Arkansas Delta, 82, 117, 217; lack of uniformity in, 217; underlying investments of, 218; dismantling of, 219; modification of, 219
Sensenbrenner, James, 175
Serja, Fidel, 59
Service industry: in Georgia, 129; Latino working class in, 184–85, 189, 197–98, 287 (n. 95); and women as Mexican immigrants, 194
Sharecropping: of African Americans, 4, 57, 65, 92, 111; of Mexican immigrants in Mississippi, 10, 53, 55, 59–60, 64–68, 78, 80; wage labor compared to, 57, 64, 65, 80, 86, 250 (n. 32); evictions of 1930s, 80, 86, 92, 99
Sharpton, Al, 209–10
Shaw, John, 25–26
Shogren Hosiery Manufacturing, Concord, North Carolina, 196
Sifuentez, Manuel, 69
Smyrna, Georgia, 173
Smythers, Alex, 290 (n. 164)

Smythers, Anne, 290 (n. 164)
Social mobility: of Mexican immigrants in New Orleans, 28, 50, 243 (n. 84); of Mexican immigrants in Mississippi Delta, 50, 53, 55, 65–66, 67, 68, 74–76, 78–79, 81; of African Americans in Mississippi Delta, 68; in Mexico, 73–74; of Mexican agricultural migrant laborers, 122, 124, 128, 136, 140, 162; of African Americans in Georgia, 131, 171; in exurban Charlotte, 181; of Mexican immigrants in Charlotte, 183, 185
Sociedades mutualistas (mutual aid societies), 44, 58
Solís, Manuel, 67, 68, 70, 222
Solís Aguilera, Gabino, 88, 90, 94, 95
Sosa, José Dionisio, 96
Soto, Petra, 139, 169–70
Soto Amaya, Pablo, 94–95
South: history of Latino migration to, 1, 3–4, 85; invisible Mexican American history of, 4; African American out-migration in 1910s–60s, 4, 9, 51, 55, 56, 57, 63, 67, 68, 86, 88, 92, 96, 106; dependence on agriculture, 4–5; paternalistic labor systems of, 4–5; liberalism and conservatism in, 7; Mexican immigration in, 10–11, 56, 58, 183, 185, 217, 238 (n. 38); popular narrative on race in, 13, 184, 215–16, 219; African American laborers in, 51; Chinese immigrants in, 55–56; Mexicanization of agricultural labor, 119, 124–29; post–civil rights era in, 122; desegregation of education in, 130; anti-immigrant movements in, 200, 202–4, 215–16, 220; integration with national trends, 217, 220
South Americans, 184
South Carolina, 125
Southeast Georgia Communities Project (SEGCP), 149–50, 175

Southern Tenant Farmers' Union (STFU), 88, 92, 98, 99, 104, 106, 112–13
Southwest: borderlands of, 5; Mexican immigration in, 5–6, 14, 15, 185, 219, 223; Mexican American generation in, 14, 15–16; racialization of Mexican immigrants in, 25, 106, 116; working-class Mexican immigrants in, 26; settlement patterns of Mexican immigrants in, 29, 30; attitudes toward Mexican Americans in, 35, 55, 91; effect of Mexican Revolution on, 43; and deportation campaigns, 45, 49; Mexican immigrants petitioning Mexican consulates, 72; Mexican Caucasian strategy on educational desegregation, 76; educational segregation in, 79; and welfare for undocumented Mexican immigrants, 186
Spain, colonization of Louisiana, 17, 24
Spanish language: and white middle-class attitudes toward bracero program, 93, 259 (n. 65); and Mexican agricultural migrant laborers, 129, 130, 149, 153; and white middle-class charity and mission work, 153, 154; exurb developers' advertisements in, 199
Spanish-language press: in New Orleans, 17; in Texas, 37, 46, 59; on Mexican laborers in South, 60; on Mississippi River flood, 66; white southern planters advertising for labor in, 87; on Mexican immigrants to Charlotte, 183; recruitment of Latino workers in, 196; on anti-immigrant movement, 208. *See also specific newspapers*
Stubblefield, Royce, 94
Suburbs: Mexican immigrants moving to, 11, 189, 196, 198; of Charlotte, 180–81, 194, 196, 281 (n. 3); conservatism of, 201; anti-immigrant movements in, 202, 203, 204, 206–7, 208, 216,

288 (n. 129); defining of, 281 (n. 3); emerging suburbs, 281 (n. 3)
Sun Valley High School, Indian Trail, North Carolina, 213
Swann v. Charlotte-Mecklenburg Board of Education (1971), 179
Swartz, Frederick, 30
Sycamore Bend Plantation, Hughes, Arkansas, 86

Tabasco, Mexico, 19
Tampa, Florida, 37, 244 (n. 113), 245 (n. 127)
Tancredo, Tom, 209
Tejanos: as Mexican Americans born in Texas, 9; migration to New Orleans, 21–22; white violence against, 58, 87; as laborers in Mississippi Delta, 61–62, 64, 79, 80–81; citizenship rights of, 61–62, 79, 97, 218; demographic profile of, 64; intermarriage with whites in Mississippi Delta, 69; as crew leaders in bracero program, 84, 87, 88–89, 96; as laborers in Arkansas Delta, 87–88, 91, 93, 114, 115, 266 (n. 206); as laborers in Texas, 102; discrimination in Arkansas Delta, 107; as laborers in Florida, 124–25; as crew leaders of Mexican agricultural migrant laborers, 125, 126, 127–28, 131, 267 (n. 9); as laborers in Georgia, 126
Tellez, Manuel, 39
Texas: Jim Crow system in South Texas, 5–6, 22, 55, 58, 59, 61, 68; African Americans' attitude toward Mexicano migrants, 8; Mexican immigration to, 9, 10, 18, 19, 20, 44, 139, 190; north-central Mexico as origin of Mexican immigrants in, 9, 18, 19, 21–22, 23, 36, 44; anti-Mexican violence in, 9, 22, 56, 58, 59, 87; white attitudes toward Mexican immigrants in, 22, 28, 38, 55, 91, 93, 131, 219; Spanish-language press in, 37, 46, 59; Mexican mutual aid societies in, 44, 58, 67; and enganchadores, 57–58, 59; Mexican migration from, 58–59, 61, 64, 67, 222, 251 (n. 42); Mexican agricultural laborers in South Texas, 61, 147, 250 (n. 32); bracero program in, 80, 87, 96, 100, 102; Mexican agricultural migrant laborers in, 122, 124, 126, 128–29, 131, 137; and anti-immigrant movement, 202; Mexican American activism in, 274 (n. 163)
Texas Farm Placement Service (TFPS), 87
Thurman, Howdy, 162, 165, 166–67, 170, 210
Thurman, Mary Ann: and charity work with Mexican agricultural migrant laborers, 153, 154–55, 162, 165, 166–67, 170, 210; on white elites' influence on law enforcement, 275–76 (n. 191)
Tifton, Georgia, 125, 126, 127, 129–31, 153, 157, 174, 176
Till, Emmett, 114
Times-Picayune, 22, 23, 46, 247 (n. 178)
Toombs High School, Georgia, 175
Torbett, John, 204, 206
Torres, Frank, 69
Transnationalism: and Mexican immigrants, 3, 7, 217, 221, 223; and bracero program, 85, 113, 117; political pressure of, 106
Treaty of Guadalupe Hidalgo, 70
Trentes family, 21
Trumann, Arkansas, 107, 108, 113
Turner, John Raymond, 131
Tuskegee Institute, 40
Tyson chicken plants, Union County, North Carolina, 196

Undocumented Mexican immigrants: in Arkansas Delta, 87, 114, 266 (n. 206); in Texas, 102; U.S. government's policy toward, 102; limited protections for, 119, 222; as agricultural migrant laborers, 127, 136, 171, 276 (n. 191); legalization of seasonal agricultural workers, 128, 129, 185, 282 (n. 12); increase in, 139, 221; in Georgia, 171–73, 177; legislation targeting, 184, 188; in Charlotte, 185, 188; welfare for, 186; public services for, 186, 203–4, 205, 207; in North Carolina, 188, 190, 196–97, 198, 200, 207, 211, 212; border crossing conditions for, 193

Union County, North Carolina: population of, 180–81, 282 (n. 4); white middle class in, 180–82, 194–96, 197, 198; Mexican immigrants in, 181–82, 183, 184, 189, 191–93, 197, 198, 207–8, 213, 223; commuters in, 194–95; median income of white residents, 195; anti-immigrant movement in, 202

United Fruit Company, 22, 47

United Negro Improvement Association, 62

United States: World War II and post–World War II economic expansion in, 10; neoliberalism in, 122, 123. *See also* Mexico-U.S. border; Midwest; Northwest; South; Southwest; *and specific states*

U.S. Border Patrol, 58, 97

U.S. Department of Justice, 59–60, 63

U.S. Employment Service, 56, 60, 101, 103, 107

U.S. Immigration and Naturalization Service (INS): and deportation campaigns, 46–47, 248 (n. 183); and bracero workers, 97; deportation of Mexican agricultural migrant laborers, 126; immigration enforcement in Georgia, 171–73, 175, 177

U.S. Internal Revenue Service, 156

U.S. Labor Department, 100, 104, 105, 113, 134, 151

U.S.-Mexican War, 5, 17, 70

U.S. Supreme Court: *Plessy* case, 16, 50; *Gong Lum* decision, 70; *Brown v. Board of Education* ruling, 82; separate but equal doctrine, 82, 117; and tax-exempt status of private schools, 156; school desegregation decisions, 179; on public services to undocumented immigrants, 186

University of North Carolina at Charlotte, 187

Urban areas: free trade agreements promoting growth in, 11; Mexican immigrants participating in immigrants' rights movement in, 183, 184; immigrants' rights movement in, 183, 184, 190, 208–9, 211, 221–22; Latino population of, 184–85; and anti-immigrant movements, 204, 206–7; defining of, 281 (n. 3)

Urban League, 111–12

Urrutia, Aureliano, 19

Uvalda, Georgia, 177–78

Valles, Agustín, 38

Vargas, Teresa, 38

Vargas family, 81

Vasconcelos, José, 39

Vázquez Martínez, Cristóbal, 94–95, 117

Vega Aguiniga, Antonio, 88

Velasco Mendoza, Bernardo, 46

Velasco Mendoza, Manuel, 46

Veracruz, Mexico, 19–21, 20, 43–44

Victory Tabernacle Church of God, Tifton, Georgia, 154, 157

Vidalia, Georgia, 127–31, 136, 148, 151, 152, 168, 172–73, 279 (n. 273)

Vielma, Tomás, 76

Villa, Manuel, 27–28

Villa, Pancho, 43

Villareal, Pedro, Jr., 89

Violence: African Americans' experiences of, 1, 4, 57, 92, 218; Mexican immigrants' experiences of, 6, 9, 10, 15; in Texas, 9, 22, 56, 58, 59, 87; in Southwest, 15; of white supremacy, 17, 118; in Louisiana, 37; in Mississippi Delta, 60, 61, 66, 69; and labor organizing, 62; and labor control in Arkansas Delta, 86; in Arkansas Delta, 92, 114, 118; Mexican agricultural migrant laborers' experiences of, 122, 132–33, 134; in Georgia, 132–33, 135, 139–40; in South, 134; in Florida, 135; in Mexico, 138

Virginia, 125, 202, 204, 274 (n. 169)

Voting Rights Act (1965), 116

Wage labor: sharecropping compared to, 57, 64, 65, 80, 86, 250 (n. 32); wages in Mississippi Delta, 61, 62–63, 76; wages in Arkansas Delta, 86, 89, 90–91, 92, 93, 94, 100–101, 110, 111, 112, 118; and bracero program, 89–91, 93, 94, 96, 99, 100–101, 110, 111–12, 113, 117, 118; and Mexican agricultural migrant laborers, 122, 135–36, 139, 140, 154, 155, 157, 172; and seasonal labor, 125–26; Mexican immigrants women's participation in, 193; wages in Texas, 250 (n. 37)

Wagner Knitting Factory, Lowell, North Carolina, 196

Wainright, Jeff, 152

Walker, L. D., 131

Walker, Wanita, 131

Walmsley, T. Semmes, 43

War on Poverty programs, 148–50

Washington, D.C., 202, 204

Welfare, 48, 122, 126, 148, 152, 186–87, 203, 216

Welfare capitalism, 100, 146

Westfield School, Perry, Georgia, 155–56

West Memphis, Arkansas, 109

White assimilation: of Mexican immigrants in New Orleans, 9, 14–15, 16, 17, 24–35, 36, 37, 38, 41, 43, 49–50, 55, 72, 76, 104–5, 219; of Mexican immigrants in Mississippi Delta, 10, 55, 64, 68–72, 76, 77–78, 79, 81, 91, 219; and cultural ideas of race, 16, 76, 239 (n. 12); of bracero workers in Arkansas Delta, 85, 106, 107, 108–9, 115–16, 117, 219, 220

White elites: control of African American laborers, 3, 60, 61, 62, 66, 84, 92; alternative sources of workers for, 4, 5, 6, 10, 55–56, 57, 59, 63, 78, 80, 86, 128, 129; global ambitions of, 11; control of Mexican laborers, 60, 61, 62–63, 64, 66; and racial classification of Mexican immigrants, 69; and Depression era, 80; and bracero program, 82, 83–84, 85, 87–88, 89, 90–91, 93, 96, 98, 101, 102, 104, 110, 113, 114–16, 117, 118; and New Deal, 83, 85, 99, 100, 104; and crop reduction payments, 86, 90, 99; control of bracero workers, 96; resistance to labor rights, 113, 117; and neoliberal ideology, 123–24; seasonally labor-intensive crops of, 127–28; and working conditions of Mexican agricultural migrant laborers, 134–35; and legal aid programs in Georgia, 148–49; in Georgia, 150–51, 156; and church programs for Mexican agricultural migrant laborers, 154–55, 156, 157–62, 165, 166, 168; and federal immigration enforcement in Georgia, 171–73; and Mexican immigrants in Charlotte, 185–86

White middle class: racial entitlement sensibilities of, 12; attitudes toward bracero program, 92–93; and charity work with Mexican agricultural migrant laborers, 153–54, 155, 156, 165–66, 170; and school desegregation, 180–81; in exurban Charlotte, 181–82, 189, 194–96, 198–99, 200, 201, 203–4, 206

White middle-class families, photo albums of, 141, 273 (n. 145)

Index 343

White supremacy: ideology of, 4, 16, 150; politics of, 7, 40, 41, 50, 113; violence of, 17, 118; and resistance of Mexican immigrant upper class, 39, 40, 41–42; mestizaje ideology compared to, 40, 76; in Mississippi Delta, 63, 76; and Mexican Caucasian strategy on educational desegregation, 77, 78; and New Deal, 99; and anti-immigrant movements, 203

White working class: in Arkansas Delta, 86, 88, 89, 90, 91, 92–93, 101, 109, 110–11, 116, 125; organizational efforts of, 88, 92, 98, 112–13; populist rhetoric of, 112; and neoliberal ideology, 122; as migrant laborers, 125; in Georgia, 133; attitudes toward Mexican immigrants, 204

Wike's Drive Inn (Restaurant), Marked Tree, Arkansas, 82, 107

Willis, Harry, 40

Wilson, Lee, 87

Wisconsin, 137, 146, 147, 149, 274 (n. 163)

Women, Infants, and Children (WIC) social program, 148

Women as Mexican immigrants: and middle-class ideal, 11–12, 192, 193–94; in New Orleans, 26–27, 242 (n. 76); as single working women, 27, 192, 193, 242 (n. 75); gender balance of, 27, 242 (n. 74); marriage patterns of, 31–32, 190, 193; characteristics of, 189–90, 193–94, 284 (n. 42); settlement patterns of, 189, 190–91; in Union County, 197

Wood, Bobby, 93

Woodard, Valerie, 206

Woody, Jerome, 131

World's Fair (1884), 17

World War I, 20, 56, 57

World War II, 14, 49, 83, 86, 92

Yepes, J. P., 88

Yucatán, Mexico, 19, 20, 21

Zamudio, Casiano, 133

Zapata, Emiliano, 43

Zervigón, Carlos, 245 (n. 131)